Hawaii The Big Island Revealed
The Ultimate Guidebook

Second Edition

Andrew Doughty
Harriett Friedman

Wizard
Publications

D0311529

Hawaii The Big Island Revealed
The Ultimate Guidebook; Second Edition

Published by Wizard Publications
Post Office Box 991
Lihu'e, Hawai'i 96766–0991

ISBN# 0–9639429–6–4   2/3j
Library of Congress Catalog Card Number 98–61055
Printed in China

Publisher's Cataloging-in-Publication

Doughty, Andrew
    Hawaii the big island revealed : the ultimate
guidebook / Andrew Doughty, Harriett Friedman. --2nd ed.
    p. cm.
    Includes index
    Preassigned LCCN: 98-61055
    ISBN: 0-9639429-6-4

    1. Hawaii--Guidebooks.   I. Friedman, Harriett.
II. Title.

    DU622.D68 1999   919.96904'41
                                   QBI98-1448

All photographs (except the cover) taken by Andrew Doughty.
Cartography by Andrew Doughty.
All artwork and illustrations by Andrew Doughty and Harriett Friedman.

Past and present lava flow information for maps was graciously provided by an overworked and under-appreciated United States Geological Survey, the silent partner to all mapmakers. Keep up the good work!

Cover imagery courtesy of NASA. Note the smoke from Kilauea's Pu'u 'O'o vent (in the southeast part of the island) being carried to the north during unusual Kona winds.

Pages 4–5: Kilauea's Pu'u 'O'o vent up close.

We welcome any comments, questions, criticisms or contributions you may have. Please send to:

Wizard Publications
P.O. Box 991
Lihu'e, Hawai'i 96766–0991
E-mail us at **aloha@wizardpub.com**
For additional information visit our web site at **www.wizardpub.com**

To Harry and Mary.
Their love of travel lives on…

The Big Island has it all. Nowhere else in the world will you find the diversity available here. Pristine rain forests, lava deserts, world-class beaches, snow-covered mountains, an active volcano, dazzling sunsets and just about every activity you can think of. The island is huge—about the size of Connecticut. Navigating your way through this maze of opportunity can be daunting.

We first came to the islands as visitors and decided we could never live anywhere else. Currently we share our time between Kaua'i and the Big Island. When we released our book, *The Ultimate Kaua'i Guidebook,* we were delighted by the overwhelming response it generated. As a result, we decided to do a book about the Big Island. Knowing that most guidebooks to Hawai'i are put together by mainland writers sent over for six weeks or so to become "experts," we predicted that for our first edition of *Hawai'i The Big Island Revealed,* we would need at least eight months full time to put our book together. It took two years full time.

Long time locals have been surprised at some of the items described in our book. We have found many special places that people born and raised here didn't even know about because that's *all* we do—explore the island. Visitors will find the book as valuable as having a friend living on the island.

We recognize the effort people go through to visit the Big Island, and our goal is to expose you to as many options as possible so you can decide what you want to see and do. We took great pains to structure this book in such a way that it will be fun, easy reading and loaded with useful information. This book is not a bland regurgitation of the facts arranged in textbook fashion. We feel strongly that

guidebooks should present their information so that you don't have to read through every single page every time you want to find something. If you are here on vacation, your time is extremely precious. You don't want to spend all your time flipping through a book looking for what you want. You want to be able to locate *what* you want, *when* you want it. You want to be able to access a comprehensive index, a thorough table of contents, and refer to high quality maps that were designed with you in mind. You want to know which helicopter, SCUBA, boat tour, or lu'au is the best on the island. You want to find special hidden gems most people overlook. You want to be shown those things that will make this vacation the best of your life.

A quick look at this book will reveal features never before used in a guidebook. Let's start with the maps. They are more detailed than any other maps you will find, and yet they omit extraneous information that can sometimes make a chore out of reading a map. We know that people in unfamiliar territory sometimes have a hard time determining where they are on a map, so we included landmarks. Most notable among these are mile markers. At every mile on main roads, the government has erected numbered markers to tell you where you are. We are the first to put these markers on a map so you can use them as reference points. In addition, we repeatedly drove or walked every inch of every road on the maps. This is important because *many* of the roads represented on existing maps have been shifted, moved, or eliminated, making "current" maps obsolete. Where needed, we've drawn legal public beach access in yellow, so you'll *know* when you are legally entitled to cross someone's land. Most guide-books have the infuriating habit of mentioning a particular place or sight, but *fail to mention how to get there!* You won't find that in our book. We tell you exactly how to find the hidden gems and use our own special maps to guide you.

As you read this book, you will also notice that we are very candid in assessing businesses. Unlike some other guide-books that send out questionnaires asking a business if they are any good (gee, they *all* say they're good), we've had *personal* contact with the businesses listed in this book. One of the dirty little secrets about guidebook writers is that they sometimes make cozy little deals for good reviews. Well, you won't find that here. We accept no payment for our reviews, we make no deals with businesses for saying nice things, and there are *no advertisements* in our book. What we've seen and experienced is what you get. If we gush over a certain company, it comes from personal experience. If we rail against a business, it is for the same reason. All businesses mentioned in this book are here by *our* choosing. None have had any input into what we say, and we have not received a single cent from any of them for their inclusion. (In fact, there are some that would probably pay to be left out, given our comments.) We always approach businesses as anonymous travelers and later as guidebook writers if we need more information. This ensures that we are treated the same as you. What you get is our opinion on how they operate. Nothing more, nothing less.

Sometimes our candor gets us into trouble. For instance, this book used to be the only guidebook sold at the Visitors Center in Hawai'i Volcanoes National Park. After undergoing a rigorous multi-month review process by government bureaucrats, this book was deemed "the most accurate book we've ever seen for the Big Island." They even wanted to sell our *Kaua'i* book there, a first at the park, because they liked the way we thoroughly researched things. But thoroughness cuts both ways. When those same bureaucrats later realized that we had revealed a secret but *public* trail (previously unknown to the general public) that led to the erupting Pu'u 'O'o vent through a beautiful forest, they stopped selling this book and fumed over the loss of control to the vent. (The trail is outside the park and therefore outside the control of the bureaucrats.) It's not the first time this book has been pulled from shelves for being too honest, and it won't be the last. (Perhaps they were also mad because we revealed that it was park personnel, not vandals as they tell people, who accidentally ruined the cherished 200-year-old footprints embedded in the ash at the park.)

This book is intended to bring you independence in exploring the Big Island. We don't want to waste any of your precious time by giving you bad advice or bad directions. We want you to experience the best that the island has to offer. Our objective in writing this book is to give you the tools and information necessary to have the greatest Hawaiian experience possible.

We hope we succeeded.

Andrew Doughty
Harriett Friedman

Kailua-Kona, Hawai'i

Brand new liquid land flows in a scene as primordial as the island's birth.

How it Began

Sometime around 70 million years ago a cataclysmic rupture occurred in the Earth's mantle, deep below the crust. A hot spot of liquid rock blasted through the Pacific plate like a giant cutting torch, forcing magma to the surface off the coast of Russia, forming the Emperor Seamounts. As the tectonic plate moved slowly over this hot spot, this torch cut a long scar along the plate, piling up mountains of rock, producing island after island. The oldest of these islands to have survived is Kure. Once a massive island with its own unique ecosystem, only its ghost remains in the form of a fringing coral reef, called an atoll.

As soon as the islands were born, a conspiracy of elements proceeded to dismantle them. Ocean waves battered unmercifully against the fragile and fractured rock. Abundant rain, especially on the northeastern sides of the mountains,

easily carved up the rock surface, seeking faults in the rock and forming rivers and streams. In forming these channels, the water carried away the rock and soil, robbing the islands of their very essence. Additionally, the weight of the islands ensured their doom. Lava flows on top of other lava, and the union of these flows is always weak. This lava also contains countless air pockets and is crisscrossed with hollow lava tubes, making it inherently unstable. As these massive amounts of rock accumulated, their bases were crushed under the weight of subsequent lava flows, causing their summits to sink back into the sea.

What we call the Hawaiian Islands are simply the latest creation from this island-making machine. Kaua'i and Ni'ihau are the oldest of the eight major islands. Lush and deeply eroded, the last of Kaua'i's fires died with its volcano a million years ago. O'ahu, Moloka'i,

The wonder of creation can still be seen at night at Kilauea Volcano.

Lana'i, Kaho'olawe—their growing days are over, as well. Maui is in its twilight days as a growing island. After growing vigorously, Hawaiian volcanoes usually go to sleep for a million years or so before sputtering back to life for one last fling. Maui's volcano Haleakala has entered its final stage and last erupted around 1790.

The latest and newest star in this island chain is Hawai'i. Born less than a million years ago, this youngster is still vigorously growing. Though none of its five volcano mountains is considered truly dead, these days Mauna Loa and Kilauea are doing most of the work of making the Big Island bigger. Mauna Loa, the most massive mountain on Earth, consists of 10,000 *cubic miles* of rock. Quieter of the two active volcanoes, it last erupted in 1984. Kilauea is the most boisterous of the volcanoes and is the most active volcano on the planet.

Kilauea's most recent eruption began in 1983 and was still going strong as we went to press. Up and coming onto the world stage is Lo'ihi. This new volcano is still 3,200 feet below the ocean's surface, 20 miles off the southeastern coast of the island. Yet in a geologic heartbeat, the Hawaiian islands will be richer with its ascension, sometime in the next 100,000 years.

These virgin islands were barren at birth. Consisting only of volcanic rock, the first life forms to appreciate these new islands were marine creatures. Fish, mammals, and microscopic animals discovered this new underwater haven and made homes for themselves. Coral polyps attached themselves to the lava and succeeding generations built upon these, creating what would become a coral reef.

Meanwhile, on land, seeds carried by the winds were struggling to colonize the rocky land, eking out a living and breaking down the lava rock. Storms brought the occasional bird, hopelessly blown off course. The lucky ones found the islands. The even luckier ones arrived with mates or were pregnant when they got here. Other animals, stranded on a piece of floating debris, washed ashore against all odds and went on to colonize the islands. These introductions of new species were rare events. It took an extraordinary set of circumstances for a new species to actually make it to the islands. Single specimens were destined to live out their lives in lonely solitude. On average, a new species was successfully deposited here only once every 20,000 years.

As with people, islands have a life cycle. After their violent birth, islands grow to their maximum size, get carved up by the elements, collapse in parts, and sink back into the sea. Someday, all of the Hawaiian Islands will be nothing more than geologic footnotes in the Earth's turbulent geologic history. When a volcanic island is old, it is a sandy sliver, devoid of mountains. When it's middle aged, it can be a lush wonderland, a haven for anything green, like Kaua'i. And when it is young, it is dynamic and unpredictable, like the Big Island of Hawai'i. Of all the Hawaiian Islands, none offers a larger range of climates and landscapes than

does the Big Island. The first people to discover Hawai'i's treasures must have been humbled at their good fortune.

THE FIRST SETTLERS

Sometime around the fourth or fifth century A.D. a large double-hulled voyaging canoe, held together with flexible sennit lashings and propelled by sails made of woven pandanus, slid onto the sand on the Big Island of Hawai'i. These first intrepid adventurers, only a few dozen or so, encountered an island

Hi'ilawe Falls in Waipi'o Valley vividly demonstrates how the land is transformed by scouring water and catastrophic fault collapses.

The ancient Polynesians were exceptional navigators. These stones, at the navigational heiau near Mahukona, were aligned to point the way to other Hawaiian islands, Tahiti, and other places.

chain of unimaginable beauty.

They had left their home in the Marquesas Islands, 2,500 miles away, for reasons we will never know. Some say it was because of war, overpopulation, drought, or just a sense of adventure. Whatever their reasons, these initial settlers took a big chance and surely must have been highly motivated. They left their homes and searched for a new world to colonize. Doubtless, most of the first groups perished at sea. The Hawaiian Islands are the most isolated island chain in the world, and there was no way for them to know that there were islands in these waters. (Though some speculate that they were led here by the golden plover—see box on facing page.)

Those settlers who did arrive brought with them food staples from home: taro, breadfruit, pigs, dogs, and several types of fowl. This was a pivotal decision. These first settlers found a land that con-

tained almost no edible plants. With no land mammals other than the Hawaiian bat, the first settlers subsisted on fish until their crops matured. From then on, they lived on fish and taro. Although we associate throw-net fishing with Hawai'i, this practice was introduced by Japanese immigrants much later. The ancient Hawaiians used fishhooks and spears, for the most part, or drove fish into a net already placed in the water. They also had domesticated animals, which were used as ritual foods or reserved for chiefs.

Little is known about the initial culture. Archeologists speculate that a second wave of colonists, probably from Tahiti, may have subdued these initial inhabitants around 1,000 A.D. Some may have resisted and fled into the forest, creating the legend of the Menehune.

Today Menehune are always referred to as being small in stature. Initially referring to their social stature, the legend evolved to mean that they were physically short and lived in the woods away from the Hawaiians. (The Hawaiians avoided the woods when possible, fearing that they held evil spirits, and instead stayed on the coastal plains.) The Menehune were purported to build fabulous structures, always in one night. Their numbers were said to be vast, as many as 500,000. It is interesting to note that in a census taken of Kaua'i around 1800, 65 people from a remote valley identified themselves as Menehune.

The second wave probably swept over the island from the south, pushing the first inhabitants ever-north. On a tiny island north of Kaua'i archeologists have found carvings, clearly not Hawaiian, that closely resembling Marquesan carvings, probably left by the doomed exiles.

This second culture was far more aggressive and developed into a highly class conscious culture. The society was governed by chiefs, called Ali'i, who established a long list of taboos called kapu. These kapu were designed to keep order, and the penalty for breaking one was usually death by strangulation, club, or fire. If the violation was serious enough, the guilty party's family might also be killed. It was kapu, for instance, for your shadow to fall across the shadow of the Ali'i. It was kapu to interrupt the chief if he was speaking. It was kapu to prepare men's food in the same container used for women's food. It was kapu for women to eat pork or bananas. It was kapu for men and women to eat together. It was kapu not to observe the days designated to the gods. Certain areas were kapu for fishing if they became depleted, allowing the area to replenish itself.

While harsh by our standards today, this system kept the order. Most Ali'i were sensitive to the disturbance their presence caused and often ventured outside only at night, or a scout was sent

Hawai'i's First Tour Guide?

Given the remoteness of the Hawaiian Islands relative to the rest of Polynesia (or anywhere else for that matter) you'll be forgiven for wondering how the first settlers found these islands in the first place. Many scientists think it might have been this little guy here. Called the kolea, or golden plover, this tiny bird flies 2,500 miles nonstop to Alaska every year for the summer, returning to Hawai'i after mating. Some of these birds continue past Hawai'i and fly another 2,500 miles to Samoa and other South Pacific islands. The early Polynesians surely must have noticed this commute and concluded that there must be land in the direction that the bird was heading. They never would have dreamed that the birds leaving the South Pacific were heading to a land 5,000 miles away, and that Hawai'i was merely a stop in between, where the lazier birds wintered.

ahead to warn people that an Ali'i was on his way. All commoners were required to pay tribute to the Ali'i in the form of food and other items. Human sacrifices were common, and war among rival chiefs the norm.

By the 1700s, the Hawaiians had lost all contact with Tahiti, and the Tahitians had lost all memory of Hawai'i. Hawaiian canoes had evolved into fishing and inter-island canoes and were no longer capable of long ocean voyages.

THE OUTSIDE WORLD DISCOVERS HAWAII

In January 1778 an event occurred that would forever change Hawai'i. Captain James Cook, who usually had a genius for predicting where to find islands, stumbled upon Hawai'i. He had not expected the islands to be here. He was on his way to Alaska on his third great voyage of discovery, this time to search for the Northwest Passage linking the Atlantic and Pacific Oceans. Cook approached the shores of Waimea, Kaua'i, at night on January 19, 1778. The next morning Kaua'i's inhabitants awoke to a wondrous sight and thought they were being visited by gods. Rushing aboard to greet their visitors, the Kauaians were fascinated by what they saw: pointy-headed beings (the British wore tricornered hats) breathing fire (smoking pipes) and possessing a death-dealing instrument identified as a water squirter (guns). The amount of iron on the ship was incredible. (They had seen iron before in the form of nails on driftwood but never knew where it originated.)

Cook left Kaua'i and briefly explored Ni'ihau before heading north for his mission on February 2, 1778. When Cook returned to the islands in November after failing to find the Northwest Passage, he visited the Big Island of Hawai'i.

The Hawaiians had probably seen white men before. Local legend indicates that strange white people washed ashore at Ke'ei Beach sometime around the 1520s and integrated into society. This coincides with Spanish records of two ships lost in this part of the world in 1528. But a few weird looking stragglers couldn't compare to the arrival of Cook's great ships and instruments.

Despite some recent rewriting of history, all evidence indicates that Cook, unlike some other exploring sea captains of his era, was a thoroughly decent man. Individuals need to be evaluated in the context of their time. Cook knew that his mere presence would have a profound impact on the cultures he encountered, but he also knew that change for these cultures was inevitable, with or without him. He tried, unsuccessfully, to keep the men known to be infected with venereal diseases from mixing with local women, and frequently flogged infected men who tried to sneak ashore at night. He was greatly distressed when a party he sent to Ni'ihau was forced to stay overnight due to high surf, knowing that his men might transmit diseases to the women (which they did).

Cook arrived on the Big Island at a time of much upheaval. The mo'i, or king, of the Big Island had been badly spanked during an earlier attempt to invade Maui and was now looting and raising hell throughout the islands as retribution. Cook's arrival, and his physical appearance, assured that the Hawaiians would assume him to be the god Lono. Lono was responsible for land fertility. Every year the ruling chiefs and their war god Ku went into abeyance, removing their power so that Lono could return to the land and make it fertile again, bringing back the spring rains. During this time all public works stopped and the land was left alone. At the end of this *Makahiki,* man would again seize the land from Lono so he could grow crops and otherwise make a living upon it. Cook arrived at the beginning of the Makahiki and the Hawaiians naturally thought *he* was the god Lono, coming to make the land fertile. Cook even sailed into Kealakekua Bay, exactly where legend said Lono would arrive.

The Hawaiians went to great lengths to please their "god." All manner of supplies were made available. Eventually they became suspicious of the visitors. If they were gods, why did they accept the Hawaiian women? And if they were gods, why did one of them die?

The day the gods cried...

At the south end of Alii Drive in Kona, just before it dead ends, there is a lava road leading toward the ocean. This field of lava and an area around the point called Kuamo'o have an extraordinary past. Here occurred an event that forever changed a people. For it was here that the Hawaiians abolished their ancient religion one day in 1820.

The Hawaiian religion was based on the kapu system. A myriad of laws were maintained, with death being the usual punishment for violation. The Hawaiians believed that rigid enforcement for a single violation was necessary or else the gods would punish the whole community in the form of earthquakes, tsunamis, lava flows and famine. When Captain Cook came, he and his men were unaware of the many laws and inadvertently violated many of them. When natural punishments failed to materialize, many Hawaiians concluded that the gods would not enforce the laws. Since many found the kapu laws burdensome and oppressive, there was pressure to abolish them. While King Kamehameha I was alive, however, none dared challenge the kapu system. Almost as soon as he died, King Kamehameha II, pressured by his mother Ka'ahumanu, decided to put an end to the kapu system and destroy the temples around the island. This was before any missionaries ever came to these islands.

It was decided that the action would be consecrated by the simple act of having the king eat with women in public in November 1819. This had heretofore been kapu, and the penalty for breaking this law was death. In breaking this kapu in public, Kamehameha II declared an end to the old ways. One of his cousins, Kekuaokalani, was to be king of the spiritual world and challenged him. The ferocious battle took place near here in early 1820. His cousin was hit by Kamehameha II's forces, and the man's grieving wife ran to his side as he fell. She cried out, begging that her wounded husband's life be spared. Instead she and her husband were summarily executed on the spot, with her body falling on top of his. The Hawaiian religion, as a dominant force, died with them on that bloody day. If you look to the south, you can see what look like terraces cut into the side of the mountain. These are the graves of the many hundreds who died from that very battle.

Today there is a resurgence of the Hawaiian religion. Hawaiians are grappling with their role in the world and are reaching back to their roots. The religion that seemingly died on that raw lava field is being reborn in the hearts of some contemporary Hawaiians.

Cook left at the right time. The British had used up the Hawaiians' hospitality (not to mention their supplies). But shortly after leaving the Big Island the ship broke a mast, making it necessary to return to Kealakekua Bay for repairs. As they sailed back into the bay, the Hawaiians were nowhere to be seen. A chief had declared the area kapu to help replenish it. When Cook finally found the Hawaiians, they were polite but wary. Why are you back? Didn't we please you enough already? What do you want now?

As repair of the mast went along, things began to get tense. Eventually the Hawaiians stole a British rowboat (for the nails) and the normally calm Cook blew his cork. On the morning of February 14, 1779, he went ashore to trick the chief into coming aboard his ship where he would detain him until the rowboat was returned. As Cook and the chief were heading to the water, the chief's wife begged the chief not to go.

By now tens of thousands of Hawaiians were crowding around Cook, and he ordered a retreat. A shot was heard from the other side of the bay and someone shouted that the Englishmen had killed an important chief. A shielded warrior with a dagger came at Cook, who fired his pistol (loaded with small shot). The shield stopped the small shot, and the Hawaiians were emboldened. Other shots were fired. Standing in knee-deep water, Cook turned to call for a cease-fire and was struck in the head from behind with a club, then stabbed. Dozens of other Hawaiians pounced on him, stabbing his body repeatedly. The greatest explorer the world had ever known was dead at age 50 in a petty skirmish over a stolen rowboat.

When things calmed down, the Hawaiians were horrified that they had killed a man they had earlier presumed to be a god. See page 68 to see what finally happened to Cook's body.

The Hawaiians built a highly structured society around the needs, desires, and demands of their gods. This place of refuge is called Pu'uhonua o Honaunau.

KAMEHAMEHA THE GREAT

The most powerful and influential king in Hawaiian history lived during the time of Captain Cook and was born on this island around 1758. Until his rule, the Hawaiian chain had never been ruled by a single person. He was the first to "unite" (i.e., conquer) all the islands.

Kamehameha was an extraordinary man by any standard. He possessed herculean strength, a brilliant mind, and boundless ambition. He was marked for death before he was even born. When Kamehameha's mother was pregnant with him, she developed a strange and overpowering craving—she wanted to *eat* the eyeball of a chief. The king of the Big Island, mindful of the rumor that the unborn child's real father was his bitter enemy, the king of Maui, asked his advisors to interpret. Their conclusion was unanimous. The child would grow to be a rebel, a killer of chiefs. The king decided that the child must die as soon as he was born, but the baby was instead whisked away to a remote part of Waipi'o Valley to be raised.

In Hawaiian society, your role in life was governed by what class you were born into. The Hawaiians believed that breeding among family members produced superior offspring (except for the genetic misfortunes which were killed at birth), and the highest chiefs came from brother/sister combinations. Kamehameha was not of the highest class (his parents were merely cousins) so his future as a chief would not come easily.

As a young man Kamehameha was impressed by his experience with Captain Cook. He was among the small group that stayed overnight on Cook's ship during Cook's first pass of Maui. (Kamehameha was on Maui valiantly fighting a battle in which his side was getting badly whopped.) Kamehameha recognized that his world had forever changed, and he shrewdly used the knowledge and technology of westerners to his own advantage.

Kamehameha participated in numerous battles. Many of them were lost (by his side) but he learned from his mistakes and developed into a cunning tactician. When he finally consolidated his rule over the Big Island (by luring his enemy to be the inaugural sacrifice at the Pu'ukoholā Heiau near Kawaihae) he fixed his sights on the entire chain. In 1795 his large company of troops, armed with some western armaments and advisors, swept across Maui, Moloka'i, Lana'i and O'ahu. After some delays with the last of the holdouts, Kaua'i, their king finally acquiesced to the inevitable and Kamehameha became the first ruler of all the islands. He spent his final years governing the islands peacefully from his Capital at Kailua Bay and died in 1819.

MODERN HAWAI'I

During the 19th century, Hawai'i's character changed dramatically. Businessmen from all over the world came here to exploit Hawai'i's sandalwood, whales, land, and people. Hawai'i's leaders, for their part, actively participated in these ventures and took a piece of much of the action for themselves. Workers were brought from many parts of the world, changing the racial makeup of the islands. Government corruption became the order of the day, and everyone seemed to be profiting, except the Hawaiian commoner. By the time Queen Lili'uokalani lost her throne to a group of American businessmen in 1893, Hawai'i had become directionless. It barely resembled the Hawai'i Captain Cook had encountered the previous century. The kapu system had been abolished by the Hawaiians shortly after the death of Kamehameha the Great. The "Great Mahele," begun in 1848, had changed the relationship Hawaiians had with the land. Large tracts of land were sold by the Hawaiian government to royalty, government officials, commoners, and foreigners, effectively stripping many Hawaiians of land they had lived on for generations.

The United States recognized the Republic of Hawai'i in 1894 with Sanford Dole as its president. It was annexed in 1898 and became an official territory in 1900. During the 19th and 20th centuries, sugar established itself as king. Pineapple was also heavily grown in the islands, with the island of Lana'i being purchased in its entirety for the purpose of growing pineapples. As the 20th century rolled on, Hawaiian sugar and pineapple workers found themselves in a lofty position—they became the highest paid workers for these crops in the world. As land prices rose and competition from other parts of the world increased, sugar and pineapple became less and less profitable. Today, these crops no longer hold the position they once had. The "pineapple island" of Lana'i has shifted away from pineapple growing and is looking toward tourism. The sugar industry is now dead on the Big Island, and sugar lands are being converted to other purposes while the workers move into other vocations, often tourist-related.

The story of Hawai'i is not a story of good versus evil. Nearly everyone shares in the blame of what happened to the Hawaiian people and their culture. Westerners certainly saw Hawai'i as a potential bonanza and easily exploitable. They knew what buttons to push and pushed them well. But the Hawaiians, for their part, were in a state of flux. The mere existence of westerners seemed to bring to the surface a discontent, or at least a weakness, with their system that had been lingering just below the surface. In fact, in 1794, a mere 16 years after first encountering westerners and under no military duress from the West, Kamehameha the Great volunteered to cede his island over to Great Britain. He was hungry for western arms so he could defeat his neighbor island opponents. He even declared that as of that day, they were no longer people of Hawai'i, but rather people of Britain. (Britain declined the offer.) And in 1819, immediately after the death of the strong-willed Kamehameha, the Hawaiians, on their own accord, overthrew their own religion, dumped the kapu system, and denied their gods. This was before any western missionaries ever came to Hawai'i.

Nonetheless, Hawai'i today is once again seeking guidance from her heritage. The echoes of the past seem to be getting louder with time, rather than diminishing. Interest in the Hawaiian language and culture is at a level not seen in many decades. All who live here are very aware of the issues and the complexities involved, but there is little agreement about where it will lead. As a result, you will be exposed to a more "Hawaiian" Hawai'i than those who might have visited the state a decade ago. This is an interesting time in Hawai'i. Enjoy it as observers, and savor the flavor of Hawai'i.

Going with the flow—Big Island style.

GETTING HERE

In order to get to Hawai'i, you've got to fly here. While this may sound painfully obvious, many people spend time trying to find an ocean cruise to the Islands. With the advent of jets, the long span of open ocean makes regular cruises here infeasible.

When planning your trip, a travel agent is *strongly* recommended. They are a vastly underutilized resource and can obtain incredible bargains. Their commission is paid directly by the travel industry. If you don't want to or can't go through a travel agent, there are several large wholesalers that can get you airfare, hotel, and a rental car, often cheaper than you can get airfare on your own. **Pleasant Hawaiian Holidays** (800) 242–9244, **Suntrips** (800) 786–8747, and **Creative Leisure** (800) 426–6367 are reputable providers of complete package tours. The first two are renowned for their impossibly low rates. We've always been amazed that you can sometimes get round trip airfare from the mainland, a hotel, and car for a week for as low as $600 per person, depending on where you fly from and where you stay. That's a small price to pay for your little piece of paradise. **Cheap Tickets** (800) 377–1000 usually gets tickets for unbelievably low prices.

If you arrange everything yourself, you can often count on paying top dollar for each facet of your trip. The prices listed in the WHERE TO STAY section reflect the RACK rates, meaning the price you and I pay if we book direct. Rates can be significantly lower if you go through a travel agent or tour company.

When you pick your travel agent, shop around—the differences can be dramatic A diligent agent can make the difference between affording a *one-week* vacation, and *two-week* vacation. They don't all check the same sources for bargains; there is an art to it. Look in the Sunday travel section of your local newspaper—the bigger the paper, the better.

Flight schedules change all the time, but United and Hawaiian Airlines often have *direct* flights to Kona from San Francisco and Los Angeles. Not having to cool your heels while changing planes on O'ahu is a *big* plus. Otherwise, inter-island flights are like busses; you can always take the next one, and you can sit anywhere you want. Flight attendants zip up and down the aisles hurling juice at you for the short, inter-island flight. If you fly to the Big Island from Honolulu, either into Kona (where most arrive) or Hilo, sit on the left side (seats with an "A") coming in (right side going out) for superb views of several other islands. When flying to O'ahu from the mainland, seats on the left side have the best views. Inter-island flights are done by Aloha (800 367–5250) and Hawaiian (800 367–5320).

WHAT TO BRING

This list may assist you in planning what to bring. Obviously you won't bring everything on the list, but it might make you think of a few things you may otherwise overlook.

Waterproof sunblock (SPF 15 or higher)
Two bathing suits
Shoes—Thongs, trashable sneakers, reef shoes, hiking shoes
Mask, snorkel, and fins
Camera with lots of film
Warm clothes (for Mauna Kea, Waimea or horseback riding) and junk clothes for bikes, etc.
Light rain jacket
Flashlight if you like caves or the lava field at night if there's a surface flow.
Mosquito repellent for some hikes. (*Lotions*—not liquids—with DEET seem to work the longest.)

Large insulated water jug to keep in car
Shorts and other cool cotton clothing
Fanny pack—also called waist pack, to carry all your various vacation accouterments; waterproof ones are convenient for snorkeling
Cheap, simple backpack—you don't need to go backpacking to use one; a 10-minute trek down to a secluded beach is much easier if you bring a simple pack
Hat or cap for sun protection

GETTING AROUND
Rental Cars

The rental car prices in Hawai'i are cheaper than almost anywhere else in the country, and the competition is ferocious. Nearly every visitor to the Big Island gets around in a rental car, and for good reason—it's a *big* island.

At Kona Airport, rental cars can easily be obtained from the booths across the street from the Main Terminal. It's good idea to reserve your car in advance since companies can run out of cars during peak times.

Many hotels, condos and rental agents offer excellent room/car packages. Find out from your hotel or travel agent if one is available. You can rent a car in Hilo and return it to Kona (or vice versa). There's usually an extra fee of about $35–$75 (depending on the company and car). It's sometimes less if you pick up in Kona and return to Hilo.

If you're wondering why you can't get any radio stations—it's usually because the rental car companies push the antenna down to wash it. So when you get *da car,* pull *da buggah* out!

On the facing page is a list of rental car companies. The local area code is 808. Some have desks at various hotels.

Alamo (800) 327–9633
329–8896 in Kona
961–3343 in Hilo

Avis (800) 321–3712
327–3000 in Kona
935–1290 in Hilo

Budget (800) 527–0700
329–8511 in Kona
935–6878 in Hilo

Dollar (800) 800–4000
329–2744 in Kona
961–6059 in Hilo

Harper (800) 852–9993
329–6688 in Kona
969–1478 in Hilo

Hertz (800) 654–3011
329–3566 in Kona
935–2896 in Hilo

National (800) 227–7368
329–1674 in Kona
935–0891 in Hilo

Thrifty (800) 367–5238
329–1339 in Kona

If you are between the ages of 21 and 25, **Alamo** and **Dollar** are your best bets. You'll pay about $15–$20 extra for being young and reckless, but at least you won't have to take the bus. If you're under 21—rent a bike or take the bus.

Cruzin Paradise (331–1179) rents replicas of 1965 Cobras for $275 per day. *Very* steep, but I gotta admit they look pretty cool. $1,500 credit card security deposit required.

4-Wheel Drive JEEPs

We strongly believe that the best vehicle for the island is a 4-wheel drive vehicle. They come closed (like an Explorer or a Trooper) or open (like a Wrangler). They are more expensive, but there are several roads, beaches and sights that you can't visit without 4WD. Even the short paved road into Waipi'o Valley requires the low gear offered in 4WD. Saddle Road (described on page 127) is contractually off limits to most cars. That means that if you take it, the insurance you take out with the rental company is void, so you or your insurance company back home would have to eat it. But JEEPS rented at **Harper** go without this restriction. Different companies have different restrictions, but from a *practical* standpoint, 4WD is the way to go. The drawbacks to *open* JEEPS are more wind and heat and no trunk. Closed 4WDs are best. Expect to pay up to $60–$90 per day for the privilege of cheating the road builders.

Motorcycles and Scooters

If you really want to ham it up, you can try renting a hog. (*Disclaimer*— Wizard Publications will not be held liable for bad puns.) **Kona Harley-Davidson** (326–9887) rents Harleys for $125–$135 per day. **DJ's Rentals** (329–1700 in Kona rents Harleys for $145 per day and scooters for $45. DJ's selection is good, though they seem easy to dislike with their brusque service.

A few tips...

Gasoline is *obscenely* expensive here. You may want to have some FedExed to you from home to save money. (OK, maybe not *that* expensive.) Kona is said to have the highest gas prices in the United States (about 15¢ higher than expensive Hilo). Whether that's true or not, prepare to get hammered at the pump. If you're in the Kohala resort area, there's a station off the road to the Waikoloa Resorts at the 76 mile marker. When returning your car to the Kona airport, fill up either at the station at Honokohau Harbor or the station near Costco (both marked on the map on page 151) for your cheapest alternatives and least distance to the airport. Chevron on the highway is a bit more expensive. Many companies charge a top off fee due to the airport's distance to town, so fill it to the top.

Seat belt use is required by law, and the police will pull you over for this alone. Wide open roads and frequently changing speed limits make it easy to accidentally speed here. Police usually cruise in their own private, unmarked vehicles so you won't see them coming. I'm not supposed to tell you this, but local protocol dictates that you flash your headlights for a couple of miles when you pass a police car to warn drivers coming the other way.

So if you see someone flashing their lights at you, you'd better check your speed.

It's best not to leave anything valuable in your car. There are teenagers here who pass the time by breaking into cars. Hapuna Beach and several Hilo waterfalls are notorious for car break-ins. (There was a thieving weasel breaking into cars at Kua Bay at press time.) When we park at a beach or waterfall, or any other place frequented by visitors, we take all valuables with us, leave the windows up, and leave the doors unlocked. (Just in case someone is curious enough about the inside to smash a window.) There are plenty of stories about someone walking 100 feet to a waterfall in Hilo, coming back to their car, and finding that their brand new video camera has walked away. And don't be gullible enough to think that trunks are safe. Someone who sees you put something in your trunk can probably get at it faster than you can with your key.

JEEPS can unlock some of the Big Island's more secluded beaches, such as this empty black sand beach at Road to the Sea.

Kailua-Kona possesses the dry town syndrome: At the first drop of rain, a certain segment of the population becomes vehicularly uncoordinated, driving like a drunken cat on ice. So beware of this.

Buses

Our main island bus is called **Hele-On** (961–8744). It was designed for local use, so it doesn't go to all the places that visitors want to go. However, it does go between Hilo and Kona and they do take luggage (for an extra fee). Call them for a schedule and rates. The **Alii Shuttle** (775–7121) goes up and down Alii Drive in Kona regularly. There are also bus tours from **Roberts Hawai'i** (329–1688), and **Jack's** (329–2555).

GETTING MARRIED ON THE BIG ISLAND

If you're looking to get married in paradise, there are full-service companies on the Big Island that offer wedding services. Contact them to discuss your wedding plans, whether for a conventional wedding or something a little bit different. You may also want to consider a renewal of your vows. Either way, these companies will be able to help.

Paradise Weddings Hawaii
(800) 428–5844 or (808) 883–9067
Beaches n' Dreams Weddings, Etc.
(800) 298–7012 or (808) 325–5213

Major resort hotels can also be contacted about their wedding services. Ask for the wedding coordinator. The **Hilton Waikoloa Village, Four Seasons, Kona Village,** and **Mauna Lani** stand out. Also consider the diminutive **St. Peter's Catholic Church** (808) 326–7771 on Alii Drive overlooking Kahalu'u Bay. Non-denominational for weddings. Fee is $100. Very popular and quaint, a bit

noisy on weekends. In Hilo, consider **Nani Mau Gardens** (959–3541) or the **Hawaiian Tropical Botanical Garden** (964–5233), though the latter has many restrictions that may not fit in with your plans. How about a reception in a royal palace? **Hulihe'e Palace** (329–9555) described on page 58 is available with restrictions. Pretty novel, huh?

Obtaining a License

Contact the Department of Health at (808) 974-6008 for the name and phone number of the marriage license agent nearest where you will be staying. If you are under 20 years of age, there are special requirements you can discuss with them. Both bride and groom appear *in person* before the marriage license agent with $50 in cash and picture ID for both. The license is good for 30 days. No health testing is required.

WEATHER

The weather on the Big Island is more diverse than any island or other comparably sized chunk of land *in the world.* You name it, we got it. According to the Köppen Climate Classification System (which is probably *your* favorite system too, right?), the Big Island has 10 of the 15 types of climactic zones in the world. (Only Cold Continental Climate categories are absent.) It includes tropical, monsoonal, desert and even *periglacial* climates, among others. So no matter what kind of weather you like, we are sure to have it here. As you ascend the slopes of the volcanoes, you lose about 3 degrees for every thousand feet. Call 961–5582 for a recording of today's forecast.

Kailua-Kona has weather that can best be described as eternal springtime.

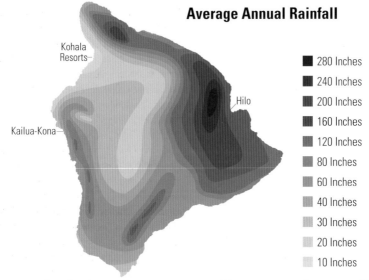

Average Annual Rainfall

Kohala Resorts

Hilo

Kailua-Kona

- 280 Inches
- 240 Inches
- 200 Inches
- 160 Inches
- 120 Inches
- 80 Inches
- 60 Inches
- 40 Inches
- 30 Inches
- 20 Inches
- 10 Inches

Quite simply, it's almost always sunny. The average high and low in February (the coldest month) is 80° and 64°, whereas the high and low in August (the warmest month) is 87° and 69°. Humidity is usually between 50% and 80%. The temperature change between night and day is greater than the temperature change between winter and summer, hence the saying that "nighttime is the winter of the tropics." Balmy wraparound onshore breezes usually keep it comfortable. The exception is during Kona winds (so named because they come from the Kona direction, rather than out of the northeast as is usually the case). Kona winds occur about 10% of the time and bring stillness or warm air to Kona, creating uncomfortably hot conditions. Normal conditions in Kona and Kohala mean clear mornings with afternoon clouds created by thermal heating, so morning is usually better for activities such as air tours. During the summer, evening showers often occur as warm moist air is cooled, squeezing rain out of the humidity. Because it is totally protected from the trade winds by Hualalai, Kona is the only place in the state that gets most of its rainfall in the summer. The higher up the mountain, the more rain you get.

Hilo's weather is almost always described with one word—*rain*. Hilo is the wettest city in the United States. Annual rainfall is rarely less than 100 inches, usually much more. But rain is not a constant here. Hilo has times of drought like anywhere else. (Like when rainfall was—*gasp!*—a *mere* 85 inches in 1995.) Most of the rain falls at night. When daytime showers do occur, they are often intense but short lived. That said, rain or cloudiness *will* be a factor here. One of the reasons that Kailua-Kona is so much more popular than Hilo is that visitors like sunny weather, and Hilo can't compete in that area. Also, all that rain has to go somewhere, which is why the ocean off Hilo is not nearly as clear as Kona's runoff-free waters.

The resort area of **Kohala** is the driest part of the island, with rainfall usually around 10 inches per year. Sunshine is almost assured (which is why it is so popular). The weather penalty here is the wind. As the lava fields heat up during the day it causes the air to heat and rise. Air from the ocean rushes in to fill the void, creating strong afternoon convective breezes. The hotter, drier and sunnier it is that day, the breezier it may be that afternoon.

The general rule of thumb is that in wet areas like Hilo, most of the rain falls at night and early morning. Dry areas like Kona and Kohala get their rains in the late afternoon and early evenings.

Water temperatures range from 75° at it's coldest in February to 82° at its warmest in September/October. It's colder in some areas where freshwater springs percolate from the ocean's floor.

PLANNING YOUR TRIP

Visitors are usually unprepared for the sheer size and diversity of the Big Island. The island is over 4,000 square miles, and a circular trip around, on Highways 19 and 11 is a hefty 222 miles. During that drive you pass through dozens of different terrains and climates. (And that doesn't even include Saddle Road, Lower Puna, any of North Kohala or scores of other places.) Put simply, this island is too big and too diverse to try to see in a few days. The graphic at right will put it in perspective.

If you are on the island three days or less, it's our recommendation that you don't try to see the whole island; you'll only end up touring Hawai'i's exotic blacktop. Pick a side. Since one of your days should be spent at the volcano, that leaves you with a scant two days to experience either Hilo's and Puna's beauty or the Kona side's diversity and activities.

Deciding which side of the island to spend the most time on is a difficult decision, but the numbers are definitely skewed. Most visitors spend most of their time on the western, or Kona, side. There are several reasons for this:

Kona Side

The Kona side has the sunshine. The climate in Kona is as perfect as weather gets, and the Kohala resort area has the highest number of sunny days of anywhere in the state. The Kona side also has *far* more activities available. This leads to another reason—the ocean. Since it's on the leeward side of the island, and because there are no permanent streams on the entire west side of the island (except, some say, for the one from Kona to Hilo that is filled with tax money), Kona has the calmest, clearest water in the state. Water sports such as swimming, snorkeling, SCUBA, fishing—you name it—are usually unmatched on

Just How Big is The Big Island of Hawai'i?

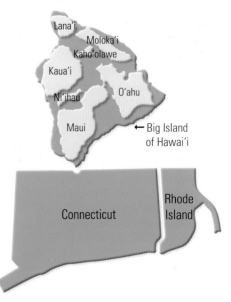

THE BASICS

the Kona side. This side also has the best beaches on the island, with some, such as Hapuna, consistently rated in the top five in the United States. (With a few notable exceptions, the Hilo side has poor beaches.) All this adds up to a traveler's delight, one of the reasons that the Kona side has such a high visitor repeat ratio.

But stand by for a shock when you fly into Kona Airport for the first time. Kona makes a *rotten* first impression on the uninitiated airborne visitor. Part of the airport sits atop a lava flow from 1801, and the first thing you think when you fly in over all that jet black lava is, "I came all this way for *this?*" Don't worry, it gets much better.

Hilo Side

On the other hand, the Kona side is short of what Hilo has in abundance—green. Whereas much of the Kona side is dominated by lava, Hilo is plant heaven. The weather usually comes from the northeast, so Hilo gets around 140 inches of rain per year. This is paradise for anything that grows. Hilo also has breathtaking waterfalls. You won't find *one* on the Kona side. Hilo's weather has created beautiful folds and buckles in the terrain. The unweathered Kona side lacks angles—it's mostly gentle slopes. Lastly, Hilo is *much* more convenient for exploring Kilauea volcano.

The Two Sides

The schism between the two sides of the island is wide and deep. Because the two sides are so different and the distances so large (for Hawai'i, that is), most people who live on the west side haven't been to Hilo or Kilauea volcano in years. Most Hilo residents haven't been to Kona in years. Both sides tend to play-

fully badmouth the other.

If you have a week on the Big Island, you might want to spend four to five days on the Kona side and two to three days in Hilo. The volcano itself can take one to two days, and you're better off exploring it from Hilo than from Kona. Be aware that Hilo all but closes on Sundays, with most business, even the few tourist-related ones, taking the day off.

GEOGRAPHY

The Big Island is made up of five volcanoes. (See map on the foldout back cover.) Kohala in the north is the oldest. Next came Mauna Kea, Hualalai, Mauna Loa, and finally Kilauea. None are truly dead, but only Mauna Loa and Kilauea make regular appearances with an occasional walk-on by Hualalai. Nearly the size of Connecticut, all the other Hawaiian Islands could easily fit inside the Big Island's 4,000 square miles. It's the only state in the union that gets bigger every year (thanks to Kilauea).

Gentle slopes are the trademark of

Driving Distances in Miles

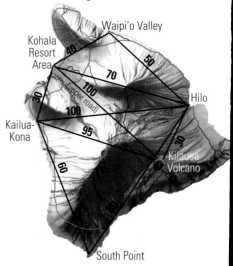

Only on the Big Island can you experience both conditions on the same day a few dozen miles apart.

this young island. It hasn't had time to develop the dramatic, razor-sharp ridges that older islands such as Kaua'i possess. The exception is the windward side of Kohala where erosion and fault collapses have created a series of dramatic valleys. Two of our mountains rise to over 13,000 feet. Mauna Kea, at 13,796 feet, is the tallest mountain in the world when measured from its base, eclipsing such also-rans as Mount Everest and K-2. Mauna Loa, though slightly shorter, is much broader, earning it the moniker as the *largest* mountain in the world. It contains a mind-numbing 10,000 cubic *miles* of rock.

Another of our mountains is not really a mountain at all. Kilauea, looking more like a gaping wound on Mauna Loa, is the undisputed volcano show-off of the planet. Hundreds of thousands of cubic yards of lava per day issue from its current outlet, Pu'u 'O'o, creating and repaving land on a daily basis.

All this adds up to an exciting and dynamic geographic location. Things change faster here than anyplace you will ever visit. There have been lots of times that we have gone to a certain beach or area only to find that it has changed beyond recognition. A new black sand beach shifts to another location. Trails become absorbed by a restless and vigor-

ous Mother Nature. Whole roads get covered with lava. Island hopping in this state is like traveling through time. This is an exciting time in the life cycle of this particular island. Enjoy the island in its youth, for like all youths, this, too, shall pass.

SO IS HAWAI'I AN ISLAND OR A STATE?

Both. This island, more than any other in this state, is a bit schizophrenic when it comes to names. This is the biggest island in the state, so it is commonly referred to as (brace yourself) *the Big Island.* Its Hawaiian name is *Hawai'i.* So far, so good. But the whole *state* is called Hawai'i. So you figure the capital must be here, right? Nope, Honolulu is on O'ahu. This must be where most of the people live, right? Uh-uh, O'ahu has 80% of the population. Well, this must be where Pearl Harbor is, correct? Wrong answer—it's on O'ahu, too. So why is the state named after *this* island? Because it's the *biggest* island, and this is where King Kamehameha the Great was from. It was he who brought all the islands under one rule for the first time. His first capital was here at Kailua (another naming headache—see below). When you do all that, you have some historical influence. In this book we will refer to this island as *the Big Island.* When we say Hawai'i, we mean the whole state. (Even my brother, when he came to visit us on the Big Island, bought two tickets to Honolulu; assuming it must be on the "main" island.) In short, *in Hawai'i* could be anywhere—*on Hawai'i* is on the Big Island.

I won't even get into the name confusion for the town of Waimea. (Or is it Kamuela?—See page 123.) Let's tackle the more annoying naming problem. The main town on the west side is called, **Kailua-Kona, Kona, Kailua,** or sometimes **Kailua Town.** In the old days it was simply Kailua. Though there are also towns named Kailua on O'ahu and Maui, it didn't present much of a problem to anyone until the Post Office discovered these islands. In order to keep from messing up the mail *(don't say it!)* they decided to rename the town. (Technically, they renamed their post office, but the subtlety is lost on those who have to address mail.) Since this is the *kona* side of the island (kona being the name of the less common wind that comes from this direction), they cleverly named the Post Office *Kailua-Kona.* To complicate matters further, the builders of the first airport here named it the *Kona Airport,* so people began to refer to a trip here as "going to Kona." All this leaves you with a quandary. What do you call this place? Well, in keeping with our editorial policy of taking gutsy stands, we'll call it Kailua-Kona...except when we call it Kona or Kailua Town. In fairness, that's because most who live here do the same.

HAZARDS
The Sun

The hazard that affects by far the most people is the sun (excluding the accommodations tax). The Big Island, at 19–20° latitude, receives sunlight more directly than anywhere on the mainland. (The more overhead the sunlight is, the less atmosphere it filters through.) If you want to enjoy your *entire* vacation, make sure that you wear a strong sunblock, even while snorkeling. We recommend a waterproof sunblock with at least an SPF of 15. We've had good luck with BullFrog and Neutrogena. Try to avoid the sun between 11 a.m. and 2 p.m. when the sun's rays are particularly strong. If you are fair-skinned or unaccustomed to the sun and want to lay out, 15-20 minutes per side is all you should consider the first day. You can increase it a bit each day. *Beware of the fact that our ever constant trade winds will hide the symptoms of a burn until it's too late.* You might find that trying to get your tan as golden as possible isn't worth it. Tropical suntans are notoriously short lived, whereas you are sure to remember a bad burn far longer. If, after all of our warnings, you *still* get burned, aloe vera gel works well to relieve the pain. Some come with lidocaine in them. Ask your hotel front desk if they have any aloe plants on the grounds. Peel the skin off a section and make several crisscross cuts in the meat, then rub the plant on your skin. *Oooo,* it'll feel so good!

Water Hazards

The most serious water hazard is the surf. Though more calm in the summer and on the west side, high surf can be found anywhere on the island at any time of the year. The sad fact is that more people drown in Hawai'i each year than anywhere else in the country. This isn't said to keep you from enjoying the ocean, but rather to instill in you a healthy respect for Hawaiian waters. See BEACHES for more information on this.

Ocean Critters

Hawaiian marine life, for the most part, is quite friendly. There are, however, a few notable exceptions. Below is a list of some critters that you should be aware of. This is not mentioned to frighten you out of the water. The odds are overwhelming that you won't have any trouble with any of the beasties listed below. But should you encounter one, this information should be of some help.

SHARKS—Hawai'i does have sharks. They are mostly white-tipped reef sharks and the occasional hammerhead or tiger shark. Contrary to what most people think, sharks are in every ocean and don't pose the level of danger people attribute to them. In the past 25 years there have been a handful of documented shark attacks off the Big Island, mostly tigers attacking surfers. Considering the number of people who swam in our waters during that time, you are more likely to choke to death on a bone at a lu'au than be attacked by a shark. If you do happen to come upon a shark, however, swim away slowly. This kind of movement disinterests them. *Don't* splash about rapidly. By doing this you are imitating a fish in distress, and you don't want to do that. The one kind of water you want to avoid is murky water, such as that found in river mouths. Most shark attacks occur in murky water at dawn or dusk since sharks are basically cowards who like to sneak up on their prey. In general, don't go around worrying about sharks. *Any* animal can be threatening. (Remember when President Carter was attacked by a rabbit?)

PORTUGUESE MAN-OF-WAR—These creatures are related to jellyfish but are unable to swim. They are instead propelled by a small sail and are at the mercy of the wind. Though small, they are capable of inflicting a painful sting. This occurs when the long trailing appendages are touched, triggering the spring-loaded stinger, called a nematocyst, which injects poison. The resulting burning sensation is usually very unpleasant but not fatal. Fortunately, the Portuguese Man-of-War is not a common visitor to the Big Island. When they *do* come ashore, however, they usually do so in great numbers, jostled by a strong storm offshore. If you see them on the beach, don't go in the water. If you do get stung, immediately remove the stinger

and as much of the venom as possible with a cloth or sand. Be careful not to stimulate any inactivated nematocyst on your skin or you'll be stung some more. Remove them carefully or use white vinegar to destroy them. Then apply baking soda, diluted ammonia, or alcohol and see a physician. The folk cure is urine but you might look pretty silly applying it.

SEA URCHINS—These are like living pin cushions. They also eat coral, so we don't like them. If you step on one, or accidentally grab one, remove as much of the spine as possible with tweezers. See a physician if necessary.

CORAL—Coral is very sharp, and since it is made up of millions of individual living organisms, a scrape can leave proteinaceous matter in the wound, causing infection. This is why coral cuts are frustratingly slow to heal. Immediate cleaning and disinfecting of coral cuts should speed up healing time. One type of coral you may have heard of is fire coral. It'a apparently absent from the islands, so you don't have to worry about brushing up against it the way they do in the Caribbean.

SEA ANEMONES—Related to the jellyfish, these also have stingers and are usually found attached to rocks or coral. It's best not to touch them with your bare hands. Treatment for a sting is similar to that of a Portuguese Man-of-War.

Bugs

Though devoid of the myriad of hideous buggies found in other parts of the world, there are a few evil critters, brought here from elsewhere, that you should know about. The worst are **centipedes.** They can get to be six or more inches long and are aggressive predators. They shouldn't be messed with. If you get stung, even by a baby, the pain can range from a bad bee sting to a bad gunshot wound. Some local doctors say the only cure is to stay drunk for three days. Others say to use meat tenderizer. **Scorpions** are present on the dry, western side of the island. Though not as nasty as the ones you see in the movies, a sting is unpleasant nonetheless. They're usually a couple inches across and mildly aggressive. **Cane spiders** are big, dark, and look horrifying, but they're not poisonous. (But they seem to *think* they are. I've had *them* chase *me* across the room when *I* had the broom in my hand.) We *don't* have no-see-ums, those irritating sand fleas

With no permanent streams on the west side of the island, freshwater sometimes collects inside lava tubes at the shoreline, such as this one at Kiholo Bay.

common in the South Pacific and Caribbean. (A Hawaiian voyaging canoe that traveled to and from Tahiti on a cultural mission several years ago unknowingly brought them back. The crew was forced into quarantine against their will where the tiny biting insects were discovered and exterminated. No-see-ums would have easily spread here and change Hawai'i forever.)

Mosquitoes were unknown in the islands until the first stowaways arrived on Maui on the *Wellington* in 1826. Since then they have thrived. A good mosquito repellent containing DEET will come in handy, especially if you plan to go hiking. *Lotions* (not thin liquids) with DEET seem to work and stick best. Forget the guidebooks that tell you to take vitamin B12 to keep mosquitoes away; it just gives the little critters a healthier diet. If you find one dive bombing you at night in your room, turn on your overhead fan to help keep them away. Local residents and resorts often rely on genetically engineered plants such as Citrosa, which irritates mosquitoes as much as they irritate us.

Bees are more common on the drier west side of the island. Usually, the only way you'll get stung is if you run into one. If you rent a scooter, beware; one of us received his first bee sting while singing *Come Sail Away* on a motorcycle. A bee sting in the mouth can definitely ruin one of your precious vacation days.

Regarding **cockroaches,** there's good news and bad news. The bad news is that here, some are bigger than your thumb and can fly. The good news is that you probably won't see one. One of their predators is the **gecko.** This small, lizard-like creature makes a surprisingly loud chirp at night. They are cute and considered good luck in the Islands (probably because they eat mosquitoes and roaches).

Leptospirosis is a bacteria that is found is some of Hawai'i's freshwater. It is transmitted from animal urine and can enter the body from open cuts, eyes, and by drinking. Around 100 people a year in Hawai'i are diagnosed with the bacteria, which is treated with antibiotics if caught relatively early. You should avoid crossing streams such as Waipi'o with open cuts, and treat all water found in nature with treatment pills before drinking. (Filters are ineffective for lepto.)

Though not a bug, one animal you are almost sure to see is the **mongoose.** Think of it as a stealth squirrel with mean-looking red eyes. Mongooses (no, not mongeese) are bold enough to take on cobras in their native India and were brought here to help control rats. Great idea, except mongooses are active during the day and rats work the night shift, so never the twain shall meet. It was a disaster for local birds since mongooses love bird eggs. Kaua'i is the only major island to avoid the mongoose (and vice versa), and the difference between its bird population and the Big Island's is dramatic.

There are no snakes in Hawai'i (except for some reporters). There is concern that the brown tree snake *might* have made its way onto the islands from Guam. Although mostly harmless to humans, these snakes can spell extinction to native birds. Government officials aren't allowed to tell you this, but we will: If you ever see one anywhere in Hawai'i, please *kill it* and contact the Pest Hotline at (800) 468–4644, ext. 67378. At the very least, call them immediately. The entire bird population of Hawai'i will be grateful.

Vog

Vog is a mixture of water vapor, carbon dioxide, and sulfur dioxide. Each day (since the current eruption began) Kilauea belches 2,500 *tons* of sulphur dioxide, which reacts with sunlight, oxygen, dust particles, and water in the air to form a mixture of sulfate aerosols, sulfuric acid and other oxidized sulfur compounds. Why should *you* care? Because our trade winds blow toward the southwest, carrying the vog from its source, down the coast where the winds wrap around Mauna Loa and head up the coast. Then daytime onshore breezes and nighttime offshore breezes rake it back and forth across Kona. If you have a severe lung condition or are very asthmatic, you *may* experience discomfort. (When our asthmatic nephew visits us, he has no problems, for what it's worth.) Those who stay in Kohala and Hilo are usually free from vog. In all, it's probably less than the smog most mainland cities, but we did want to alert you to one of the few negatives to living on an active volcano. Call 885-7143 for the vog index. The scale is between 1 & 10, with 10 being the worst.

Dehydration

Bring and drink lots of water when you are out and about, especially when you are hiking. Dehydration sneaks up on people. By the time you are thirsty, you're already dehydrated. It's a good idea to take an insulated water jug with you in the car or one of those 1½ liter bottles of water. Our weather is almost certainly different than what you left behind, and you will probably find yourself thirstier than usual. Just fill it before you leave in the morning and *such 'em up* (as we say here) all day.

Curses

Legend says that if you remove any lava from the island that bad luck will befall you. *Balderdash!* you say. Hey, we don't know if it's true or not. You don't have to be a believer, but talk to any resort or local post office, and they will tell you about boxes of lava that come in all the time from visitors who brought a souvenir of lava home, only to have their house burn down, have their foot fall off, or get audited by the IRS. Coincidence? Maybe. But if you decide to do it anyway, remember…you have been warned.

TRAVELING WITH CHILDREN

Perhaps we should have put this section under HAZARDS. The Hilton Waikoloa probably has the most extensive children's activity program. Their Camp Menehune (ages 5–12) is a youngster's dream. Several other Kohala resorts also try hard to cater to families. If your keiki (kid) is looking for an adventure, check out page 211 where we have a dandy adventure just for them. **Baby's Away (329-7475)** has the usual assortment of keiki paraphernalia for rent, such as car seats, strollers, cribs, bathtubs, etc.

For swimming, the beach in front of the King Kamehameha's Kona Beach Hotel or the tide-pools at the National Energy Lab in Kona, and Onekahakaha in Hilo are probably the safest on the island. (Check them out yourself to be sure.) We don't need to tell you that keikis and surf don't mix.

There's a great playground at **Higashihara Park** just south of Kona past the 115 mile marker. Another on is **Waimea Park** in Waimea. See Waimea map.

If you want to eat at a nice restaurant but are afraid the little ones might get restless, we've noticed that many parents

The island is crisscrossed with lava tube caves. Sometimes the ceilings are thin (as more than one bulldozer operator working above one has discovered in the past).

often eat at the Kona Inn, where the strip of grass between the restaurant and the shoreline serves as a convenient romping area for kids when they are finished. You can still keep an eye out for them so they don't wander too far.

Lastly, you should know that it's a big fine plus a mandatory safety class if your keiki isn't buckled up.

THE PEOPLE

There's no doubt about it, people really *are* friendlier in Hawai'i. You will notice that people are quick to smile and wave at you here. (Those of us who live here have to remember to pack our "mainland face" when we journey there. Otherwise, we get undesired responses when we smile or wave at complete strangers.) It probably comes down to a matter of happiness. People are happy here, and happy people are friendly people. Some people compare a trip to an outer island in Hawai'i to a trip back in time, when smiles weren't rare, and politeness was the order of the day.

Ethnic Breakdown

The Big Island has an ethnic mix that is as diversified as any you will find. Here, *everyone* is a minority; there are no majorities. The last census revealed the ethnic makeup below:

White	47,736
Japanese	25,044
Hawaiian	23,120
Filipino	15,540
Chinese	2,518
Other Asian or Pacific Islander	975
Korean	921
American Indian	868
Black	615
Samoan	382
Other	2,598
Total	**120,118**

Many endemic Hawaiian birds, such as these nenes, are endangered and protected. At one time the Volcano House restaurant served nene like turkey, with a side dish of golden plover on toast.

Some Terms

A person of Hawaiian blood is Hawaiian. Only people of this race are called by this term. They are also called Kanaka Maoli, but only another Hawaiian can use this term. Anybody who was born here, regardless of race (except whites) is called a local. If you were born elsewhere but have lived here awhile, you are called a kama'aina. If you are white, you are a haole. It doesn't matter if you have been here a day or your family has been here for over a century, you will always be a haole. The term comes from the time when westerners first encountered these islands. Its precise meaning has been lost, but it is thought to refer to people with no background (since westerners could not chant the kanaenae of their ancestors).

The continental United States is called the Mainland. If you are here and are returning, you are not "going back to the states" (we *are* a state). When somebody leaves the island, they are off-island

Hawaiian Time

One aspect of Hawaiian culture you may have heard of is Hawaiian Time. The stereotype is that everyone in Hawai'i moves just a little bit slower than on the mainland. Supposedly we are more laid-back and don't let things get to us as easily as people on the mainland. This is the stereotype... OK, it's *not* a stereotype. It's real. Hopefully, during your visit, you will notice that this feeling infects *you* as well. You may find yourself letting another driver cut in front of you in circumstances that would incur your wrath back home. You may find yourself willing to wait for a red light without feeling like you're going to explode. The whole reason for coming to Hawai'i is to experience beauty and a sense of peace, so let it happen. If someone else is moving a bit slower than you want, just go with it.

Shaka

One symbol you will see often and should not be offended by is the *shaka* sign. This is done by extending the pinkie and thumb while curling up the three middle fingers. Sometimes visitors think it is some kind of local gesture indicating *up yours* or some similarly unfriendly message. Actually it is a friendly act used as a sign of greeting or just to say *Hey*. Its origin is thought to date back to the 1930s. A guard at the Kahuku Sugar Plantation on Oʻahu used to patrol the plantation railroad to keep local kids from stealing cane from the slow moving trains. This guard had lost his middle fingers in an accident and his manner of waving off the youths became well known. Kids began to warn other kids that he was around by waving their hands in a way that looked like the guard's, and the custom took off.

THE HAWAIIAN LANGUAGE

The Hawaiian language is a beautiful, gentle, and melodic language that flows smoothly off the tongue. Just the sounds of the words conjure up trees gently blowing in the breeze and the sound of the surf. Most Polynesian languages share the same roots, and many have common words. Today, Hawaiian is spoken *as an everyday language* only on the privately owned island of Niʻihau. Visitors are often intimidated by Hawaiian. With a few ground rules you will come to realize that pronunciation is not as hard as you might think.

When missionaries discovered that the Hawaiians had no written language, they sat down and created an alphabet. This Hawaiian alphabet has only twelve letters. Five vowels; A, E, I, O, and U as well as seven consonants; H, K, L, M, N, P, and W. The consonants are pronounced just as they are in English with the exception of W. It is often pronounced as a V if it is in the middle of a word and comes after an E or I. Vowels are pronounced as follows:

> A—pronounced as in *Ah* if stressed, or *above* if not stressed.
> E—pronounced as in *say* if stressed, or *dent* if not stressed.
> I—pronounced as in *bee.*
> O—pronounced as in *nose.*
> U—pronounced as in *stew.*

If you examine long Hawaiian words, you will see that most have repeating syllables, making it easier to remember and pronounce.

One thing you will notice in this book are glottal stops. These are represented by an upside-down apostrophe ʻ and are meant to convey a hard stop in the pronunciation. So if we are talking about the a type of lava called aʻa, it is pronounced as two separate As.

Another feature you will encounter are diphthongs, where two letters glide together. They are ae, ai, ao, au, ei, eu, oi, and ou. Unlike many English diphthongs, the second vowel is always pronounced. One word you will read in this book, referring to Hawaiian temples, is *heiau* (hey-ee-ow). The e and i flow together as a single sound, then the a and u flow together as a single sound. The ee sound binds the two sounds making the whole word flow together.

Let's take a word that might seem

impossible to pronounce. When you see how easy this word is, the rest will seem like a snap. The Hawaiian State Fish used to be the humuhumunukunukuapua'a. At first glance it seems like a nightmare. But if you read the word slowly, it is pronounced just like it looks and isn't nearly as horrifying as it appears. Try it. Humu (hoo-moo) is pronounced twice. Nuku (noo-koo) is pronounced twice. A (ah) is pronounced once. Pu (poo) is pronounced once. A'a (ah-ah) is the ah sound pronounced twice, the glottal stop indicating a hard stop between sounds. Now you can try it again. Humuhumunukunukuapua'a. Now, wasn't that easy? OK, so it's not easy, but it's not impossible either.

Below are some words that you might hear during your visit:

'Aina (eye-nah)—Land.
Akamai (ah-kah-MY)—Wise or shrewd.
Ali'i (ah-LEE-ee)—A Hawaiian chief; a member of the chiefly class.
Aloha (ah-LOW-ha)—Hello, goodbye, or a feeling or the spirit of love, affection, or kindness.
Hala (hah-la)—Pandanus tree.
Hale (hah-leh)—House or building.
Hana (ha-nah)—Work.
Hana hou (ha-nah-HO)—To do again.
Haole (how-leh)—Originally foreigner, now means Caucasian.
Heiau (hey-ee-ow)—Hawaiian temple.
Hula (hoo-lah)—The story-telling dance of Hawai'i.
Imu (ee-moo)—An underground oven.
'Iniki (ee-nee-key)—Sharp and piercing wind (as in Hurricane 'Iniki).
Kahuna (kah-HOO-na)—A priest or minister; someone who is an expert in a profession.
Kai (kigh)—The sea.

Kalua (KAH-loo-ah)—Cooking food underground.
Kama'aina (kah-ma-EYE-na)—Long-time Hawai'i resident.
Kane (kah-neh)—Boy or man.
Kapu (kah-poo)—Forbidden, taboo; keep out.
Keiki (kay-key)—Child or children.
Kokua (koh-koo-ah)—Help.
Kona (koh-NAH)—Leeward side of the island; wind blowing from the south, southwest direction.
Kuleana (koo-leh-AH-nah)—Concern, responsibility, or jurisdiction.
Lanai (lah-NIGH)—Porch, veranda, patio.
Lani (lah-nee)—Sky or heaven.
Lei (lay)—Necklace of flowers, shells, or feathers. The lehua blossom lei is the lei of the Big Island.
Liliko'i (lee-lee-koy)—Passion fruit.
Limu (lee-moo)—Edible seaweed.
Lomi (low-mee)—To rub or massage; lomi salmon is raw salmon rubbed with salt and spices.
Lu'au (loo-ow)—Hawaiian feast; literally means taro leaves.
Mahalo (mah-hah-low)—Thank you.
Makai (mah-kigh)—Toward the sea.
Malihini (mah-lee-hee-nee)—A newcomer, visitor, or guest.
Mauka (mow-ka)—Toward the mountain.
Moana (moh-ah-nah)—Ocean.
Mo'o (moh-oh)—Lizard.
Nani (nah-nee)—Beautiful, pretty.
Nui (new-ee)—Big, important, great.
'Ohana (oh-hah-nah)—Family.
'Ono (oh-no)—Delicious, the best.
'Okole (oh-koh-leh)—Derrière.
Pakalolo (pah-kah-low-low)—Marijuana.
Pali (pah-lee)—A cliff.
Paniolo (pah-nee-OH-low)—Hawaiian cowboy.

Pau (pow)—Finish, end; i.e. pau hana means quitting time from work.

Poi (poy)—Pounded kalo (taro) root that forms a paste.

Pono (poh-no)—Goodness, excellence, correct, proper.

Pua (poo-ah)—Flower.

Pupu (poo-poo)—Appetizer, snacks, or finger food.

Puka (poo-ka)—Hole.

Wahine (vah-hee-neh)—Woman.

Wai (why)—Fresh water.

Wikiwiki (wee-kee-wee-kee)—To hurry up, very quick.

Quick Pidgin Lesson

Hawaiian pidgin is fun to listen to. It's like ear candy. It's colorful, rhythmic, and sways in the wind. Below is a list of some of the words and phrases you might hear on your visit. It's tempting to read some of these and try to use them. If you do, the odds are you will simply look foolish. These words and phrases are used in certain ways and with certain inflections. People who have spent years living in the islands still feel uncomfortable using them. Thick pidgin can be incomprehensible to the untrained ear (that's the idea). If you are someplace and hear two people engaged in a discussion in pidgin, stop and eavesdrop for a bit. You won't forget it.

Pidgin Words and Phrases

An' den—And then? So?

Any kine—Anything; any kind.

Ass right—That's right.

Ass wy—That's why.

Beef—Fight.

Brah—Bruddah; friend; brother.

Brok' da mouf—Delicious.

Buggah—That's the one; it is difficult.

Bummahs—Bummer; too bad.

Bus laugh—To laugh out loud.

Bus nose—How one reacts to a bad smell.

Chicken skin kine—Something that gives you goose bumps.

Cockaroach—Steal; rip off.

Cool head main ting—Stay cool; relax.

Cornbeef eye—Same as stink eye.

Da kine—A noun or verb used in place of whatever the speaker wishes. Heard constantly.

Fo Days—plenty; "He got hair fo days."

Geevum—Go for it! Give 'em hell!

Grind—To eat.

Grinds—Food.

Hold ass—A close call when driving your new car.

How you figga?—How do you figure that? It makes no sense.

Howzit?—How is it going? How are you? Also, Howzit o wot?

I owe you money or wot?—What to say when someone is staring at you.

Lesgo—Let's go; let's do it.

Make house—Make yourself at home.

Mek ass—Make a fool of yourself.

Mo' bettah—This is better.

No can—Cannot; I cannot do it.

No, yeah?—No, or is "no" correct?

'Okole squeezer—Something that suddenly frightens you ('okole meaning derrière).

O wot?—Or what?

Poi dog—A mutt.

Shahkbait—Shark bait, meaning pale, untanned people.

Shaka—Great! All right!

Shredding—Riding a gnarly wave.

Sleepahs—Flip flops, thongs, zoris.

Stink eye—Dirty looks; facial expression denoting displeasure.

Suck rocks—Buzz off, or pound sand.

Talk story—Shooting the breeze; to rap.

Tanks eh?—Thank you.

To da max—All the way; the most you can get.

Waddascoops?—What's the scoop? What's happening?

Yeah?—Used at the end of sentences.

MUSIC

Hawaiian music is far more diverse than most people think. Many people picture Hawaiian music as someone twanging away on an 'ukulele with their voice slipping and sliding all over the place like they have an ice cube down their back. In reality, the music here can be outstanding. There is the melodic sound of the more traditional music. There are young local bands putting out modern music with a Hawaiian beat. There is even Hawaiian reggae. *Hawaiian Style Band,* the late *Israel Kamakawiwo'ole* (known locally as Bruddah Iz) and *Bruddah Waltah* are excellent examples. Even if you don't always agree with the all the messages in the songs, there's no denying the talent of these groups. If you get a chance, stop by **Tempo Music** in Hilo at Prince Kuhio Plaza, or in Kona at Kopiko Plaza. They have a good selection of Hawaiian music. **Borders Books** (331–1668) in Kona or in Hilo (933–1410) also has a good selection.

THE HULA

The hula evolved as a means of worship, later becoming a forum for telling a story with chants (called mele), hands, and body movement. It can be fascinating to watch. When most people think of the hula, they picture a woman in a grass skirt swinging her hips to the beat of an 'ukulele. But in reality there are two types of hula. The modern hula, or hula 'auana, uses musical instruments and vocals to augment the dancer. It came about after westerners first encountered the Islands. Missionaries found the hula distasteful, and the old style was driven underground. The modern type came about as a form of entertainment and was practiced in places where missionaries had no influence. Ancient Hawaiians didn't even use grass skirts. They were later brought by Gilbert Islanders.

The old style of hula is called hula 'olapa or hula kahiko. It consists of chants and is accompanied by percussion only and takes years of training. It can be exciting to watch as performers work together in a synchronous harmony. Both men and women participate, with women's hula being softer (though no less disciplined) and men's hula being more active. This type of hula is physically demanding, requiring strong concentration. Keiki (children's) hula can be charming to watch as well.

The world's best gather each year for a week starting the first Thursday after Easter Sunday for the **Merrie Monarch Festival** (named after the 19th-century king credited with reviving the hula). Tickets are often hard to come by if you wait until the end. Call (808) 935–9168 *several* months in advance if you want to be assured of getting a seat. Otherwise, check it out on TV. It will utterly dazzle you.

MISCELLANEOUS INFORMATION

Traveler's checks are usually accepted, but you should be aware that some merchants might look at you like you just tried to offer them Mongolian money. You should also know that the American Express Card seems to be less welcome here than other destinations. *Many* places will not accept it.

It is customary here for *everyone* to remove their shoes upon entering someone's house (sometimes their office).

If you are going to spend any time at the beach, woven bamboo beach mats can be found all over the island for $1–$2 dollars. Some roll up, some can be folded. The sand comes off these easier than it comes off towels.

It's a good idea to get your photos developed here. That's because developers are more familiar with the colors. (Just try to get a black or green sand beach to look right from a mainland developer, and you'll see what I mean.) If you don't want to pay retail-retail, try Costco, Wal-mart, Kmart or Longs. Most have cheap one-hour service and are surprisingly good. Most will redo the photos to make the color right.

Around the island you'll see signs saying VISITOR INFORMATION or something similar. Allow me to translate. That's usually code for WE WANT TO SELL YOU SOMETHING.

There are no large **grocery stores** in the Kohala resort area, but you'll find one six miles up Waikoloa Road (which is across from the 75 mile marker) in Waikoloa Village. They're easy to find in Kona and Hilo. If you are staying at a condo, those in the know head over to **Costco** (334–0770) just north of Kona (shown on map on page 151) to stock up. If you're not a member of this national warehouse store, you *might* qualify for membership. If so, the savings on food and everything else are incredible. Otherwise, ask around to see if any residents you are dealing with will let you go with them.

If you want to arrange a lei greeting for you or your honey when you disembark the airplane at Kona Airport, **Greeters of** Hawai'i (800) 366–8559 can make the arrangements for around $20. Nice way to kick off a romantic trip, huh?

A WORD ABOUT DRIVING TOURS

The Big Island is, to use the scientific term, *one big bugga*. With this in mind, we have decided to describe the various parts of the island in a series of tours. You're not being pigeonholed into seeing the island in this order, but we had to organize the regions in some fashion, and this seemed the logical way to do it rather than a scattershot description. You can take these tours from anyplace you are staying, but we have described most of them (except the Hilo Tour and the Hamakua/Waimea tour) on the assumption that you are starting from the west (Kona) side because the majority of Big Island visitors do just that. The Hamakua/Waimea section is described from Hilo side first because it is convenient to see it that way after traveling to Hilo via Saddle Road.

Nearly every guidebook divides the Big Island and its sights by districts. (See

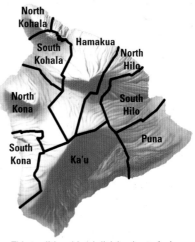

This traditional land division is confusing and irrelevant to the modern traveler.

graphic.) While this land division made perfect sense to the ancients who divvied up the island amongst themselves, it is not real helpful to the modern traveler who cruises the island by car. So we have divided the island up in a way that makes more sense to today's visitor. It takes into account where most people stay and how they drive. Look at the inside *front* cover to see how we have divided the island and on what pages we describe the sights.

Most main roads have mile markers erected every mile. Since Hawai'i is mostly void of other identification signs, these little green signs can be a big help in knowing where you are at a given time. Therefore, we have placed them on the maps represented as a number inside a small box ⑯. We will often describe a certain feature or unmarked road as being, "⁴⁄₁₀ miles past the 22 mile mark." We hope this helps.

For directions, locals usually describe things as being on the *mauka* side of the highway (meaning toward the mountains) or *makai* (toward the ocean).

Beaches, activities and adventures are mentioned briefly, but described in detail in their own separate sections.

BOOKS

There is an astonishing variety of books available about Hawai'i and the Big Island. Everything from history, legends, geology, children's stories, and just plain ol' novels. **Borders Books** at Henry Street and Highway 11 in Kona (331–1668) and in Hilo at the Waiakea Center on Highway 11 (933–1410) have dazzling selections. Walk in and lose yourself in Hawai'i's richness. **Basically Books** on Kamehameha in Hilo (961–0144) also has a superb col-

lection of Hawaii titles. They also have the best selection of topographic maps on the island. A good resource.

THE INTERNET

Our web site, **www.wizardpub.com** has recent changes, links to cool sites and the latest satellite weather shots, aerial photos of the resorts, and more. We also show our own aerial photos of nearly every place to stay, so you'll know if oceanfront *really* means oceanfront. It also has links to every company listed in the book that has a site—both those we like and those we recommend against. For the record we don't charge a cent for links (it would be a conflict of interest), and there are no advertisements on the site. (Well...except for our own books, of course.) We could have listed all of the addresses in the book, but it seemed pretty mean to make you type in all of those URL addresses.

In the past we printed a **Calendar of Events** mentioning festivals, island celebrations, and special events. *Waste of time!* Organizers make changes so often (including days before scheduled events) that it wasn't reliable enough to continue printing it in advance. But the internet is perfect for that. So the web site has updated listings of island events.

If you're on-island and need web access (to check your mail, etc.), most of the big resorts have business services available for around $20 an hour. **Hawai'i Online** (800 733–5638) can arrange unlimited local internet access for $10 a week. Call them in advance. **Zac's** (329–0006) in Kona has internet access for $6 per hour. The various libraries around the island sometimes offer free surfing from their computers if you need internet access while on-island.

'Anaeho'omalu Beach is a sunset photographer's dream come true.

Kohala is the oldest volcano on the island, having last sputtered 60,000 years ago. It contains lush forest, dry lava desert, windswept grassy plains, and outrageous beaches. Some of the most expensive resorts on the island are along the Kohala Coast.

This is a large, diverse area to cover in one section, but because of the way the island's resorts are distributed and the roads are laid out, most will see this area in a circular driving tour. Therefore, that's how we will describe it.

We're going to start as you leave Kona (see map) heading up Highway 190. If you are staying in Kohala, you can come up Waikoloa Village Road and pick up the description on Highway 190 heading north. If staying in Hilo, pick it up from Waimea.

UP HIGHWAY 190 FROM KAILUA-KONA

As you leave Kona, you'll take Palani Road, which becomes Mamalahoa Highway (190) heading north. (See map on next page or page 59.) From near sea level, you will be heading up to 3,564 feet then down again into Hawi, so gas up on that cheap *(ha!)* Kona gasoline.

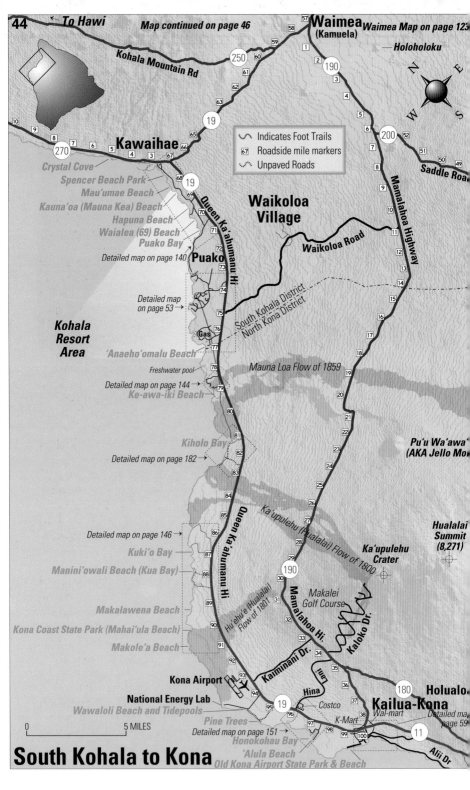

South Kohala to Kona

44

To Hawi

Map continued on page 46

Kohala Mountain Rd

250

Waimea (Kamuela)

Waimea Map on page 123

Holoholoku

190

200

Saddle Road

19

Kawaihae

270

Crystal Cove
Spencer Beach Park
Mau'umae Beach
Kauna'oa (Mauna Kea) Beach
Hapuna Beach
Waialea (69) Beach
Puako Bay

Detailed map on page 140

Puako

Waikoloa Village

Waikoloa Road

Queen Ka'ahumanu Hi.

Mamalahoa Highway

Detailed map on page 53 →

Indicates Foot Trails
67 Roadside mile markers
Unpaved Roads

Gas

Kohala Resort Area

'Anaeho'omalu Beach

Freshwater pool

South Kohala District
North Kona District

Detailed map on page 144 →
Ke-awa-iki Beach

Mauna Loa Flow of 1859

Kiholo Bay

Detailed map on page 182 →

Ka'upulehu (Hualalai) Flow of 1800

Pu'u Wa'awa' (AKA Jello Mo

Hualalai Summit (8,271)

Detailed map on page 146 →

Queen Ka'ahumanu Hi.

Kuki'o Bay
Manini'owali Beach (Kua Bay)

Makalawena Beach
Kona Coast State Park (Mahai'ula Beach)
Makole'a Beach

Ka'upulehu Crater

Makalei Golf Course

Kaloko Dr.

190

Hu'ehu'e (Hualalai) Flow of 1801

Mamalahoa Hi.

Kaiminani Dr.

Hina

Kona Airport

National Energy Lab
Wawaloli Beach and Tidepools
Pine Trees

Detailed map on page 151
Honokohau Bay
'Alula Beach
Old Kona Airport State Park & Beach

19

Costco

K-Mart

Wal-mart

180

Holualo

Kailua-Kona

Detailed ma page 59

11

Alii Dr

0   5 MILES

Leaving Kailua-Kona, it's hard to believe that just above the town is a fern and 'ohi'a cloud forest steeped in fog and moss. Weather here is determined by altitude. You can see it by taking Koloko Road just south of the 34 mile marker. Follow it as it winds itself into another world. The road dead ends at 5,000 feet, but you don't have to go that far to appreciate the green slopes of Hualalai.

As you leave Kona, you'll get some good views down the coast. Keep an eye out for renegade peacocks from the Makalei Golf Course around the 32 mile marker.

The highway bisects several channels and tubes in the lava between the 28 and 26 mile markers. Rivers of molten stone coursed down the mountain here during the 1800 Hualalai lava flow. If you look down the coast you'll get an idea of the scale of a "typical" lava flow.

By the 19 mile marker you have passed from Hualalai Mountain to the slopes of Mauna Loa. Proof is in the form of a lava flow here that ran for 30 miles in 1859 all the way to Kiholo Bay, destroying Kamehameha's fishpond (see BEACHES). If clouds are absent, you may see the top of Mauna Kea and its many dome-enclosed telescopes ahead and on your right.

As you continue, you'll notice cactus scattered about, and trees appear again. Parker Ranch starts at the 14 mile marker, part of a colossal 225,000 acre cattle ranch.

At the 11 mile marker is the road through Waikoloa Village, which leads down to the Kohala mega-resorts. It's marked by a giant obelisk erected by Waikoloa Land Co. in a fit of psychedelic creativity. Waikoloa Village is a relatively new and stark community. Due to its location, on the leeward side of the

saddle between Mauna Loa and Mauna Kea, it's usually pretty windy. *(How often? When the wind stops, the cows fall down.)* If you are staying at a mega-resort in Kohala, you'll want to know that there is a fairly large grocery store here.

Between the 5 and 2 mile markers off to your right (up mauka) is a large hill, called Holoholoku. Everyone has seen the famous WWII photo and statue of the scene where Marines on Iwo Jima raised the American flag over Mt. Suribachi. Possibly the most dramatic war photo ever taken, it puts a lump in your throat every time you see it. What you don't know is that those very guys practiced storming the hill right there on Holoholoku because it was thought to be similar to Suribachi in size and shape.

As you approach the town of Waimea (Kamuela), you may decide to check it out now. Since this is the crossroads between the east and west sides of the island, we could have included it here or in the section on Hamakua. After careful analysis of driving patterns, accommodation indexes, and topography...we flipped a coin and put it in the Hamakua section. Waimea has an incredibly colorful history and is worth exploring. If you do it now, turn to page 123 before continuing on.

KOHALA MOUNTAIN ROAD

See map on next page or on page 123 to get to Highway 250. (Left at the Chevron station.) You are traveling up the spine of the sleeping Kohala Volcano. (They say you shouldn't honk your horn or you may wake it up.) You're still on the dry leeward side and will crest at 3,564 feet before descending to the sea.

Around the 14 mile marker you'll start to see a huge mountain looming in front of you. That's not on this island; it's Maui 30 miles across the sea. On clear days,

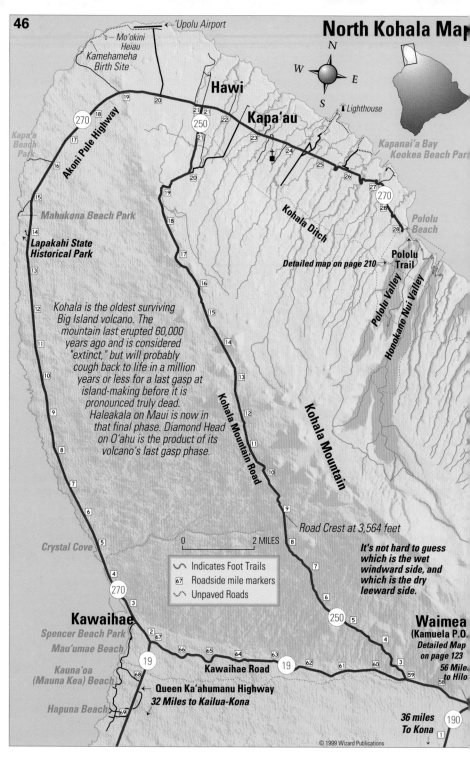

North Kohala Map

'Upolu Airport

Mo'okini Heiau
Kamehameha Birth Site

N
W   E
S

Hawi

Kapa'au

Lighthouse

Kapa'a Beach Park

Akoni Pule Highway

270

19   20

18

17

16

15

Mahukona Beach Park

14

Lapakahi State Historical Park

13

12

21 21

250

22

21

23

24

25

26

27   270

28

28

Kapanai'a Bay
Keokea Beach Park

Kohala Ditch

Detailed map on page 210

Pololu Beach

Pololu Trail

Pololu Valley

Honokane Nui Valley

Kohala is the oldest surviving Big Island volcano. The mountain last erupted 60,000 years ago and is considered "extinct," but will probably cough back to life in a million years or less for a last gasp at island-making before it is pronounced truly dead. Haleakala on Maui is now in that final phase. Diamond Head on O'ahu is the product of its volcano's last gasp phase.

11

10

9

8

7

6

5

Crystal Cove

4

270

3

Kawaihae

Spencer Beach Park
Mau'umae Beach

*Kauna'oa
(Mauna Kea) Beach*

Hapuna Beach

19

2
67

68

69

16

15

14

13

12

11

10

Kohala Mountain Road

Kohala Mountain

9

Road Crest at 3,564 feet

It's not hard to guess which is the wet windward side, and which is the dry leeward side.

7

6

250   5

4

3

59

58

Waimea
(Kamuela P.O.
Detailed Map on page 123

56 Miles to Hilo

0   2 MILES

⌇ Indicates Foot Trails
67 Roadside mile markers
⋯ Unpaved Roads

66   65   64   63

19

62   61   60

19

Kawaihae Road

Queen Ka'ahumanu Highway
32 Miles to Kailua-Kona

**36 miles
To Kona**

190

1

© 1999 Wizard Publications

the island of Maui seems to tower over the little town of Hawi even more than the Big Island's own volcanoes. Sometimes it looks gigantic, and sometimes less impressive. It's the same reason the moon always looks enormous when it's near a mountain horizon or through trees—it gives your brain some scale to compute its size. Maui looks biggest when you see it *with or through* something other than the ocean's horizon.

NORTH SHORE OF KOHALA

Be sure to take the road to Hawi, not Kapa'au, near the 20 mile marker. As you pull into Hawi, you're greeted by a couple of old banyan trees on your right. You'll want to head right (east), but if you're hungry, **Bamboo Restaurant** on your left is your best bet. There you will also find **Kohala Koa Gallery,** which has excellent wood carvings and silk paintings. Also consider stopping by **Tropical Dreams.** They have *outstanding* ice cream made here on the island. We unselfishly review it every time we are on the north shore, just to be thorough.

The sleepy little towns of Hawi and Kapa'au lie at this northernmost point of the island. Until the 70s, this was sugar country. When Kohala Sugar pulled out, this area was left high and dry. Rather than let their towns die, residents stuck it out, opening shops and other small businesses. Today, this area is enjoying a comeback of sorts. There are lots of artists who call this area home. A Japanese investment company bought most of Kohala Sugar's land assets (19,000 acres) in 1988 and has *plans* for a resort at Mahukona, a restaurant at the end of the road overlooking Pololu Valley, and more. But they've been *planning* for a long time. In the meantime, this is a quiet, peaceful community. It's said that the investor bought all this land after simply flying over in a helicopter—without ever touching it!

Heading east, you come to the town of **Kapa'au.** On the mauka side of the

Horseback riding in North Kohala is a wide-open affair.

highway in Kapaʻau is a statue of **King Kamehameha the Great**. If it looks just like the famous one standing in front of the Judiciary building in Honolulu, that's because it's the same…sort of. When the Hawaiian Legislature commissioned the statue in 1878, it was cast in Paris and put on a ship. Unfortunately, the ship and its cargo were lost at sea near the Falkland Islands in the South Atlantic. Since they had shipping insurance, they used the money to order a new one. Meanwhile, the captain of the wrecked ship later spotted the "lost" statue standing in Port Stanley (somebody had salvaged it). He bought it for $500 and shipped it (this time successfully—must have FedExed it) to Hawaiʻi where its broken arm was repaired, and it was erected where you see it now. On King Kamehameha Day (June 11) the statue is piled high with leis and other decorations and is quite a sight to see. There are public restrooms here behind the building.

Continuing east, just before the 24 mile marker is the road to **Kalahikiola Church**, built in 1855. Guidebooks usually tell you to stop by, check it out, and talk story with the caretaker or minister. Sounds sweet, but most of the times we've stopped by it's been empty and locked. (Another myth shattered!)

If you're into lighthouses or want to see some raw coastline, take the next left, past Sun Lumber and Kohala Carriages. After the gate (remember to close it behind you), the bumpy road (a car is *usually* OK) leads to the **Kauhola Point Lighthouse**. This area is wild and undeveloped and sports nice views of the sea cliffs that wrap around the north shore. The area just to the right (east) is full of abandoned sugar equipment and cars. Many are actually embedded in the *side* of the cliff, evidence of the rapid pace of

cliff erosion. Just a few decades ago the cars were buried in "stable" ground and the cliffs were much farther out. The road just to the left, before the lighthouse, has even better views. Park at the top of the hill and walk down to the overlook. Daring local youngsters sometimes bring their boogie boards down here.

Back on the highway look to your left just before the 25 mile marker. There is a large banyan tree with a nifty **tree house**. Wouldn't you have *loved* a tree house like that when you were a kid?

Though you're above the ocean and there are no navigable rivers, a popular activity here is **kayaking** in an unlikely place—the old Kohala Ditch. There are also ATV **tours** along the coastal cliffs, both described under ACTIVITIES.

POLOLU VALLEY

The end of the road is the **Pololu Valley Lookout**. This outstanding vista displays the raw, untamed side of the Big Island. **A Real Gem** Nearly vertical cliffs are battered unmercifully by the north shore surf. Four hundred feet below is **Pololu Beach**, accessed via a 15–20 minute (each way) trail through lush vegetation. If it's been raining much, the trail may be slippery. At several spots you'll find black sand dunes over 100 feet high, now mostly covered with vegetation. This type of black sand beach is formed as water constantly chips away at the lava river bed. Though the beach is not very swimmable (the surf and current are usually too violent), it's very picturesque and a nice place to observe Mother Nature's force. During the week you may have it mostly to yourself down there. Halfway down the trail is a small natural

Thousands of tons of stones have been hauled from here to build temples, houses, and other structures. The massive Pu'ukohola Heiau 25 miles away at Kawaihae was built from stones from this valley. A gigantic chain of people passed stones hand to hand all the way. If one was dropped, it was left where it lay (unless it was on his foot) to prevent the cadence from being interrupted. When you're ready, head back west past Hawi.

MO'OKINI HEIAU

Near the 20 mile marker is a sign saying simply "Upolu Airport." This loop road (unpaved in parts) leads to the northernmost tip of the island and past two important sites. You head left when you reach the quiet 'Upolu Airport. The county does a terrible job maintaining this road and there *may* be large puddles past the airport if it's been raining much, which will dissuade those without JEEPS.

The Pololu Lookout is your reward for driving to the end of the road in North Kohala.

platform that looks out over the beach—a good photo op. Be sure to close the gate at the bottom of the trail. The beach is prettier from below than above. On the opposite side of the valley, a trail leads up the wall over to the next valley, called Honokane Nui. (See ADVENTURES.) These seven valleys, from Pololu to Waipi'o, are the only part of this new island that show much sign of erosion.

In ancient times Pololu Valley was a bountiful source for waterworn stones.

This area is dominated by the legacy of two influential men—an ancient priest named Pa'ao and Kamehameha the Great. Pa'ao is said to have arrived in the 12th century and changed the islands. He was born in Tahiti or on one of its neighbor islands. It is said that the islands were in a state of anarchy when Pa'ao arrived. He restructured society, introduced the concept of human sacrifice, and brought other similar traditions. Here he built the Mo'okini Heiau, where countless people were put to death to please Pa'ao's hungry gods.

You'll probably have to park at the gate and walk five minutes to the heiau.

Even before we knew the gory details about Mo'okini Heiau's history, the place gave us the heebie-jeebies. We aren't the only ones who have noticed that the area around the temple is filled with an eerie, ghostly lifelessness, and it's the only place on the island that we like to avoid (not counting the Department of Motor Vehicles). Used for human sacrifices, the area feels devoid of a soul. The quiet is not comforting, but rather an empty void. The walls of Mo'okini are extremely tall and thick—oral tradition says that some of the rocks were passed by hand from Pololu Valley, 9 miles away. Just in front of the heiau is a large lava slab with a slight dip in it. In front of it is a raised stone. It takes little imagination to see that this slab was the *holehole* stone, where unfortunate victims were laid while the flesh was stripped from their bones. These bones were then used to make fishhooks and other objects. The number of Hawaiians sacrificed here ran into the tens of thousands.

There may be plaques at Mo'okini indicating "conclusive evidence" that the temple was built around 300 A.D. Don't you believe it! This is contrary to nearly all archeological and other evidence and should be given little merit. (Long story.) Farther down the road is the **Kamehameha Akahi Aina Hanau Heiau.** This is where Kamehameha the Great, who conquered all the islands, was said to have been born. (Actually, many think he was born nearby, but not right here.) Kamehameha means "the lonely one," which seems ironically befitting given the almost palpable lonely feeling that this area of the island exudes.

After Kamehameha's birthplace you will pass through an old Coast Guard LORAN station. (Despite incorrect signs you may see, driving through *is* permitted on this *federal* land—We checked.) Then you're back on the highway. You may encounter boulders blocking the road near the LORAN station illegally erected by squatters. If so, retrace your route to the highway.

As you pass the tip of Kohala on 270, take note of how quickly you go from green, to lots of dry scrub and an arid feel. That's the rain shadow effect, the mountain causing it to rain more on one side than the other.

There are a couple of places along this stretch to swim or snorkel. **Kapa'a Beach Park** and **Mahukona,** both described in BEACHES.

Near the 15 mile marker, toward the ocean in the distance, you can see stones sticking up in the air from a fascinating *navigational* heiau where the stones are aligned to point to other Hawaiian islands, Tahiti, and more. You can walk to it from Mahukona.

By the way, Mahukona is also the name given the Big Island's first and forgotten volcano, located offshore. It started it all, but sank beneath the water less than half a million years ago.

On a clear day, you can't miss seeing Maui from here. But on *very* clear late afternoons, in addition to Maui's two mountains, you may see the islands of Lana'i, Kaho'olawe (in front of Lana'i from northern angles), and Moloka'i between Lana'i and Maui. Look at the island chain map on the back cover to orient yourself. Sunsets from this area can be superb.

LAPAKAHI STATE HISTORICAL PARK

At the 14 mile marker is **Lapakahi State Historical Park,** which consists of the remains of an old Hawaiian village. There is a trail running through the village, complete with markers noting interesting spots. Admission is free. This self-guided tour takes around 45 minutes, and the brochure does a reasonable job of explaining what you are seeing. Lapakahi is interesting at times and worthwhile for anyone interested in a taste of how the ancient Hawaiians may have lived in such an inhospitable place. That said, this is the worst run state park you'll find on the island. On those occasions when the staff shows up, they convey some of the worst and most inaccurate information we've run across in any park in the state. An example: "This area was once lush rain forest until western man came along and cut it down, causing the rainfall to go from 100 inches to 10 inches annually." (In reality, this was originally a thin, rocky, and scrubby *dryland* forest until *the Hawaiians* burned it down to plant crops after they discovered Hawai'i. This area is dry because it is, and always has been, in the rain shadow of Kohala mountain.)

Also be careful if you open the brochure box near the road entrance at Lapakahi. The first time we did, we got a handful of bees instead of a brochure.

One often overlooked aspect to Lapakahi is the fabulous water in **Koai'e Cove** (described in BEACHES). But don't expect to get the warmies from the staff who seem to resent snorkelers here.

The highway between Kawaihae (2 mile marker) and the 14 mile marker is replete with dirt roads leading toward the ocean. You may be tempted to explore them, especially if you have a JEEP. With that in mind, using a variety of vehicles and on foot, we traversed nearly every inch of all of them, including their branches (and we can cough up the dust-balls to prove it). The result? We can say with complete confidence that all of these roads are utterly wretched and lead to absolute squat. The entire coastline in this area is rocky and mostly unprotected. There are *no* beaches. It's pretty but not beautiful, and the land is harsh and unforgiving. (The real beauty of this area is underwater, with lots of extensive coral formations.) The only people who bother to make their way to the coast along this stretch are shoreline fishermen. So don't bother unless you have *way* too much time on your hands. The only exception is a cove about 100 feet south of the 5 mile marker. The SCUBA is outstanding and fairly easy to access. (See SCUBA in ACTIV-ITIES.) Some

Kamehameha was instructed to build Pu'ukohola Heiau in order to conquer all the islands.

local shoreline fishermen have driven pole holders into the lava to practice shoreline fishing. I'm sure they won't mind if you borrow them. Otherwise, kiss this area off.

KAWAIHAE

The tiny port town of Kawaihae has a few places to eat, and is the launching area for some fishing and SCUBA operations. Otherwise, there's not much to see. There's an ice cream place on the back side of Kawaihae Center that changes names and ice creams a lot; it may or may not be good. Café Pesto is your best bet for food.

This is the driest part of the state, with annual rainfall averaging less than 10 inches. (Contrast that with 240 inches on the slopes northwest of Hilo.)

At the junction of Highways 19 and 270 is the impressive Pu'ukohola Heiau. This massive structure was built by King Kamehameha in 1790–1791. He had sent his wife's grandmother to visit a kahuna on Kaua'i to ask how he could conquer Hawai'i. The kahuna said that if he built a fabulous heiau (temple) at Kawaihae and dedicated it to his war god, he would prevail. Thousands of "volunteers" worked on the project, carrying boulders from miles away. Workers were routinely sacrificed at different portions of the structure during construction to ensure that the gods would be pleased. When completed, Kamehameha dedicated the temple by inviting and then sacrificing his enemy Keoua (see page 84). During construction Kamehameha himself participated to inspire his workers. When his brother picked up a boulder to help, Kamehameha slapped the rock out of his hand saying, "No, brother, one of us should keep the kapu (meaning staying pure)." Kamehameha then instructed that the rock his brother had touched be taken far out to sea and dumped into deep water. Pu'ukohola Heiau is best viewed from Kawaihae Harbor Road (the one that leads out to the breakwater) in the late afternoon with Mauna Kea in the background. Just offshore are said to be the remains of a shark heiau, called Hale-o-Kapuni where human remains were offered to sharks. Its precise location is unknown, and it has been buried for decades.

KOHALA RESORT AREA

Continuing *south* onto Highway 19 (called *Queen K* by most locals, short for Ka'ahumanu) toward Kailua-Kona, you will pass the Kohala mega-resort area. Ensconced in this desolate sea of lava and scrub, multi-zillion dollar resorts dot the coastline offering the luxury and amenities that have made this region famous. Golfing is top notch (and *expensive*) here, see ACTIVITIES. Ocean activities, such as snorkeling and SCUBA, are very good. Though you wouldn't suspect it from the road, some of the best beaches in the state lie between here and Kailua-Kona. Some, such as Hapuna and Mauna Kea, are well known. Others, such as Kua Bay and Makalawena, are less known or deliciously secluded. The section on BEACHES describes them all in detail and tells you *exactly* how to get to each one of them.

See that barren lava field on the mauka (mountain) side of the highway? A Japanese company purchased the 3,000 acres in 1990 for a *mere* $45 million. They had big plans for it including six golf courses and 2,600 homes. After paying taxes on it for nine years, the shrewd investors unloaded it in 1998 for $5 million.

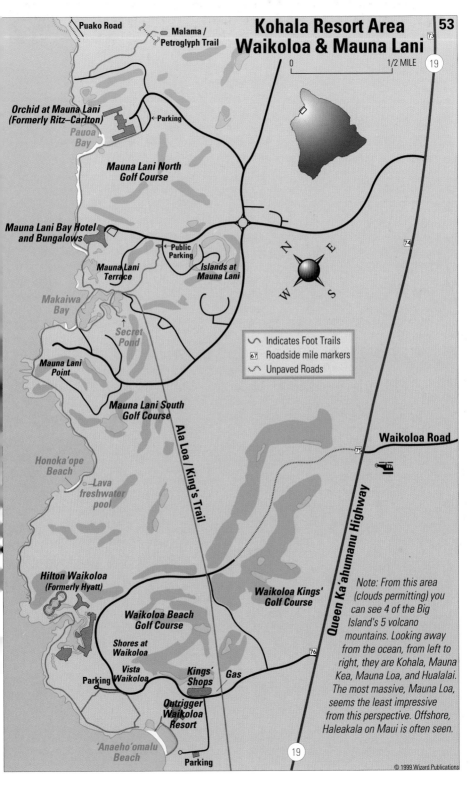

Kohala Resort Area
Waikoloa & Mauna Lani

53

73

19

Puako Road

Malama / Petroglyph Trail

0   1/2 MILE

Orchid at Mauna Lani
(Formerly Ritz–Carlton)

← Parking

Pauoa
Bay

Mauna Lani North
Golf Course

74

Mauna Lani Bay Hotel
and Bungalows

← Public
Parking

Mauna Lani
Terrace

Islands at
Mauna Lani

N
E
W
S

Makaiwa
Bay

↑ Secret
Pond

Indicates Foot Trails
67 Roadside mile markers
Unpaved Roads

Mauna Lani
Point

Mauna Lani South
Golf Course

Ala Loa / King's Trail

Waikoloa Road

75

Honoka'ope
Beach

Lava
freshwater
pool

Waikoloa Kings'
Golf Course

Queen Ka'ahumanu Highway

Hilton Waikoloa
(Formerly Hyatt)

Waikoloa Beach
Golf Course

Shores at
Waikoloa

Vista
Waikoloa

Parking

Kings'
Shops

Gas

76

Note: From this area
(clouds permitting) you
can see 4 of the Big
Island's 5 volcano
mountains. Looking away
from the ocean, from left to
right, they are Kohala, Mauna
Kea, Mauna Loa, and Hualalai.
The most massive, Mauna Loa,
seems the least impressive
from this perspective. Offshore,
Haleakala on Maui is often seen.

Outrigger
Waikoloa
Resort

'Anaeho'omalu
Beach

Parking

19

Hold onto your hat along this stretch. The wind can be fierce in late afternoon. As the lava fields heat up during the day, it causes the air to heat and rise. Air from the ocean rushes in to fill the void, creating strong afternoon breezes.

Hapuna Beach is off the road near the 69 mile marker. This beach is often featured in travel shows and is a *superb* place to frolic. We like to snorkel from there to 69 Beach on calm days, or boogie board till we're raw. Otherwise, just gallivant on the fine sand.

The road to the Mauna Lani between the 73 and 74 mile markers is worth consideration. See map on previous page. To the north is the **Malama Petroglyph Trail.** This simple 25-minute walk through kiawe forest leads to a very large field of petroglyphs, or carvings, in the lava. Though not as extensive as the Pu'u Loa field at Kilauea Volcano, it's one of the largest in the state and worth a stroll if you want to see how ancient Hawaiians expressed themselves through their tenacious carvings.

The **Mauna Lani Bay Hotel** sits adjacent to some of the most fascinating grounds of any Big Island resort. Huge fishponds surrounded by palm trees to the south make for wonder-filled strolling. We like to wander back to Secret Pond (see map) for a cool, refreshing dip in the crystal clear water. (I know, the other ponds aren't clear—*this* one is.) Park at the public parking area and wander along the trail towards the fishponds. Allow an hour for this pleasant diversion.

Continuing south, the road at the 76 mile marker leads to 'Anaeho'omalu **Beach.** If you're low on gasoline, there is relief on this road. 'Anaeho'omalu has a gorgeous palm-fronted fishpond behind the beach. If you're looking for the perfect location to take a **sunset photo,** the backside of the fishpond is as good as it gets. When clouds cooperate, even the most photographically challenged (present reader excluded) can take postcard quality shots.

KOHALA LAVA DESERT AREA

Back on Highway 19 heading South, the large cluster of palms towards the ocean at the 79 mile marker surround a large freshwater pond and a pretty but secluded beach called **Ke-awa-iki.** The pond itself is not available to visitors (the barbed wire, half-starved dobermans, and snipers with night vision glasses see to that), but the beach is accessible via a 15-minute walk, and there is a special freshwater golden pool available to hikers. (See Ke-awa-iki hike under ACTIVITIES.)

Take a look at the "graffiti" strewn about the lava field. It's sort of an island tradition to compose messages from pieces of coral, and families often come out here to do it together. They're almost always friendly messages, like *Al* ♥ *Sandy, I Love You Mom,* or *In Memory of Dan,* and rarely contain the nasties often seen in real mainland graffiti.

The scenic turnout at the 82 mile marker overlooks **Kiholo Bay.** Down there you will find a saltwater bay with fresh water calmly floating on top, lots of turtles, and a lava tube with fresh spring water just a few dozen feet from the ocean. Intrigued? I hope so. You can drive there…maybe. Access is a little unusual. (See ACTIVITIES on page 182.)

Throughout this part of the island you'll occasionally see palm trees along the barren coastline. These are almost always an indication of freshwater spring-fed pools. Since there's no permanent stream on the entire west side of the island, water percolates into the lava and often bubbles to the surface near the shore, forming pools. We look for them when we're hiking along the coast. When you're hot and tired, you can't beat splashing like a fool in a cold, clean freshwater or brackish pool.

If you're looking for a stunning secluded beach, and don't mind walking for 15–20 minutes, **Makalawena Beach** (described in BEACHES) is west of the 89 mile marker.

There's a small herd of wild donkeys that crosses the highway at night and early mornings on the older lava north of the 85 mile marker. (You'll see warning signs posted, but for some reason the donkeys just ignore them.) They come down out of the mountains to lick the salt off rocks by the shore, drink from springs, and occasionally putt on the Hualalai Golf Course. (Now *there's* a hazard.) Known locally as **Kona Nightingales**, they are the descendants of coffee-hauling pack animals that

escaped a century ago. Every so often one gets whacked by a passing car, leaving both pretty bent out of shape.

Just north of the 91 mile marker is a **large lava tube** from the Hualalai lava flow of 1801 that bisects the highway. On the ocean side of the road it has collapsed, leaving a large chasm in the lava. On the mauka side it forms a cave, which is collapsing in several spots. This cave looks rickety and unstable.

Located just south of the Kona airport is the **National Energy Laboratory** (329–7341). They are experimenting using seawater temperature differences to generate electricity. The ocean drops to over 4,000 feet deep less than one mile offshore, so tapping that deep cold water is relatively easy. Whether it ever becomes practical on a large scale is uncertain, and you can expect a litle bit of subtle propaganda. *(Government funded agencies protecting their turf, on the next 20/20.)* They do a number

Even the harsh lava deserts hide jewels, such as the golden pools of Ke-awa-iki.

of other things with cold water here, including housing Maine lobsters. When the lobsters arrive from the mainland they have a nasty case of jet lag. (If you flew here from the east coast you can probably relate.) The beasties are put in the cold water to rejuvenate so that they are bright and alert when boiled for dinner. You can pick up lobsters here (Kona Cold Lobster at 329–4332) fairly cheap if you like. The lab gives free hour-long lecture/presentations every Thursday at 10 a.m.

An excellent tide-pool is nearby at Wawaloli Beach. (See page 149.)

Near the 97 mile marker is the parking lot for Kaloko-Honokohau National Historical Park. Despite its appearance, this was once a thriving community, and Hawaiian artifacts are still scattered about the lava field. There's even a holua (stone slide) that was used by chiefs. They would cover it with grasses and leaves and go zooming down on a sled. Commoners weren't allowed to do it, but they could cheer. (Yippee!) See BEACHES for more.

If you are into deep sea fishing, you'll want to check out Honokohau Harbor listed under BEACHES. Fishing boats leave from here and weigh-ins take place daily at 11 a.m. and 3 p.m. (You can tell what they caught by the fish flags they hoist.) If you want to buy some, Marina Seafoods (326–2117) gets the fish right off the boats as they come in.

KOHALA SHOPPING

In Hawi, Kohala Koa Gallery (mentioned earlier) is excellent. Go upstairs to view additional art work and furniture as well as the one-room Hawaiian Moon shop for their line of Omodt Art Designs. Across the street As Hawi Turns has clothing worth browsing.

All of the mega-resorts have shopping areas, but especially noteworthy are the shops at the Hilton Waikoloa and the Mauna Lani. Many fine quality Hawaiian-made products are available at Makana O' Hawaii at the Mauna Lani. All offer great shops for browsing after a memorable meal at either hotel.

The main shopping area in South Kohala is the Kings' Shops located at the Waikoloa Beach Resort. Keep an eye out for Paradise Walking Co. for a large selection of shoes, Endangered Species, Crazy Shirts, Sgt. Leisure, and the Gecko Store for tees, Kane by Malia and Malia (men's & ladies aloha wear), Noah's Ark for kids and Liberty House (resort dept. store). The prices are higher here because it's a resort shopping area.

KOHALA'S BEST BETS

Best Sunsets—Behind the fishponds at 'Anaeho'omalu Beach

Best Place to Get the Willies—Mo'okini Heiau, Hawi

Best Treat—Tropical Dreams, Hawi

Best Pizza—Café Pesto, Kawaihae

Best Koa Carvings—Kohala Koa Gallery

Best Secluded Beach—Makalawena

Best Resort Grounds to Stroll Around— Mauna Lani Bay Hotel and Bungalows

Best Lu'au—Kona Village

Best Golf—Mauna Kea

Best View of Maui—Coming down Highway (250) into Hawi

Best Overlook—Pololu Valley

Best Hawaiian Petroglyphs—Malama Petroglyph Trail

Best Boogie-Boarding—Hapuna or Mauna Kea Beach

Best Remnant of Ancient Hawaiian Art—Puako Petroglyph Field

Best Place for a Cocktail at Sundown— Beach Tree Bar at the Four Seasons or Ocean Bar at the Orchid Mauna Lani

Kamehameha the Great, the first king to rule all the islands, could live anywhere he wanted. He chose Kailua-Kona. This is his 'Ahu'ena Heiau.

Kailua was a tiny fishing village in days gone by. Fishermen would haul in giants from the deep, bountiful waters, while farmers tended their fields up the slopes of Hualalai. Many of the great chiefs of old chose this part of the island as their home. Kona weather and Kona waters were known throughout the islands as being the very best, and that hasn't changed. Though no longer the sleepy little village of yesteryear, this is a charming seaside town where the strolling is pleasant, the sunsets are mesmerizing, the food is diverse, and the activities are plentiful. Some guidebooks badmouth Kona because it's not the same as it was 20 years ago—what is? Kona is still great; there're simply more people who know it.

The town is alternately referred to as Kailua-Kona, Kona, Kailua, or sometimes Kailua Town. See page 30 for an explanation of this confusing situation.

Kailua-Kona is nestled in the lee of Hualalai Volcano, meaning that it is sheltered from the trade winds coming from the other side of the island. The winds we do get are usually from wraparound sea breezes. The rains from them have already been wrung out.

The heart of Kailua-Kona is the mile-long oceanfront stretch of Alii Drive starting at the Kailua Pier. As with any town, traffic can be heavy at pau hana (quit work) time. Alii Drive is a particularly good area to take a walk after a meal. Public parking is somewhat limited and is shown on the Kailua-Kona Map. This part of town has lots of shops and restaurants overlooking the water. If you start strolling from the Kailua Pier, keep an eye out for some of these sights.

AROUND DOWNTOWN KAILUA-KONA

To the right (north) of the pier is the 'Ahu'ena Heiau. Now wonderfully maintained and very picturesque, this was King Kamehameha the Great's personal heiau (temple) that he had restored in 1812, and it was here that he spent his later years until his death in 1819. Note the bird on top of the tallest ki'i akua (statue of a god). It is a golden plover, the bird that may have guided the first Polynesians here. (See page 15.) Kamehameha dedicated this heiau to the god Lono and filled it with European and Chinese furniture. Nearby is Nane Mahina 'Ai, where the King went to get away from it all. There was a famous portrait painted here of Kamehameha wearing a red vest, white shirt, and a yellow silk necktie. The artist pleaded with him not to wear the fancy sailor's outfit but Kamehameha insisted.

The tiny beach in front of the heiau is **Kamakahonu Beach**, one of the calmest beaches on the island. There you can rent kayaks, paddle boats, snorkel gear, etc.

To the left of the pier is a starting gate to end all starting gates. Every year in October an athletic event occurs on the Big Island which draws national attention. The **Ironman Triathlon** is a profound testimony to the power to challenge. To the ability to reach down to the

very core of our spirit and summon the impossible. Three events, any one of which would seem insurmountable to most of us mere mortals, stitched together in a triathlon that seems almost ludicrous. Swim 2.4 miles in the open ocean, then get out and ride a bike 112 miles on a hot road cut through a lava field. Finally, dismount and run a 26.2 mile marathon. All this is done consecutively under the tropical sun. This is the best opportunity you'll ever have to look into the faces of mass excellence.

The seawall near the pier is usually a great place to fish. During abnormally high seas, water crashes over the wall and is quite a sight to see. Even better fishing is at the wall in front of the **Hulihe'e Palace** (329–1877) farther down. This palace, built in 1838 by Governor Kuakini, quickly

A Real Gem

became the house of choice for vacationing Hawaiian Royalty until 1914. Now a museum lovingly run by the Daughters of Hawai'i, inside you'll find a nice collection of koa furniture, including some stunning armoires, and a 6 foot diameter table cut from a single piece of koa. Most of the furniture was auctioned off in the 1920s but was fortuitously cataloged. Later, the buyers were contacted, and many have graciously lent the items to the museum for display. There are photos of many Hawaiian royalty, including Princess Ruth. (History books *never* mention her without mentioning her size, but we're above that...no, we're not. Estimates range from 6-foot-2 to 6-foot-10, 400–450 lbs. She slept in a hut outside.) Spears, fishhooks, and other artifacts make this museum a worthwhile stop. Most who give the tours (under an hour)

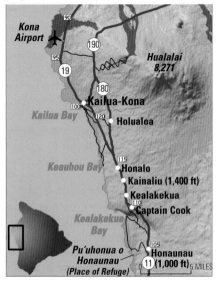

Kona Airport ✈

90

190

95

19

Hualalai 8,271

180

Kailua-Kona

100

Kailua Bay

120 Holualoa

Keauhou Bay

115

Honalo

Kainaliu (1,400 ft)

Kealakekua

110

Captain Cook

Kealakekua Bay

Pu'uhonua o Honaunau
(Place of Refuge)

105

Honaunau

11 **(1,000 ft)**

0   5 MILES

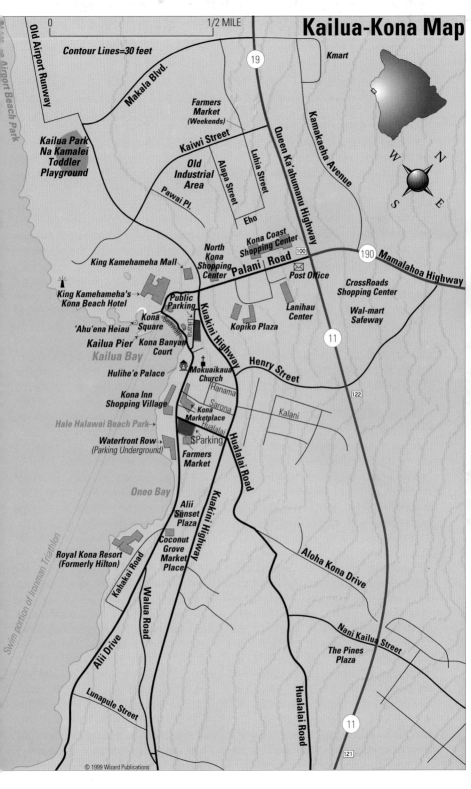

are very knowledgeable and friendly, but occasionally you'll get some bad historical information. Admission is $5. The Palace Gift Shop next door has some interesting items and hard-to-find books and is worth a peek.

Outside, on the south side of the Palace to the right of the drinking fountain, is a rock with a hole in it. It is the top of a Pohaku Likanaka. It was used for executions out at Kahalu'u Beach Park. People would be forced to stand in front of it while a rope was passed through the hole, around the neck, and back out. The executioner would then pull back for a few minutes...and that was that.

Across the street from the seawall are two places to get good shave ice, Ocean View and Scandinavian Shave Ice (farther down). For around $2 you get your choice of 50 flavors. (Ocean View is better.)

Across the street from Hulihe'e Palace is the Mokuaikaua Church. This was the first Christian church built in the islands in 1820. The initial building was a thatched hut, with the current structure erected in 1837. You're welcome inside, admission is free. Built of lava rock and crushed coral with koa hardwood gracing the tall interior, this is a magnificent remnant of the era. Look at the joints inside the building, which were painstakingly attached with pins made from gnarly 'ohi'a trees. There are exhibits relating to early Hawai'i and the work of the missionaries, along with a model of the *Thaddeus,* which brought the first missionaries here. Sometimes referred to as the Mayflower of Hawai'i, the *Thaddeus* left Boston in October 1819 for a five-month trip to the islands. These men and women left comfortable lives in the U.S. to come to an alien and mysterious land. Unbeknownst to them, their chances for success were greatly enhanced en route when Kamehameha II and his mother Ka'ahumanu orchestrated the overthrow of the Hawaiian religion less than a month into their journey.

There's a large shopping area at Kona Inn. If you're looking for a place to watch the sunset or have a picnic, the grass on the ocean side of this center is ideal. Also at this center is Mrs. Barry's Kona Cookies (329–6055) with their delicious homemade treats. Try the chocolate chip/mac nut cookies.

If you want to watch the sunset from a restaurant along here, the best views (from south to north) are: Tropics Cafe (at Royal Kona Resort), Huggo's, Jolly Roger, Chart House, Kona Inn, Hard Rock Café and Don Drysdale's. Lulu's sunset views are not quite as good. See individual reviews under DINING. During months around the summer solstice (June 21), the sun may set behind the point from the northernmost restaurants.

ELSEWHERE ALONG ALII DRIVE

As you drive further south along Alii Drive, keep an eye out for joggers. They trot up and down Alii Drive in large enough numbers to constitute a flock. (Or is it a gaggle?) There are mile markers every half mile here (with the number 50 on the half mile signs), so we put them on the map that way. Between Kona-By-The-Sea and Kona Isle is a 100-yard access trail that leads to something that even most longtime Alii Drive residents don't know about. It's a public saltwater swimming pool fed by the splashing of waves. It was privately built decades ago and reverted to the state when the owner died without heirs. The pool directly abuts the ocean and even has some fish in it most of the time. There's a smaller tide-pool to the left. If you want to swim in seawater but are hesitant to go into the ocean, here's your chance. Unmaintained, the pool occasionally isn't refreshed enough if the surf has been flat for too long, meaning it sometimes gets green.

Keep an eye out on the mauka side of Alii Drive for a farmers market. Near the 3½ mile marker is Pahoehoe Beach Park. No sand here, but it's a nice place to have a picnic, or to just sit on a bench and watch the surf. White Sands Beach (it has several other names) is a little farther down with good boogie boarding when the sand is in town. (See BEACHES.)

There are scads of oceanfront condos and apartments along this road. Traffic noise is going to be your penalty for staying on Alii Drive, but it's a penalty most are quite willing to endure.

Soon you'll come to the quaintest little church you've ever seen. St. Peter's Catholic Church is known locally as the "Little Blue Church." This tiny building, with its picturesque location, ever-open doors, and less than a dozen simple *small* pews, is the most photographed in the islands. Weddings of all denominations take place there almost every weekend. Sunsets through the etched glass can offer dramatic photo opportunities.

To the right of the church is the Ku'emanu Heiau. This is the only heiau (temple) in the state known to be associated solely with surfing. This sport was available only to chiefs (commoners caught surfing were put to death) and they came here to pray for gnarly conditions. (They usually got it, too. Even today this is one of the most dependable breaks in Kona.) To this day Hawaiians still come here to pay homage to the spirits. The small notch in front was a luapa'u, where discarded bones were tossed—perhaps

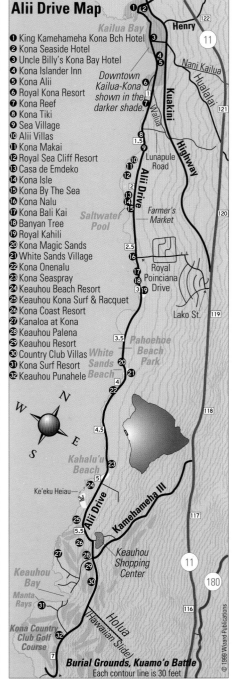

Alii Drive Map

❶ King Kamehameha Kona Bch Hotel
❷ Kona Seaside Hotel
❸ Uncle Billy's Kona Bay Hotel
❹ Kona Islander Inn
❺ Kona Alii
❻ Royal Kona Resort
❼ Kona Reef
❽ Kona Tiki
❾ Sea Village
❿ Alii Villas
⓫ Kona Makai
⓬ Royal Sea Cliff Resort
⓭ Casa de Emdeko
⓮ Kona Isle
⓯ Kona By The Sea
⓰ Kona Nalu
⓱ Kona Bali Kai
⓲ Banyan Tree
⓳ Royal Kahili
⓴ Kona Magic Sands
㉑ White Sands Village
㉒ Kona Onenalu
㉓ Kona Seaspray
㉔ Keauhou Beach Resort
㉕ Keauhou Kona Surf & Racquet
㉖ Kona Coast Resort
㉗ Kanaloa at Kona
㉘ Keauhou Palena
㉙ Keauhou Resort
㉚ Country Club Villas
㉛ Kona Surf Resort
㉜ Keauhou Punahele

Kailua Bay

Henry

Downtown Kailua-Kona shown in the darker shade.

Lunapule Road

Farmer's Market

Saltwater Pool

Royal Poinciana Drive

Lako St.

Pahoehoe Beach Park

White Sands Beach

Kahalu'u Beach

Ke'eku Heiau

Keauhou Shopping Center

Keauhou Bay

Manta Rays

Kona Country Club Golf Course

Holua (Hawaiian Slide)

Burial Grounds, Kuamo'o Battle
Each contour line is 30 feet

© 1999 Wizard Publications

With moonlight on one side and sunlight on the other, altars (called lele ho'okau), such as this one at the Hawaiian heiau Ku'emanu, are still used by some for a morning prayer.

bones of commoners caught surfing. Incidentally, surfing in the old days was usually done naked (giving new meaning to the term *hang loose*).

Next to the church is Kahalu'u Beach Park where you'll find some of the easiest access to good snorkeling on the island. It gets crowded on weekends. See BEACHES for more on this gem. Kahalu'u had a large population in the old days, and there are very extensive lava tube caves tucked away in the jungle up mauka (toward the mountain). Across the street is a massage school (322–0048) where you can get cheap massages by training pupils.

As you pass Keauhou Beach Resort, you'll see its former sister hotel, the Kona Lagoon. A Japanese company bought the lease to the 454-room hotel along with the Keauhou Beach for $23 million and quickly closed the Lagoons in 1988 for renovations. It never reopened. When

the Japanese economy took a dive a couple years later, and local environmentalists stalled their renovation plans, the company ran out of money. In 1995 they walked away, giving it to the land owner, Bishop Estate. Time will tell what happens to it. The land contains several heiaus, including one where thousands of Hawaiians were sacrificed to their gods. Local lore has it that any business that operates there is cursed, and guards at the closed Lagoon Hotel have lots of strange stories to tell. Fronting the hotel, on some of the lava at low tide, you can see petroglyphs carved in the rock. They are at the northern end of the salt-and-pepper sand and gravel beach. In the 16th century, Kamalalawalu, the King of Maui, was impaled by Lonoikamakahiki at Ke'eku Heiau for 10 or 11 days. Kamalalawalu was then taken to a flat rock nearby and slain. His body was towed out to sea and fed to the sharks.

The petroglyphs on the rock date back to that incident and detail the event. (Lonoikamakahiki had a good reason to be miffed. His general had been captured by Maui forces, had his eyes gouged out, and his eye sockets pierced with darts *before* being killed. That was considered savage even by the standards of the time.)

As you ascend Alii Drive toward the Keauhou Shopping Center (the bakery at KTA there has wicked taro bread pudding), keep an eye on your right, in the golf course, for the strangest corkscrew-shaped palm tree we've ever seen. No interesting story here—just weird. There's a flock of imported wild parrots that cruises around these parts. Keep an eye (and ear) out for them.

If you stay on Alii for a mile, it'll go back toward the ocean. There is a lava road before the dead end. If you walk on the road for a minute (actually you can see it from your car), you'll be able to see, on your left, terraces in the side of the mountain. You are at an extraordinary place. It might not look like much, but this is where the battle between Hawaiians to kill their religion took place one day in 1820. (See page 17 for the extraordinary story.)

UP MAUKA OF KAILUA-KONA

Hualalai Volcano erupts sporadically every few hundred years. The last time was in 1801 when it covered part of what is now Kona Airport. The top of Hualalai is mostly covered with 'ohi'a and eucalyptus forest with occasional koa and pine. The clouds usually roll in around mid-morning, blanketing the 8,271-foot summit in a rich fog that can reduce visibility to zero. Wild goats and pigs scramble about the uninhabited top portion of the mountain. The views of Mauna Kea and Mauna Loa, as well as its own caldera, make Hualalai a hiker's haven.

The Hawaiians planted coconut trees wherever they could. In ancient times Kahalu'u Beach was heavily populated. Today, it is heavily snorkeled.

A Fish Story

Keauhou was dominated by the legacy of a King in the 1600s named Lonoikamakahiki (called Lono by his friends). Lono (not to be confused with the Hawaiian god of the same name) got into a series of bets with the king of O'ahu. Each time Lono won. On one occasion, Lono and the O'ahu king were out fishing. Lono's advisor told Lono not to go because he (Lono) didn't know how to fish. They went anyway, and while fishing, Lono got all worked up while the O'ahu king was hauling in a beauty and asked to borrow fishing gear. As Lono's advisor feared, the O'ahu king mocked Lono for not bringing his own gear. Lono's advisor, in order to save his master's honor, volunteered the solution to Lono. He whispered it into his ear and Lono accepted. Lono then shouted, "Hey, I don't need your gear. I'll bet you I can catch a fish on my own." The O'ahu king accepted, knowing that Lono had not brought any fishing gear with him. Then Lono, *at his advisor's suggestion,* clubbed his advisor to death, ripped open his belly and used his intestines for fishing line. Lono splintered the man's thigh bone for a fishhook. His flesh was used for bait and his head for a sinker. He lowered the gear into the water and immediately caught an ahi. Lono won the bet (a large piece of O'ahu) and later went on to win all of O'ahu in another bet.

The moral: If you think you sacrifice a lot for your boss, try working for Lono.

(Incidentally, Lono's bones were in Bishop Museum in Honolulu until 1994 when they were stolen by Hawaiian activists and buried in Waipi'o Valley.)

Unfortunately, it's all owned by Bishop Estate, which routinely denies access to the public. (Bishop Estate is a trust set up in the last century to help Hawai'i's kids. It has grown to where it now owns 11% of the state and has astonishing power. Many of the houses you see on the island are actually on Bishop land leased for several decades by individuals.)

Hovering above the town of Kailua-Kona is the "artist community" of Holualoa on Highway 180. There are several galleries worth stopping for if you are in the neighborhood. Hours can be sporadic. Otherwise, there is not as much to offer the visitor in this quiet, peaceful bedroom community as visitor literature might imply.

SOUTH OF KAILUA-KONA

If you head south out of Kona, you'll come to a series of small towns, all above 1,000 feet. It's usually cool up here, sometimes even foggy. The theme to these towns is often coffee. Free samples are offered at many establishments. Some, such as Bad Ass Coffee, are just what the name implies. *(There's* a truthful name if I ever saw one.)* Others, such as Greenwell, sell very good quality coffee to take with you. There are several places to eat along here, such as Aloha Theater Cafe, Kona Theatre Cafe, and The Coffee Shack, all good for breakfast. Look for Antiques—Art—Ice Cream on the ocean side of the highway in Kealakekua. They serve Tropical Dreams ice cream, as sinful here as in Hawi on the north shore. Keep an eye out for a portable rotisserie BBQ called Island Style Kiawe Chicken on the side of the road. They sell tasty, whole

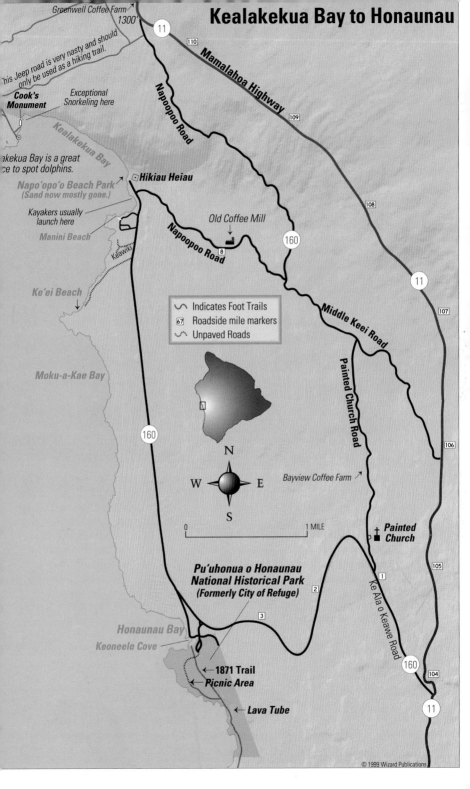

Kealakekua Bay to Honaunau

Greenwell Coffee Farm
1300'

11

110

Mamalahoa Highway

109

This Jeep road is very nasty and should only be used as a hiking trail.

Cook's Monument

Exceptional Snorkeling here

Napoopoo Road

Kealakekua Bay

akekua Bay is a great ce to spot dolphins.

Hikiau Heiau

Napoʻopoʻo Beach Park (Sand now mostly gone.)

Kayakers usually launch here

Manini Beach

Keawiki

Napoopoo Road

Old Coffee Mill

8

160

108

11

107

Middle Keei Road

Ke'ei Beach

Painted Church Road

106

Moku-a-Kae Bay

⌇	Indicates Foot Trails
67	Roadside mile markers
⋯	Unpaved Roads

N

W E

S

Bayview Coffee Farm

160

1 MILE

0

† **Painted Church**

105

Puʻuhonua o Honaunau National Historical Park (Formerly City of Refuge)

1

2

Ke Ala o Keawe Road

160

104

Honaunau Bay

Keoneele Cove

3

← **1871 Trail**
Picnic Area

← **Lava Tube**

11

© 1999 Wizard Publications

Hawaiian BBQ chickens for $7.

In Kealakekua (you'll be forgiven if you don't readily see the transition between towns up here) between the 112 & 111 mile markers on the ocean side of the road is the Kona Historical Society Museum (323–2005). Located in an old general store built during the last century, there's lots of old coffee related photos and other items of historical interest.

Worth a stop if you have an interest in the past. $2 admission.

There are good views down the coast from some spots along here. After you pass the 111 mile marker on Highway 11, you'll see Napoopoo Road on the ocean side of the road—take it. There are lots of coffee farms down here. (See gray box below.) A coffee tour might be worth the effort. You may get to try deli-

Kona Coffee

Of all the products produced on the Big Island, none is more well known or has received more accolades than Kona coffee. Though now out-produced *in quantity* by Kaua'i, Kona coffee is unmatched in terms of quality. With the *possible* exception of Jamaican Blue Mountain coffee, Kona coffee is widely considered the best in the world. Good Kona coffee lacks the bitterness of coffees from other parts of the world. By the way, contrary to nearly *everyone's* belief, lighter roasts have *more* caffeine than darker roasts. (Caffeine cooks away during the roasting process.)

A truly quality cup of coffee has little resemblance to mass-produced coffee you see on most supermarket shelves. (Of course, you pay more for the good stuff.) Good Kona coffee will set you back $18 or more per pound. Surprisingly little profit is made by the farmer at that price. Most small farmers grow coffee as a labor of love. If you see 100% Kona coffee (not a blend) selling for $9 per pound, it might be poorly chosen, broken, or poorly roasted beans. You *usually* get what you pay for. And if you're told in a restaurant that they serve Kona blend because pure Kona is too strong, it's like saying that champagne needs to be blended with gasoline because pure champagne is too strong. Kona blends (which are blended with cheap beans from elsewhere) are *less* mellow than pure Kona. Blends are usually served because it's cheaper, not better.

Being wretched coffee addicts, we've tried them all. For what it's worth, we like **Auntie Loraine's** (808 322–1675), **Fike Farms** (808 328–2265), **Holualoa** (800 334–0348), **Greenwell** (808 323–2862), and **Bayview** (800 662–5880). Some aren't available in stores, only by phone or mail order.

Coffees that we've tried and *didn't* like are Bad Ass Coffee, Ferrari Mountain Gold, Royal Aloha, and Starbuck's Kona coffee. (The last one is surprising.) We are not saying that these companies are bad, just that we didn't like their coffee and didn't think it was worth the money.

Coffee tours are available from many growers, but coffee farms that claim to offer tours are often poorly marked and owners and employees sometimes seem shocked when you show up to buy coffee. Greenwell and Bayview have nice tours. They are on the map on the previous page.

cious coffee or meet offbeat characters that you'll remember for years to come.

Napoopoo comes to an intersection of itself and Middle Keʻei Road. Turn right here and head toward the ocean. The old Mauna Loa Coffee mill near the 6 mile marker is now a tourist shop run by another company and is of marginal interest. Stop if you need to stretch.

KEALAKEKUA BAY AND PLACE OF REFUGE

A Real Gem

When you get to the sea, hang a right to Napoʻopoʻo Beach Park. The stone structure you see in front of you at this southern end of Kealakekua Bay (at the end of the road) is Hiki-au Heiau. This was a luakini (a temple where human sacrifices were made). Here Captain Cook was first worshiped as the returning god Lono. During the ceremony, an elder priest named Koa, in the honored tradition of the Hawaiians, chewed the food first before spitting it out and offering it to Cook. (He politely declined.) It was also here that the first Christian ceremony was held in Hawaiʻi. Ironically it may have contributed to the death of Captain Cook. When one of his men died, Cook ordered him buried near this heiau and personally read the service. This event was proof to some Hawaiians that the strangers were mere mortals, not the gods some felt them to be.

Napoʻopoʻo Beach used to be a fabulous beach fronting the heiau. Most "current" guidebooks still rave about it. Too bad it doesn't really exist anymore. It had been eroding for years, being gradually replaced by boulders. When Hurricane ʻIniki sideswiped the island in 1992, its surf removed most of what sand was left. Only time will tell if it ever comes back, but so far very little has.

One mile across the bay you can see a white obelisk, the Captain Cook Monument, which was erected in 1874 by British sailors. It was near this spot (a rarely visited plaque at the end of the "road" marks the *actual* spot) in 1779 that Cook was killed by the Hawaiians. (See INTRODUCTION for more on this event.) You won't need your passport to go there, even though it is British soil that the monument rests on. The small plot was deeded to the United Kingdom by Princess Likelike.

Kealakekua Bay is also popular with dolphins. A large number of spinners reside in the bay, so keep an eye out for them. We see them almost every time we kayak to the monument. Toward the monument side on the bay, but up on the steep cliff, there is a grayish impression in the cliff. Local lore says this was made by a cannonball fired from Cook's ship.

These cliffs hold even more secrets. In the past, important chiefs were buried in small caves on the cliff face. After the bones had been separated, volunteers were lowered down the face of the cliffs by rope to place the bones in crevices. Few people had a long résumé for doing this. That's because the person doing the burying, once finished with his task, would signal to those above that he was done. The officials on top would promptly cut the rope, sending the burial person, and all knowledge of the location of the bones, crashing to the rocks below. (It was actually considered an honor to be the volunteer at the end of the rope.) All this was to prevent the bones from being desecrated. Bones were often turned into fishhooks and other implements.

Today, if you hear something fall from the cliff, it won't be a person. Cows from above occasionally wander off the ledge, pleasing fish that are sick of seafood.

The waters near the monument are crystal clear and teeming with coral and fish. This is perhaps the best snorkeling in the state. The local community wants to keep it somewhat difficult to access to prevent it from being overrun with "casual" visitors. If you are wondering how to get there, you have several choices:

You can swim it. This takes us about an hour each way with fins and is guaranteed to tucker you out.

You can walk along the edge of the bay for about 98% of the distance. You'll have to scramble on boulders the whole way and will have to swim for a couple of short patches. You expose yourself to the ocean's whims with this method.

You can rent a kayak and paddle over. (See KAYAKING on page 190.) This is our favorite method. It's a pretty easy 30-minute paddle across the usually peaceful bay, and you stand a good chance of cruising among dolphins along the way. Make sure you bring water, lunch, and snorkel gear. This is an excellent way to spend the morning.

Another way to get to the monument is to take the trail near the intersection of Highway 11 and Napoopoo Road. (The trailhead is a little over ⅒ mile from the highway across from 3 large palm trees. See map.) It used to be a road but is now suitable only for hiking. It's two miles each way with a 1,300-foot constant descent to the water. It's a pretty good puffer coming back up with little shade and some obnoxious footing. It takes most people more than an hour each way. Drink *plenty* of water before and during the ascent, and be careful not to pull your calves during the steady climb. Along the way you'll pass (but won't see due to brush) the Puhina o Lono Heiau. It was here that Cook's bones were...well,

cooked. (See below.) For $95 per person Kings' Trail Rides (323–2388) brings small groups down this trail on horseback for a four hour ride and snorkel tour. (See HORSEBACK under ACTIVITIES.)

Lastly, you can take one of the boat trips on page 192. They stop for snorkeling near the monument. They also offer SCUBA, SNUBA, and all-around fun.

What Finally Happened to Cook?

The Hawaiians traditionally scraped the flesh off the bones of great men. The bones were then bundled together and burned or buried in secret so they wouldn't be desecrated. If the dead person was really loved, the bones were kept in a private home for a while. Because Cook was so respected by the Hawaiians, his body parts were distributed among the chiefs. His head went to the king, his scalp went to a high-ranking chief, his hair went to Kamehameha, etc. Some of his organs, including his heart and liver, were stolen and eaten by some local children who mistook them for dog innards. *(Yuck!)* Eventually, when two Hawaiians brought a bundle to the ship, the British solemnly unwrapped the bundle and discovered a pile of bloody flesh that had been cut from Cook's body. Even though the Hawaiians were bestowing an honor upon Cook, the British sailors didn't see it that way and were naturally shocked and horrified. The anguished sailors begged Captain Clerke to allow them to go into the village and extract revenge, but he refused, fearing a bloodbath. Some went anyway, killing several villagers. Most of the bones were eventually returned to the British, and Cook was buried at sea in Kealakekua Bay. The ship's surgeon wrote, "In every situation he stood unrivaled and alone. On him all eyes were turned. He was our leading star which, at its setting, left us in darkness and despair."

The steeper cliffs and hills from Kealakekua Bay south seem strangely out of place on this otherwise gently sloping mountain. There's a good reason, and it happened in one day. See page 74 for the explanation.

As you leave Napo'opo'o Beach, stay on the oceanmost road heading south. There is a side road leading to Ke'ei Beach. Pretty but not real usable, its historical legacy is a Hawaiian legend, bolstered by Spanish records, which states that white men straggled ashore in the 1520s, 250 years before Cook arrived.

Lots of blood has been spilt on this part of the island. One particularly important battle took place just south of Ke'ei Beach at Moku-a-Kae Bay. You can't access it, but it was near here in 1782 that Kamehameha the Great finally became king of this half of the island after defeating Kiwala'o. During a bloody battle, one of Kamehameha's generals, named Ke'eaumoku (call him Ke for short), tangled in his own spear and tripped, savagely impaling himself. Presuming Ke to be mortally wounded, Kiwala'o ran over to the enemy general to finish him off and seize his prized neck ornament. (Taking it off your enemy's body was symbolic of defeating him.) As he was leaning over Ke's body, he was beaned on the head by a sling stone hurled by one of Kamehameha's warriors, falling backward. Ke, who wasn't dead from his spear wound, painfully crawled to the unconscious Kiwala'o and slit his throat with a leiomanu (a Hawaiian version of brass knuckles, but with razor sharp shark's teeth embedded on the outside). Thus Kamehameha was able to defeat his nemesis and rule western Hawai'i.

Battles such as these are a constant throughout Hawaiian history after the 12th century. Rival chiefs or kings were quick to take each other on. Warriors would often congregate on opposite sides of the battlefield and shout insults at each other to in an attempt to intimidate. (Insults about lineage were always a real hit.) During battles, spears, sling stones, and clubs were used with remarkable efficiency. Shark tooth-studded leiomanus were often given to old men who would go out onto battlefields after the fighting was over to slit the throats of all of those still alive. Though it may sound harsh (OK, OK—it *is* harsh), this was their way and not considered abhorrent to them.

Soon you come to Pu'uhonua o Honaunau (pronounced HOE-NOW-NOW). Also called Place of Refuge, this is a *great* place to visit. It is a site of great importance and a fun place to explore. In ancient times, commoner's lives were governed by the kapu system. There was a dizzying number of laws to observe. Those of lower classes weren't allowed to look at or even walk on the same trails as upper classes. Men and women were forbidden to eat together, citizens were not allowed to get close to a chief or allow their shadows to fall across them, etc. All manner of laws kept the order. The penalty for breaking any of the laws was usually the same—death by club, strangulation, fire or spear. (It's nice to have choices, huh?) If the offense was severe enough, the offender's entire family might be executed. It was believed that the gods retaliated against lawbreakers by sending tidal waves, lava flows, droughts and earthquakes, so communities had a great incentive to dispatch lawbreakers with haste. If a lawbreaker could elude his

NOT TO BE MISSED!

Lawbreakers had one chance to escape the inevitable death penalty: Reach the area's place of refuge before your enemies reached you and all was forgiven.

club or spear-wielding pursuers, however, he had one way out of his mess—the area's Pu'uhonua (place of refuge). This predesignated area offered asylum. If a lawbreaker could make it here, he could perform certain rituals mandated by the kahuna pule (priest). After that, all was forgiven and he could return home as if nothing had happened, regardless of the violation. Defeated warriors could also come here to await the victor of a battle. They could then pledge their allegiance to whoever won and live out their lives in peace.

Pu'uhonua o Honaunau is such a place. Designated as a national park by Congress in 1961, it is the finest example of a Place of Refuge in all the islands. Here you will find neatly kept grounds featuring a remarkable stone wall, called the Great Wall. Built in the 1500s, this massive wall is 1,000 feet long, 10 feet high and 17 feet thick in most places. It

separated the Pu'uhonua from the Ali'i's palace grounds. Though the wall has a chiseled appearance, it was made without dressed (cut) stones and without mortar. Also on the grounds you will find reconstructed Hawaiian houses, temples, and a few petroglyphs (rock drawings). There are wood carvings of gods (including one that is anatomically correct, assuming that's how the gods were endowed). The reconstructed thatched structure called **Hale-o-Keawe** was originally a mausoleum, containing the bones of 23 chiefs. Bones were thought to contain the supernatural power, or *mana,* and therefore ensured that the place of refuge would remain sacred.

There are many other sights here as well. Overall, this place is easy to recommend. The walk around the grounds is gentle, and there are facilities such as drinking water and restrooms. Coconut trees (which have an almost magical, calming effect) are scattered all over. There is a $2 entrance fee but sometimes no one is there to collect it because they "can't afford the manpower to collect the money." (Only the government could come up with that kind of logic.) At the visitor's desk you'll find an informative brochure with a difficult-to-follow and inaccurate map. Ask if they have any other literature.

Honaunau is particularly enchanting an hour before sunset, the best time to visit. Swaying coconut trees have a golden glow as large turtles munch near the canoe landing. You won't find a more relaxing or soothing place to finish off the day. Then head over to the middle/southern end of the park where picnic tables and BBQS await. Local families often bring their keikis (kids) to play in the nearby tide-pools. Drive to that area using the dirt road to the left of the visitor center as you enter the park.

For the less cerebral, you'll find unbeatable snorkeling and SCUBA diving in Honaunau Bay to the right of the boat launch. There are also hiking trails. An unusual hiking destination is the 1871 Trail, so named because area residents paid their taxes in 1871 by fixing up this formerly dilapidated trail. (I'll have to ask the IRS if the offer's still good.) About 15 minutes into the walk you will come to a rock ramp. To the left are grates sealing off caves containing ancient bones. Past that is a lava tube that runs for a minute through the mountain and stops suddenly 15–20 feet above the water. This tube has fascinating textures and is not well known, but beware of the ceiling. Harriett smacked her head good the first time in the cave, and the floor has been known to

The Green Flash

Ever heard of the Green Flash? No, it's not a super-hero. We'd heard of the Green Flash for years before we moved here. We assumed that it was an urban myth, or perhaps something seen through the bottom of a beer bottle. But now we know it to be a real phenomenon, complete with a scientific explanation. You may hear other ways to experience the Green Flash—but this is the only *true* way.

On days when the horizon is crisp and clear with *no* clouds in the way of the sun as it sets, you stand a reasonable chance of seeing it. Avoid looking directly at the sun until the *very last* part of the disk is about to slip below the horizon. Looking at it beforehand will burn a greenish image into your retina, creating a "Fool's Flash" (and possible wrecking your eyes). The *instant* before the last part of the sun's disk disappears, a vivid flash of green is often seen. This is because the sun's rays are passing through the thickest part of the atmosphere, and the light is bent and split into its different components the way it is in a rainbow. The light that is bent the most is the green and blue light, but the blue is less vivid and is overwhelmed by the flash of green, which lingers for the briefest of moments as the very last of the sun sets.

For a variety of reasons, including our latitude, Hawai'i is one of the best places in the world to observe the Green Flash. North Kohala is usually better than Kona due to the clarity of the horizon, but we've seen excellent Green Flash from all along the west coast.

If you aren't successful in seeing the real Green Flash, try the beer bottle method— at least it's better than nothing.

And so ends another day in paradise...

twist an ankle or two. Once at the end of the tube, many people jump into the deep water below. We won't stick our necks out and vouch for its safety, but suffice it to say that plenty of people (including one of us) do it and we have not heard of any problems as a result.

Leaving Honaunau, you'll continue up Ke Ala o Keawe Road to Painted Church Road. Hang a left onto it to get to Saint Benedict's Catholic Church,

A Real Gem

known simply as the **Painted Church.** It's a charming little building dating back to the last century. Between 1899 and 1904 Father John Velge dedicated himself to creating frescos on the inside walls and ceiling. Everything from hell, to the Temptation of Christ is represented in loving detail. There is a sign on the door explaining in detail Father Velge's efforts. Termites and age are starting to take their toll, but

this is a always worth a stop.

Either continue on Painted Church Road to Middle Keei Road, or backtrack to get back up to the highway. (See map.)

When deciding where to eat in Kailua-Kona, see DINING.

KONA SHOPPING

Along Alii Drive from the King Kamehemeha Beach Hotel down to the Royal Kona Resort there are countless places to shop and walk. Starting at the King Kamehemeha Hotel shops, you'll find the **Made on the Big Island Outlet.** If you're interested in the bonsai plants you see on many counters around the island, this is where to get them. Also good for Kona coffee. Across the street from the King Kamehemeha Hotel is **SandalStop** and **Country Samurai Coffee Company.** One is great for hiking sandals and the other for Buzz Beans, a coffee and chocolate jolt that will wake the dead. Down Alii Drive, stop by **Middle**

Earth Bookstore, tucked away behind Crazy Shirts if you need some topographic maps. At Kona Inn Shopping Village, some of the better stops are Island Life, Island Salsa, Hula Heaven, and Sgt. Leisure for clothing. Across the street at Kona Marketplace, Kona Sports has a good selection of T-shirts. Next door is Paradise Clothing if you're looking for shoes. At Alii Sunset Plaza, is Sol-Sations where every item changes color in the sunlight. Continuing down Alii Drive near the Hard Rock Cafe are lots of shops and Kona Ono Cookies.

There are three Farmer's Markets in Kona. One at the corner of Hualalai Rd. and Alii Dr. (Wed.–Sun.) one at Kaiwi Square. (Sat. & Sun.) and a new one on Alii Dr. just south of downtown on the mauka side, irregular days.

While you're on Kaiwi Street, stop by the French Bakery or Kailua Candy Company to sample some delicious baked goods or Kona-made chocolate.

For an exceptional treat, Kona Wine Market at King Kamehameha Mall (Aloha is on the roof) on Kuakini has locally grown Hawaiian Vintage Chocolate. This is the only chocolate grown in the U.S. and is unusually full bodied, similar to a high quality Belgian chocolate. (*Occasionally* we've found the chocolate there a bit old.) They also have a huge selection of wines (including Volcano Winery) and gourmet foods.

Some other stops in Kona are Hilo Hattie near Kopiko Plaza behind Burger King for reasonable prices and a great selection of aloha wear and souvenirs. Hawaii's version of a mainland department store is Liberty House near K-Mart. Our K-Mart and Wal-mart offer good prices on coffee, T-shirts, hats, souvenirs, reef shoes, and suntan lotion. Near the Wal-mart is Borders Books for Hawaiian music or videos of island sights.

Keauhou Shopping Center south of Kailua-Kona has the Showcase Gallery of fine gift items. Stop by for a slice of macadamia nut pie at the Mac Pie Store. If you're into crafts, Ben Franklin Crafts offers Hawaiian craft items.

The Bong Brothers in Honaunau on Highway 11 is a good place for a smoothie (try to ignore the rude sign telling you not to walk behind the counter), some fresh fruit, or some Bong Brothers logo items. Gotta love the name.

KONA'S BEST BETS

Best Place to Meet Fish for the First Time—Kahalu'u Beach Park

Best Lu'au—Royal Kona Resort

Best Kona Coffee—Auntie Loraine's

Best Pizza—Bianelli's or Kona Brewing Company & Brewpub

Best Fish Sandwich—Hard Rock Cafe or Quinn's (pretty close call)

Best Oceanside Breakfast—Royal Kona Resort

Best Place for a Coffee and Cinnamon Roll in the Morning—Island Lava Java

Best Snorkeling—Captain Cook Monument or Honaunau

Best Place to Spot Dolphins—Kealakekua Bay

Best Dessert to Go—Mac Nut Pie, Mac Pie Store in Keauhou Shopping Cntr.

Best Sunset Picnic—The BBQS at Honaunau or the tide-pools of Wawaloli Beach if the surf is crashing

Best Shave Ice—Ocean View Inn

Best Place to Lose Your Lunch—Upside down in an aerobatic ride at Classic Aviation

Best SCUBA Adventure—Manta Ray Night Dive

Best Place For a Man to End Up Wearing a Coconut Bra—Captain Beans' Cruise

The black sand beach at Punalu'u is the most accessible black sand beach on the island.

The southern end of the island from Honaunau (near the 104 mile marker on Highway 11) to Hawai'i Volcanoes National Park is the least developed part of the Big Island. Long stretches of lava fields on the western side of Mauna Loa's flank give way to green as you round the southern part of the island, where rain is allowed to fall with less interference from Mauna Loa volcano. Along the way you'll pass roads leading to, among other things, a (usually) deserted black sand beach, a mostly uninhabited 11,000+ acre housing subdivision, and the southernmost place in the United States. Since most people drive this stretch on their way to the volcano from Kailua-Kona or Kohala, we'll describe it from that direction.

These districts, called **South Kona** and **Ka'u**, are littered with the financial corpses of big businessmen with big plans and big wallets who took a big bath. Most didn't have a clue how business in Hawai'i works and lost their 'okoles as a result. Three examples, all mentioned in detail later, are:

H.O.V.E.—*If you build it, they won't come.*
Hawaiian Riviera—*He who underestimates his opponents will ultimately be crushed by them.*
SeaMountain—*How to turn $30 million in cash into $3 million in real estate.*

From Highway 11 heading south from Honaunau, you'll have several opportunities to visit beaches below the road. **Ho'okena** (a decent gray sand beach) and **Pebble Beach** (a violent 'okole kicker) are described under BEACHES. Distances between gas stations are large, so gas up when you can. Just after Honaunau between the 104 and 103 mile marker is the best fruit stand we know of on the west side. **South Kona Fruit Stand** usually has excellent quality fruits all organically grown on the adjacent farm.

While driving along the flanks of Mauna Loa along here, consider this:

Mauna Loa was built from countless thin layers of lava flows, usually less than 15-feet thick. (Flows since 1800 are shown on the map.) About 120,000 years ago, there was a plain below you where there are now steep hills. At that time, a humongous piece (that's a technical term) of the island, from roughly around the 109 mile marker to an area north of Miloli'i (20 miles to the south) broke off and slid into the ocean, creating what is now Kealakekua Bay and the steep hills south of Honaunau. The resulting tsunami (tidal wave) was so huge that it washed completely over the 1,427-foot-high island of Kaho'olawe, continued on, and washed almost completely over the 3,370-foot-high island of Lana'i, where it deposited chunks of coral over a thousand feet up the mountain. This area is, geologically speaking, still unstable. Just didn't want you to run out of things to worry about.

Usually referred to as the last fishing village on the island, Miloli'i, is just past the 89 mile marker. As a beach destination, it won't offer you much (especially on the weekends—see BEACHES for more information). From the highway, 2²⁄₁₀ miles into the beach access road, look off to your left, and you will see a narrow a'a lava flow. The nearby village of Ho'opuloa was wiped out entirely when the lava marched down the slopes of Mauna Loa in 1926. Miloli'i's residents gained notoriety when they and their lawyer managed to kill the Hawaiian Riviera Resort, 17 miles to the south. (See next page.) A 20-minute walk from Miloli'i leads to an exceptionally picturesque coconut-lined bay called Honomolino. It's usually deserted and worth the walk. See page 157 for more.

A Real Gem

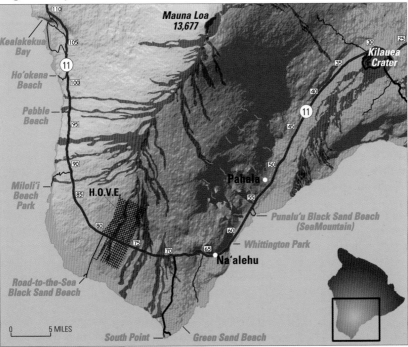

The main highway, called the Hawai'i Belt Road, follows an old Hawaiian road called the Mamalahoa Highway. If you want to see what driving this area used to be like (and why it took so bloody long to circle the island), take the 2-mile stretch of the old road. The intersections are at the 88 and 86 mile markers on the mauka (mountain) side of the road.

You'll see lots of macadamia nut trees along this stretch of the island. (By the way, keep the mac nuts away from dogs; they cause paralysis in certain species.) The Big Island is rapidly becoming a major player in the macadamia nut world. The inner shell of the macadamia nut is impossibly hard. We've been told by nearly every macadamia farmer we know that if you roll over them with your car, they won't break. So we did it. The result? They all broke. Another urban legend shot to...

Back on the highway, **Manuka State Park** is near the 81 mile marker. There's a 2-mile loop trail that wanders through lava flows of several ages, giving you perspective on how things grow over different times. See HIKING for more info. There are restrooms and phones.

The straight dirt road between the 79 and 80 mile markers off Highway 11 is a perfect example of why 4WD vehicles are so useful here. It's called **Road to the Sea**. (Gee, I wonder where it goes?) Two stark, deserted black sand beaches, unknown even to the vast majority of island residents, are at the end. With a regular car you *might* be able to reach the first (smaller) one. (See BEACHES on page 157 for an explanation.) But for the second and better beach, JEEPS only need apply. It's hard to conceive of a lifeless, arid area being inviting, yet this beach somehow is. We've seen plankton-eating whale sharks more than once near the beach.

Another beautiful bay south of here is called **Pohue,** but access to it from the dirt road was scuttled by petty lawsuits between Kahuku Ranch and a Norwegian bank. (They *each* put up gates, one just a hundred feet from the other, and deny each other use.) Separately, there was a several *thousand* acre resort called **Hawaiian Riviera** slated to be built from Road-to-the-Sea to Pohue Bay. Even though the developer had big bucks, he was thwarted by a handful of residents from Miloli'i, 17 miles to the north, who protested that a planned marina here (and the resort in general) would interfere with their rich fishing grounds and their way of life. They got a lawyer to take up their cause, and together they successfully killed the project.

Continuing along, Hawaiian Ocean View Estate (known locally as H.O.V.E.) lies up mauka of the highway along here. Look at the map on the previous page. Notice all those roads? If you drive on them you will notice something missing—houses. About 11,000 one-acre lots on harsh lava, are sparsely populated by 1,500 or so people. Signal Oil built it in the '60s, with the dream of creating a new community. Acre lots originally sold for $500 each. It's changed owners many times since then. Most residents live without water or power, and they used party line phones until 1998. Rain catchment is their lifeline. There's not even a school. Streets have lovely sounding names like *Paradise Parkway* and *Tree Fern Lane*. But after driving around, you'd expect names like *Lava Lane* and *Rocky Road*. Most of the lots have been sold or given away free with a full tank of gas *(just teasing)*, but not many have built. So if you're trying to decide whether to go out for an expensive meal, or buy an acre of Hawai'i, consider H.O.V.E. (O.K., maybe not *that* cheap.) Oh, by the way, part of it lies in an area that was overrun by lava from Mauna Loa in 1907. Just thought you'd like to know. Not to be outdone, another company built a subdivision below the highway (also shown on the map) with 600 three-acre lots. They've had marginally better success.

To be fair, everyone we've met who lives in H.O.V.E. loves it there. They have formed a tight-knit community and seem happy as can be with their location. Whenever I drive around here, however, I'm reminded that the Big Island is often rumored to be one of the largest repositories of people from the FEDERAL WITNESS PROTECTION PROGRAM. What a perfect place to lose one's self.

The Ka'u Drive Inn is a surprisingly good place to stop for a quick bite in these parts. Good, simple food, nice folks. Located near H.O.V.E., an informative sign says simply, "Food." Farther south, the South Point Bar & Restaurant is considerably more avoidable.

SOUTH POINT

Between the 69 and 70 mile markers is the road to South Point (called Ka Lae meaning "the point"). This is the south-ernmost part of the island, making it the southernmost spot in the entire nation. (Not the Florida Keys, as most trivia books claim.) At one time the road was nasty and very hard on rental cars. It has since been repaved and is in fine condition the whole way. The only hazard is that the road is one lane for most of its length. It is mostly straight and there is space to pull over for oncoming cars. Try to resist the temptation to speed on the seemingly wide open parts of this road; there are several surprise blind hills and turns.

NOT TO BE MISSED!

The wind is always blowing out on this grassy plain, hence this location for the Kamoa Wind Farm you cross on South Point Road. (The generators make a

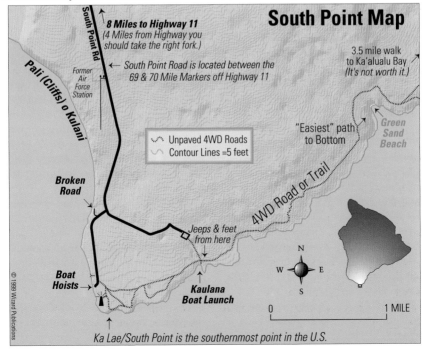

South Point Rd

8 Miles to Highway 11
(4 Miles from Highway you should take the right fork.)

South Point Map

Former Air Force Station

← South Point Road is located between the 69 & 70 Mile Markers off Highway 11

Pali (Cliffs) o Kulani

3.5 mile walk to Ka'alualu Bay →
(It's not worth it.)

Green Sand Beach

"Easiest" path to Bottom

Unpaved 4WD Roads
Contour Lines =5 feet

4WD Road or Trail

Broken Road

Jeeps & feet from here

N
W ⊕ E
S

Boat Hoists →

Kaulana Boat Launch

0   1 MILE

© 1999 Wizard Publications

Ka Lae/South Point is the southernmost point in the U.S.

Bring your extra-strength hairspray when you visit South Point.

strange sound; stop and listen.) The trees here are all wind-blown in the same direction (west), vividly showing what happens to deflected trade winds coming from the northeast. (The foldout back cover map puts it in perspective.) South Point is the site of some of the oldest artifacts yet discovered in Hawai'i (as early as 300 A.D.) and was probably the first place the Polynesians came ashore and settled when they discovered these islands. Dry and desolate with no permanent streams, this might seem a surprising place for people to settle. The reason for its settlements, however, lies offshore. The waters off South Point are incredibly rich fishing grounds. Large pelagic game fish, such as tunas, mahimahi, and marlin, are plentiful. The ancient Hawaiians quickly discovered this but had a problem harvesting the fish. The wind and current together form such a strong offshore force that it would require all your attention just to stay put in a canoe. Those who went out too far were considered lost due to these forces since fishing canoes were not as maneuverable as voyaging canoes, and since the currents are uninterrupted all

the way to Antarctica. The bottom drops to great depths quickly, so anchors aren't the answer. Their clever solution was to carve holes into the rock ledge and feed ropes through them so their canoes could be tied to shore while fishing. Some of those holes are still visible near the boat hoists at the cliffs.

Fresh water is very scarce here, even from wells, and what is available is barely potable. In the 1700s a chief named Kalani'opu'u, tired of having to bathe several miles away, asked his kahunas if there was water under the ground. One know-it-all assured him there was water at a certain spot if he dug *really* deep. After much digging, they found nothing. The big-mouth kahuna was promptly executed for his bad advice.

Today, you're likely to see long lines strung from the sea cliffs just to the northwest of the actual South Point. These lines are usually held afloat by empty bleach bottles and are sometimes pulled so taut by the wind and current that you'd swear you could walk on them. Fishermen use toy sailboats to drag the rope out to sea and dangle 10 foot leaders from the main line at every bleach bottle. When they get a strike, they haul the whole line in.

At the cliffs near South Point are hoists, used to lower small boats from the low cliffs. Metal cliffside ladders are present, as well. Larger boats use the Kaulana boat launch less than a mile to the east. People lived at Kaulana until the turn of the century. Most visitors make the mistake of assuming that the cliffs with the boat hoists *are* South Point. The real South Point is past the light beacon at a place where a rock wall trails down into the sea. There is no cliff there. The beacon will be behind you. Next to the beacon is the small Kalaea Heiau.

Since ancient times this entire area has had a reputation of having exceptionally strong currents, and during all but calm seas this is no doubt true. Even so, we know people who love nothing better than to leap into the water from the boat hoist area and come back up via the ladders adjacent to many boat hoists. There are also a few spots along the cliffs where you can scramble down to the water. Some people even like to snorkel here at night when fish and clouds of small, beautiful shrimp greet the eye. The water is unbelievably clear and seems quite inviting when calm, especially when you can see lots of fish swimming below. With this in mind, I've repeatedly snorkeled here below the boat hoists to assess the currents. I was so wary the first time out that I tied myself to one of the cliff ladders with a long rope—just to be safe. It turned out to be unnecessary. *When calm,* I have yet to detect much current *below the boat hoist area,* probably because it's protected by the point. The water is teeming with life and visibility is usually over 100 feet. But (and I can't stress this enough) I've *never* gone into the water when it's not calm, I don't

swim too far, and I don't endorse swimming there. The surge there demonstrates the extreme power of the ocean and I'm excited and nervous every time I swim at that spot. South of the cliffs at the actual South Point, the water is always violent and unswimmable. I mention all this so you will know what I've experienced here in case you are crazy enough to do it on your own. Check to see that your life insurance policy is in order before you go, and buy a good guidebook to Antarctica—just in case.

South Point was used during WWII for army barracks. Later, the Navy installed a missile tracking station on 33 acres. Not to be left out, the Air Force later took over the facilities and renamed it South Point Air Force Station. The station was closed in 1979, and little remains except the shabby buildings on your right as you are approaching South Point.

Just north of the boat hoists (see map) is a road that leads you off a cliff. There is nothing to stop you except your own good judgment, so don't take it all the way. The road was built in 1955 along with a concrete landing below to service fishing boats. Representing the finest county quality, it lasted less than a year. The surf erased the landing and part of the road. What remains is called (you see this one coming, don't you?) **Broken Road.** The view from the end of Broken Road is spectacular, but the snorkeling isn't as good here as it is below the boat hoists. Off in the distance you see Pali o Kulani, which rises 350 feet from the ocean. At the place where the cliff appears to end, it actually turns inland and runs north to an area just south of Highway 11. The inland cliff was caused by another catastrophic landslide, similar to (but pre-dating) the one described earlier. It slid to the west and caused a similar splash.

Don't adjust your book. The sand really is green here.

A Real Gem

Off to the east of South Point is a strange phenomenon called **Green Sand Beach.** (See BEACHES.) It features a beautiful mixture of green and black sand and is a fascinating place to visit. JEEPS can drive all the way out there, everybody else will have to hoof it for the 4½-mile round trip on the flat, grassy plain.

Back on Highway 11, as you continue you'll wrap around the island and enter the wetter, windward side. Almost instantly, our old friend green has returned to the scene. This was the edge of sugar country. Big Island sugar died here in 1996 (as a business—some of the cane still lives on), and most of the fields here are supposed to be replaced with the more profitable macadamia nut trees. **Waiohinu** and **Na'alehu** are the first towns you come to. Waiohinu's claim to fame was the **Mark Twain Monkeypod Tree,** planted by the author himself. It blew down in the '50s, but its shoots

have grown into a respectable new tree. There are restrooms here.

While in Na'alehu, stop by the **Na'alehu Fruit Stand.** This is a good place to pick up some Ka'u oranges or other fruits. (Remember, the uglier the Ka'u orange, the better it tastes.) They also make a wicked macadamia nut shortbread that, when fresh, is *very* ono. Pizza (which is only fair) is also available.

As you come down the hill near the 62 mile marker, you'll see **Whittington Park** and the remains of its wharf in the distance. Picturesque from a distance but less so close up. Best to drive past or see BEACHES. From the vantage point up there you truly appreciate the vastness of this Big Island.

Just after the 56 mile marker is the road to **Punalu'u Black Sand Beach.** This is the easiest genuine black sand beach to access on the island now that the more famous one in Puna is gone. (That one was

NOT TO BE MISSED!

buried by lava in 1990—see page 110.) The water here is cold due to the large amounts of fresh water percolating from the floor just offshore. At one time the ancient Hawaiians at Punalu'u (which means *spring dived for*) obtained their fresh water here by diving down with an upside-down, dried, hollow gourd to where the fresh water was streaming out. There they would flip the gourd, fill it with fresh water, put their thumbs over it, and come to the surface.

There are scads of turtles in the bay. There is also a picturesque fishpond backed by lots of coconut trees. (Incidentally, there were no coconuts in Hawai'i before the Polynesians came. Though ubiquitous in the South Pacific, Hawai'i is fed by the North Pacific Current, precluding the possibility that a live coconut could have floated here from any place warm. Just thought you needed to know that for your next appearance on *Jeopardy*.) The only eyesore at this exotic black sand beach is the closed and ramshackle restaurant behind the fishpond. The beach is being unfairly affected by the misfortunes of the adjacent complex mentioned below.

When the Japanese attacked Pearl Harbor in 1941, Army troops dynamited the concrete wall over near the boat launch to keep it from being used by the enemy in case of an invasion.

Tour buses sometimes bring groups to Punalu'u, but it *usually* isn't crowded since it is 60 miles from both Hilo and Kona. Forgive us for nagging, but please resist the temptation to take black sand home as a souvenir. Since it is finite, it would eventually deplete the beach for everyone. (Or you can see CURSES under BASICS.) The sharp edges of the sand grains ensures that swimmers will inadvertently take some home anyway. You will find plenty of stowaways in the lining of your bathing suit, which will stay there for years. The concessionaire at Punalu'u sells black sand, but they claim it's from another beach consumed by the volcano. OK, end of nag.

This area is sometimes called SeaMountain, named by a developer for the Lo'ihi Seamount. That undersea volcano, 20 miles offshore from here, will be the Big Island's next volcano attraction. It's still 3,200 feet underwater and won't surface for another 100,000 years, but be sure to look for it when we release our 99,000th edition of this book. (Call now to reserve your copy early.) The whole property was purchased by a Japanese investment company for more than $30 million at the height of the real estate boom in 1989. After five years and countless challenges to their plans by local residents, they sold it for less than $3 million, not even a *tenth* of what they paid for it. *(Ouch!)* There are places to stay here and a golf course. See BEACHES for more on Punalu'u.

From Punalu'u you'll start your gradual 4,000-foot ascent to Kilauea Volcano. Along the way you pass Pahala, a former sugar town now learning to live without the plantations. (This is a speed trap so watch it. Another bad speed trap is when the limit changes after the 38 mile marker.) The coastal land below Pahala was slated to be a spaceport where private satellites would be launched. Again, local residents were able to successfully fight the plan, even though it was backed by the state, the governor, and the mayor.

A couple miles past the edge of Hawai'i Volcanoes National Park, take note of the rugged looking a'a lava. It's hard to believe that barefoot armies marched through this stuff, but they did—sometimes under extraordinary circumstances like those described on page 84.

Lava sometimes forms surreal images as it's flowing.

If you had to name the one thing the Big Island is most famous for, it would undoubtedly be **Kilauea Volcano**. In all the world there isn't a more active volcano, and none is as user friendly as Kilauea. People often refer to it as the drive-in volcano.

Kilauea is an enigma—you can't really see the mountain from anywhere on the island, or even recognize it when you are standing on it. It seems more like a growth on Mauna Loa, whose flanks it resides upon. In the past, everyone thought that it was *part* of Mauna Loa, but today we know that it is separate and distinct, with its own separate magma chamber. One part of Kilauea, the actual Pu'u 'O'o vent itself, is teasingly inaccessible. You can't get very close to it without a long hike. The "quickest" way is described in ADVENTURES on page 212.

We feel strongly that most people allow far too little time for visiting **Hawai'i Volcanoes National Park.** Many simply blow through on an around-the-island driving frenzy, stopping long enough to snap a shot of Kilauea Caldera. There is much more here than meets the eye, and this might be the highlight of your Hawaiian trip. Whether Kilauea is erupting or not, this park is the most fascinating place you may ever visit, and you *surely* don't have anything like this back home. The finest hiking on the island is here. The lushest rain forest you've ever seen is here to stroll through. Vents spewing steam, brand new land, birds-a-plenty, giant chasms, ancient Hawaiian petroglyphs, lava craters, walk-through lava tubes, unrivaled vistas—it's all here. Once you know what to look for, you will want to spend at least a whole day, preferably two. Since a trip to the Volcano can take four hours round trip from Kona and five hours from Kohala, many people plan the trip by reserving a place to stay at Volcano House or in the town of Volcano (see WHERE TO STAY). This allows you to experience it at a more leisurely pace and is a nice way to go, if you can swing it.

You'll probably want to stay until after dark if there are accessible surface lava flows, and the drive back to Kona or Kohala is a drag (with no place to eat at night until Kealakekua). If you are staying in Hilo, it's an easy drive back.

WILL I GET TO SEE LAVA FLOWING?

Historically (meaning since 1778), most eruptions have lasted days or weeks, rarely months. Until this eruption, only once, from 1969–1974 at Mauna Ulu, has an eruption outside the crater lasted more than a year. The current eruption, originating from a newly created vent called Pu'u 'O'o, is redefining our understanding of an eruption. It started on January 3, 1983, shifted to a vent called Kupaianaha from 1986 to 1992, then shifted back toward Pu'u 'O'o and was still going strong as we went to press with an occasional hiccup in its flowing activity.

When you visit Kilauea, you either *will* or *won't* get to see a surface lava flow. (Now *there's* a gutsy prediction!) Hawai'i Volcanoes National Park has a recording at 985–6000, but it's not always updated when it should be. They also have weather updates. As we went to press, there were no signs of an impending work stoppage by Madam Pele, the fire goddess of Hawai'i, but that doesn't mean you can come here and be assured

of being able to stick your toe into liquid lava. Madam Pele can be kind of a tease. The lava has stopped and started many times, shifted from vent to vent, gone straight into the ocean from underground lava tubes, and flowed in inaccessible places. It has also flowed just feet from the end of Chain of Craters Road, in Kilauea Caldera, and other very accessible places. It's a gamble as to whether you will get to see it. Kilauea might go months without *accessible* lava flows, then put on a flawless show for months after that. If you have internet access, we have an eruption update on our site at www.wizardpub.com. We also have links to other eruption web sites.

When you hear that the volcano is erupting, you might think of a cone-shaped mountain, of going up to the top and peering into a boiling lake of molten rock. Maybe some will be pouring rapidly down the mountain, consuming everything in its path as people flee in panic. In Hawai'i, things are *far* different. Here, even the volcano is laid-back. Though it has erupted from the main crater in the past, most of the time (including the current eruption) the lava breaks out from a vent along what's called the rift zone, a linear belt of fractured rock on the flank of the volcano. From this vent the lava travels downhill, usually to the sea. After it starts flowing,

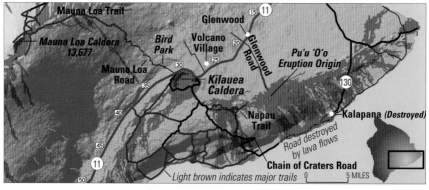

The Explosion That Changed History

Mild mannered Kilauea has exploded only twice in recorded history, once in 1790 and once in 1924. (There is evidence that it may have exploded more often in the distant past.) These eruption are phreatomagmatic, meaning steam induced (but you knew that). In 1790, Kamehameha ruled much of the island. While he was distracted with plans to invade Maui, a rival chief named Keoua seized control of this part of the island. Kamehameha sent troops to do battle. Eventually both armies pulled back to their strongholds. As Keoua's troops and their families camped at Kilauea that night, fire and rock spewed from Kilauea caldera. Keoua thought he had offended Pele, the volcano goddess, by rolling stones into the crater the day before, and spent two days trying to appease her. It didn't work. On the third day they tried to leave, organized in three divisions. Right after the first division left, the mountain exploded. Darkness enveloped the area, punctured by volcano-induced thunder and lightning, and streams of red and blue light from the crater. Huge amounts of hot ash rained down, then a suffocating gas belched up from the volcano.

The first division to depart escaped mostly intact. The second division disappeared. When the third division came to the scene they found their comrades of the second division huddled in circles, some hugging each other with their noses pressed together. Relieved, the third division rushed forward to greet them, only to discover that every last member of the second division—around 400 men and their wives and children—were dead. (Not 85 as the park sign says.) Most had been asphyxiated by the noxious gas. The only survivor was a solitary hog. If you take the Ka'u Desert Trail (page 100) you can see the faint outline of steps preserved in the ash—steps created by other soldiers at the time of the disaster.

As for Keoua, everyone now knew that Pele was against him and his army. He kept fighting more battles but never turned the tide. Not yet defeated, he was invited by Kamehameha to peacefully dedicate the new Pu'ukohola Heiau in Kawaihae. When Keoua's boat approached the shore of Kawaihae he was immediately murdered by one of Kamehameha's officers and had the dubious honor of being the temple's first official human sacrifice. Thus was Kamehameha's rule over the island forever solidified.

pahoehoe lava rivers crust over, forming tubes. These tubes act as excellent insulators (the lava usually loses a mere 20°F over miles of travel in these tubes) and carry the lava to the ocean. Sometimes these tubes break the surface downhill of the source, forming surface flows. When this happens, you can often walk right up to it. Otherwise, there might be an enormous steam plume at the sea (which glows at night).

Many activity companies and nearly every guidebook shows photos of a helicopter or viewer directly in front of gigantic fountains of lava. You won't see any pictures like that in our book for two reasons. One, you're more likely to see *Elvis* than to see that. It might happen a few times each decade for a few hours. What are *your* chances? The other reason is that a few of those photos are fake. (A stock government photo of a

Beaches of jet black sand can form almost overnight when lava shatters as it's quenched by the sea.

Kilauea lava fountain taken by scientists, a shot of a helicopter or person, a computer, and *voilà*—the unreal looks real.) The close-up photographs of surface lava flows you see in this book were all taken by us at accessible sites. We didn't get special permission to go to special spots or go through any unusual procedures. We didn't use a camera lens longer than a rental car to make it *seem* like it was close (and I had the singed leg hairs to prove it). We also didn't charter helicopters and use zillion dollar cameras on loan from NASA. Granted, we didn't get to see this kind of lava our first time out there, but these are the kinds of things that mere mortals like us might get to see *if* Madame Pele is cooperating.

THE SCENE

We've been to the volcano countless times, with and without surface lava. It's always a fantastic experience, though not what people expect.

During a relatively calm flow, pahoehoe lava is silvery coated, red, or yellow as it oozes its way toward the sea. It is a humbling experience to stand there and observe Earthly creation, like seeing the planet during its fiery adolescence. In most parts of the world, people dread active volcanoes, fearing death and destruction. A huge explosion will send clouds of ash and pumice into air, killing everything in its path. In Hawai'i, people drop whatever they are doing and drive out to see it. Rather than apocalyptic explosions, Kilauea mostly drools and dribbles. (In historic times, it has exploded only twice, one had astonishing consequences—see facing page.) Though the total volume of lava erupting ranges from 300,000 to more than a million cubic yards *per day,* it is so spread out that it rarely rushes down the mountain in a hellish river of liquid stone. Usually, it's small rivulets of molten lava separated by large distances from other rivulets.

A'a lava on the left (named by the first Hawaiian to walk on it bare-footed?) is rough and clinkery. Pahoehoe on the right is smooth and ropy, like thick cake batter.

When it hardens (which occurs very quickly), it crunches beneath your feet like shards of glass.

There are not many places on this planet where you can walk on ground younger than you are, where you can be assured that there is absolutely nothing alive beneath your feet except for the earth itself. We've been there when people from all over the world stand in awe, tears streaming down their cheeks as they tell their children, "You may never see anything like this again in your lifetime."

As freshly hardened pahoehoe lava cools, it stresses the silica coating on the outside. This natural glass then crackles and pops off the rock creating subtle sounds that bewitch viewers. Heat from the flows can be intense. Many times we've been less than a yard from the molten lava and felt like we would suddenly burst into flames. Other times, the wind has blown the other direction so we could enjoy the liquid earth in com-

fort. Sometimes there is unpleasant black smoke and fumes (especially when the volcano is gobbling up more road or forest). Other times it seems to have absolutely no fumes or smoke and no offensive smell. (What smell it does have is hard to describe but never forgotten.)

At night, the lava may glow in numerous spots like a prehistoric scene from yesteryear. Sometimes, as the lava flows into the ocean, brilliant red and orange steam clouds light up the immediate area, creating dazzling light shows as the flow drips or gushes into the ocean. Sometimes, when it burns scrub vegetation at night, the methane emits a blue flame. A scene at night might go like this: A crowd of about 50 people on a bluff overlooking a field of fresh pahoehoe. It pops, crackles, and glows as the night consumes all. What amazes us is how reverent everybody is. Couples hold each other tight. People speak in soft whispers. They try not to move much for fear of disturbing others as they watch Earth's most primordial show. Nobody wants to leave. Watching the lava enter the sea at night never fails to impress, and we been told more times that we can count by visitors that it is an unsurpassed highlight.

A FEW BASICS

Despite the fact that it is operated by the federal government, the park seems very well run. Much of the staff are friendly and professional. (We've seen other parks where the staff can be real curmudgeons.) The rangers are pretty good at letting you see the action close up. We've been there when they lead people across smoldering lava, the heat coming up through their shoes. They will only keep you away if they *truly* perceive danger, unlike some other parks where they sometimes keep you away from imaginary dangers on orders from the lawyers. Because of this, you should heed their cautions seriously. If they say you can't go to a certain area because they expect a lava bench might collapse, don't go there. At least one person has died because he didn't heed this warning. (The ocean drops quickly off the coast of the park, and new lava land is usually destined to break off when it reaches a critical mass.) If rangers say an area is off limits because of the dangers of methane explosions, believe it. Methane from plant matter in older

flows can heat up when a new flow covers it. This usually escapes by hissing or by small pops, but sometimes it can be more dramatic. We were there once with many other visitors when a large methane explosion occurred 25 feet from us. It was powerful enough to rip through 12-inch thick lava, pieces of which jumped into the air. Under certain circumstances, these explosions occur 100 yards in advance of a lava flow.

In the park we like to arrive at surface flows about an hour or two before sunset. That way we get to see it during the day, and at night. As the sun sets, the light-emitting lava doesn't have to compete with the sun, resulting in brighter and seemingly more abundant lava.

A river of stone plunges into the sea.

Bring plenty of film and a polarizing filter if you have a camera that will accept it. (Wipe your camera off when you are finished; the air can be acidic and is hard on electronics.) The best shots will be late in the afternoon. If you get close to the lava, the heat might consume your camera battery faster than you think. (Trust me on that one.) Bring water—you'll get hot and thirsty. If it rains, you'll be grateful for something waterproof, and so will your camera. Depending on the flow, a flashlight might be invaluable. At times, they let you walk to places at night that can be spectacular. Contact lens wearers will want to bring drops—maybe even your glasses if it gets uncomfortable. Bring sunscreen if you are there for the day. Add more film and water. During really good flows the question you hear most is, "Does anybody have any film I can buy?" What you don't want to bring are your preconceptions. No matter what you expect, the flow will be different. Come with a blank slate, and you will leave full of wonder.

And remember, if there are no accessible surface flows (which is quite possible), don't despair. The volcano area is eminently fascinating and exciting, with or without surface flows, and is always worth at least a day of exploration. Below are some of the other delights waiting for you at Hawai'i Volcanoes National Park.

Why You Shouldn't Pick a Lehua Blossom Off an 'Ohi'a Tree

According to legend, 'Ohi'a was a young, handsome Big Island chief. The volcano goddess Pele knew that 'Ohi'a was courting a beautiful young girl named Lehua. Pele became enamored with 'Ohi'a and desired him for a husband. One day as 'Ohi'a went up into the mountains to cut kukui bark to stain his surfboard, Pele appeared to him. She was dressed in her finest clothes and was quite striking. After a time, she announced to 'Ohi'a who she was and asked him to be her husband. Nervous but very diplomatically, he turned her down, professing his eternal love for Lehua. In her anger, Pele told him he was as gutless as a piece of wood, and changed him into a gnarled tree with grey-green leaves. When the other gods saw what Pele had done, they felt bad and tried to reverse it, but failed. The best they could do to reunite the brokenhearted Lehua with her beloved 'Ohi'a was to turn Lehua into a beautiful blossom on the same tree. To this day, it is said that picking a lehua blossom off an 'ohi'a tree will produce rain. These are the tears from heaven for separated lovers everywhere.

AROUND KILAUEA CRATER

A quick note: We decided not to use our **Real Gem** and **Not To Be Missed** icons in this section because they would fill the pages. The entire park is *a real gem* and is *not to be missed*.

As you arrive at the park, which is open 24 hours a day, there is a recording playing on 530 AM radio. It has information that is promptly updated every leap year or so, so don't expect up-to-the-minute reports.

Remember that Kilauea Caldera is located at an altitude of 4,000 feet, so make sure you bring your warmies for those days that it's misty and chilly at the summit.

After paying your $10 car entrance fee (what a deal!) at the gate, stop by the Visitor Center on your right. They have up-to-date information, a nice display of books, videos, artifacts, a movie showing, and—most important if you've driven a long way—restrooms. Check out the 3-D miniature of the island near the restrooms to get a perspective of the island. Some guided hike notices are sometimes posted at the Visitor Center if you're interested. From the Center, you might want to walk across the street to **Volcano House** for your first peek of Kilauea Caldera from their enviable view. You can also eat at the restaurant or snack bar there. (See DINING for review.) This is the only place to eat *in* the park.

We should probably take the opportunity to confess here that the park used to sell this book at the Visitors Center. After undergoing a lengthy reviewing process, they called it the most accurate book they'd ever seen on the Big Island, and it became the only guidebook sold there. Quite a coup. The book's not there anymore. Why? Because some park bureaucrats became upset when they realized that we revealed things, such as a trail to Puʻu ʻOʻo that doesn't go through their park, the hike to Mauna Ulu, and several other things. Well, we're not going to stop telling you about these attractions even if it means they won't carry our book at the Visitors Center. The trail is described under ADVENTURES on page 212, Mauna Ulu is on page 207. (A few other things we revealed also got under their skin.)

You'll want to do a counter-clockwise tour of the caldera to start. The first thing you come to is **Sulphur Banks** on your right. There is a road to this stinky phenomenon, where hydrogen sulphide gas and steam form deposits of sulphur, gypsum and hematite on the ground. This should be avoided by those with a heart condition, respiratory problems, children, or anyone eating lunch in the car.

Going further on Crater Rim Road, you see the **Steam Vents** on your left. Here, rain that has seeped into the ground is heated by Kilauea and issues forth as steam. The amount varies daily depending on the level of rain in the past few days, and it is rarely smelly like Sulphur Banks—in fact, there is usually no smell at all. Make sure you take the trail for 2–3 minutes toward the crater rim for a smashing view of the crater, and where additional, more powerful and unobstructed steam vents are present.

Rounding the crater, you come to **Kilauea Overlook**. This is a different perspective on Kilauea Crater and its progeny, **Halemaʻumaʻu Crater**, and is definitely worth a stop. Look for white-tailed tropic birds soaring on the thermals down in the crater.

Just past the overlook is **Jagger Museum** and the **Hawaiian Volcano Observatory**. The museum has some very interesting exhibits and is worth a stop. (The view is *da kine* as well.)

Kilauea Crater Map

This map is rendered at an angle in order to convey the lay of the land at Kilauea. Visualize it as a solid cast of the land sitting on a table. Each "terraced" contour line represents an elevation change of 20 feet.

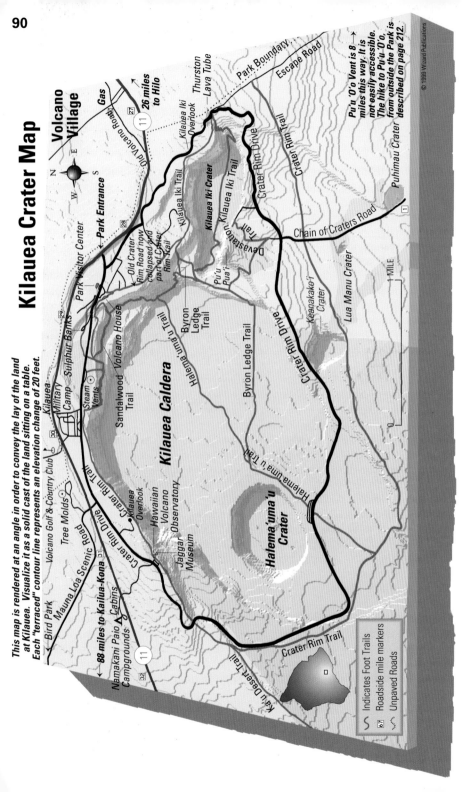

Volcano Village

Gas

26 miles to Hilo

Old Volcano Road

Park Entrance

Park Visitor Center

Military Camp

Sulphur Banks

Steam Vents

Sandalwood Volcano House

Old Crater Rim Road now collapsed and part of Crater Rim Trail

Kilauea Iki Overlook

Kilauea Iki Crater

Kilauea Iki Trail

Thurston Lava Tube

Park Boundary

Escape Road

Crater Rim Drive

Devastation Trail

Chain of Craters Road

Pu'u Pua'i

Byron Ledge Trail

Kilauea Caldera

Halema'uma'u Trail

Byron Ledge Trail

Keanakako'i Crater

Lua Manu Crater

Crater Rim Drive

Halema'uma'u Trail

Halema'uma'u Crater

Crater Rim Trail

Puhimau Crater

Pu'u 'O'o Vent is 8 miles this way. It is not easily accessible. The hike to Pu'u 'O'o, from outside the Park is described on page 212.

1 MILE

Bird Park

Mauna Loa Scenic Road

Volcano Golf & Country Club

Tree Molds

Crater Rim Scenic Road

Crater Rim Drive

Kilauea Overlook

Hawaiian Volcano Observatory

Jaggar Museum

Namakani Paio Campgrounds Cabins

88 miles to Kailua-Kona

Ka'u Desert Trail

Crater Rim Trail

Indicates Foot Trails

Roadside mile markers

Unpaved Roads

Continuing on, you start to round the bottom of the crater. Note that there are no walls here. The crater summit is tilted, and lava has spilled over the sides at the southern end many times in the past. Soon you come to **Halema'uma'u Crater.** This crater-within-a-crater is said to be the home to Madame Pele, the Hawaiian volcano goddess. Though crusted over now, for most of the 19th century this was a boiling lava lake. Mark Twain and other celebrities of his time visited here, and described it as viewing the fiery pits of hell. When Isabella Bird saw it in 1873, she wrote:

"Suddenly, just above, and in front of us, gory drops were tossed in air, and springing forwards we stood on the brink of Halemau-mau, which was about 35 feet below us. I think we all screamed, I know we all wept, but we were speechless, for a new glory and terror had been added to the Earth. It is the most unutterable of wonderful things. The words of common speech are quite useless. It is unimaginable, indescribable, a sight to remember forever, a sight which at once took possession of every faculty of sense and soul, removing one altogether out of the range of ordinary life. Here was the real "bottomless pit"—the "fire which is not quenched"—"the place of hell"—"the lake which burneth with fire and brimstone"—the "everlasting burnings"—the fiery sea whose waves are never weary. There were groanings, rumblings, and detonations, rushings, hissings, and splashings, and the crashing sound of breakers on the coast, but it was the surging of fiery waves upon a fiery shore."

Halema'uma'u is quieter now with the lava action occurring elsewhere. It takes a few minutes to walk to the crater overlook and is well worth the walk. Though usually not as strong, fumes *can* call for similar warnings as at Sulphur Banks. The crater has risen and fallen over time—going from 1,335 feet deep to overflowing its top. Right now, it's less than 300 feet deep and 3,000 feet across.

Some Hawaiians today still make offerings to Pele. You might see these gifts near the edge of the crater, though most of the time these come from visitors and are considered an irritant by park personnel. It is said that Pele will appear as a beautiful young woman in the mountains and as a very old and very ugly woman at the shoreline. (Hence the Hawaiian saying, "Always be nice to an old woman; it might be Pele.") Though Halema'uma'u is said to be her home, she seems to be spending more time these days at her summer house at Pu'u 'O'o.

Continuing, you come to another crater called **Keanakako'i.** The Hawaiians used to fetch abnormally hard rock from here until it was covered by subsequent lava flows. Across the road from Keanakako'i is a lava fissure. These fissures are usually long cracks where lava erupts in a curtain of fire, as this one did in 1974.

Past Keanakako'i you will notice a gravel-like substance on the ground. That's **tephra,** airborne gas-frothed lava from fountains, which cools as pumice cinders.

Soon you pass **Chain of Craters Road,** which leads 20 miles down to the shore and ends abruptly where the current lava flow has cut it off. Just pass it by *for now.*

The road will pass through an incredibly lush area. Ferns and 'ohi'a trees rule this forest—it's hard to believe that a few minutes ago you were in a lava desert.

On your left will be a road to the **Pu'u Pua'i Overlook.** The overlook just past the parking lot is great. It overlooks **Kilauea Iki Crater** and Pu'u Pua'i. This crater (meaning little Kilauea) had been asleep for almost a century when it became active in 1959. Then it erupted into gargantuan fountains of lava, some reaching a staggering 1,900 feet—that's more than four times the height of the crater walls and is the highest on record. Scientists had warnings that an eruption was going to occur. Earthquake swarms and a swelling of Kilauea told them it was coming. So they set up their instruments and waited for the inevitable—*at Halema'uma'u.* They were stunned when the lava instead shot from the southwest wall of Kilauea Iki (right below you) 2 miles away. Ground zero was near the Pu'u Pua'i (meaning gushing hill) cinder cone. It was created as fountains of lava, blown southwest by the trade winds piled high into a cone. The vent spewed enough lava at one point to bury a football field 15 feet deep in lava—*every minute!* Each time the showers ended, the lava would drain back into the vent opening, only to be shot out again. When it ended, 36 days after it began, the crater floor was a dead zone with a lava bathtub ring above the floor to tell how high the lava had reached. The lava lake cooled and cracked as sheets of lava buckled and warped, giving the crater the look of dried, crusted-over gravy. Today, steam usually issues from cracks in the crater floor, and the rock is still molten a couple of hundred feet down. There are still vents on the crater, though the main vent was covered by falling cinders. Kilauea Iki offers one of the best hikes on the Island. See HIKING on page 178.

From here you could stroll for 10–15 minutes along the **Devastation Trail.** This is where the fallout from the 1959 Kilauea Iki eruption killed the fern and 'ohi'a forest. The line of demarcation is abrupt, going from healthy forest to a field of tephra littered with bleached tree trunks. The forest is working to come back, and you will see the results along the way. You can either walk back the way you came, loop around on Crater Rim Road, or have someone pick you up at the other end.

Back on Crater Rim Road, you come to a parking lot (probably full of buses). This is **Thurston Lava Tube.** If you are looking for an easy way to see what the inside of natural lava plumbing looks like, Thurston Lava Tube is worth a stop. It is considered one of the "must sees" at the volcano. If you get there between tour buses, it can be an interesting experience. The entrance is a few minutes walk from Crater Rim Drive (see map). You exit about halfway through the tube. This part of the tube is lighted and is the most widely visited. Most of the lava stalactites have been removed over the decades, but you can still see enough tube detail to get the idea of how the lava travels. Undisturbed tubes often have floors littered with rocks that fall from the ceiling (either from when the tube cooled or from rainwater seeping through the cracks over the years). Thurston has been cleaned up and lighted to make it easy to visit. The more adventurous might want to see Thurston's *darker* half. At the stairs at the end of the tube tour and past the gate, Thurston continues for another 1,000 feet (it seems like more) before it ends abruptly. You are welcome to go. (The rangers used to keep a book for visitors to sign at the end of the tube, protected by a PVC pipe, but say they had to pull it out because visitors kept mistaking the PVC for a pipe bomb.) Make sure you bring a good flashlight (or two) for the journey, as you will be in total darkness most of the way. At the end turn off the light. You've never seen *real* blackness until you've seen *this* blackness.

The 1959 eruption of Kilauea Iki punished this part of the forest when it showered the land with falling bits of gas-frothed lava from the 1,900-foot-high fountains. But it's the forest that will prevail. Take the short Devastation Trail and see for yourself.

If you want to get a feel for what Thurston Lava Tube looked like before it was tamed, see ADVENTURES.

That dirt road that leads south of Thurston Lava Tube is an **escape road.** It is well maintained in case Chain of Craters road is ever obliterated by a lava flow (again). That dirt road is the only place in the park where **mountain bikes** are allowed. It goes through very lush forest and is a delight. Just make sure you close all gates behind you. Some areas are fenced off to prevent pig damage. Wild pigs are amazingly destructive and rangers fight an unending war to minimize their impact.

Just past Thurston Lava Tube is the **Kilauea Iki Overlook.** This, too, is worth stopping for. You look at Kilauea Iki from the other side. The Kilauea Iki hike mentioned a moment ago starts from here. Kilauea Iki is separated from Kilauea by a narrow shelf of land called **Byron Ledge.** It was on this ledge in 1824 that Princess Kapiolani publicly stood and, to the horror and fear of many, denied the volcano goddess Pele and embraced Christianity. She initiated this by eating 'ohelo berries without offering any to Pele first. (It was thought that Pele would strike you dead if you didn't offer her some first by tossing a fruiting branch into the crater.) When the Princess didn't die after snubbing and denying Pele, Christianity was greatly bolstered among the people.

If you continue on Crater Rim Drive, you will end up back at the Visitor Center. If you need a break, walk over to the building on your left, the **Volcano Art Center Gallery.** Built in 1877, this was the original Volcano House before it was moved it here to make way for another building. Now an art gallery, they have an exquisite selection from some of the island's top artists, including higher-end wood carvings, glassworks, paintings, and the like. This is also a good place to check out what's going on in the area in terms of events and demonstrations. Open 9–5.

There is another nice hike that starts near Volcano House. (See HIKING on page 180.) Part of it is on the *old* Crater Rim Drive—before it fell into the crater in 1983—and the results are dramatic.

DOWN CHAIN OF CRATERS ROAD

From the Visitor Center, you could head back the way you came on Crater Rim Drive, past Kilauea Iki and onto **Chain of Craters Road.** This is a 20-mile descent to the sea. (At least it was 20 miles when we went to press, and getting shorter all the time.) The road was so-named because it passed numerous craters along the rift zone before veering off to the shore. It was rerouted after Madam Pele repaved 12 miles of the road with lava during the 1969–74 Mauna Ulu flow, and now visits fewer craters than in used to. Mile markers are on alternating sides of the road and we will refer to some of them. There are still some craters along the way you might want to check out (but don't bother with Ko'oko'olau). Remember to check your gas gauge; we've seen people run out of gas coming back up.

A little more than 2 miles into Chain of Craters Road is **Hilina Pali Road,** 8³⁄₁₀ miles long. It may be closed during nene nesting or if there is a perceived fire danger. The drive isn't impressive, but at the end is **Hilina Pali Lookout.** Walk down the path for 100 feet or so and you are treated to an amazingly expansive view. You're perched above the vast shoreline below, and on a clear day you can see the entire shoreline for over 30 miles south. It's very quiet, desolate, and peaceful, with the sound of the distant ocean sometimes present. They close this road often for fire hazards and when nenes (the Hawaiian goose) are breeding. If you take it,

Lava sometimes bursts from fissures such as this one from the 1970s Mauna Ulu eruption. But life always reclaims the land.

please drive very slowly as the endangered nenes are usually in the road and aren't very impressed by cars. The Kulanaokuaiki campgrounds are also on Hilina Pali Road. Less than ⅟₁₀ mile past Hilina Pali Road, on the left (east) side is a 60 second walk to **Devil's Throat.** (It's unmarked.) This small collapsed crater is impressively sheer. It's *Straight* down. Be careful at the edge, it looks pretty fragile.

The Hawaiians, like people since the dawn of time, were compelled to leave a lasting legacy of themselves to the ages. These ancient petroglyphs are on the short Pu'u Loa trail.

Along this stretch of Chain of Craters Road, keep an eye to your left. You *might* see steam coming from a hill. This is **Mauna Ulu,** the source of the second longest flank eruption of Kilauea. From 1969–1974 it poured lava and harassed park road builders, forcing Chain of Craters road to be rerouted. There is a trail off the spur road past Pauahi Crater that goes near Mauna Ulu. (See ADVENTURES on page 207.) In 1997 a couple camping way out at Napau Crater (3½ miles east of Mauna Ulu) were awakened when lava suddenly began gushing from the ground a half mile away.

Just south of the 4 mile marker is a field of tephra. We've walked to the east along here and discovered incredible lava fissures from 25 years ago (such as the one shown on the facing page), with ferns and trees already growing in them. But there is no trail, so you are on virgin, and untested, ground.

Proceeding down the road, you will get an appreciation in several spots of how lava actually flowed down the mountain during the 1969–74 Mauna Ulu eruption. At the **Alanui Kahakai turnout** (near the 14 mile marker) you will see a segment of the old, partially covered Chain of Craters Road. At the **Holei Pali Lookout,** just before the 15 mile marker, there is a great view of the mountain flows where you get a feel for the volume of a'a and pahoehoe that drooled down the mountain. The newer highway cutting through the lava flow is dramatic.

About ⅓ mile past the 15 mile marker, you will pass by a lava tube on your left. Road crews bisect them every time they cut a new road in this area.

Past the 16 mile marker you will see the **Pu'u Loa Petroglyph Trail.** This fairly easy 15–20 minute walk is over an old pahoehoe lava flow with cairns (mounds of rock) marking the way. It leads to an area studded with thousands of petroglyphs (rock carvings) representing everything from birth to death. This is the largest petroglyph field in the state. A circular boardwalk (which they may remove) has been built near some of them to allow you to view them without walking on them. *Many* more carvings are located

96

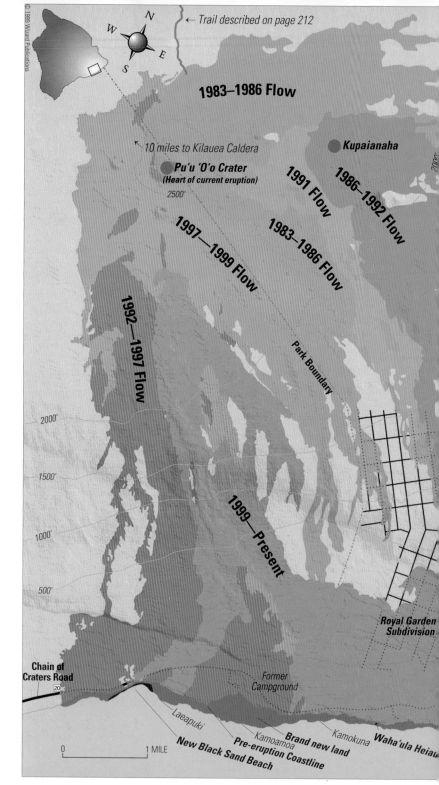

← Trail described on page 212

N
W   E
S

1983–1986 Flow

● **Kupaianaha**

← 10 miles to Kilauea Caldera

● **Pu'u 'O'o Crater**
(Heart of current eruption)

2500'

1991 Flow

1986–1992 Flow

1983–1986 Flow

1997—1999 Flow

1992—1997 Flow

Park Boundary

2000'

1500'

1000'

500'

1999—Present

**Royal Garden
Subdivision**

**Chain of
Craters Road**
20

*Former
Campground*

Laeapuki

Kamoamoa

Brand new land

Kamokuna

Waha'ula Heiau

Pre-eruption Coastline

New Black Sand Beach

0   1 MILE

© 1999 Wizard Publications

The Current Eruption

Since the eruption began at Pu'u 'O'o (which conveniently materialized just within the park boundary) on January 3, 1983 the lava flows have been quite prolific. Each day 300,000 to 1,000,000 cubic yards of lava erupts which has dramatically changed the landscape. Note how the lava concentrates in one area until another area opens up. The town of Kalapana was erased from the map in 1990. The famous Black Sand Beach at Kaimu is gone, now under 50–75 feet of lava. But a new, unnamed black sand beach now exists a third of a mile in front of where the old one was.

One of the most important heiau on the island was Waha'ula Heiau. Oral tradition states that it was constructed by Pa'ao, a priest from Tahiti who arrived during the second wave of colonization in the 12th century. It was he who was said to have introduced the concept of human sacrifice. Mu, whose role was to gatherer people to be sacrificed, would go out at night in parties of three and eavesdrop on houses, listening for any breach of kapu (rules of conduct). When one occurred they would rush in and seize the victims and lead them off to this heiau. Sacrifices here were deemed so important that priests were sometimes sacrificed if others could not be found by the required time. Even smoke from its altars was sacred and it was death to anyone who passed under the shadow of the smoke. Abraham Fornander states in his epic work of the late 19th century that this was the last heiau to be destroyed after the kapu system was abolished by King Kamehameha II in 1819. The heiau was buried by lava in 1997.

The doomed village of Kalapana is said to be named after an old man from Kaua'i trying to make a pilgrimage to Pele. He landed at what was Kaimu Beach and tried to make it to Kilauea but was unsuccessful due to severe storms. That night Pele came to his hut and appeared to him. The next morning nearly all of the old man's long hair was burned off. When he died some time later, the people named their village after him. It is said that because Kalapana could not make it to Pele's house, she sometimes visits his.

Interesting facts at a glance…

Total amount of lava erupted—2,250,000,000 Cubic Yards
Temperature lost while traveling in lava tubes—20°
Average temperature of flowing lava—2,000°
Length of public highway covered—8 Miles
Amount of new land created—575 Acres
Owner of all new land—State of Hawaii
Total area covered—38 Square Miles
Number of homes destroyed—182

1500'

1000'

500'

apana Gardens and
st of Royal Gardens
were destroyed by
lava flows in 1990.

Kalapana

D Lava Road

Former Kaimu
Black Sand Beach

Kalapana Gardens
Subdivision

Pre-eruption Coastline
New Unnamed Black Sand Beach
Brand new land
Cave of Refuge

Brand new land

apau Point

130

19

20

21

137

past the boardwalk, but they request that you avoid walking around to protect the perishable petroglyphs from wear. The small holes bored in the rock were usually cut by parents who placed the umbilical cords from their newborns there for good luck. The area is very peaceful and worth your time if you wish to see a direct expression of ancient Hawaiian life. It's about 1½ miles round trip.

Just before the 19 mile mark is the **Holei Sea Arch,** where the ocean has undercut the rock, leaving an arch. You walk less than a minute to it.

Past here should be the **end of Chain of Craters Road** (unless the lava advances to the sea arch). This is where the lava was pouring as we went to press, sometimes on the surface, sometimes into the sea, sometimes too far inland to walk to. Old maps showing Kamoamoa Campgrounds, a visitor center, Waha'ula Heiau, Lae 'Apuki, Waiaka Pond, Queen's Bath, Royal Garden, Kalapana Gardens, and more are all tragically out of date. These were victims of the current eruption. Before you is a newly paved lava wasteland, where liquid rock has poured above and below ground, reaching the ocean and building more land. The park "Visitor Center" at the bottom is now a motor home, which has had to be moved many times to avoid the fate of the last visitor center down here. Check with the rangers to see what's shakin'. Ask if nighttime offers good viewing conditions. Often at night the skylights, holes in the ceiling of a lava tube, are visible in the distance. Usually the only way to see a skylight during the day is on a helicopter flight. (See Helicopters under ACTIVITIES.) When the lava is flowing

inland you are usually allowed to hike to it. (They'll *imply* that you can't but will usually admit that it is permitted if pressed.) See ADVENTURES on page 214.

HIKING IN THE PARK

Much of the best hiking on the island is in Hawai'i Volcanoes National Park. The ACTIVITIES section has a HIKING section on page 177, which lists scads of great hikes in the Park. There's also a couple of spookier park hikes listed under ADVENTURES. Note that strolls of less than 30 minutes were described above in the tour of the volcano.

OUTSIDE THE PARK ENTRANCE

Just outside the park entrance there are a few sights that are worth checking out, either before or after your park visit.

Mauna Loa Scenic Road leads past the **Tree Molds.** These holes are created when a lava flow encounters a sopping wet tree trunk, which resists bursting into flames just long enough to harden the lava around it, giving the holes the texture of the tree bark. Better tree molds are found on the easy beginning of the **Napau Crater Trail** hike listed on page 179. Farther up the road is **Kipuka Puaulu (Bird Park).** This 30-minute hike goes through a kipuka, an old growth of forest surrounded by newer lava flows. This kipuka features many native trees and plants. Birds abound in this park, hence its nickname, Bird Park. The entire 1-mile stroll takes only 30 minutes plus stopping time. There are several benches scattered along the trail, which ascends gently the first half.

Mauna Loa Scenic Road becomes very winding past here and switches to

one lane (with several blind turns), as it passes through forest. At the end of the 13-mile road (at 6,650 feet) is the trailhead to Mauna Loa Trail. This is where you start your multi-day trek through the cold and altitude to ascend the summit of Mauna Loa. (Maybe another day.) There are picnic tables and a nice view of the park at the road's end. Though pleasant, this road is dispensable if you are budgeting your time.

Off the main highway south of the park entrance near the 38 mile marker is the Ka'u Desert Trail, which leads less than a mile to Footprints. These were created during the explosion of 1790. You may read or be told that the footprints are worn away because they were vandalized. The truth is apparently a little more embarrassing. Park sources have told us that Park personnel tried to protect the footprints many years ago by placing a glass case over them. Their intentions were pure, but when it rained, water condensed on the underside of the cracked glass and dripped onto the prints, wearing them away. That's why the case is gone, but the vandalism rumor persists. Most personnel believe the vandalism explanation to be true to this day. Regardless, if you look around, you can still find better footprints elsewhere when shifting ash dunes permit.

Just outside the park is Volcano Golf and Country Club (see GOLFING under ACTIVITIES). Their restaurant (see DINING) has pretty good food. A little ways down Volcano Golf Course Road, you'll find Volcano Winery. This is a good place to stop for a sip of some locally made wines. (Actually four sips is your limit.) They have several unusual wines, including a local favorite, Lehua Blossom Honey Wine. They also have wines made from fruits—*even grapes*. Hard core oenophiles might turn up their

noses. But less finicky palates might enjoy a snort or two of the exotic. We've encountered both good and snotty service there—hope you c'em on a good day.

THE TOWN OF VOLCANO

When you first see the town of Volcano on a map, you figure they must spend all their time biting their nails over the active volcano crater less than 2 miles away. In fact, since they're upslope of the crater, they're safer from lava flows than Hilo or even the Kohala Resort area 50 miles away, as far as the geologists are concerned. Volcano Village's threat is from Mauna Loa, which hasn't sent anything their way for thousands of years. And as for volcano smoke, normal trade winds send the smoke around the bottom of the island and up the coast where it harasses Kailua-Kona. It's ironic that this dreamy little community, set in a misty, lush fern-filled forest, can be so snug living on an active volcano. Volcano is also a convenient place to pick up some supplies and gas. If you enter the loop road from near the 27 mile marker, you pass by the Volcano Store and Kilauea General Store and gas station farther down. If you're driving back to the west side of the island, you can grab some gas or a snack before the long drive back. We often pick up some tasty pumpkin bread, 'ohelo berry turnovers, or sandwiches on Hawaiian sweetbread at Kilauea General before heading back.

In addition to the Volcano accommodations listed under WHERE TO STAY, there are cabins and free tent camping at Namakani Paio Campgrounds and Kulanaokuaiki both in CAMPING on page 163. Current and retired military can rent clean cabins at Kilauea Military Camp (967–8333) right in the park. Higher rank, higher rent.

Hilo is rich with tranquil parks.

Hilo is a charming mix of old and new Hawai'i. Once a thriving town bolstered by limitless sugar revenues, the demise of the sugar industry has kept Hilo in a time warp. And that's the charm. Though a full-fledged city, things move slower here, and the community is tight. They've been through a lot. Lashed by tsunamis, threatened by lava flows, racked by a changing economy, Hilo has withstood it all. Hilo is also a strikingly beautiful town. Abundant rains give the flora a healthy sheen that soothes the soul. Though the exodus of business has left many of its buildings looking worn and neglected, Hilo's charms lie deeper.

Hilo's Achilles' heel is weather. Only in Hilo would water officials quake in fear and declare a drought, even encouraging water conservation, when they receive *only* 70 inches of rain in a year. (All you Arizona residents can stop laughing now!) This translates to an unacceptable gamble to many visitors. People are hesitant to spend precious Big Island days in a place that might get rained out. But they forget that even if it's rain-city here, elsewhere along the eastern side things might be sunnier. Hilo is the logical gateway for exploring Puna, the easternmost part of the island, where you'll find lush rain forests, a black sand beach, thermally heated pools, and volcano-ravaged towns. Puna is also famous for its outlaws from the '60s, guerrilla gardeners, and bizarre characters.

Hilo has a reputation of being less friendly to visitors than other parts of the island. Sort of a *let da buggahs go to Kona* mentality. Though this reputation is not entirely unearned, it is also not entirely accurate. Some of the friendliest, nicest, and most helpful people that we've run into have been in Hilo. But we've also gotten more blank expressions and outright nastiness here.

Hilo is a ghost town on Sundays. Don't expect much of anything to be open. We'll describe sights around Hilo in a scattershot manner before heading toward Puna.

AROUND HILO TOWN

Starting at the corner of Kamehameha (which fronts the bay) and Waianuenue (in northern Hilo), head northwest on Waianuenue. (See map on facing page.) When you pass the Hilo Public Library on your right, take a look at that oblong stone out front, six full strides long. Think you can move it? At 14, Kamehameha risked death (if he failed) and agreed to try to move that Naha Stone (estimated at 7,000 pounds). He did it because legend said that whoever could overturn the stone would be the first king of all the islands. At that time the stone was slightly imbedded in the ground. The ox-like youth, whose strength was unprecedented, squatted and gave a huge push— nothing. He tried and tried but could barely nudge it. As people gathered around and the priest started to come over (to condemn him), he summoned a final burst of strength and overturned the boulder, shocking everyone and begin-

ning the fulfillment of his destiny.

Farther up Waianuenue the Lyman Museum (935–5021) is worth a stop.

A Real Gem

The museum has a fine collection of Polynesian artifacts, wooden bowls, and a display of the voyages of Captain Cook, along with Bibles, diaries, and other books from the 1800s. Upstairs there is an *incredible* rock and mineral collection with specimens from all over the world. This alone is worth the $5 admission price. Tours of the Lyman missionary house next door are given on the hour.

Take the right fork after the 1 mile marker and follow the signs to Rainbow Falls. These falls change dramatically depending on water flow. Moderate flow is best. (Too little and the wishbone shape

NOT TO BE MISSED!

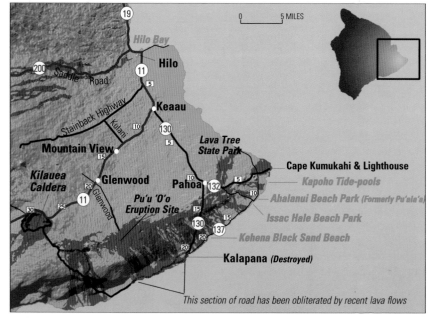

Hilo Bay

19

Hilo

11

5

200 Saddle Road

Stainback Highway

Kulani

Keaau

10 130

5

Mountain View

15

Lava Tree State Park

Kilauea Caldera

20 Glenwood

11

Pahoa 132

5

10

Cape Kumukahi & Lighthouse

Kapoho Tide-pools

Ahalanui Beach Park (Formerly Pu'ala'a)

30 25

Pu'u 'O'o Eruption Site

15

130 137

15

10

Issac Hale Beach Park

20 Kehena Black Sand Beach

Kalapana (Destroyed)

0   5 MILES

This section of road has been obliterated by recent lava flows

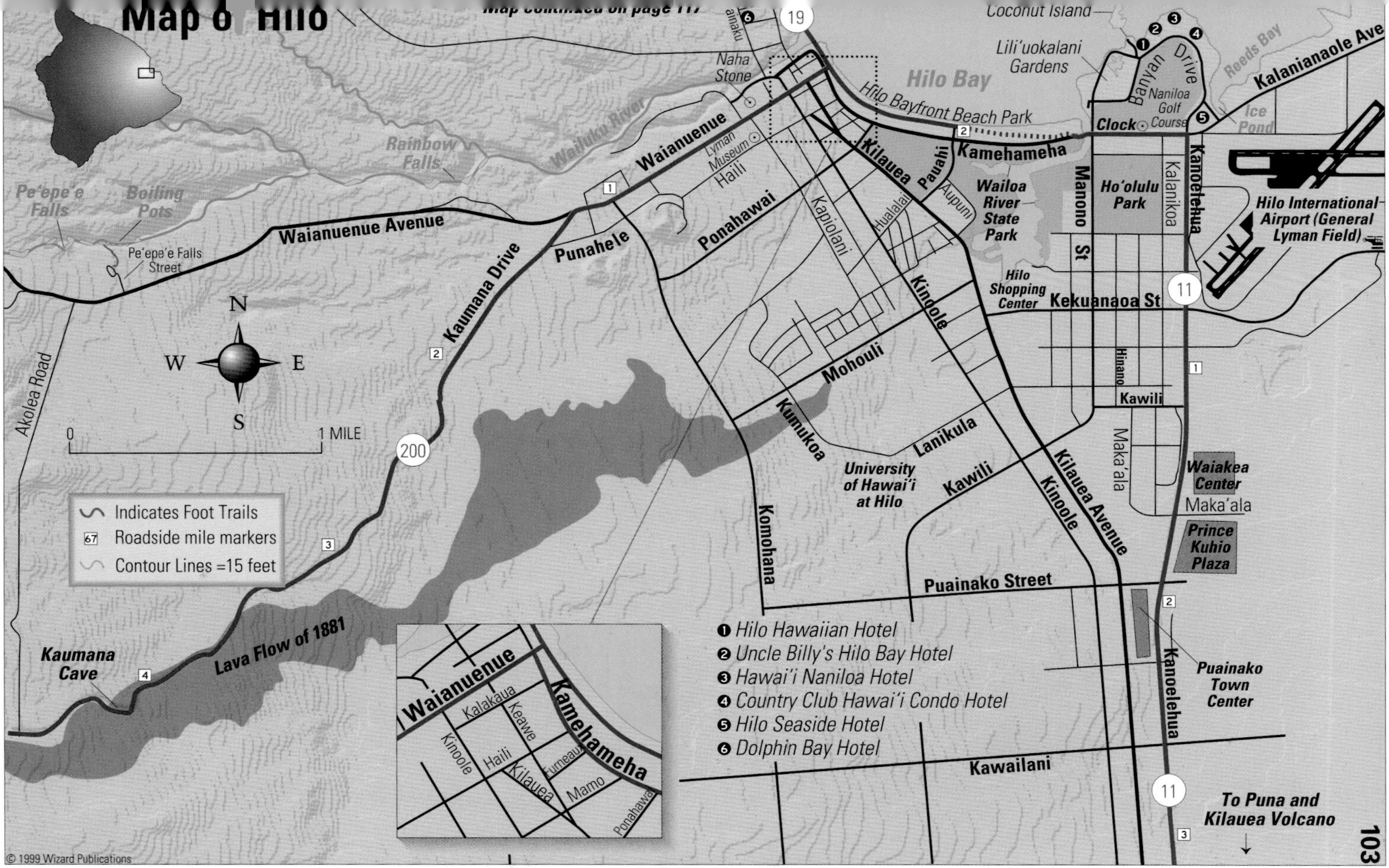
Map 6 Hilo
Map continued on page 117
Coconut Island
Lili'uokalani Gardens
Hilo Bay
Hilo Bayfront Beach Park
Reeds Bay
Kalanianaole Ave
Banyan Drive
Naniloa Golf Course
Clock
Ice Pond
Naha Stone
Lyman Museum
Haili
Waianuenue
Wailuku River
Rainbow Falls
Pe'epe'e Falls
Boiling Pots
Pe'epe'e Falls Street
Waianuenue Avenue
Kaumana Drive
Punahele
Ponahawai
Kapiolani
Hualalai
Aupuni
Kilauea
Pauahi
Kamehameha
Wailoa River State Park
Manono St
Ho'olulu Park
Kalanikoa
Kanoelehua
Hilo International Airport (General Lyman Field)
Hilo Shopping Center
Kekuanaoa St
Kinoole
Mohouli
Kumukoa
Hinano
Kawili
Lanikula
University of Hawai'i at Hilo
Maka'ala
Waiakea Center
Prince Kuhio Plaza
Kilauea Avenue
Komohana
Puainako Street
Puainako Town Center
Kawailani
To Puna and Kilauea Volcano
Akolea Road
N
W
E
S
0
1 MILE
200
19
11
Indicates Foot Trails
Roadside mile markers
Contour Lines =15 feet
Lava Flow of 1881
Kaumana Cave
1 Hilo Hawaiian Hotel
2 Uncle Billy's Hilo Bay Hotel
3 Hawai'i Naniloa Hotel
4 Country Club Hawai'i Condo Hotel
5 Hilo Seaside Hotel
6 Dolphin Bay Hotel
Waianuenue
Kalakaua
Keawe
Kamehameha
Kinoole
Haili
Kilauea
Furneaux
Mamo
Ponahawai
© 1999 Wizard Publications

is gone; too much and it's an undefined, roiling mess.) The falls are best seen in the morning when the sun is behind you. (Rainbows can only be seen when the sun is behind you, so if you ever see a photo with the sun and a rainbow in the same frame, it's fake.) The cave below the falls is where Kamehameha is said to have buried the bones of his father. Take the trail to the left for different views and the shady comfort of a large banyan tree. From the left a trail leads to the top of the falls, but you are on your own in assessing whether to go down there.

A mile farther up the road is Boiling Pots. This series of bowl-shaped depressions roil and boil when the water flow is heavy, creating dramatic photo opportunities. To the left is Pe'epe'e Falls. (No, it's not pronounced pee-pee, but rather peh-eh peh-eh, so wipe that smirk off your face.) One look and it's obvious you can't swim in Boiling Pots. But there's a trail to the right of the viewing area that leads down to the rocks below. From there you could scramble over the boulders to the other side (without getting your feet wet if the flow is low enough, as in this photo) and continue to Pe'epe'e Falls. This waterfall and deep pool are an idyllic place to sit in your solitude and ponder. You'll usually have it to yourself. Be careful on the rocks; don't go if the river is raging, and don't fall in. Though sometimes absent, if the mosquitoes are in the right mood, they can suck you dry down there without bug juice. While I'm nagging, this is prob-ably a good time to tell you that Boiling Pots and Rainbow Falls are common places for car break-ins. We often see thieving scum casing the lots looking for unsuspecting tourist cars to rob while they are away lost in the beauty.

Over on Kaumana Drive (see map) is Kaumana Cave. This lava tube can make for fun exploring and is described in detail in the SADDLE ROAD section on page 134 since it's usually visited by those coming into Hilo from the Saddle.

Along the bay, the grassy park fronting the town is the Hilo Bayfront. It used to be the home of numerous

Offerings are common at Pe'epe'e Falls.

Japanese sugar workers. On April Fool's day 1946 a tsunami (tidal wave) of unprecedented size was generated from a horrific earthquake off Alaska. The tsunami lashed the entire state, but punished this part of the Big Island the most. 159 people, including 21 school children in Laupahoehoe, were killed in the worst natural disaster in Hawai'i's history. After another tsunami killed another 38 people in 1960, town fathers decided to make this area a park rather than risk more lives during the next tsunami. (The clock on the side of the road on Kamehameha Street in front of Naniloa Golf Course stands with its hands frozen in time—1:04 a.m.—from the 1960 tsunami. Townsfolk refurbished the clock but refused to rebuild it in honor of those who died.) Tsunamis have unimaginable power. The water first recedes, exposing the ocean's floor, and then bulldozers of water come crashing in wave after wave. The event can last for hours.

The Pacific Tsunami Museum (935–0926) is on Kamehameha and Kalakaua. (10 a.m. to 3 p.m. but they close for lunch.) It's in the old First Hawaiian Bank Building, which explains why there's a bank vault inside. (And it's probably a good place to hide during a tsunami.) The narrated tour, video, and photo exhibit are all excellent and worth your time.

Banyan Drive, where most of Hilo's hotels are located, is named after the graceful and stately banyan trees that line the road. If a tree can look wise, then banyan trees definitely qualify. Each tree was named after the person who planted it. Familiar names such as Amelia Earhart, King George V, Babe Ruth, FDR, and Richard

A Real Gem

Nixon. (In one of those ironies of life, the first one he planted was washed away on election day when he became VP.) Also on Banyan Drive is Lili'uokalani Gardens. This is one of several graceful and serene parks in the area worth checking out. If you're a bit warm, look for the nearby ice pond. (See map.) Cold water intruding into this part of the bay (you can sometimes see it percolating to the surface) creates water so cold it'll give you *chicken skin kine.*

Nearby, the Suisan Fish Auction Market on Lihiwai is the largest fish auction in the state. Local fishermen fish at night (because, they say, the boat doesn't cast a shadow and scare away the fish) and their results are auctioned at 7:30 a.m. Monday–Saturday. Restaurants from all over the state buy here, so smile at that fish being sold—he may end up on your plate later that day.

If you were to continue east along the shoreline on Kalanianaole, you would pass by most of Hilo's beach parks. See BEACHES for more on these. Don't go past the part where the road is paved; you won't like what you see. (Hilo's underbelly.) On your way out to them check out a beach access across from Lokoaka Street. It is very jungly and draped with vines. The beach is worthless, but the short road is kind of cool. You'll also pass the Hilo Homemade Ice Cream (969–9559) on the ocean side. This mom-and-pop operation serves ice cream that is not as sweet or rich as other gourmet ice creams. Lots of exotic flavors like ginger and 'ohelo.

HEADING SOUTH ON HIGHWAY 11

As you head out of town, you will pass by Hilo's biggest shopping area. Prince Kuhio Plaza, Waiakea Center, and Puainako Town Center are where you will find Safeway, Longs, Wal-mart,

Borders, and a zillion fast food restaurants. On Hinano St. off Kekuanaoa is Big Island Candies (935–8890). Their locally made chocolates and cakes are excellent, though their prices are confiscatory (this is a favorite stopping place for tour buses). Good place for chocolate if you don't mind paying double-extra-super-retail. On the Highway before the 4 mile marker, Makalika Street heading east leads to Nani Mau Gardens (959–3541), 20 acres of flawlessly groomed tropical and sub-tropical plants. Most of their business comes from Japanese tour groups (who are fussy about their gardens). Whereas the mother of all gardens, the Hawai'i Tropical Botanical Garden (on your way out of town heading north, described on page 115) is much more exotic, this garden will appeal to those who want a more manicured, controlled, and artistically arranged setting. This is also a popular place to get married. Allow 30–60 minutes; cost is $7.50. (For the garden, not the wedding.) They also have a Polynesian buffet for $10.

Either of the roads past the 4 mile marker heading west leads to Stainback Highway and the Panaewa Rain Forest Zoo (959–7224). They have a handful of exhibits sprinkled about. (Good luck spotting the tiger.) Wailing peacocks, which sound a lot like cats being tortured, strut about the small but pleasant and well-maintained grounds. Despite the exotic-sounding name, this zoo may disappoint if you live in an area with a nice zoo, but kids may find it interesting. The price is the best asset—free. Don't expect crowds.

Between the 5 and 6 mile marker on Macadamia Road is the Mauna Loa Visitor Center (966–8618). This is the mac nut giant's main processing plant. You can see the process through the glass or pick up some of their products; otherwise, it's expendable.

If you're going to explore Puna, your best route is to take Highway 11 to 130, then take 132 to 137, 137 to Kalapana where you link back up to 130. See map on page 102 if you aren't too dizzy to flip the page. If you want a meaningless diversion, you could continue along Stainback Highway until it ends at our least popular visitor attraction—our prison. This one-lane road goes for miles through an otherwise impenetrable forest. There are signs saying that it is illegal to drive the road, but they were put up by the prison to cover their 'okole—they told us that it's perfectly OK to drive it as long as you're not planning to spring anyone. Some 13¾ miles into the one-lane (and dead-on straight) road is the Pu'u Maka'ala Forest Reserve. The roads in there are 4WD only, and the trails (if you can find them) are lush and wet.

EXPLORING PUNA

Head south on Highway 130 and you come to the town of Pahoa. Known as the Big Island's outlaw town, this is where guerrilla gardeners (pakalolo farmers), dreadlock enthusiasts, FBI fugitives, and the never–bathe crowd coexist without stepping on each other's toes. You'd be surprised to learn how many homes you see are built on vacant land—at least according to the County Tax Assessor's Office. Permit? What's that? To be honest, their reputation is a little exaggerated—probably. There are a couple places to eat here that you may like, reviewed under DINING.

Stay on Hwy. 132 and you come to Lava Tree State Park. Lava trees form when fast flowing pahoehoe encounters wet 'ohi'a trees. As the flow drains away, it leaves a thick coating around the dying tree. Most of these free-standing tubes are moss-covered. You can saunter around the park in 30–60 minutes. Look for the huge chasms created during the explosive eruption of 1790. Even if you don't want to hike (there are better lava trees on the Napau Crater Trail), take a minute to drive into the park and gawk at the regal monkeypod trees that dominate the area, and listen to the cacophony of birds which echo through the forest.

Shortly after Lava Trees take the left fork (near a papaya grove) where 132 continues toward Kapoho. Ever wonder where people on an island get their electricity? Well, here on the Big Island 25% of our juice is volcano-powered. There are deep wells in this area that pump superheated water to the surface where it turns turbines before being returned to the source.

The end of Hwy. 132 is on lava flows from 1960. This area was ravaged during that flow and an earlier one in 1955. Having hiked through countless lava fields on the island, this wins the prize as the harshest and most difficult to walk through we've ever encountered. (You'd have an easier time walking through the minefields of the demilitarized zone between North and South Korea than hiking through this stuff.) At the end of the unpaved road leading to the sea is a light tower.

Take a deep breath. Because this is the easternmost part of the island and because our winds come from that direction,

scientists use it to test "virgin air" that has drifted over the landless Pacific for many weeks. Air from here is considered as pristine as any in the world and it is analyzed by governments around the globe and used as a benchmark to compare to their air. From Hwy. 132 you'll want to head right (south) on 137. But if you feel like a different kind of forest drive, for no particular reason, head north first for 5 miles or so. It goes from stark lava to luxuriant forest filled with birds almost instantly. Return to this spot when you get to the subdivision.

Heading south on Hwy. 137 leads

Free energy. In Puna they don't drill for oil, they drill for steam.

past Kapoho-Kai Road. This road goes to one of the more unusual locations on the Big Island. Dozens and dozens of spring-fed, brackish pools and tide-pools, some volcanical- ly heated, are strewn throughout the area known as the Kapoho Tide-pools. Many of the smaller pools have been incorporated into people's front and back yards as swimming pools. The large pools adjacent to the ocean (called Wai'opae Ponds) and *on public property* contain some of the most fascinating snorkeling around. The local residents have done their best to ruin the area by posting countless unfriendly and ungracious signs, but despite their best efforts they have been unable to take away from the tide-pool's innate charms. If you wish to snorkel here, take Kapoho–Kai Road (just before the 9 mile marker). When it seems to dead end (on Waiopae), turn left, go ¹⁄₁₀ mile and park when the ocean is visible near a No Parking sign. At least, that's what the neighborhood watch official told us was allowed. Exploration is possible even for novice snorkelers. The largest pool snakes its way to the ocean and rises and falls each day with the tide. This creates slight currents that are fun to ride if the surf's not high. These pools are usually very calm and protected. Closer to the reef edge brings more fish but sometimes there's a current.

There are lots of vacation rentals available here at the "*DON'T*" community (called Vacationland). Make *sure* you see what you're getting beforehand because there are a number of charming sounding dumps there. Nicer homes are in the nearby gated Kapoho Beach Lots.

Farther down Highway 137 past the 10 mile marker is Ahalanui. (Formerly

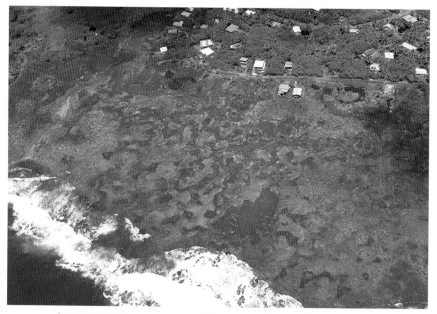

A vast area of often interconnected tide-pools await you at Kapoho, providing endless snorkeling possibilities if you can put up with the grouchy residents.

There's no such thing as a quick dip in the soothing volcanically heated pool of Ahalanui.

called Puʻalaʻa, the state recently discovered that they had accidentally misnamed it for decades—*oops.*) Rarely mentioned anywhere, this delightful gem is definitely worth stopping for. It's a spring and ocean fed pool with a manmade wall and an inlet separating it from the ocean. *Big deal,* you say! But this one is different, because the 1960 Kapoho eruption reworked the lava plumbing here so that now, instead of coming out ice cold (as it used to), this pool is *volcanically heated* to a toasty 90 or so degrees. With palm trees all around and the sound of the surf over the seawall, you may have trouble hauling yourself out once you've experienced this genuine Pele bath. You may notice a slight sulphur smell on your skin when you get out, but it's worth it.

A Real Gem

Isaac Hale Beach Park farther down the road is where local fishermen launch their boats, and they are not known for extending gobs of aloha to visitors. (There's also a lunch wagon here that serves the worst shave ice we've had on the island.) The swimming is poor and the surfing is for experts. So why bother? Because if you take the shoreline trail to the right of the boat launch for two minutes where it veers inland, you'll come to a surprise. There, set in the vine-covered jungle but only 40–50 feet from the shore, is a small (8-feet by 14-feet) warm water pool similar to Ahalanui but completely natural. The setting is heaven sent. The only caveat is that some residents don't always appreciate the paradise that they live in and occasionally spoil the area with litter. But if you come during the week, there's a chance you may have it all to yourself.

As you drive along this stretch, realize that this is one of the least known parts of the Big Island. The vast majority of island residents and visitors never see this area, and that's a shame. It is mostly

A lonely Puna highway.

the right of the turnout, it leads to the stone steps, which, upon descent, end abruptly 10 feet above the beach. Those wishing to use Kehena should go back up and take the trail to the eastern section of the beach, which is marked by two yellow poles. Swimming is dangerous during high surf.

Shortly after the 22 mile marker, you're confronted with the consequences of the current Kilauea eruption. A rolling sea of hardened lava stretches in front of you. This particular flow occurred in 1990, annihilating the town of Kalapana and the Royal Gardens subdivision beyond. (See map on page 96 so you can get an idea of the scale of the devastation.) Kalapana was a treasured Hawaiian fishing village, richly steeped in the traditions of the past. Its loss was a stunning blow to those wishing to keep the old ways alive.

Until the 1990 lava flow, this was also the site of the most famous black sand beach in the world. A long curving bay of jet black sand with numerous stately palm trees sprinkled about, the black sand beach at Kaimu was universally regarded as the finest. Today, it is gone, buried under 50–75 feet of lava.

When the road stops, and if you walk to the top of the lava and look toward the shore, you may notice young, sprouting coconut trees in the distance. The campaign to bring the plantings was begun by a local resident. She encouraged others in the community to take trees out to the new black sand beach ⅓ mile in front

untouched and exceptionally beautiful. Take your time here. If you're not driving too fast, you may see Hawaiian ruins along the side of the road.

Near the 19 mile marker is Kehena Beach. This is a powerful testament to the changing nature of the Big Island. This beach wasn't even here until it was created by the 1955 lava flow you just drove through. Officials created stone steps leading down to the western part of the beach. Then an earthquake in 1975 sank the beach 3 feet in one moment. The lower portion of the stone steps collapsed. If you take the path to of you to begin the process of rebuilding their precious beach. Even as she was dying of cancer, residents continued the tradition in her honor. Today, there are vast numbers of sprouting coconuts along the new black sand beach, a testament to the vision of one resident who refused to let her community die, even in the face of her own death.

If you walk out to the new beach, look for indentations in the lava from the palm trees that were killed when the lava inundated the old beach. Some have perfect molds of the tree bark. A 15–20 minute walk straight out leads to the black sandy area. Don't even consider swimming there for the surf is treacherous. The state (or more likely their lawyers) posted signs telling you to stay away—one of the great disregards of all time. The ground is new and there are opportunities to test its flaws if you walk. But residents and visitors do it all the time, ignoring the signs with abandon.

We're not telling you to do it; we're just telling you that everyone else does it.

If you look at the map on page 96 you'll see another road, Highway 130, leading toward the buried subdivision. It's now buried under lava. But a junky new lava road was cut on top of the old road out to the park boundary. Though private, it's on *state land,* so they can't legally stop you from driving on it if you have a 4WD, according to state personnel we contacted. There's not much to see in the subdivision itself: a handful of hardy souls still live in the ravaged subdivision without power or water. Birds have rediscovered this island of green in a sea of lava (called a kipuka). During the devastating lava flows, the media and the public focused their sympathy on the people who lost their houses. The *real* people to feel sorry for are the people who *didn't* lose their houses. You see, insurance covers loss of property, not loss of *access* to property. Imagine an

The sprouting coconut trees of the new Kaimu Beach are a tribute to one woman's dream and represent community hope for another beautiful family beach for tomorrow's generation.

insurance adjuster walking up to your now worthless house, surrounded but untouched by a sea of hardened lava and saying, "Nothing wrong with this house; claim denied." (The state also took their sweet time reassessing property values in the ravaged areas for property taxes. Oversight, no doubt.)

Depending on where the lava is entering the ocean at the time you're reading this (it changes all the time), this lava road *may* end near a current lava flow. See ADVENTURES on page 214 for more on this road and accessing the lava flows from this area.

You may be wondering what happens if you own oceanfront property and the volcano creates new land in front of you (called *accreted land* for the trivia deprived). Do you now own a larger parcel? No. You don't even own oceanfront anymore! Apparently Madam Pele signed a quit claim deed over to the state, because all newly created land goes to our hungry state government.

As you head north on Hwy. 130 on your way back toward Highway 11, look for the church on the right (east) side of the road near the 20 mile marker.

Formerly the Star of the Sea church built in 1928 by the same priest who did the painted church near Honaunau, the building was in the path of an advancing lava flow in 1990. Community members had to wrench it from its foundations to save it just in the nick of time. After sitting on the side of the road for years without a home, it was finally decommissioned and is being turned into a Hawaiian cultural center.

Here's something I'll bet you've never seen. Just before you get to the 15 mile marker (south of it) is a pullout area, a scenic overlook with seemingly no attraction. Take the very quick trail to the 'ohi'a trees (60 seconds or so), and from there a maze of short trails lead to natural lava steam rooms ranging in size from one person pukas (holes) to rooms large enough for large groups. Unusually pasty lava flowed here in 1955, and, depending on how much rain we've had lately, varying amounts of steam issue from the ground. The pukas have been enhanced by regular users with wooden benches and even a ladder for the deepest room. Occasionally, regular local users can be found basking in the steam in their altogether.

When you take Hwy. 130 back to Hwy. 11, you can either head to Hilo or toward the volcano. If you head to the volcano, look for the Hirano Store before the 20 mile marker. From their parking lot you get the easiest view on the island of **Pu'u 'O'o** belching off in the distance. This is the headline-grabbing vent that has been the lava source for most of the current eruption. Look across the road and slightly to your right. Unless you hike to it or fly over it, this is as close as you'll come. If you *are* up to a long hike, the trek through the

Hilo is the orchid capital of the U.S. In 1995, the first 747 to land at the Hilo Airport in a decade was a Federal Express plane, which left with 60,000 pounds of fresh cut flowers. (It was for Mother's Day, of course.)

virgin rain forest to Pu'u 'O'o is the trek of a lifetime. See ADVENTURES on page 212 for more on this beautiful hike.

Kilauea Volcano is just ahead.

HILO SHOPPING

Shoppers may want to visit Hilo on Wednesday as this is Farmers Market day. Park along the bayfront (Kamehameha Avenue) and walk around downtown Hilo. There are many one-way streets and walking is easier than trying to navigate with your car and parallel park.

Begin on Kamehameha and head north along Kamehameha, turn left on Waianuenue, turn left (south) on Keawe, left (east) on Mamo, up Furneaux, back to Kamehmeha and end up back where you started. See inset map. Parking in downtown was free at press time.

On Kamehameha, Big Island Woodworks has a good selection of Hawaiian wood pieces; stop only if you missed the better Woodshop Gallery at Akaka Falls, otherwise skip it. Tropical Dreams at the Kress Building has excellent ice cream. Hana Hou has aloha wear, gift and food items. Nearby is Basically Books which has an unparalleled selection of Hawaiian books and maps.

Turn left on Waianuenue for Hilo Seeds & Snacks. Try the large Shave Ice for $2. Next door is Ets'ko with an exceptional collection of fine gifts. Don't miss this one. Head up to Keawe Street for KD's Gifts and Crafts, Bears' Coffee, the Hilo Surplus Store, and Mauna Kea Galleries for fine vintage Hawaiiana. There's something for all price ranges and interests on Keawe Street. When you reach Mamo, turn left for the Farmers Market on the corner of Mamo and Kamehameha. Everything from tropical flowers, to baked goods, to fresh fish.

Turn left up Furneaux for the Rock Island Gallery and their excellent selection of rocks and minerals. Return to Kamehameha and your car.

Exquisite original gold jewelry designs can be found at Ming's, a Hilo landmark, at the corner of Hualalai and Kinoole Streets.

On Highway 11 heading south you'll see Waiakea Center which has Borders Books and Wal-mart. Across the street is Prince Kuhio Plaza and Hilo Hattie at the corner of Maka'ala and the Hwy. Hilo Hattie is the favorite stopping place for visitors, and for good reason—Their aloha wear is excellent and priced right.

If you're interested in the beautiful bonsai plants you've seen on many countertops around the island, Fuku–Bonsai (982-9880) is 10 miles outside of Hilo in Kurtistown. Call first to be sure they'll be open when you'll be driving through.

HILO AND PUNA'S BEST BETS

Best Cerebral Stimulation—Lyman Museum

Best Buffet—Hilo Hawaiian Hotel's Queen's Court

Best Dessert—Double Chocolate Truffle Cake at Pescatore

Best Snorkeling—Tide-pools at Kapoho

Best Place to Soak Your Bones—Ahalanui Beach Park

Best Way to Pull Your Back—Duplicating Kamehameha's Feat of Lifting the Naha Stone

Best Waterfall—Rainbow Falls

Best *Secluded* Waterfall—Pe'epe'é Falls

Best Healthy Food—Island Naturals' Deli in Waiakea Center

Best Place to Nuke Your Cholesterol Count—Café 100

Best Local Food—Super Coma Foot Long Lau Laus at Ka'upena.

Best Place to Catch an Easy Glimpse of Erupting Pu'u 'O'o—Hirano Store

Waterfalls and thick, lush gulches bursting with life are Hamakua's trademark.

When local residents speak of driving between Hilo and Kona, they either "drive the saddle" or they "take the upper road." The upper road is the stretch of Highway 19 between Hilo and Waimea. It passes through magnificent country reminiscent of old Hawai'i. Along the way you can check out numerous waterfalls, drive along stunning gorges, gaze over (or go into) an Eden-like valley, or check out Hawai'i's premiere ranch town, home of the nearly quarter-million acre Parker Ranch. Part of this drive is actually in the districts of North and South Hilo, but that distinction is lost on the driver.

We'll start our description from the Hilo side. (If you're coming the other way, just turn the book upside down.) It's best to start this drive in the morning since the waterfalls and much of the best scenery faces east.

Highway 19 was constructed to make it easier and faster to travel this part of the island. Consequently, most people are totally unaware of the almost forgotten stretches of roads that made up the old highway. We have a particular fondness for these diversions off the highway and point them out as DIVERSION ALERTS.

LEAVING HILO BEHIND

Heading north (see map on page 117) you will see a sign on the ocean side past the 4 mile marker that says ALAE. Take

Nahala Road there, then turn left at the T. You pass by **Honoli'i Beach Park.** This is the primo surfing and boogie boarding spot on this side of the island. There are stairs leading down to the black sand beach. The road continues around the back of the stream. When it ends, hang a right to go back to the highway, then left. This is probably a good time to mention that, while stopping at scenic spots along here, during certain times of the year, it's a good idea to have mosquito repellent.

Sometimes they are absent; other times they are ferocious. Feeling lucky?

Past the 7 mile marker is the only part of the old highway that is marked. This 4 mile scenic route is breathtaking and leads past the **Hawai'i Tropical Botanical Garden** (964–5233). (Consider the 4 mile drive a NOT TO BE MISSED.) You don't have to be a "garden person" to appreciate this stunningly beautiful area that fronts Onomea Bay. For $15 (no credit cards for admission fee, kids 16 and under are free) you wander on a self-guided tour for about an hour through over 2,000 exotic types of marked flora. (Mosquito repellent and umbrellas are thoughtfully provided.) Birds abound in this Eden-like setting. The smell of flowers and fruit (especially mangos) fills the air. Onomea Falls is located on the grounds, which makes a nice place to stop and take in the surroundings. Views of the bay are unbeat-

A Real Gem

able. $15 is pretty steep for a garden, but this is the Big Island's best. Past the garden is a food stand called **What's Shakin'** that serves exceptionally good smoothies.

Back on the highway between the 13 and 14 mile marker is a 3¾-mile road through old sugar land to **Akaka Falls**. This free-fall plunge of 420 feet is best seen early in the day. (This is a popular place with tour buses.) If you're in a hurry, walk left 2–3 minutes to the falls, where silver/white strands form as the water hits the rocks on the way down. Otherwise, there is a 15–20 minute amble (and a few hills) through the lush bamboo-filled woods along with another waterfall. The latter is recommended if you have the time. After visiting Akaka Falls you want to stop at the **Woodshop Gallery and Cafe** for some homemade ice cream and the best collection of Hawaiian wood products we've seen on the island. Wood workers can even purchase a plank of Hawaiian

NOT TO BE MISSED!

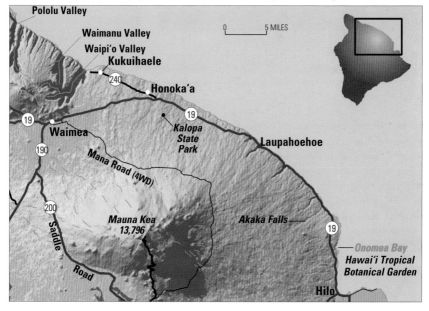

Akaka Falls tumbles 420 feet.

ables to make good use of the stone BBQs, full facilities, and tranquil setting. (Though quiet during the week, it gets too rowdy on weekends to recommend.) The small waterfall and swimming hole is where most swim when the river isn't raging, since the black sand beach itself is too hazardous to swim. This is where the water from Akaka Falls ends up, so if you lost something up there, maybe you'll see it again here.

If you stay on this road, it crosses the highway, curves left, and empties into Hakalau Bay. A rich, vine-filled forest dripping with life ushers you into the bay. The ruins near the mouth were from a mill destroyed during the tsunami. The swimming here is poor, but you can't say that about the view. Backtrack to the highway.

The bridge past the 16 mile marker boasts nice views of two waterfalls. As impressive as they are, they don't even come close to the multi-tiered beauty of Umauma Falls upstream. This may be the most stunning waterfall setting in the state. You can either hike to these falls (described on page 186 along with a photo) or visit the World Botanical Gardens (934–8355). This is a relatively new garden, so don't expect much. A short stroll called the Rain Forest walk has a few things to see. The garden below the visitor center has numerous plants, such as chocolate and blueberry, all neatly marked, and visitors are given free fruit. But their exclusive view of Umauma Falls almost makes it worth the $5 price without the garden.

hardwood to take home.

As you continue on Highway 19, there is another piece of old road to take. It's shortly after the 14 mile marker on the mauka (mountain) side. It leads past Kolekole Park. The massive highway bridge in front of you was part of an old railway. The great tsunami of 1946 carried away many of the girders, rendering the bridge useless. This was the deathblow for the railway, sparking the construction for the entire highway. During the week this is a great place to bring your Briquettes and cook-

DIVERSION ALERT!

DIVERSION ALERT!

Whether you plan to pay for the gardens or not, *be sure* to backtrack ²/₁₀ mile from the highway bridge turnout and take the road on the mauka side across from the 16 mile marker and turn right at the T. This 4-mile long, one lane country road passes through sugar land before it takes you to a small tree tunnel and several striking gulches. This is the Hawai'i of yesteryear, when life moved a bit slower. You might want to do the same. Stop at one of the old bridges and enjoy the peace. Vine-covered trees and ever-chirping birds give this area an unforgettable feel. One of the small Depression-era bridges crosses Nanue Stream (stamped into the bridge). The guard-rail beyond the bridge has a crude and steep trail that leads down to the stream. From there a person could walk over to the top of the falls (don't fall off), or go upstream where taller waterfalls await. If you don't have mosquito repellent, be prepared for the bloodletting of a lifetime.

Bypass any opportunities to reconnect with the highway until you pass rarely used Waikaumalo Park near a pretty stream. There are trails along the stream leading to more pools and waterfalls.

When you reacquire the highway just north of the 19 mile marker, you may want to backtrack less than a mile to see the densely jungled gulch and waterfall visible from the highway that you missed before continuing north.

As you effortlessly cruise these gulches on our modern bridges of today, try to visualize what a nightmare it must have been to cross them in days gone by. It took many days to get from Hilo to Waipi'o Valley. When Isabella Bird toured this area by horse in 1873, she writes of the utter dread she felt as she plunged down and then trudged up gulch after harrowing gulch on her way to Waipi'o, fording raging streams on a terrified horse. Today, the hardest part about traversing these gulches is resetting the cruise control after a sharp bend.

Just past the 25 mile marker is the road leading mauka to the town of Laupahoehoe. (The short road on the ocean side sports a nice view of the point mentioned below.) The town itself doesn't offer much other than Big Island Bakery (which has such squirrely hours that you probably won't be able to buy anything) and the Laupahoehoe Train Museum. This assortment of artifacts and photos of Hamakua's history with trains is marginally interesting. I'm sure they have informative

To Waipi'o and Waimea

Hamakua Coast Map

Laupahoehoe Point and Memorial

Laupahoehoe Town

Maulua Stream

Waikaumalo Park

Nanua Falls

Multi-tiered Umauma Falls

Hakalau Bay

Kolekole Beach Park

Akaka Falls

4 Mile Scenic Dr.

Onomea Bay

Hawai'i Tropical Botanical Garden

Honoli'i Beach Park

© 1999 Wizard Publications

Map continued on page 103

people working with them...we just haven't met any.

Just past the 27 mile marker is a road on the ocean side that leads 1 mile down the cliffs to **Laupahoehoe Point.** To many on the Big Island, Laupahoehoe is associated with tragedy. During the April Fool's Day tsunami of 1946, twenty-one schoolchildren and three adults were swept to their deaths. Following this, the village was moved topside. The views from the road down to the rugged point sport dramatic views of the sea cliffs beyond and is well worth the stop. There is a memorial at the bottom to those who lost their lives. The surf pounds against the twisted and jagged lava and is spectacular to watch, especially when surf's up, but don't even *think* of swimming here at any time. In 1985 a barge full of brand new Toyotas broke loose from from its tug and washed ashore near here, spilling the entire cargo. According to local lore, an insurance adjuster from Lloyd's of London landed on the deck in a helicopter where a wave knocked the chopper over, drowning the adjuster. Surf is almost always violent here.

DIVERSION ALERT!

This whole area was once dominated by sugar. Over 70,000 acres of the Big Island were under cultivation. Even with generous government subsidies, the last mill shut down in 1996, ending 150 years of sugar production. Now this part of sugar country is getting a new look. More than 24,000 acres of fast-growing eucalyptus trees are being planted, and soon Hamakua will be known as tree-farming country.

Between the 39 and 40 mile markers is the road to **Kalopa Native Forest State Park,** which offers nice hiking and camping. See ACTIVITIES.

HONOKAʻA

Near the 42 mile marker is a road through the town of **Honokaʻa**. Most merely use it to get to **Waipiʻo Valley,** described below, but while on the main road in Honokaʻa, stop by **Mamane Bakery** for limited but extremely delicious baked goods. You have a few other eating options described in DINING.

WAIPIʻO VALLEY

Waipiʻo Valley is as beautiful a place

A Real Gem

as you will ever visit. With unimaginably steep walls on all sides, waterfalls etching the perimeter, fields of taro, and a luscious mile-long black sand beach, Waipiʻo never fails to impress. The instant you arrive at the lookout above this awesome spectacle, you realize why this place was so special to the ancient Hawaiians. Because of its inspiring and tranquilizing effects, Waipiʻo was often chosen as the meeting place for chiefs when important decisions, such as the succession of the king, were made. Even the kings that resided in sunny Kona had residences in Waipiʻo Valley. According to Hawaiian legend, Waipiʻo Valley was gouged out by a powerful warrior with his club to demonstrate his power. (Unfortunately, the warrior was himself clubbed to death by the one he was trying to impress.)

At one time thousands of people lived here, meticulously cultivating the lush valley floor with everything from bananas to taro to coconuts. Even Waipiʻo pigs were considered tastier here in the Big Island's bread-basket. During times of famine, you could always count on Waipiʻo Valley for much-needed sustenance. Fifty generations of Hawaiians have lived and died here, and they believe that the spiritual *mana,* or supernatural power left by those departed, is preserved and felt to this day.

As an infant, Kamehameha was hidden away here soon after he was born to avoid a death sentence by the king of the Big Island, who feared the prophecy that the child would one day rule the island.

The peace of Waipi'o Valley was shattered by the great tsunami of 1946 that washed away nearly everything. Most people moved away and the valley was left mostly wild for two decades. Then in the '60s and early '70s people started trickling back in. Most were "hippies" and recently discharged veterans who wanted to "get away from it all." Others soon joined. These days Waipi'o is populated by a colorful assortment of 40 or so characters. Many have turned their backs on traditional

Waipi'o Valley is a lush wonderland where taro farming is still the main occupation.

society; others simply live there to experience the grace of nature at its grandest. There are some who live "topside" and come down on weekends to tend their taro patch. Those who live on the far side of the valley have no power, water, or phones. Solar power provides the electricity they need. (Nearside residents have power and phones courtesy of a line stretching down into the valley.) They share their valley with wild horses that were left by the departing residents after the tsunami of '46.

Today the allure of Waipi'o Valley is beckoning others as well. Visitors and residents alike enjoy the splendor of Waipi'o. Experienced surfers and boogie boarders ride the waves off the black sand beach. Hikers are enthralled by the scenery. Horseback rides are becoming popular. Waipi'o Valley Shuttle takes groups down the steep road. Even Kevin Costner found Waipi'o and the adjacent uninhabited valley of Waimanu the perfect place to film the "dry land" scenes for his movie, *Waterworld.* Does all this mean that Waipi'o is ablaze with activity? Not really. To you and me, Waipi'o is still

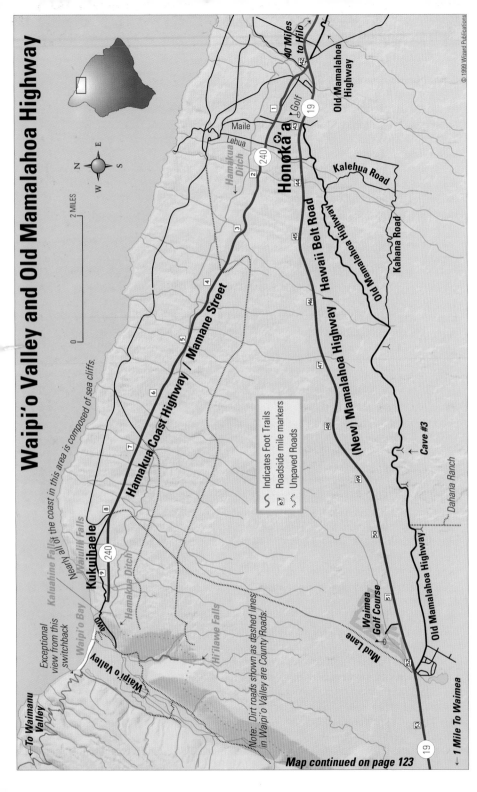

Waipi'o Valley and Old Mamalahoa Highway

© 1999 Wizard Publications

← To Waimanu Valley

Nearly all of the coast in this area is composed of sea cliffs.

Kaluahine Falls

Exceptional view from this switchback

Waipi'o Valley

Waipi'o Bay

Hi'ilawe Falls

Hamakua Ditch

Kukuihaele

Waiulili Falls

Hamakua Coast Highway / Mamane Street

Hamakua Ditch

240

9

8

7

6

5

4

3

2

Maile

Lehua

Honoka'a

Golf

Maile

Indicates Foot Trails

67 Roadside mile markers

Unpaved Roads

Note: Dirt roads shown as dashed lines in Waipi'o Valley are County Roads.

1 Mile To Waimea

Waimea Golf Course

Mud Lane

(New) Mamalahoa Highway / Hawaii Belt Road

Old Mamalahoa Highway

Old Mamalahoa Highway

53

52

51

50

49

48

47

46

45

44

43

42

Cave #3

Dahana Ranch

Kahana Road

Kalehua Road

Old Mamalahoa Highway

40 Miles to Hilo

1

19

N
W — E
S

2 MILES

0

Map continued on page 123

Waipi'o. But if you've had the place all to yourself for years, even a few people a week would seem like a crowd. The residents here range from the friendly to the grouchy to the *very* weird. We've found that we are less likely to get a smile or a wave in this valley than anywhere else on the island (except maybe Kapoho Tidepools), in sharp contrast to the friendly folks in Kukuihaele and Honoka'a above. Stink eye (dirty looks) and overall unfriendliness from some residents is common. Perhaps it's because they see visitors as antithetical to the reason they chose to live in Waipi'o in the first place. Whatever. At any rate, you should feel free to explore and enjoy the valley; just don't expect a big hug from some of the people who live there.

Getting into the Valley

Don't even think about driving a regular car down Waipi'o Valley Road. The paved one-lane road down into the valley has a ridiculously steep 25% grade. JEEPS with their 4WD and low gears (so you don't burn up your brakes) can make it down the 900-foot descent (in less than a mile). Regular cars simply can't. (There is a wad of metal that was once a two-wheel drive truck below one of the turns left by someone who thought otherwise. He miraculously survived by jumping from the vehicle just as it started tumbling down the almost vertical plunge.) You would probably be violating your rental car agreement if you brought your JEEP down here, meaning that they won't come save your bacon if it breaks down. Downhill traffic yields to uphill traffic, so use the turnouts.

While the overlook sports an unforgettable view of the valley and along the coast, it gives you only a taste of what the valley has to offer. The view from the valley floor with its numerous waterfalls is even better. If you don't have a JEEP (or nerve) you can take Waipi'o Valley Shuttle (775–7121). For $30 they'll take you into the valley on a 1½-hour *limited* tour. You can get off and try to catch the next shuttle back up but don't count on an open space. (Or any cooperation—they can be downright rude to deal with.) They are nearby in the town of Kukuihaele (shown on map). A better way is Waipi'o Valley Wagon Tours (775–9518). For $40 they take you on the same 1½-hour tour in a mule-driven wagon. (A half hour of it gets you into and out of the valley by 4WD.) Wagons hold 8 passengers and the driver narrates the sights in a similar way, but with the added charm of being in an open-air wagon.

If you want a real thrill, Waipi'o Na'alapa Trail Rides (775–0419) has outstanding horseback rides in the valley. They'll shuttle you down into the valley and take you back a ways. See HORSEBACK RIDING for more.

If you want to hike down into Waipi'o Valley just walk the road to the bottom. (Oh, is *that* all?) Though less than a mile going down, you'd swear it was 5 miles coming up. Just take your time. Waipi'o is a great place to spend the afternoon. At the bottom, the beach is to your right. Past the right (eastern) side of the beach at the shore is Kaluahine Falls. (Also shown in *Waterworld,* the falls are sometimes dry.) If you kept walking along the beach boulders below the cliff for 20–120 minutes (depending on your surefootedness), you'd come to the larger Waiulili Falls ⅔ mile from the beach. It drops almost directly into the ocean and is nearly always deserted. Bear in mind that even on calm days, the ocean could always toss a rogue wave at you while you are walking on the dry boulders, and that could ruin your day. Waipi'o Beach is often treacherous to swim unless the surf is real calm. Rip currents are a problem, and the power of the waves is impressive. Legend states that the door to the underworld is near Waipi'o Beach, so Hawaiians were always careful where they camped, lest they should take the one-way trip there themselves.

The back part of Waipi'o Valley is awesome. In the first nook you'll find twin falls of staggering heights. The one on the left was shut off by a sugar company when they diverted the water. *(Grumble, grumble.)* Now that sugar is dead, many are hoping they will turn it back on. The other, **Hi'ilawe Falls,** is 1,600 feet high with a free fall of 1,000 feet, the highest on the island. You see it when you head inland once you reach the bottom. Hikers can get there with some difficulty, see ADVENTURES.

Mosquito repellent should be required by law for hikers here. The bugs are not always around, but when they are in a foul mood—watch out! Remember while walking around that the roads are county roads and are public access. At one place there is a sign saying END OF COUNTY ROAD. According to the county official we spoke to, that's a crock. The sign was stolen from a construction site to dissuade you. Part of the road near the sign *looks* like a stream. Fifty feet or so is flooded with taro runoff, but it is usually driveable. See map. Other illegal signs farther back also falsely indicate road closures.

The trail you see zig-zagging up the wall on the far side of Waipi'o Valley goes up then down into the next valley, **Waimanu.** The view from the third switchback (400 feet up the trail cut pretty deeply into the mountain) offers a view of the valley far grander than the automobile lookout. You can see the back of the valley, the twin falls, and lots more. Waimanu is much farther along the trail. It is utterly gorgeous, devoid of

residents, and camping is allowed for those who are willing to make the trek. (There is an aerial photo gorgeous Waimanu Valley under Helicopters on page 175.) Call Forestry & Wildlife (974–4221) for free permits one month ahead of time. Don't try to go and come back as a day hike. It's too long and you can't see Waimanu Valley from the trail until you have mostly descended.

Believe it or not, there are places to stay in Waipi'o Valley. The unique **Waipi'o Treehouse,** and Tom Araki's *very* simple **Waipi'o Hotel** are located down here. See WHERE TO STAY.

OLD MAMALAHOA HIGHWAY

Leaving Waipi'o and Honoka'a behind, get back on Highway 19. Along this stretch of the Highway, between the 43 and 52 mile markers, there is another

forgotten piece **The Old Mamalahoa Highway.** Again the scenery on Old Mamalahoa is much nicer than 19 and worth the diversion. Lush, green hillsides bracket this old, country road. Mist and rain mean that lovers of green will be very happy. If you like caves, there are several along Old Mamalahoa Highway. The best by far is labeled on the map as cave #3. You should bring two flashlights. (There are lots of long chambers snaking pitch black into the mountain and, though tall enough to walk upright in, you'd be groping till the cows come home if you lost your only flashlight toward the back of some of these chambers.) The entrances are often dripping with ferns. Cave #3 has lots of structures inside (such as walls and platforms) presumably built by early Hawaiians, and a few beer bottles, presumably left a bit later. The other caves labeled are much less impressive.

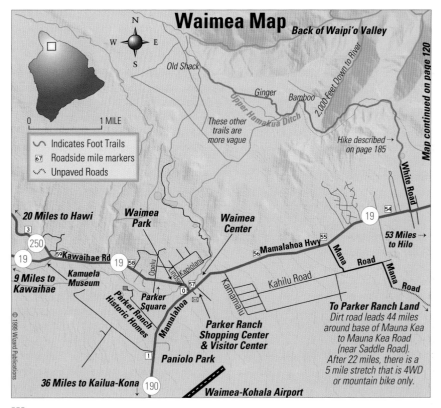

Waimea Map

Map continued on page 120

Back of Waipi'o Valley

Old Shack

Ginger Bamboo

2,000 Feet Down to River

Upper Hamakua Ditch

These other trails are more vague

Hike described → on page 185

N W E S

0   1 MILE

∿ Indicates Foot Trails
67 Roadside mile markers
⋰⋱ Unpaved Roads

White Road

20 Miles to Hawi

3

250

19

9 Miles to Kawaihae

59 Kawaihae Rd

Kamuela Museum

Waimea Park

19 58

Opelu

Kaniolani

Linus

Parker Ranch Historic Homes

Parker Square

57

0

Mamalahoa

Kamanalu

Kamanalu

Waimea Center

56 Mamalahoa Hwy 55

Kahilu Road

Mana Road

19 54

53 Miles → to Hilo

Mana Road

To Parker Ranch Land
Dirt road leads 44 miles around base of Mauna Kea to Mauna Kea Road (near Saddle Road). After 22 miles, there is a 5 mile stretch that is 4WD or mountain bike only.

Parker Ranch Shopping Center & Visitor Center

Paniolo Park

1

36 Miles to Kailua-Kona 190

Waimea-Kohala Airport

© 1999 Wizard Publications

WAIMEA

This town is often labeled Kamuela on maps. That's because there are two other Waimeas in the state, so the Post Office named the local branch Kamuela—Hawaiian for Samuel (as in Samuel Parker; see below). Many locals object to the use of Kamuela, so we will use the original name in deference.

On the surface, Waimea seems like the least Hawaiian town in Hawai'i. In fact, if Scotty had beamed you here and asked you where you were, Hawai'i would probably be the last state you'd guess. At 2,600 feet, the air has a cool crispness to it. Clouds slither over the saddle between Kohala and Mauna Loa Volcanoes often bathing Waimea in a cool fog. Evergreen trees and cactus sit side by side, and the trees all seem blown in one direction. (Kind of like your hair if you've rented a convertible.) Rather than seeing surfers in shorts and aloha shirts, you're more apt to see Hawaiian cowboys (called paniolos) wearing blue jeans and driving pick-up trucks. (A brief visit to a magazine rack, and you'll think, "I never knew there were so many *truck* magazines.")

Life runs a little slower here, and families are a bit closer knit. Many people compare its appearance to a Northern California rural town, but prettier. As you drive through town from the east side of the island, note how quickly the terrain changes from lush upland forests and green pastures to dry lava scrubland.

Don't be lulled into thinking that Waimea is a hick town. It is remarkably over-represented when it comes to fine shopping and has several restaurants that are utterly superb. Some of the homes up in the Waimea Homesteads are absolutely beautiful where the descendants of cattle magnates live.

PARKER RANCH

The town is dominated by the legacy of John Palmer Parker. When Captain George Vancouver brought long-horned cattle to Kamehameha as a gift in 1793, the king made them kapu (off limits) for 10 years to build up the numbers. By 1815 the wild herds that roamed Kohala were so ferocious that locals steered clear of them. Marauding cattle were known to drive Hawaiians from their homes by munching and goring everything in sight, even the homes themselves. Kamehameha the Great hired Massachusetts-born John Palmer Parker to shoot them, salt the meat and bring it to the harbor to sell to passing ships. This was no easy task. Long-horned cattle of that time were not like the tame, mindless morons we know today. They were wily, lean, and stealthy. They would charge men on horseback, goring them. They lived in the valleys and canyons as well, making them very difficult to detect. Good horses became the equivalent of hunting dogs—they would smell the wild cattle before they saw them, and their ears would prick up, warning their rider to the danger. Because Parker possessed a musket and good shooting skills, Kamehameha made him the first person ever allowed to kill the cattle. Parker took great pains to select cattle with favorable traits and kept them for himself as payment. These he domesticated, starting the Parker herd.

As a totally irrelevant aside, one of the casualties of these cattle was the Scottish botanist David Douglas. He's the guy for whom Douglas fir trees were named. He

was walking near Mana Road on the slopes of Mauna Kea one day when he fell into one of the covered pits used as a cattle trap. (Some said he was thrown in.) Although he was lucky enough to survive the fall, so was the bull already occupying the pit. The unhappy bovine made his displeasure known by goring Douglas to death.

John Parker himself was a colorful character. A lover of adventure, he was a natural born risk-taker who, though a long-range planner, felt strongly that part of wisdom is to know the value of today. He was well loved and respected by his contemporaries. (But he sure wasn't very photogenic—in his dour photo he makes Ebenezer Scrooge look like Mr. Rogers.)

In 1816 John Parker married Kamehameha the Great's granddaughter, forever cementing the bond between him and the royal family. He was eventually allowed to purchase two acres of land. His wife, because of her royal blood, was later granted 640 acres, and he bought another 1,000 acres. Thus was born what would become the largest privately owned cattle ranch in the entire United States, stretching over 225,000 acres (9% of the Big Island). Parker and his descendants would go on to become very powerful on the island.

Later, when Kamehameha III realized

225,000 Acre Parker Ranch Shown in Dark Areas

Mana Road→

that Hawai'i was lacking in people knowledgeable in the ways of cattle ranching, he arranged for three Mexican cowboys to come to the Big Island and teach the locals about ranching. Nearly all Big Island paniolo traditions descend from these three cowboys. Parker Ranch was severely neglected by subsequent Parkers. John Parker's grandson, Samuel Parker, was a flamboyant playboy who spent money like water and had a genius for making profoundly stupid investments. Unlike King Midas, everything *he* touched turned to manure. As the aging Parker II saw money pouring down Samuel's many ratholes, he began to squirrel away funds as fast as he could. But when the time came to retrieve the money, the old man could not remember where he had hidden most of it. To this day, much of the fortune Parker II hid away has never been found. In 1900 the family hired a Honolulu attorney named Alfred Wellington Carter to manage and rejuvenate the ranch. This he did with a vengeance, turning a dying relic into the powerful and very lucrative operation it is today.

The serenity of Waimea was broken in 1992 when Richard Smart, the descendent of John Palmer Parker, died, leaving some of his $450 *million* estate to his family, but the bulk to the Richard Smart Foundation Trust. Lawsuits started flying from disgruntled family members angry about their share, and it was beginning to look as if the ranch might be broken up and fed to the lawyers and tax collectors. Fortunately, the dispute was finally settled in 1994, and peace once again returned to sleepy little Waimea.

Most of Parker Ranch is mile after mile of rolling, grassy hills and wide open plains interrupted by rows of trees for windbreaks. Owls and pheasants crisscross the ranch while ever-chewing cows wander about. The ranch consists of several non-contiguous segments of land, and its 55,000 cattle are controlled by a mere 25 paniolo (Hawai'i cowboys). The road across from the 55 mile mark (see Waimea map, page 115, or graphic on facing page) slices through Parker Ranch. Called Mana Road, it goes 44 miles around Mauna Kea mountain to Mauna Kea Road (off Saddle Road). There is a 5-mile segment in the middle that requires 4WD, otherwise, you can go as far as your desire takes you. Close any gates that you open. According to the county, it is a *public* right of way, despite any signs you may see that *imply* the contrary. Parker Ranch no longer gives tours (liability, what else?), so this is as close as you will get.

A successful cattle ranch is first and foremost a grass farm. After being raised on sweet Hawaiian range grass for 5–6 months, most of the cattle are shipped by boat or 747 to the mainland or Canada, then fattened in various areas before slaughter. In the old days, just getting the cows to ships was a traumatic process. They were driven to Kawaihae, forced into the ocean, then lashed to the outside of small boats, which ferried them to the main ship where they were belly-hoisted aboard. Now they simply walk onto an old cruise ship, into stalls, and off they go. If you want to get an idea of what Big Island beef tastes like, the best (and most consistent) source is the Kamuela Meat Market (885–4601) located behind Sure Save in the tired-looking Parker Ranch Shopping Center. The range-fed beef is darker and stronger than grain-fed beef and is particularly good marinated. Fresh deliveries are usually MWF afternoons. Grocery stores around the island usually have beef flown in from the mainland. Visitors to Waimea often stop by the

Parker Ranch Historic Homes (885–5433). One of these homes was purchased in 1879 by John Palmer Parker II. It was used as a ranch home until it was converted to a French provincial home in the 1960s by his descendent, Richard Smart. Full of fine European art and furniture, the entrance fee is $7.50. This fee also allows admittance to the house next door. It contains the original koa interior of the Parker home located 12 miles away at Mana, which was built in the mid-1800s. With Hawaiian koa wood everywhere (floors, ceiling, stairs, etc.), you'll see the kind of house the rich lived in a century and a half ago. (Floors of that era make a surprising amount of noise when you walk on them.)

The cerebrally inclined will enjoy the Kamuela Museum 885–4724. Created by an O'ahu cop named Albert Solomon Jr. (a spry character in his mid-90s) and his wife Harriet, it is an antique lover's dream. An eclectic assortment of artifacts from the Hawaiian Islands, Japan, and China feature Hawaiian brass (actually lava) knuckles, a 34-star union flag, slippers made of ti leaves and worn by FDR, fabulous Japanese cherrywood furniture given to King Kalakaua by Japanese Royals in the 1800s, a machine gun recovered from a kamikaze plane, whale bone carvings, stuffed birds, and scads more. Extremely valuable articles sit next to trinkets. The longer you stay, the more interesting it becomes. Admission is a ridiculously cheap $5 per person. (The museum was for sale as we went to press, and there was a chance that its priceless collection might be broken up.) It's at the junction of Highways 19 and 250.

The Parker Ranch Visitors Center in the Parker Ranch Shopping Center shows a video-tape of the Parker Ranch history and has a small museum.

Sugar & Spice (on the Highway) is a *delicious* place to stop if you want to give that sweet tooth a workout.

One of the prettiest hikes on the island is above Waimea. It overlooks the back side of Waipi'o Valley and is off White Road and described under HIKING.

Past Waimea heading into Kohala, sights are described in the Kohala section.

WAIMEA AND HAMAKUA SHOPPING

In Waimea at Parker Ranch Center, check out Malia Kamuela for men's and ladies clothing, Keep in Touch for souvenir T-shirts, Parker Ranch Store for Parker Ranch mementos. Waimea Craft Mall just east of Parker Ranch Center is the place to try Hawaiian Vintage Chocolate (grown on the island!) or to pick up one of the cow-themed Ka-Moo-Ela T-shirts. (*Real* cute.)

Across the street at the Waimea Center stop at Cook's Discoveries for Hawai'i-produced food and gift items. The Kamuela Hat Company is wonderful if you're into hats. Parker Square offers the superb Bentley's and the Gallery of Great Things. You can also pick up something for your children at Imagination Toys.

After leaving the Waipio Valley lookout, drive by Kukuihaele for Waipi'o Valley Artworks featuring an outstanding selection of Hawaiian wood pieces and other gifts. Ice cream is next door.

WAIMEA AND HAMAKUA'S BEST BETS

Best Garden—Hawai'i Tropical Botanical
Best Waterfall—Umauma Falls
Best Place to Ride a Horse—Waipi'o
Best View (Easy)—Waipi'o Overlook
Best View (Hard)—From the zigzag trail on *other* side of Waipi'o Valley
Best Treat—Mamane Bakery in Honoka'a or Sugar & Spice in Waimea
Best Place to Get Stink Eye—Waipi'o

The long and winding road…

Saddle Road runs between our largest volcanoes, Mauna Loa and Mauna Kea. The entire area is called the Saddle because of the saddle-shaped valley between the two mountains. It travels through some unpopulated and very surreal looking country and is worth consideration if you are driving from one side to the other.

The saddle crests at an impressive 6,578 feet. That's some saddle. The 53-mile long road has a bad and outdated reputation. It was hastily built by the military in 1942 for strategic purposes. This was wartime and they wanted a road connecting the two sides of the island, and they wanted it fast. They didn't design it with general traffic in mind; it was meant for military vehicles. Even today, driving on Saddle Road is prohibited in many rental car agreements, meaning your Collision Damage Waiver with them won't cover you. A few years ago their fears were quite well founded. The road had been paved by *Sadists-R-Us* and was a body shop's dream. But now it's in decent shape. It's still a winding, hilly road with blind turns that aren't banked. Think of it as a roller coaster for your car. Traffic is almost always sparse. It's two (narrow) lanes wide, but most drive the center when nobody's coming their way. There are no lights and only a fool drives it at night. (We came out here in the middle of the night to watch comet awhile back and *got chicken skin fo days*—i.e., it was spooky.) The road is often licked by fog toward the center crest. But all in all, it's not as bad as when the rental car companies first made the decision to keep you off of it.

Some companies, like Harper Rentals (See BASICS), have no qualms about letting you drive on it. The government is thinking about straightening Saddle Road. The study might be completed by the year 2160 and work should commence shortly thereafter.

So why drive Saddle Road? Three reasons. First, it's the only way to drive to Mauna Kea. Second, it cuts between Mauna Kea and Mauna Loa and has some nice sights. The landscape is otherworldly in places and decidedly different.

Third, it's kind of fun (if you like winding roads). If your question is, "Yeah, but do *you* bring *your* own car on it?"—the answer is yes. (As we all know, *drive it like a rental* is like saying *drive it like it's stolen*.) It's not necessarily a short-cut, though. It's a shorter distance, but you can't drive it as fast as Highway 19, known locally as *the upper road*. Some people love taking Saddle Road; others feel intimidated. I guess it depends on your personality. We like to take it from the Kona side and return from Hilo on the upper road. In 50 miles the terrain goes from dry lava scrub land to rolling green hills and plains to young lava fields to dripping fern-covered forests. With this in mind, we'll describe it from west to east. There's no **gas** on this road; get it Waikoloa Village or Waimea in the west, Hilo in the east.

Look at the foldout back cover map to familiarize yourself with the route and to put it in context. From the intersection of Saddle Road (200) and Highway 190, you leave the lava land behind and enter rolling plains of grasses.

As you ascend to the crest of this saddle, you'll get an idea of the scale of Mauna Kea on your left and Mauna Loa on your right. The military often drive this road in their Humvees and other camouflaged vehicles. If you stop and listen, you'll often hear the booms of artillery from the Pohakuloa Military Training Area. Sometimes you'll see their choppers swooping low like a scene out of *Apocalypse Now.* Tanks and Armored Personnel Carriers also use this road on occasion. (I respectfully suggest that you *always* give armored tanks the right of way.)

Mauna Kea State Park is at the 35 mile marker. After you turn into the park, there are restrooms and a phone to your right. Cabins are available for $45. (See CAMPING.)

Back on the highway, note the rock wall just before the 29 mile marker on the right (southern) side. Follow it and you'll see where it was covered by the Mauna Loa flow of 1935.

You'll find the road up Mauna Kea (on your left) is marked by a large mound,

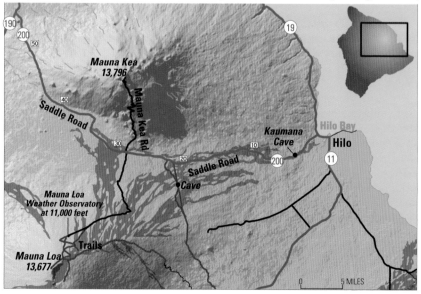

called **Pu'u Huluhulu** (hairy hill) shown on page 127. This pu'u is a good place to stretch if you want to walk to the top. (If you have kids, this is a good place to let them burn off some of that extra energy.) It's an old cinder cone created by Mauna Kea long ago

Top of the world! The moonscape terrain of Mauna Kea is like none other.

and has been surrounded by more recent lava flows from Mauna Loa. (You can tell by scars on the side that it was once mined for its cinders.) The main trail is on the far (east) side of Pu'u Huluhulu, just off the road to Mauna Loa, on your right. There are several trails on top of this forested mound. Just generally stay to the right at major intersections, and it'll take you around and to the bottom on the other side. The splendid view, as well as the birds, make it a short but worthwhile diversion.

MAUNA KEA

Question: What's the tallest mountain in the world? Answer: Mauna Kea. (All those who were going to say Mt. Everest, please lower your hands now.) It's a staggering 32,000 feet from its underwater base to its peak. Compare this to Mt. Everest, whose peak at 29,028 is really even less than that when measured from its base. The second of the five surviving volcanoes to create the island, Mauna Kea (meaning White Mountain) pokes its head 13,796 feet above sea level. In its prime, half a million years ago, Mauna

Kea was over 17,000 feet high. But it gets shorter with age. It shrinks every day, settling under its own weight, and bending the ocean floor beneath it. The ancient Hawaiians considered it the home of Poli'ahu, the snow goddess. She and Madame Pele, next door on Mauna Loa, didn't always get along very well, and the saddle between Mauna Loa and Mauna Kea was said to be their battleground. The ancient Hawaiians were uncomfortable in this region, not wishing to get in the middle of this domestic disturbance.

Atop the mountain, the air is thin and incredibly clear. Scientists recognize this spot as possibly the best place in the world to observe stars and have been placing the world's finest telescopes up here for years. (The *twinkle, twinkle* of the little star is caused by air turbulence, and the air above Mauna Kea is some of the least turbulent in the world—windy, but not turbulent.) With little precipitation (except for the occasional blizzard), little in the way of city lights below, and relatively easy access, Mauna Kea is the pride of the astronomical community. Two dozen of the finest telescopes in the world are sprinkled about the summit or are in the works. One area up there is called Millimeter Valley, since its peepers are designed to look not in the optical wavelength, but rather at the high end of the radio band, in the much longer millimeter and sub-millimeter wavelength. This allows scientists to look through cosmic clouds and watch stars being born. Some of these telescopes can look at objects over 12 billion light years away, meaning that the light they are seeing left those objects long before the earth and sun were even born. The mighty Keck telescope has a 33-foot wide viewing surface. The moveable part weighs 300 tons but is so perfectly balanced that it can be moved *with one hand.*

Here's a thought for you: Look around at all the infrastructure necessary to look at the stars—the roads, the buildings, the computers, the people, the research, the scopes themselves. All of these things and the hundreds of millions of dollars they cost are here for a single purpose: to hold *one tenth of an ounce* of metal in a specific shape. That's how much aluminum coats the giant mirrors that gather all the starlight and where all the information comes from.

Tours of the **University of Hawai'i Telescope** are given Saturdays and Sundays. Call 961–2180 beforehand for more information. Call 969–3218 for a recorded weather update of Mauna Kea. (It's not usually updated in the summer.) Except during summit tours, visitors won't be able to visit the inside of any of the telescopes except Keck (labeled on map), which has a visitors' gallery open weekdays, as well as restrooms. You'll get a glimpse through the window of the telescope itself there. (As cold as it gets outdoors, it feels even colder in the temperature-controlled rooms housing the telescopes.)

The view from atop Mauna Kea can only be described as majestic moonscape. The Apollo astronauts did considerable training up here because it was considered uniquely moon-like. Looking down on the clouds is mesmerizing. It's a cliché but true—you feel like you're on top of the world! Off in the distance, the still-active volcano of Mauna Loa seems bigger than life, especially from a place

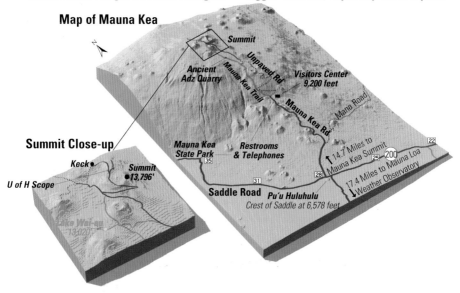

Map of Mauna Kea

Summit

Ancient Adz Quarry

Unpaved Rd

Mauna Kea Trail

Visitors Center 9,200 feet

Mauna Kea Rd

Mana Road

Summit Close-up

Mauna Kea State Park [35]

Restrooms & Telephones

14.7 Miles to Mauna Kea Summit [25] [200]

[22]

Keck•

Summit •13,796'

17.4 Miles to Mauna Loa Weather Observatory

[28]

U of H Scope

[31]

Saddle Road Pu'u Huluhulu
Crest of Saddle at 6,578 feet

Lake Wai-au 13,020'

about 2 miles down the road from the summit. Ironically, Mauna Loa's massive size makes it appear smaller than Mauna Kea. *(Huh?!)* Because Mauna Loa rises so gently to its 13,677-foot height, you don't get the sense of size that you would if it were steeper, like Mauna Kea. But that very gentle slope hides a volume of rock far greater than Mauna Kea—10,000 *cubic miles* of stone. From atop Mauna Kea, the islands of Maui, Moloka'i and Kaho'olawe can be seen on clear days. From this area people ski down the mountain to link up with the road below. The actual summit is a quick (five short-of-breath minutes) hike from the University of Hawaii Observatory. (You'll see a faint trail.) Sunsets from up here when clouds cooperate are an unrivaled splendor of unequaled expansiveness. The summit appears utterly lifeless except for a few unlucky bugs blown up from below and a few flightless native insects that feed on them. No trees, no plants. Just a lifeless void. The mountain last erupted 4,500 years ago and is considered dormant. (If it erupts when you are up there, please disregard this last statement.)

Also located near the top are two oddities. **Lake Wai-au,** at 13,020 feet, is one of the highest lakes in the United States and at first its existence defies explanation. What could be feeding it? There are no rivers at the top of a mountain, and natural springs need a higher source to gravitationally feed them (like water in a siphon tube). Rain and snow are insufficient, and the lake is here year round. The answer is *permafrost.* During the last Ice Age, Mauna Kea was covered by a 20-square-mile glacier that was up to 350 feet thick and extended 3,200 feet below the summit. It carved and scoured the mountain and left permafrost several feet below the surface. Each day, as the sun heats up the mountain, it melts a fraction of the permafrost, which then works its way into Lake Wai-au. Though shallow, the ancient Hawaiians thought the lake was bottomless—probably because they couldn't find anyone crazy enough to venture into it at this frigid altitude. Lake Wai-au can be accessed by a 15–30 minute walk from the road. (See map and turn right when the trail intersects another trail. The upper trail, near the hairpin turn on Mauna Kea Road, is the easier trail.) Many of the gulches you see on the side of Mauna Kea were created when the glacier melted, sending the snowmelt to scour the sides of the mountain.

The other oddity up here is **Keanakako'i,** an ancient Hawaiian adz quarry. (Adz is a stone cutter used for shaping wood.) When Mauna Kea erupted during the last ice age, the glacier cap cooled the lava very quickly. The result is the densest and hardest rock in all the islands (harder than spring steel) and was

The only one of its kind—a tropical lake fed by permafrost.

As the snow begins to melt, the summit of Mauna Kea becomes a land of many contrasts.

the hardest substance in the state (except for the bread at a Kona restaurant we reviewed recently). What's impressive is that the ancient Hawaiians discovered this site (at 12,400 feet) and were able to successfully mine it for generations, trading it to other islanders for assorted goodies. The only trail to the adz quarry is down from Lake Wai-au. Coming back up involves a grueling 800-foot ascent, a genuine 'okole kicker at this altitude.

DRIVING UP TO MAUNA KEA

From Saddle Road it's 14⁷⁄₁₀ miles to the summit. About 2 miles into Mauna Kea Road is a dirt road on your right called **Mana Road.** It leads 44 miles *around* Mauna Kea Mountain all the way to Waimea and passes through tranquil forest. There's rarely anyone on the road, and you need 4WD (or a mountain bike) to take it. The **Onizuka Center for International Astronomy** is 6 miles up Mauna Kea Road at 9,200 feet. Ellison Onizuka was a native of Kona and part

of the crew of the Space Shuttle Challenger in 1986 that *"slipped the surly bonds of Earth to touch the face of God."* The Visitor Center has a few displays. Friday—Sunday evenings they have star gazing sessions using their small telescope at the Visitor Center. Their hours are squirrely, so don't expect them to be open for you. There are restrooms here. While driving up this part of Mauna Kea Road, watch out for mindless wayward cows occasionally wandering about.

After the Visitor Center the road is unpaved for 5 miles before it becomes paved again for the last 3⁷⁄₁₀ miles. You are allowed access to the top of the mountain, but astronomers *request* that 4WD vehicles only drive past the Visitor's Center. That's because the unpaved portion of the somewhat steep road coming down can get a bit slippery at times, especially when wet. 4WD vehicles *usually* have a gear low enough to obviate this situation. We've found, however, that 4WD vehicles seem to fishtail *going up* as much as 2WD cars do. The more vexing problem for them is that two-wheel drive vehicles cause severe wear on the dirt road, making the trek to the summit rougher for astronomers and causing higher maintenance costs. If you don't want to bring a JEEP, **Waipiʻo Valley Shuttle** at 775-7121 will carry you up for a *mere* $80 per person. (You can rent a JEEP for a day for that price.) **Paradise Safaris** at 322-2366 will pick you up on the west side and take you to the summit for sunset, then come down a bit for some stargazing and hot chocolate sipping for $130 per person. They provide warm coats for you, and the total time is 7½ hours. If you are going to be shuttled up, **Paradise** is a *much* better experience.

Those who *really* want a challenge can opt to hike the trail from the Visitor's Center to the top. (See Map.) It's 15 miles round-trip and a *very* tough day hike, even for the fittest. You need a very early start and should take precautions mentioned in the hiking section.

If you drive up, drink plenty of water before, during, and after, as dehydration is a severe problem at that altitude. Children, pregnant women, and those with respiratory problems should avoid the summit. Try to avoid soft drinks and (how do I put this delicately?) foods that produce gas. (You figure it out.) Don't come up here within 24 hours of a SCUBA dive. As far as your nitrogen is concerned, you're flying. Altitude sickness can strike anyone, causing weakness, dizziness and nausea. Some claim that an ibuprofen *before* the trip will help this, similar to the way aspirin is said to forestall hangovers, but we won't swear by it. Go slow and don't exert yourself too much. Acclimating for a half hour or so at the 9,200-foot visitor center can help.

Then there's the cold. Between November and April, snow is common. Even summertime brings the occasional freak snowstorm. During the rest of the year, it's often bone-chilling up there. Dress warm. *(Like you packed your parka for your Hawaiian vacation!)* The wind can be exceptionally fierce. It's often warm and calm up there, but you shouldn't *count* on it being this way. During the winter, you can snow ski short distances. See Snow Skiing under ACTIVITIES. When it snows, local residents often rush up the mountain to frolic. We've seen people dashing down the hill below the summit on *every* conceivable mode of transportation. Skis, snowboards, sleds, boogie boards, surf boards, tarps—we've even seen people sliding down in *ocean kayaks,* complete with paddles!

According to King Kalakaua, the Hawaiians had their own version of the Ironman Triathlon. Here, the objective was to climb Mauna Kea during the winter, grab all the snow you could carry, bolt back down the mountain, and run all the way to the ocean. If you had enough snow for a snowball, you won. (If you didn't, you probably grabbed the winner's snowball and stuck it in his pants.) Ironically, this is still done. Only today people bring the snow back in pickup beds and throw a party when they get home. This may be the only place in the world where you can experience snow less than 40 miles from an 85° tropical resort area.

On your way down, a couple of miles below the Visitor's Center, you *may* (clouds permitting) see the smoldering Puʻu ʻOʻo cone (not the same Puʻu ʻOʻo mentioned below) at Kilauea Volcano 30 miles to the southeast. Without question the best views from Mauna Kea are while coming down, not going up.

MAUNA LOA

Across the saddle from Mauna Kea is the more active Mauna Loa (long mountain). This is the most difficult volcano summit on the island to access. You've got two choices, and both are a *buggah*. (See HIKING.) However, off Saddle Road a quarter mile east of the road up Mauna Kea, there is a narrow, paved road leading 17⁴/₁₀ miles up to the **Mauna Loa Weather Observatory,** just above the 11,000-foot level. From there the view across the saddle to Mauna Kea is stunning, especially if there is snow on top. Otherwise, Mauna Loa Observatory Road offers little for you. Created in 1958, the observatory is used to measure gases to determine if global warming is occurring. Built near the top of a semi-active volcano, it is protected by a first-of-its-kind lava barrier on the upslope side designed to redirect any lava flows long enough to get the scientists out during an eruption. Someone (with *way* too much time on his hands) has painted a squiggly line on this entire road, creating the illusion that this is a two-lane road. You might want to check out the pit crater across the street from telephone pole #200. It's about 50 feet from the road and 50 feet deep where lava drained after overflowing.

APPROACHING HILO

As you continue on Saddle Road, you'll descend toward Hilo. There's a pristine mile-long cave that you can hike to. See ADVENTURES on page 216. The *old* **Pu'u 'O'o Hike** mentioned on under HIKING starts between the 22 and 23 mile markers. Look at the foldout back cover map to get an idea of where the lava has flowed during historic times. You'll be periodically passing through fields of it.

You're on the windward side now, and things will start to get greener. As you approach Hilo, before the 4 mile

marker, you'll see **Kaumana Cave** on your left. Created by the Mauna Loa lava flow of 1881 that traveled 25 miles and threatened Hilo, this lava tube skylight is saturated with green. Full grown trees and ferns have taken over the cave and its entrance. It stands in stark contrast to other caves throughout the island. Elsewhere, a century-old lava tube would be little changed from when it was created. But here, in lush, wet Hilo, geologic time marches at a rapid pace. The cave looks old, worn, and rickety. You can take the stairs to the bottom and peer in. Once down there, most people are immediately attracted to the large opening to the right, never even noticing the cave entrance to the left. Remember, this is simply an interruption in a 2-mile long lava tube. If you have a flashlight (make that two—it's so dark you can't tell whether your eyes are open or closed) and sufficient nerve, you can go cave exploring. (Called spelunking—in case that's the only word you forgot in your last crossword puzzle.) The cave to your right has more low overhangs between long stretches of tall ceilings, but the formations are more fascinating. To your left, after an initial low overhang, the cave is more cathedral-like. Tree roots occasionally poke through the ceiling. You could spend hours exploring this lava tube if you wanted.

This flow came within 1½ miles of Hilo Bay. Princess Ruth was sent from Honolulu to save Hilo. She stood in front of the lava flow beseeching Pele to stop the lava. That night she slept next to the advancing flow and by morning it had stopped. Today several hundred homes are built on the 1881 flow and can easily be recognized by their rock gardens.

Rainbow Falls and Boiling Pots are off Waianuenue Road in this area. See HILO SIGHTS for more on these.

In addition to the better known beaches, hidden gems such as this one at Kua Bay are scattered along the west side of the island.

The Big Island has the reputation of being the island without beaches. That's because in the past, lack of roads and lack of knowledge caused most of its more glorious beaches to go unnoticed. Granted, the island has fewer sand beaches per mile of shoreline than any of the other islands. It's newer, and plentiful beaches are the blessings of older, more mature islands. However, what beaches we *do* have, especially on the west side, are among the very best in the state. The water off the west side of the Big Island is the clearest, cleanest and often calmest water in all the islands. There is not one permanent stream on the entire west side, so cloudy river runoff is not a problem. And the shape of the island, along with the prevailing current, often gives the west side relatively gentle water. Rough water usually comes from the northeast. Kona and Kohala's calmer waters can be dramatically seen from the air. During normal conditions, the inbound flier will notice that the transition from coarse, choppy channel waters to fine textured leeward waters is almost instantaneous, just south of the northernmost tip of the island.

On the Big Island we have white sand, black sand, salt-and-pepper sand, even green sand beaches. As for beach quality, Hapuna Beach is consistently named the best beach *in the entire country* by travel magazines. Mauna Kea Beach is not far behind. Kahalu'u and Honaunau offer outrageous snorkeling. And secluded gems like Kua Bay, Makalawena, and Road to the Sea along with unusual delights such as Kiholo Bay, Kapoho Tide-pools, and Green Sand Beach probably make beach-going on the Big Island the best in the state.

The biggest danger you will face at the beach is the surf. Though it is calmer on the west side of the Big Island, that's a relative term. Most mainlanders are unprepared for the strength of Hawai'i's surf. We're out in the middle of the biggest ocean in the world and the surf has lots of room to build up. We have our calm days where the water is like glass. We often have days where the surf is moderate, calling for respect and diligence on the part of the swimmer. And we have the high surf days, perfect for sitting on the beach with a picnic or a mai-tai, watching the experienced and the audacious tempt the ocean's patience. Call 935–1666 ext. 9800 for a surf forecast. Don't make the mistake of underestimating the ocean's power here. Hawai'i is the undisputed drowning capital of the United States and we don't want you to join the statistics.

Other hazards include rip currents, which can form, cease, and form again with no warning. Large "rogue waves" can come ashore with no warning. These usually occur when two or more waves fuse at sea, becoming a larger wave. Even calm seas are no guarantee of safety. Many people have been caught unaware by large waves during ostensibly "calm seas." We have swam and snorkeled most of the beaches described in this book on at least two occasions (usually more than two). But beaches change. The underwater topography changes throughout the year. (White Sands Beach is a dramatic example.) Storms can take a very safe beach and rearrange the sand, turning it into a dangerous beach. Napo'opo'o Beach vanished after a storm in 1992 and has yet to come back. Just because we describe a beach as being in a certain condition does not mean it will be in that same condition when you visit it.

Consequently, you should take the beach descriptions as a snapshot in calm times. If seas aren't calm, you probably shouldn't go in the water. If you observe a rip current, you probably shouldn't go in the water. If you aren't a comfortable swimmer, you should probably never go in the water, except at those beaches that have lifeguards. There is no way we can tell you that a certain beach will be swimmable on a certain day, and we claim no such prescience. There is no substitution for your own observations and judgment.

A few standard safety tips: Never turn your back on the ocean. Never swim alone. Never swim in the mouth of a river. Never swim in murky water. Never swim when the seas are not calm. Don't walk too close to the shorebreak; a large wave can come and knock you over and pull you in. Observe ocean conditions carefully. Don't let small children play in the water unsupervised. Fins give you far more power and speed and are a good safety device in addition to being more fun. If you're comfortable in a mask and snorkel, they provide considerable peace of mind in addition to opening up the underwater world. Lastly, don't let Hawai'i's idyllic environment cloud your judgment. Recognize the ocean for what it is—a powerful force that needs to be respected.

If you're going to spend any time at the shoreline or beach, reef shoes are the best investment you'll ever make. These water-friendly wonders accompany us whenever we go to any beach. Wal-mart or Kmart in Kona sell cheap ones, perfect for your short-duration usage. Even on sandy beaches, rocks or sea life seem magnetically attracted to the bottom of feet. With reef shoes, you can frolic without the worry. (Though don't expect them to protect you from everything. Some beaches are backed by kiawe trees, and their thorns could probably penetrate an armored car.)

The ocean here rarely smells fishy

since the difference between high and low tide is so small. (In other words, it doesn't strand large amounts of smelly sea plants at low tide like other locations.)

Theft can be a problem when visiting beaches. Visitors like to lock their cars at all beaches, but piles of glass on the ground usually dissuade island residents from doing that at secluded beaches. We usually remove anything we can't bear to have stolen and leave the car with the windows rolled up but unlocked. That way, we're less likely to get our windows broken by a curious thief. Regardless, don't leave anything of value in your car. (Well...maybe the seats can stay.) While in the water, we use a waterproof fanny pack (available at many outdoor stores) for our wallet, checkbook and keys, and leave everything else on the beach. Sometimes we only bring car keys and tie them to bathing suit drawstrings. We don't take a camera (except disposables) to the beach unless we are willing to stay there on the sand and baby-sit it. This way, when we swim, snorkel or just walk, we don't have to constantly watch our things.

Use sunblock early and often. Don't pay any attention to the claims from sunblock makers that their product is waterproof, rubproof, sand blast proof, powerwash proof, etc. Reapply it every couple of hours and after you get out of the ocean. The ocean water will hide sunburn symptoms until after you're toast. Then you can look forward to agony for the rest of your trip. (And yes, you *can* get burned while in the water.) Of the sunblocks we've tried, Bullfrog and Neutrogena seem to work the best.

Consider one of those disposable underwater cameras. Even if you don't go in the water, they will withstand the elements. Their quality is better than most people think. Between the Kodak and the Fuji, we give a slight quality edge to the Fuji, as it seems to have a sharper lens, though a slightly inferior film.

Always remember that in Hawai'i, all beaches are public beaches. This means that you can park yourself on any stretch of sand you like. The trick, sometimes, can be access. You might have to cross private land to get to a public beach. We'll try to point out a way to nearly all beaches

In general, surf is higher and stronger during the winter, calmer in the summer, but there are exceptions during all seasons. When we mention that a beach has facilities, it usually includes restrooms, showers, picnic tables, and drinking water.

Lastly, remember that just because *you* may be on vacation doesn't mean that residents are. Consequently, beaches are more crowded on weekends.

Tell me a lawyer didn't write this beach sign!

To get ocean safety information, call County Aquatics at 935-2725. The beaches that had year-round lifeguards at press time were:

West—Hapuna, Kahalu'u, White Sands
Puna—Ahalanui (north of Isaac Hale)
Hilo—Onekahakaha, Honoli'i, Richardson's

Those with lifeguards on weekends and whenever school's out were:

West—Spencer
Hilo—Leleiwi, James Kealoha

We'll start our descriptions at the end of the road at the top of the island and work our way counter-clockwise. The first few beaches have marginal swimming.

❖ **Pololu Beach**—Located at the end of Highway 270 on the northern end of the island, this beach is very pretty. High surf and currents usually make this a poor swimming or snorkeling beach. Access is via a 15–20 minute trail from the Pololu Valley Overlook 400 feet up. No facilities.

❖ **Kapanai'a Bay**—Tell anyone outside North Kohala that there is a beach below Kapa'au, and they'll look at you like you're crazy. Kapana Bay is one of the best kept secrets in North Kohala. This small pebble-and-sand beach is backed by trees and was carved out of the cliffs by a small brook. Even during moderate surf, you may see keikis boogie boarding in the back part of the bay. Surfers venture farther out where the waves are completely unobstructed. While there's not much sand and the water is a bit murky, the bay is very picturesque and a wonderful place for a picnic. The catch is that the access road is junky and suitable for only 4WD (see map on page 46). One qualifier: This is the only place in the book where we request

this (there is one other place where we *recommend* it for your own benefit), but if you visit this beach, please do so during the week. On an island that cherishes water activities, North Kohala residents have very few choices and this place is very special to them on weekends and holidays. We are the first to reveal this beach and want to avoid shocking local residents with lots of weekend visitors.

❖ **Keokea Beach Park**—Although the swimming is usually poor, the exception is a small cove created by a man-made boulder breakwater. It was constructed as a community project by locals with the help from some heavy equipment donated by a sugar company. Not worth driving to unless you're in the neighborhood. Access road near the 27 mile marker on Highway 270 in North Kohala. Full facilities.

❖ **Kapa'a Beach Park**—No sand at this beach, just rocks and a little coral rubble. The attractive assets here are the exceptionally clear water for snorkeling and SCUBA, usually abundant fish (sometimes large pelagic fish), coupled with somewhat protected waters except during periods of high surf (which can bring rips and surges). Be careful of surge here. Clear water makes it a good place to take underwater fish pictures. Not much coral (a recent invasion of urchins has wiped out much of what little there was). Rarely visited during the week, but easy to access just north of the 16 mile marker on Highway 270. Facilities include restrooms, as well as a BBQ and picnic tables. Excellent view of Maui and a nice place to watch the sunset.

❖ **Mahukona**—When the seas are calm, it's *really* calm here. Not a beach, but an old abandoned sugar company harbor, Mahukona boasts crystal clear water and ridiculously easy access for snorkeling or swimming. You can practically drive up, open your door and fall in. (But use the ladder at the entrance at right, OK?) Though not much coral, the underwater relief is interesting. There's usually a large variety of fish as well as abandoned sugar equipment (giant chains, wheels, etc.) and sparse remains of an old shipwreck. If the surf's up, don't go. When it's calm, check for surginess. During the week you'll most likely have it all to yourself. Facilities, except drinking water. (Don't drink the shower water!) The dirt road heading north leads to the navigational heiau shown on page 14.

❖ **Lapakahi**—We feel kind of funny putting this in the beaches section. Located in Lapakahi State Historical Park near the 14 mile marker on Highway 270, this is a reserve and there is no real beach here. (See page 51.) In fact, swimming is not even allowed. But *snorkeling* is and it's exceptional. (Yes,

they *do* differentiate.) The water is clean and clear in **Koaiʻe Cove** between site 11 and site 7 near the coconut grove (see brochure at entrance). Not much coral but usually *lots* of fish. Stay inside the cove; the waters get unfriendly outside of its protection. Speaking of unfriendly, don't expect to be overwhelmed with aloha from park personnel. They seem to resent snorkelers here.

❖ **Spencer Beach Park**—A great family beach. Located just south of Kawaihae Harbor, the beach is protected by a long offshore reef and the extensive landfill of the harbor to the north. The beach slope is very gentle and the swimming is usually quite good. Keikis (kids) enjoy the usually calm waters of Spencer. Though the water is a bit cloudy due to its proximity to the harbor, this shouldn't deter you from enjoying the ocean here. If you snorkel, you will probably see miniature underwater volcanoes from small amounts of cold freshwater seeping from the floor. The

Normally placid, Spencer Beach Park is a popular place for families with keikis (kids).

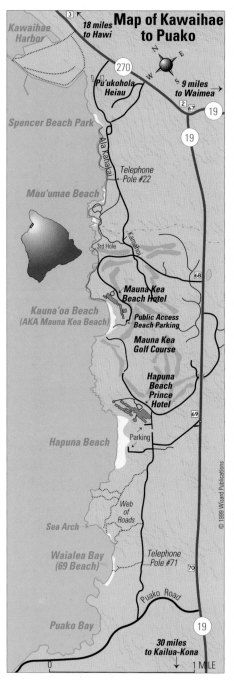

Map of Kawaihae to Puako

Kawaihae Harbor

18 miles to Hawi

Pu'ukohola Heiau

9 miles to Waimea

Spencer Beach Park

Ala Kahakai

Telephone Pole #22

Mau'umae Beach

3rd Hole

Kamahoi

Mauna Kea Beach Hotel

Public Access Beach Parking

Kauna'oa Beach (AKA Mauna Kea Beach)

Mauna Kea Golf Course

Hapuna Beach Prince Hotel

Hapuna Beach

Parking

Sea Arch

Web of Roads

Waialea Bay (69 Beach)

Telephone Pole #71

Puako Road

Puako Bay

30 miles to Kailua-Kona

1 MILE

amenities include several showers, restrooms, a pavilion, lifeguard, picnic tables, barbeques, a lawn area, lots of shade, and basketball/volleyball courts. Camping is permitted by county permit (see Camping). As you approach the park from the access road between the 2 and 3 mile marker on Highway 270, you can go to the right or left side of the park. Whether by design or not, the right (northern) side seems to be used mostly by locals and the left side by visitors. Since it's so popular with locals, expect it to be a little messier than other, more pristine beaches.

Just north of here is a small beach in front of the Pu'ukohola Heiau called **Pelekane Beach.** No swimming or sunbathing is allowed there out of deference to the sacred heiau complex.

The **Ala Kahakai Trail** between **Spencer** and **Hapuna Beach** hugs the shoreline. It crosses hole #3 on the golf course but otherwise is easy to follow and passes some pretty shoreline.

❖ **Mau'umae Beach**—Pretty, secluded, uncrowded during the week and decent swimming when calm. Nice place for a picnic, and you may have it to yourself during the week. Snorkeling is only fair due to slightly cloudy water. Access is through the Mauna Kea Resort entrance, right on Kamahoi, park at pole #22. 10-car maximum is rarely a problem (see map). Less than 5-minute trail walk from your car. No facilities. Usually pronounced MOW-MY. This is one of the most underrated and unknown beaches in this part of the island. Winter usually thins the sand out a bit.

❖ **Mauna Kea Beach (AKA Kauna'oa Beach)**—This is a great beach! Probably the most classically perfect beach in the state. This gorgeous crescent of sand over ¼-mile long offers *very fine swimming* and boogie boarding during calm seas. On the left side of

Luscious Mauna Kea Beach offers some of the best swimming—or frolicking—on the Big Island.

the beach are a bunch of rocks composing a linear reef which offers outstanding snorkeling. Don't venture too far out unless calm (the outer portion of this reef is more surgy and unpredictable). The northern (right) side of the beach also offers interesting snorkeling but is more exposed and should only be snorkeled by strong swimmers. There is a big light there that attracts plankton at night, which in turn attracts large manta rays. This beach and Hapuna are **the two best frolicking beaches on the island,** if not the state. This beach is usually less windy than Hapuna. Full facilities. Only 30 cars allowed in the Mauna Kea Resort parking lot at a time which is sometimes a problem on weekends or holidays so try to arrive before 10 a.m. Located 32 miles north of Kona in the Kohala resort area off the 68 mile marker. See map.

A Real Gem

❖ **Hapuna Beach**—If you close your eyes and picture a perfect beach, there's a good chance you'll see Hapuna in your mind's eye. Half a mile long and 200 feet wide during the summer, beautiful Hapuna is the ultimate frolicking beach. Fine golden white sand slopes gradually into the ocean. Clean, clear water and excellent swimming conditions during calm seas, full facilities, easy access, and gorgeous scenery. The **boogie boarding** here, when the surf's not too high, is exceptional. These are some of the elements that account for the fact that *Condé Nast Traveler* magazine has often voted this beach the best in the entire nation. During the week it usually isn't too crowded, but weekends and holidays bring lots of locals who know a great beach when they see one. Most people who live here bring their guests

A Real Gem

to Hapuna at least once to gloat. The lifeguard is usually stationed near the sign saying that there's no lifeguard on duty. Swimming is not safe during periods of high surf which will kick the living daylights out of you. Also note that the wind sometimes kicks up in the afternoon. We've noticed that the southernmost (left) part of the beach is usually more protected during strong winds. All in all, this is a beach to savor. The only shade *on* the beach is a tree at the southern end. (Though there are shaded pavilions behind the beach.) You know how frenzied dogs can get when they go to the beach? That's how most people act when they come to Hapuna or Mauna Kea Beach.

For the more advanced snorkelers on calm days, the area directly south of the sand beach offers superb snorkeling, and it's usually empty during the week because no one knows about it. The waters are usually teeming with fish, and coral is abundant. The sea is unprotected here, so don't do it if it isn't calm or you'll get beaten up. Check for currents. If it starts to get rough, get out. We often start at the southern end of the beach and snorkel along the rocky coastline all the way to a little black gravel cove half a mile down the coast near a sea arch. Then we walk back along the shore in our reef shoes via a poor trail or use the dirt road (don't do it bare-footed). Be careful of the wicked kiawe thorns—they can penetrate nearly any shoe and probably most bullet-proof vests. If you have some energy left, keep snorkeling past the little gravel cove to Waialea (69) Beach. The area just past the cove is absolutely heavenly.

Hapuna is located 30 miles north of Kailua-Kona in the northern part of the Kohala mega-resort area near the 69 mile marker off Highway 19. The only ding is that the state has historically done a terrible job of maintaining the facilities. Sometimes the restrooms look like they're from the third world.

❖ **Waialea (Beach 69)**—*Sigh!* Just another kickin' Kohala beach. This

A Real Gem

beach slopes gently into the water, giving it nice swimming conditions most of the year when the sea is calm. Not as long or as well known as Hapuna or Mauna Kea, this beach is popular with *akamai* (savvy) residents who sometimes bring their families for a day at the beach on weekends. To the north (right) of the main beach is a secluded little cove, which people sometimes claim for the day. The snorkeling around the northern part of the beach can be excellent. There's a sea arch at the northern tip, but refrain from walking on it; it looks like it's getting ready to go. Located 30 miles north of Kona near the Kohala resort area off Puako Road. (See bottom of map on page 140.) Walk a couple minutes toward the houses on the short, junky road near telephone #71 (it used to be pole #69—hence the name). Veer to left and the trail/road ends at the shoreline parallel to a wooden wall. No facilities, just a lazy day in paradise.

❖ **Puako**—Great snorkeling and SCUBA (see page 199 for directions to best spots, and photo of the reef), but the swimming is marginal. The reef at Puako is *very* extensive. The somewhat cloudy water on entry usually gives way to very clear water at the reef's edge. You stand an excellent chance of sharing the water with multiple turtles. (Oh yeah, what's a multiple turtle?) The tops of the reefs are not the most interesting part (and can subject you to the prospect of being raked over them). The best fish and scenic action are at the outer edges of the reef. Check for currents and give the ocean respect. People occasionally bring their dogs to this beach (which end up chasing the catfish, no doubt). Wind often creates chop on the water here, but that doesn't usually affect the underwater experience much. There are 6 legal public accesses along the bay from the boat launch. Some are *conveniently* unmarked. A check of the county tax map and a site check shows us that they are by telephone poles #106, 110/111, 115, 120, 127/128 & 137, plus the dirt road at 143.

❖ **Mauna Lani**—The Mauna Lani Bay Hotel and the Orchid at Mauna Lani both have small, manmade (or enhanced) beaches. The Mauna Lani Bay Hotel beach to the south is usually *very* protected. Access is via the public parking lot shown on the map on page 53. You'll have to walk for about 15 minutes, but the trip through the fishpond area is worth it.

❖ **Honoka'ope Beach**—This small beach is located between the Hilton Waikoloa and the Mauna Lani. It's almost never visited and is virtually unknown. That's because it is only reachable via the ancient Ala Kahakai shoreline lava trail and takes 30–60 minutes to reach. (See map on page 53.) But this trail segment, which starts near the Mauna Lani fishponds and seemingly ends here, goes through some fabulous lava cliff scenery, which, when surf's up, features waves exploding onto the twisted, gnarled lava fragments in the ocean. At the beach the swimming and snorkeling are good if it's calm, ugly if it's rough. There's an unmaintained outhouse and picnic tables, as well as plenty of shade.

The best bonus is an outstanding cool, clear freshwater pool nearby to wash the salt off. It's ironic that a beach situated between two large resort areas could be so unknown to both locals and visitors. County officials have been planning to make this a park with an access road for years, but it never happens. Until it does, you'll almost certainly have it to yourself.

❖ **'Anaeho'omalu Bay**—Another nice Kohala beach. (Even those born and raised here usually call it **A** Bay.) This long, curving salt-and-pepper sand beach is popular with both locals and visitors. The swimming is best in the sandy center, whereas the snorkeling is best on the right side past the sandy area. The water is not as clear as it used to be, but acceptable. Protected by an offshore reef, this bay is usually safe except during very high surf. Windsurfing is popular here.

A Real Gem

'Anaeho'omalu is well known throughout the islands for its two large fishponds. These exceptionally picturesque and placid pools were used by ancient Hawaiians for raising mullet. Passing royalty were the beneficiaries of these ponds—commoners weren't allowed to partake. The ponds are ringed by palm trees, making sunset photos from behind the trees a sure-fire winner.

There's a pleasant paved path on the mauka side of the fishpond that's worth a stroll. Numerous informational plaques along the way give information about the fishponds and the area in general. Toward the center of the path are the remains of an ancient dwelling, probably a combination of sleeping and eating quarters as well as a shrine. The pond itself contains brackish water; fresh water flows from a natural spring and mixes with ocean tide water. The ancient Hawaiians covered the opening to the fishpond with a grate, which allowed small fry to enter from the ocean. Once inside, they gorged themselves on algae and small shrimp and became too fat to get back through the grate, at which time they were sitting ducks (so to speak) for the Hawaiian pond keepers.

On the right (northern) side of the beach is a hut that rents snorkel gear, kayaks, boogie boards, windsurfers, etc. (at confiscatory rates). They also have guided snorkel and SCUBA tours.

There's a marvelous shoreline trail north between the two Waikoloa hotels that leads through sand, lava, and large amounts of brilliant white coral rubble. All along the trail you'll find various tide-pools tucked against the shoreline. Turtles tend to hang out at one particular tide-pool just a few feet from shore. At the north end of this trail is the Hilton Waikoloa. What a way to see this place for the first time! A sunset stroll along this path is unforgettable. Footwear is a must. There is an alternative place to park along this stretch—see map on page 53.

A few minutes walk south of A Bay on a narrow ribbon of sand leads to **Kapalaoa Beach**, a series of sand pockets. There is shade and a pleasant cove for snorkeling at the last pocket. If the surf's not high, the cove is amazingly protected. The short walk to this beach goes by numerous Hawaiian petroglyphs, some ancient and some modern. The more ambitious will want to take the lava trail farther south for about half an hour until you reach a lone palm tree in the lava, a hundred feet or so from the shore. Here, you are rewarded with an outstanding spring-fed brackish pool with lots of charm. It is very deep in

spots and is great for dipping after a hike. You will rarely see anybody else here as it is only accessible by foot and is a favorite stopping place of ours. The lava trails in this area offer good hiking, but they can get a bit hot in the middle of the day. The trail leads mostly along the shoreline for miles, all the way to Ke-awa-iki below.

❖ **Ke-awa-iki Beach**—This black sand and gravel lined bay is never crowded due to the access, half of which you walk on a lava road, the other is on a rougher a'a trail off to the right of the fence. Few on the island even know it's there. (It takes about 15 minutes to walk to.) The water off the left (south) is clear and offers good snorkeling when calm, but be wary of currents. There's also some shade there (and sometimes a swing from one of the trees). The best snorkeling is usually in the center of the bay. If you keep walking past the southern edge of the bay, there are lots of tide-pools to explore on older smooth pahoehoe lava shelf at low tide. (This is

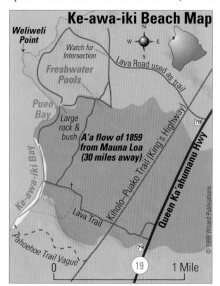

Ke-awa-iki Beach Map

a good place to be wearing reef shoes.) Past that are numerous salt deposits from evaporated seawater. These deposits attract goats from the dry scrub inland who warily come and lick the salt off the rocks. Past the right (northern) side of Ke-awa-iki Bay is **Pueo Bay,** lined with black pebbles and semi-protected with nice swimming on calm days. There are off-shore freshwater springs here, causing areas of perturbations in the water, visible as waves of underwater distortion. You will almost certainly have this bay to yourself. No shade here because it's backed by an a'a field. If you feel like an extended stroll, you can walk past Weliweli Point and take a lava road inland to circle back to the highway. Mauka of Pueo Bay are some beautiful golden pools, described under HIKING on page 184 and shown on page 55.

Both of these beaches were created in 1859 when a'a from Mauna Loa drooled down the mountain and exploded when it hit the ocean, creating black sand. The eruption only covered half the bay and some white sand is still sprinkled at the southern end because there hasn't been enough time to evenly distribute the newer black sand. The entire area has a desolate but pretty character to it and is one of the least known beaches on the west side of the island. The only pockmark is the Brown Estate lining the center part of the beach with its barbed wire fence and its unwelcome feeling. Francis I'i Brown was an influential and beloved Hawaiian businessman earlier this century and in turning his estate into a historical landmark, they seem to have taken away all of its charm. They have tours of it for a few hours the third Tuesday of every month. (Gee, *that's* convenient!) Located 20 miles north of Kailua-Kona just after the 79 mile marker.

❖ **Kiholo Bay**—This beach is unique and has a few surprises. Access is unusual and requires an explanation, perhaps a hike. See HIKING on page 182. It's worth it.

A Real Gem

❖ **Ka'upulehu Beach (Kona Village)**—Most of this long sand beach is fronted by a lava bench making the swimming poor, but there is a pocket of sand in front of the Kona Village that allows easier access to the water. You can access this beach either from the Four Seasons, which is closer to the water from your car, or the Kona Village. (Kona Village guards at the guard shack imply that you can't go through. Just say these magic words— *public access.* They *have* to admit you, but expect dirty looks.) Public access is in yellow on the map on the next page.

❖ **Kuki'o Beach**—Near the Four Seasons Resort between Kona and the Kohala Resort area, this is yet another pretty Kohala beach. This long, fringing crescent of white sand is backed in parts by palm, ironwood, and kiawe trees offering inviting shade. At the southern end of the bay is a small, but very protected sandy cove. The swimming in the bay itself is only fair during calm seas, and the snorkeling offers somewhat murky water. There is public access from the resort area (see map on next page). While Kuki'o Bay might sound like a pretty name, in Hawaiian it means to *stand and defecate* (traditional definition) or *settled dregs* (modern definition). *That* doesn't look real good on the back of a postcard. The reason behind the *lovely* name has been lost to the generations, but it's probably safe to say that whoever named it was having a bad hair day.

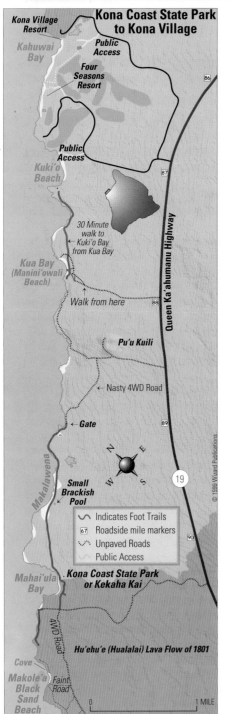

Kona Coast State Park to Kona Village

Kona Village Resort
Kahuwai Bay
Public Access
Four Seasons Resort
86
Public Access
Kuki'o Beach
87
30 Minute walk to Kuki'o Bay from Kua Bay
Kua Bay (Manini'owali) Beach)
Walk from here
88
Pu'u Kuili
Queen Ka'ahumanu Highway
Nasty 4WD Road
Gate
89
Makalawena
Small Brackish Pool
19
Indicates Foot Trails
67 Roadside mile markers
Unpaved Roads
Public Access
90
Mahai'ula Bay
Kona Coast State Park or Kekaha Kai
4WD Road
Hu'ehu'e (Hualalai) Lava Flow of 1801
Cove
Makole'a Black Sand Beach
Faint Road
0   1 MILE
Tree
© 1999 Wizard Publications

❖ **Kua Bay**—This is one of our favorite beaches. (Also called **Manini'owali**.) Off the

A Real Gem

beaten path, beautiful fine white sand, clear, clean water, gentle slope, and a picturesque setting. When the ocean is calm, the swimming is fabulous. The snorkeling off to the right (north) is interesting not for its coral, but for the underwater relief. **Boogie boarding** is excellent during moderate surf, but the waves can be strong and deserve respect. There is sand here most of the time, but it is most abundant during the summer months. During the winter, high surf sometimes shifts the sand offshore for a time, leaving the area rocky and undesirable. Many residents consider this the best swimming beach near Kona when calm, and on weekends they sometimes make their presence known. But during the week, it's blissfully uncrowded. So what's the catch? Well, if you don't have a JEEP, you'll have to walk 10–20 minutes to it. With a JEEP it's a 5–10 minute walk. People are always filling in holes with gravel here, but it would take a lot of gumption to drive to the gate in a regular rental car. This description may change as they have been contemplating fixing the road. From Highway 19 (just north of the 88 mile mark) the dirt road makes its way for 1 mile to the beach. At about 5/10 miles, you'll *probably* have to park and walk the rest. JEEPs can go farther. (See map.) But this is a beach that's worth it. Note that the waves here have a lot of power, so if the surf's up, don't go in. No shade here. One caveat: Behind the northern end of the beach are a couple of palm trees adjacent to a freshwater spring. The water looks like a nice place to splash the saltwater off. *Don't!* What looks like inviting sand on the bottom is actually quicksand created from the rotting palm fronds of countless generations of

Isolated and unknown, Makalawena is one of the finest beaches on the island. Access requires a 15–20 minute walk or a JEEP.

palm trees. If you jump in, you will find yourself up to your chest in the most putrid, disgusting rot you ever saw or smelled and will require help getting out while you revile from the stench and pull snails off you. If this warning sounds particularly detailed...let's just say we're still picking scum out of our gear.

❖ **Makalawena**—To many, this is the choicest beach on the island...if you don't mind walking to it. In fact, Maka-lawena is as idyllic a beach as you will find anywhere in the islands. Gobs of

A Real Gem

superfine, clean white sand, plentiful shade, and no crowds. The setting is utterly beautiful. Consisting of a number of coves and rocky points united by a long, curving stretch of beach, the best swimming is in the largest inlet backed by high sand dunes. **Boogie boarding** can

be great here. There's a freshwater pond (see map on facing page) where we like to rinse off the saltwater before walking back. A herd of wild goats visits this area often so keep an eye out for them.

Fronted by private (Bishop Estate) land, you get there over the trail from Kona Coast State Park (about a 20-minute walk). It's a lava trail through an a'a field and the footing is a little annoying. As you walk through this trail, try to imagine how ridiculously difficult it would be to walk through the field itself without the trail. Then imagine doing it *barefoot,* as the ancient Hawaiians did. As you approach Makalawena from the Kona Coast side, the a'a, trail suddenly gives way to sand dunes. But if you climb the dunes, rather than finding ocean you find more a'a indicating that this had been shoreline until a lava flow of a'a came along and added more real estate, cutting off the dunes from the sea.

If you have a JEEP (and your fillings are

tight), you can take the nasty road from the highway between the 88 and 89 mile marker. It'll take you just north of the beach before a gate forces you to walk like the rest of us dogs.

❖ **Kona Coast (Kekaha Kai) State Park (or Mahai'ula/Ka'elehuluhulu Beaches)**—This beach is usually uncrowded and fairly easy to get to. It

A Real Gem

was renamed Kekaha Kai but still referred to by the old name. The beach is outside of Kona town and pretty. **Mahai'ula** Beach (which you access from the first parking area) offers good swimming and interesting strolling. Just around the southern corner is a pocket of sand called **Ka'elehuluhulu Beach** (park at the end of the lava road), not as good as the northern beach. The entire area was once owned by a prominent part-Hawaiian family called the Magoons. They sold the land to a Japanese investor who had visions of a resort. When the state refused permission, the investor sold it to the state which turned it into a park. The abandoned Magoon house is still (as of this writing) located at the northern end of Mahai'ula Beach. This area abounds with freshwater springs that bubble to the surface occasionally forming ponds. At the farthest northern part of the beach near some palm trees and a rock wall, you may see strange indentations in the sand at low tide. Here, fresh water gurgles right out of the sand and into the ocean. The snorkeling is only fair as the water can be a bit cloudy, especially during Spring. This is a good beach to get away from it all yet still have fairly easy access. There's plenty of shade at the backshore. Access is via a bumpy, but driveable

semi–paved 1½-mile road halfway between the 90 and 91 mile markers on Queen Ka'ahumanu Highway north of Kailua-Kona. (They were contemplating paving it at press time.) The only negative is the occasional plane overhead as it lands at Kona Airport. Facilities include picnic tables and portable toilets. Bring your own water. From where you park your car, it's a 5–10 minute walk to Mahai'ula beach on the right. The gate to the beach is open 9 a.m. to 8 p.m., closed Wednesdays.

Legend states that before 1801 there was a 3-mile long fishpond here. That year an old lady came to the village and asked for fish. The village overseer refused, saying that it *all* belonged to the chief. On her way out she was stopped by one villager who gave her food. After eating, she told the kind stranger to place kapu (forbidden) sticks outside his house. That night lava from Hualalai roared down the mountain to the village, destroying the great fishpond but sparing the man who fed her. The villagers realized that the old woman was the volcano goddess Pele, avenging the selfishness of the chief.

Check out some of the lava on the road leading to this beach (you'll certainly be driving slow enough). There are lots of interesting formations where different flows meet. It has patches of gold/rust colored lava, streaks of blue, red, and other colors indicating the presence of numerous elements and gasses present during cooling.

❖ **Makole'a Beach**—Ask a hundred residents of Kona about a black sand

A Real Gem

beach just north of town named Makole'a Beach, and you'll get a hundred blank stares. Aside from a handful of shoreline fishermen, *nobody* seems to have known about this beach—until now. It even escaped *our* attention in the first edition; we stumbled onto it only recently. Created during the 1801 lava flow of Hualalai, this small pocket of jet black sand is the only black sand beach on this part of the island.

To get there you have two options. After driving to Kona Coast State Park (see previous page), those with 4WD can take a left at the first parking lot and take the lava road heading south. Between ⁶⁄₁₀ & ⁷⁄₁₀ mile is a faint car path marked by some coral that leads 500 feet over lava to the sea. (Though driveable, you can walk this last part if the lava there dissuades you.) The other way is to park at the beach at Kona Coast State Park and walk along the shoreline for 15–20 minutes. At one point the sandy trail is interrupted. Best to walk on the smooth pahoehoe lava behind the beach boulders for this part. Just before the black sand beach is a small cove protected at low to mid tide during calm seas. It's a perfect place to take a quick dip. At the black sand beach the snorkeling and SCUBA diving are great. Though the visibility is only fair (it's better when you get away from the beach), there is a beautiful field of coral to the north (right) of the beach and to the south farther out. Enter at the sandy part in the center, and beware of unchecked waves. If you walked here, consider cutting across the lava field on your return for different scenery.

This beach, while certainly not on par with Mauna Kea or Kua Bay, deserves the GEM rating because it's the *only real black sand beach* anywhere near Kona, it's not overly difficult to access, and you are likely to have it all to yourself on weekdays. (Some fishermen use it on weekends and sometimes leave their beer bottles.) It's that rare treat—an undiscovered black sand beach.

❖ **Wawaloli Beach**—This is our favorite tide-pool area on the west side of the island (shown on next page). The instantly accessible sand beach is cut off from the ocean by a large tide-pool that offers warm swimming when the surf is too high elsewhere. There are restrooms and showers here, making it popular with local families who bring their keikis (kids) to play in the mostly protected area. The largest pool (mostly sand-lined) is best near high tide if the surf's down, or best at low tide if the surf's up. The other, less protected tide-pool is better at low tide. In late afternoon you might want to pick up a pizza on your way out, bring the kids, if you have 'em, and watch the sunset. Take the road to the Natural Energy Lab (near the 94 mile marker on the main highway north of Kailua-Kona) and park just as it veers to the right. Some equipment to the south is an eyesore, but try to ignore it, and airplanes sometimes shatter the quiet. Near here is a 4WD road that leads a mile south to **Pine Trees**, one of the island's premier surf spots. (So named because of the mangrove in a brackish pool. Surfer dudes thought they were pine trees.) The road is fairly poor, and there may be lots of unfriendly illegal long-term campers to deal with there.

A Real Gem

❖ **Honokohau/Kaloko Fishpond**—Honokohau is an area rich in archaeological treasures. This part of the coast was inhabited for centuries and is filled with relics. Consequently, it was made a national park in 1978 in an effort to

The quiet tide-pools at the National Energy Lab are an excellent place to go when the surf's pounding.

preserve what remains. At first it might seem surprising that people thrived here. Barren and rocky with particularly harsh aʻa fields in many areas, the draw here was the freshwater springs. The Hawaiians took advantage of the water to create large fishponds to raise mullet and other fish.

Located just south of the airport, you can access the park from the park entrance near the 97 mile marker on Highway 19 just north of Kailua-Kona. A trail leads to Kaloko Fishpond. As of this writing the Park Service closes it every day at 3:30 p.m. You can also access the park from the **Honokohau Harbor,** off the paved road between the 97 and 98 mile markers. From there, a brief walk north will take you to **ʻAiʻopio Beach.** This lovely beach, located *so* close to town, has been forgotten by most Kona residents due to a nasty dispute, now settled, that intimidated residents from even *walking* there. There are scads of turtles

munching on grasses in the cloudy cove water. This was an ocean fish trap in ancient days, where fish entered at high tide and were easily captured. A protected area here is perfect for keikis (kids). An impressive heiau called Hale o Mono rests at the south end. Park at the north end of the harbor (past the restaurant) and take the trail for minute or two. Turn toward the ocean before you reach the restrooms. This is a nice beach for relaxing. Farther north is **Honokohau Beach.** You may read elsewhere that this is a nude beach, but it is no longer permitted and they now cite violators. This long stretch of salt-and-pepper sand offers reasonable swimming at the center. One nearby highlight is known as **Queen's Bath.** (Even locals get confused by Queen's Bath. There are several of these scattered throughout the islands. Essentially, any place that was considered an outstanding place to bathe was called Queen's Bath.) This

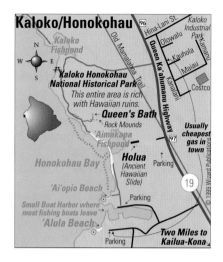

Kaloko/Honokohau

N W E S

Kaloko Fishpond

Kaloko Industrial Park

Old Mamalahoa Trail

Hina-Lani St.

Olowalu

Kauhola

Maiau

Kaloko

Kauhola

Maiau

Queen Ka'ahumanu Highway

Costco

Kaloko Honokohau National Historical Park
This entire area is rich with Hawaiian ruins.

Queen's Bath
Rock Mounds
'Aimakapa Fishpond

Honokohau Bay

Holua
(Ancient Hawaiian Slide)

Parking

96

97

19

Usually cheapest gas in town

© 1999 Wizard Publications

'Ai'opio Beach

Parking

Small Boat Harbor where most fishing boats leave

'Alula Beach

Parking

Two Miles to Kailua-Kona

15-by-20 foot natural lava pool of brackish water was lovingly enhanced by the Hawaiians to make it a fine place to congregate and splash in relatively fresh (and very cool) water. They lined the pool, located in the middle of a harsh a'a field, with smoother stones, built areas to sit, and generally made it a pleasant place to visit. These days, it is sporadically visited by hikers and beach-goers from the nearby beach. Consequently, though deserted most of the time, there may be a person or two there who still resist the nudist ban and frolic in the water in their altogether. To get there from Honokohau beach, take the shoreline trail north through the woods for a hundred yards or so until you get to a rock wall. Look mauka (toward the mountain) and you will see numerous large piles of rocks. These are also ancient in origin—the largest is 10 feet high and 15 feet thick—and are part of 12 rock piles placed in a rectangle around the Queen's Bath, possibly used for lookouts. Go toward, then between, the two largest mounds. The pool is about 100 feet north of the largest mound. Enjoy!

At the south end of the Honokohau Harbor is **'Alula Beach,** a small, pleasant crescent of sand which is fairly protected during calm seas.

❖ **Old Kona Airport Park**—This beach park is located at (do I *really* need to say it?) the Old Kona Airport, closed in 1970 because it was unable to accommodate larger aircraft. You park anywhere on the runway (you may taxi as long as you like) and enjoy the patchy beach and full facilities. On the south end are ball fields where Little League parents battle for supremacy. The long beach is an easy one to access, and the sunsets from here are nice. Though you won't be overwhelmed by an abundance of thick sand, it's rarely crowded during the week. Located ½ mile (15–20 minutes walk along the lava coastline) north

is the finer **Pawai Bay.** The **snorkeling** in Pawai Bay is very exciting, especially for the experienced snorkeler.

A Real Gem There's a little of everything with crystal clear water, lots of life, caverns, arches, dropoffs, small caves, and some pinnacles along the shoreline. Here you may see the elusive and extraordinary frog fish (an angler fish) on the coral, and Spanish dancers (a contorting nudibranch). During tricky surge, novices should stay away from the more interesting shore. Boats such as Body Glove bring groups. If you walk here, you will find the cove in the center of the bay is the best way to enter. Be careful of the channel that leads out to the bay, it can be surgy. The shady backshore of Pawai Bay has plush camping facilities, but it belongs to the Queen Lili'uokalani Trust, used for Hawaiian children. The walk to Pawai Bay from the Old Airport is best

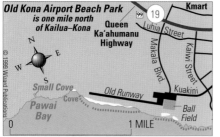

Old Kona Airport Beach Park is one mile north of Kailua–Kona

© 1999 Wizard Publications

Kmart

Queen Ka'ahumanu Highway

Makala Blvd.

Luhia Street

Kaiwi Street

Kuakini

Small Cove

Pawai Bay

Cove

Old Runway

Ball Field

0   1 MILE

experienced at low tide. Lots of pukas (holes) in the lava are exposed, creating fissures where water often surges and air escapes in loud gasping sounds. This lava fractures easily, which is why the underwater relief along here is so good.

❖ **Kailua Bay**—Located in the heart of Downtown Kailua-Kona. (See map on page 59.) Usually bays or pier areas have nasty water. This one is surprisingly clean due to the daily flushing action of the sea. There's a surprising number of fish in Kailua Bay. We've seen super-schools numbering in the many thousands off Hulihe'e Palace. On calm days we like to snorkel from the pier to the sand pocket across from Kona Islander Inn or the boulder beach across from Lulu's. If you are looking for *exceptionally* calm water and a sandy beach, the very small **Kamakahonu Beach** to the right of the Kailua Pier (in front of the King Kamehameha Hotel) is perhaps the gentlest and safest water on the island (with the *possible* exception of your hotel bathtub). Children love frolicking in the water here, though freshwater springs sometimes make it cold. This is where King Kamehameha choose to spend the last years of his extraordinary life, so you gotta figure it has something going for it. His personal 'Ahu'ena Heiau is right in front of you. The sand at the beach doesn't extend very far into the water, but it is shallow the whole way. If you swim out

from the beach you'll notice a private ocean entrance to the right. It leads to a house owned by billionaire Paul Allen, the less famous co-founder of Microsoft. He bought this gloriously located house a few years ago for (gulp) $11 million. (Don't worry, that's probably a mere rounding error in his checkbook.)

There is a concessionaire at Kamakahonu renting various beach accouterments at the usual confiscatory prices—but it's convenient. Large schools of fish sometimes congregate on the other side of the heiau. It's about 800 feet from the public parking to the beach, so you may want to drop off your stuff (and a person) at the pier first.

To the left (south) of the pier is another pocket of sand. (They sometimes do SCUBA intros there.) It's a bit less protected but still relatively calm. Boogie boarders like to ride the normally small but long lasting swells. The grueling Ironman Triathlon (see page 58) starts here. They swim 2⁴⁄₁₀ before returning to start their 112-mile bike ride and 26-mile marathon run—*all in the same day!* (Makes you sore just thinking about it, huh?) If it's rained recently, snorkelers should look for little calderas of what looks like boiling sand, like a mini volcano. It's caused by small amounts of cold fresh water bubbling to the surface.

❖ **Pahoehoe Beach Park**—Though there's no sand here to speak of, this is a nice place to have a picnic and enjoy the surf and sunset from the benches. We've never seen it crowded. Backed by pretty trees and a lawn, there is a small gravel entrance to the water, but swimmers are discouraged from entering unless equipped with snorkeling gear. Even then, advanced snorkelers only need apply. That's because there are numerous holes, arches and pockets on the lava shelf offshore, making exploration very exciting. But surf can sometimes rake you over, and even under the reef, making it *too* exciting. Lots of fish here as well. Located north of the 4 mile mark on Alii Drive in Kailua (just north of White Sands Beach).

❖ **White Sands Beach Park**—Also known as **Magic Sands, Disappearing Sands,** and **La'aloa Bay Beach.** Located just north of the 4 mile mark on Alii Drive in Kailua, this small beach has particularly nomadic sand that retreats at the first sign of a surf assault, settling in a repository just offshore. Once the surf subsides, the sand slowly drifts back onto the shoreline until the next high surf. This occasional flushing of the sand tends to keep it clean and white. Those who live here can tell you of countless instances where the entire beach washes away in less than a day. Much of the time there is a shallow sandbar just offshore making the swimming and boogie boarding quite good. (The best wave break is on the left [south] side of the beach.) Watch for undertow. When the sand's thick, the frolicking is good. (But reef shoes are recommended in case you step on a rock.) When there's no sand or it's in the process of disappearing (i.e., when the surf's high), there is a strong rip current making water activities hazardous. During weekends and summer months, this beach can become crowded. Lifeguard and facilities are here along with some shade trees. On calm days, the snorkeler will want to check out the area to the right (north), in front of Jameson's Restaurant. Especially large schools of fish sometimes hang out there. (Guess they don't know that Jameson's serves seafood.) We've also seen more moray eels here in front of the restaurant than at any other place on

the island. This beach was wiped clean during a storm in 1992, and its sand level hasn't returned to its postcard state since.

Just south of here right at the 4 mile mark is a small cove where the SCUBA diving is excellent, offering short, easy access and good underwater relief and caves. The snorkeling is not bad either. Just offshore from this location we often see a pod of dolphins patrolling the waters. Why they hang out there we don't know, but whatever the reason, keep an eye out for them.

❖ **Kahalu'u Beach Park**—This is one of the nicer snorkeling spots on the Big Island. It is teaming with fish and offers more variety of sea life than any other easily accessible spot in Kona. Among the many fish present are wrasses, parrotfishes, convict tang, porcupinefish, needlefish, and puffers as well as the occasional lobster, eel, and

A Real Gem

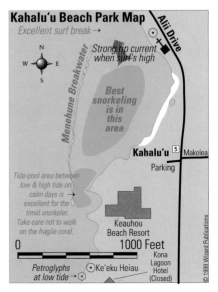

Kahalu'u Beach Park Map

Excellent surf break →

N W E S

Menehune Breakwater

Strong rip current when surf's high

Best snorkeling is in this area

Kahalu'u [5] Makolea

Parking

Tide-pool area between low & high tide on calm days → excellent for the timid snorkeler. Take care not to walk on the fragile coral.

Keauhou Beach Resort

0   1000 Feet

Kona Lagoon Hotel (Closed)

Petroglyphs at low tide → • Ke'eku Heiau •

Alii Drive

© 1999 Wizard Publications

Good reef protected by a boulder breakwater have made Kahalu'u the most popular snorkel site in Kona.

octopus. Outside the reef you may occasionally see deep sea life such as tuna, marlin, and dolphin jumping about. When you first enter the water you might think, "What's all the hubbub about?" Well…it's about 100 feet offshore. The perimeter of this small, sheltered bay has numerous freshwater springs, making the nearshore water cold and cloudy. But once you swim out toward the middle, it gets warmer and clearer, and life is abundant. One reason is the Menehune breakwater offshore. Built in ancient times, it has been partially disassembled by countless waves, creating an excellent fish environment. There's usually a truck at the beach where you can rent snorkel gear, boogie boards and take surfing lessons, and there is a full range of facilities. A family of turtles calls Kahalu'u home, and they usually won't dart away from you if you don't harass them. (We've noticed that near high tide, they often work the grasses that are otherwise exposed on the left/south-

ern side of the bay.) Your odds of swimming with turtles are probably greater here than anywhere else on the island, with the possible exception of Punalu'u Beach. The best way to keep the turtle from fleeing is to act disinterested—like you don't give a flying fish. (*Ooo*, sorry.) If you scope him out, he'll run off. If you pretend to eat the same grasses he eats, you aren't a threat. The more intrepid might venture around the breakwater on very calm days where life is also abundant. There, just before sunset, you may see manta rays commuting to dinner at the Kona Surf. Exceptionally large mixed schools of fish sometimes congregate just outside the reef, but you expose yourself the possibility of being strained through the reef—better stay inside unless it is real calm or you are real confident.

Crowds accumulate at Kahalu'u on holidays and weekends, but weekdays are *usually* not too bad. During periods of high surf, large waves can wash over the reef and form a rip current flowing out the reef opening at the north end of the bay, making it unsafe.

Though we usually recommend against feeding fish since it upsets the balance, the fish here are already junkies. Read the snorkel section for tips.

To the left is a **tide-pool** in front of the Keauhou Beach Resort. The water there is sometimes as warm as bathwater as it gets heated by the sun. Cruise around in the shallows and look for eels, which like to be fed by people at the railings of the hotel.

Eight hundred feet to the left (south) of Kahaluʻu is **Makoleʻa Beach** in front of the abandoned Kona Lagoon Hotel. (Not to be confused with the beach described on page 148 with the same name.) There are several heiaus along this beach, mostly in disrepair, like the eyesore hotel behind you. The salt-and-pepper sand and gravel beach is usually empty and has a lonely, forgotten feel. The swimming is poor since you are facing large tide-pools. Look for the petroglyphs mentioned on page 62.

❖ **Napoʻopoʻo Beach**—We only mention this here because lazy guidebook writers rave about the splendid beach at the south end of Kealakekua. *It's gone!* It disappeared when Hurricane ʻIniki sideswiped the island in 1992 and the surf wiped the beach clean, depositing boulders there. You'll find little more than a small patch of sand. This beach will probably never return to its former glory—part of the ever changing nature of the Big Island. Across the bay is the Captain Cook Monument, described on page 67. Slightly south is **Manini Beach** (shown on map on page 65). Coral rubble sprinkled with aʻa lava, and poor swimming make this another must-miss beach.

❖ **Keʻei**—Between Kealakekua and Honaunau (see map on page 65), this pretty but small stretch of sand is backed by numerous coconut trees. Though picturesque, poor swimming and difficult parking mean that it is used almost solely by the small, adjacent community and by visiting SCUBA divers. This area seems to have been a magnet for historical events. Local legend (bolstered by old Spanish records) states that foreigners washed ashore here during the 1520s. Several big battles took place nearby, including the one where Kamehameha becomes king. (See page 69.)

❖ **Puʻuhonua o Honaunau**—This is a popular place to visit for reasons other than its water. It was the place of refuge in ancient times. See detailed description on page 69. For the ocean lovers, the snorkeling and SCUBA just north of the boat launch are incredible, perhaps as good as the more difficult-to-reach Captain Cook Monument at Kealakekua Bay, making it some of the best in the state when conditions are good. There are also picnic tables near

A Real Gem

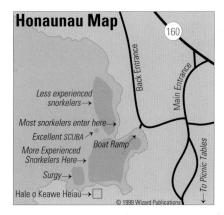

Honaunau Map

160

Back Entrance

Main Entrance

Less experienced snorkelers →

Most snorkelers enter here →

Excellent SCUBA ↗

More Experienced Snorkelers Here →

Boat Ramp

Surgy →

Hale o Keawe Heiau →

← To Picnic Tables

© 1999 Wizard Publications

the shoreline at the southern half of the park that make for absolutely splendid sunset picnics. We've made good use of the BBQs there and can recommend them highly. There's also a lava tube to jump out of—again, see full description on page 69.

❖ **Ho'okena Beach Park**—South of Kona between the 101 and 102 mile marker is a paved road leading 2³⁄₁₀ miles to Ho'okena Beach Park. This pocket of fine salt-and-pepper sand is popular with local families on weekends, but mostly empty on weekdays. Tourists are not common because the beach is not well known and is off the beaten path, though access by car is a snap. Keikis (kids) ride the waves on calm days and splash about in a few of the tide-pools adjacent to the sand beach. (Decent snorkeling is to the left of the beach.) Once used as a boat landing in the days when steamships were king, the beach offers shade and facilities.

❖ **Pebble Beach**—Located at the end of a *very* steep road at the bottom of Kona Paradise (off Highway 11 between the 96 and 97 mile markers 20 miles south of Kona), this is one of the most violent beaches we know of. Even when calm it will kick your 'okole. We've seen fish tossed out of the water on calm days. *(Seriously!)* The "beach" is actually countless large waterworn pebbles, which make a great sound when the surf's up.

❖ **Miloli'i Beach Park**—Located 30 miles south of Kailua-Kona, this is considered a very local beach, meaning that on weekends it's best to leave it to them. There is a very tight local community here, and, though Hawai'i is as friendly a place as you will find, you may get a little stink eye if you visit during "their time"—like crashing someone's family barbeque. This community beach sports a thatched pavilion used by local bands

Honomalino Beach on a crowded day.

playing outstanding Hawaiian music on weekends and holidays. There's not much sand, but the the surfing is good and the facilities are well developed.

Take the winding one-lane paved road just south of the 89 mile marker. Drive slowly at the end of the road and watch for local kids.

❖ **Honomalino Bay**—Ask most people who live here where Honomalino is, and they'll probably tell you it's on Maui. This lovely black-and-white sand beach is not well **A Real Gem** known. It's 100 yards or so long, backed by scads of coconut trees, decent swimming when calm (which is often), usually deserted, and a 20-minute walk from your car. Though one of the larger *south* Kona beaches, it has eroded considerably during this century (as black sand beaches naturally tend to do—see explanation on page 159), and will probably be mostly a memory a hundred years or so from now. To get there, start at Miloli'i Beach Park (see previous page). Go to the end of the road and take the trail heading south. There were some signs there last time saying it was private—it's *not*. 3–4 minutes into it after some tide-pools and a palm backed spit of sand, reacquire the trail at the back part of the sand and continue south for 15 minutes. The snorkeling on the right side of the bay is interesting when calm in the cluster of rocks. There is a small cave there where a 6' white tipped reef shark (with a fishing leader in his mouth) often rests. Don't worry, he's not a man eater—yet. If you plunge your hand into the sand at the water's edge at the south end of the beach the sand's cold. That's freshwater percolating into the sand from below.

❖ **Road to the Sea**—This is one of Ka'u district's best kept secrets. In BASICS we mentioned that having a JEEP can come in handy. Here's a perfect example **A Real Gem** why. First, if you don't have a JEEP, you *may* make it. It depends on the level of cruelty you normally inflict on rental cars. The first of two beaches is at the end of a 6-mile long dirt road with only a 10-foot stretch in the middle that might cause a problem for a *regular* car. But remember, you're far from Kona. If you get stuck, the first thing the tow truck driver will ask is, "Do you own your own home?" A JEEP will do nicely and is necessary to get to the second, better beach. Incidentally, misleading signs notwithstanding, you *are* permitted on the road down here.

Anyway, these two beautiful black-and-green sand beaches are nearly always deserted, especially during the week. The first beach is at the end of the road. Swimming *during calm seas* is fair and the beach is inviting; enter it from the left (south) side. Harmless plankton-eating whale sharks are often seen in the area. To the right of the end of the road is a *deep* tide-pool—7 to 9 feet in spots.

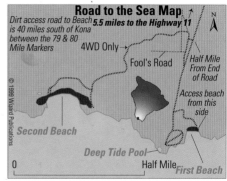

Road to the Sea Map

Dirt access road to Beach is 40 miles south of Kona between the 79 & 80 Mile Markers

5.5 miles to the Highway 11

N

4WD Only

Fool's Road

Half Mile From End of Road

© 1999 Wizard Publications

Access beach from this side

Second Beach

Deep Tide Pool

0   Half Mile

First Beach

It makes a *great* wading pool, and there's even some coral in it—unusual for a tide-pool.

The second beach is reached via a 1-mile long *rough* but driveable JEEP road ⁵⁄₁₀ mile back up from the *very* end of the road. It doglegs right, so don't take the first Fool's Road. The road leads to a much longer and finer black-and-green sand beach. (See Green Sand Beach below for explanation of green sand.) To the right are some palm trees, which means a fresh water pool. In this case it's saltier than most, but is great for dipping. There is some shade at the back part of the beach. Stay close to shore; the water can get tricky further out. (See photo on page 24)

This is a great beach to get away from it all, and you can see people coming if you and your honey are smooching.

The entire area out here is lifeless, arid, and desolate. It's been utterly assaulted by savage lava flows and on paper isn't worth a hill of beans. Yet despite this (or perhaps because of it), it is alluring. The lava field looks young and raw and the beaches are desirable. If you have a JEEP, it is a recommended trip. Located 40 miles south of Kona, see map on previous page.

❖ **Green Sand (Mahana) Beach**—So

A Real Gem
(Literally!)

you say you've seen white sand beaches. You've seen plenty of golden sand beaches. Maybe you've even seen a black sand beach. But when is the last time you frolicked on a *green* sand beach? This unique beach owes its name and color to a large deposit of a semi-precious gem called olivine liberally mixed with black sand.

After ancient volcanic eruptions created Pu'u o Mahana, a small littoral cone containing thick veins of the stuff, the ocean went to work dismantling it. It has already broken through one side, and when the surf is up, each wave rakes at the back side, revealing more and more olivine. Though most of the gem is in the form of sand particles, people occasionally find large nuggets. (Actually, your best chance of finding a nugget is at the rarely visited adjacent cove on the far side of Green Sand Beach. Access is from the far [northeast] side). See map of South Point on page 77.

Located near South Point, which (this will stun you) is at the southernmost point on the island, access to the beach requires a 2½-mile (each way) walk from Kaulana Boat Launch, unless you have a JEEP. (JEEP drivers get all the breaks!) At press time there were some people charging $5 to park shy of the boat ramp and telling you to walk to the beach. The people they *claim* to represent, Department of Hawaiian Homelands, confirm that they are *not* authorized to charge any money or do anything else, for that matter. At first the DHHL told us they were evicting them, now they refuse to return our calls. Use your best judgement. Personally we tell the people there to pound sand. We're not paying 'em diddly.

Once at the cone, most people take a "path" on the closest (southwest) side (see map), which requires a short hop off a rock at one point. Unfortunately, the path is more evident from the beach than from the top and might be tough to spot. Others walk down a path from about the middle of the cone, which can be slippery due to sand particles on the hard surface. Don't try to walk from the highest part of the cone; it's treacherous. Use your best judgment. Everyone from small keikis to the elderly go to the beach, but you are on your own in accessing it. Check to see that the waves are not inundating the entire beach before you go down. The ocean is unprotected, so the waves are at full strength. Many books tell you that you will drown if you even *think* about swimming there. We swam there plenty of times and if the surf's not up, it's not that bad. The sand bottom is thick and there are few exposed rocks. We have yet to encounter nasty currents *in the bay,* but we're not stupid enough to venture out of the bay where the prevailing current will give you a splendid tour of Antarctica. Again, use your best judgment. There is a shorebreak, and the undertow can be harsh. You might see plenty of local kids (or us) playing in the surf, but this is not Waikiki. And if the surf is high, definitely stay out. Those same large waves that expose the olivine could pull you in. There's no shade here and the wind, which has beautifully sculpted the eastern side of the bay, is also the same wind that might get on your nerves if it is blowing hard, particularly in the late afternoon. Go earlier if you can. No facilities. Please resist the urge to take any of the sand with you.

❖ **Whittington Park**—Located off the road between the 61 and 62 mile marker on the southern part of the island. Very pretty from a distance, but a bit run down and less pleasant up close. (The signs near the picnic tables say, "No Sleeping on the Tables." Need we say more?) Not worth the effort.

❖ **Punalu'u Black Sand Beach**—

A Real Gem

This is the most easily accessible black sand beach on the island (now that Kaimu Beach is under 75 feet of lava). Backed by palm trees and a freshwater pond, the sand is *genuine* black sand—the kind created when a chunky a'a lava flow meets the ocean and shatters into small pieces on contact with the water. These small chunks are quickly pulverized by the ocean, forming a delicious black sand. This differs from older black sand beaches where the sand is made up of lava chipped from a river bed by coursing water. Genuine black sand beaches are relatively fleeting since the source of the sand ends as soon as the lava flow stops. This contrasts with white and golden sand beaches, which have organic sources (coral or shells) that continue to build up sand over time. (In fact, one large, coral-munching parrotfish can produce three *tons* of white sand per year by himself!) That's why you don't see genuine black sand on old islands— the black sand erodes into the ocean over time and cannot be recovered.

The swimming is a bit different here than many other island beaches. Cold freshwater springs bubble up from just offshore. Consequently, the top 8–12 inches of the water is guaranteed to freeze your 'okole off. You can usually see the floating freshwater while swimming and will be tempted to swim below to get a semblance of warmth. The visibility here is only fair and you need to be conscious of rip currents. Generally, you want to stay fairly close to shore and be aware of currents during all but the calmest seas. Past the boat launch on the left (north) side of the beach, the rips can be a problem.

So why swim here at all? Well, one of this beach's lesser known treats are its turtles. The waters can get almost crowded with them. We've been there when you could see small groups of turtles every couple of minutes. They munch on limu that clings to rocks on the sea floor. Please remember not to disturb or play with them. In addition to the possible harm, it might cause them to find a less accessible beach to frolic.

OTHER EAST SIDE BEACHES

Past Punaluʻu your choices for beaches diminish along with their calibre. Put simply, the east shore, which is exposed to more hazardous surf and lots of river runoff, has fewer and mostly poorer beaches. Therefore, we are breaking them up into regions and deviating from our previous rules by describing many in the tours of the various regions.

❖ **Puna Beaches**—Located near the extreme eastern part of the island, **Kehena Black Sand Beach, Issac Hale Beach Park, Ahalanui Warm Springs,** and **Kapoho Tide-pools** are described in the Hilo and Puna tour because you won't encounter them unless you are touring that area anyway.

❖ **Hilo Beach Parks**—To the east on Kalanianaole (where Highways 11 and 19 meet) are Hilo's most popular beach parks. **Onekahakaha Beach Park** has a small boulder-enclosed pool that is popular with local keikis (kids). The sand lined pool is utterly protected except during very high seas. The pool to the left is rockier and has lots of urchins on the floor. Past Onekahakaha is **James Kealoha Beach Park.** Though picturesque, the swimming is difficult, and you're likely to share it with young toughs drinking too much and giving you stink eye. Best to move on to **Leleiwi Beach Park.** This last park contains **Richardson's Ocean Center** at the far end and is particularly attractive with freshwater pools sprinkled about. The county Aquatic's Division is located here and they are friendly and full of helpful information. This is an excellent place for a picnic. There's a small black sand cove where you can enter the water. It'll be cold from fresh water intruding into the area. Some of Hilo's better snorkeling is here. Dolphins often frequent the area, and turtles usually congregate a little farther down the coast toward Hilo. Check with lifeguards as this area is subject to strong surf.

Other beach parks north of Hilo are **Honoliʻi, Kolekole Beach, Hakalau Bay, Waikaumalo Park,** and **Laupahoehoe Point.** Farther north is the difficult to access but beautiful black sand beach of **Waipiʻo Bay.** All are described in the HAMAKUA AND WAIMEA SIGHTS section.

| Kua Bay White Sand | Green Sand Beach | New Black Sand Beach | White Powder Sand from Florida |

The Big Island is a snorkeler's paradise. This is at the Captain Cook Monument in Kealakekua Bay.

Take a deep breath and do some stretching before you read this section, because the Big Island has so much to see and do that you're likely to pull something just reading about it all. Among the more popular are fishing, golfing, snorkeling, SCUBA, hiking, horseback riding, kayaking, helicopter tours, boat trips, submarine rides, and whale watching. Whatever you're into—even snow skiing!—you're likely to find it here on the Big Island.

Activities can be booked directly with the individual activity providers or through activity companies. *Sometimes* you can get better deals through activity companies. Many resorts have activity directors and booths, sometimes run by the activity providers themselves, so be aware that their "recommendations" are sometimes biased. Many of the booths spread around the island are actually forums for selling timeshares. That's not a dig at timeshares, just that you need to know the real purpose of some of these

booths. They can be very aggressive: (Don't get skewered by one of the long metal hooks.) Free breakfasts and "island orientations" are often similar to activity booths. So if you are steered to XYZ helicopter company and assured that they are the best, that's fine, but consider the source. We walk up to these booths frequently. Some are reputable and honest, and some are outrageous. We have no stake in *any* company we recommend, we just want to steer you in the best direction we can.

By the way, Friday is cruise ship day in Kona, and some activities such as boating will be more crowded on these days.

With a moniker like The Big Island, you would expect an endless variety of biking choices. Unfortunately, most roads have bad or no shoulders, and most unpaved

roads have lava that is murder on bikes. With this in mind, your best opportunities are on a mountain bike.

If you are staying in Kona and want to ride on the street, cruise down Alii Drive along the coast. If you're staying in Hilo, Stainback Hwy. (described on page 106) is a great road to sail down on a mountain bike. You could then take North Kulani to Hwy. 11 where the shoulders coming back to Hilo are usually wide.

If you are willing to transport a **mountain bike** somewhere, these three rides are fun:

South Point—See map on page 77 and the description of the area. You can ride from South Point past Green Sand Beach on the JEEP roads—lots of fun. The wind is usually with you coming back. This is wide open country with good mountain bike roads.

Volcano—There's a dirt "escape" road that leads through beautiful rain forest from Thurston Lava Tube to Chain of Craters Road and the Mauna Ulu Trailhead. (See maps on pages 90 and 179.) The 4-mile road is well maintained and very scenic, with green assaulting your eyes from both directions. Return on the escape road, or take Chain of Craters road back up (right) 1½ miles, then take Hilina Pali Road as far down as you want to go before returning.

Mana Road—This road leads through Parker Ranch in Waimea and winds around Mauna Kea to near Saddle Road. It starts near the 55 mile marker on the main highway in Waimea—See maps on pages 115 and 123, and back foldout map to get an idea of the scale. It's a 44-mile dirt road to Mauna Kea Road near Saddle Road. Unless you are motivated and arrange for transportation from Saddle Road, you'll probably just want to take it as far as you like, then turn around and come back. The first 22 miles is relatively easy and passes through *fairly* flat, sometimes foggy, quiet plains of grass and cows. Past 22 miles it gets hillier and bumpier and enters a beautiful forest reserve. Be sure to close any gates you pass that are already closed. Cleverly worded or placed signs sometimes *imply* that you may not traverse the road. Actually, it's a public right of way. At $10^{4}/10$ miles is a fork—take the right one.

GUIDED TOURS

Several companies offer a variety of guided tours. Expect to pay $50–$100. Consider calling **Mauna Kea Mountain Bikes** (883–0130). **Red Sail Sports** (885–2876) also has a tour down Kohala Mountain.

BIKE SHOPS

In Kona, the best bike shop we know is **HP Bikeworks** (326–2453), visible from the highway, off Kaiwi Street. Excellent selection of bikes and bike accessories. Full suspension mountain bikes (the best you'll find on the island) rent for $30 per day, half suspensions are $25. **Hawaiian Pedals** (329–2294) rents mountain bikes, performance bikes (better mountain bikes), tandems, racks, etc. for reasonable prices. **Dave's Bikes** (329–4522) is a good repair shop, their rentals are fair at $15 per day, and Dave's a friendly guy. In Kohala, **Red Sail Sports** (885–2876) rents bikes for $7 per hour, $25 for 8 hours. Restricted to the resort area, feel free to pass. **C&S Cycle and Surf** (885–5005) is in Waimea on 19 near Kamamalu. $25 per day. **Hilo Bike Hub** (961–4452) rents mountain bikes.

Boogie Boarding

Boogie boarding (riders are derisively referred to as *spongers* by surfers) is where you ride a wave on what is essentially a sawed-off surfboard. It can be a real blast. You need short, stubby fins to catch bigger waves (which break in deeper water), but small waves can be snared by simply standing in shallow water and lurching forward as the wave is breaking. If you've never done it before, stay away from big waves; they can drill you. Smooth-bottom boards work best. Men who don't do this often should—*this is important*—wear shirts, otherwise you can rub yourself raw. (Women already have this aspect covered.)

The section on BEACHES describes whether a beach is good for boogie boarding. Our favorite is **Hapuna** in Kohala. Conditions are usually excellent. We also like Mauna Kea, Kua Bay, and White Sands Beach. You won't have any trouble finding places to rent boards, so we won't bother mentioning them individually. Just keep an eye out for signs. Expect to pay $5–$8 per day, $15–$20 per week. You can buy them at Costco, Wal-mart, Kmart etc. for $40+.

CAMPING

There's a drive-up campground at the **Kilauea Volcano** called Namakani Paio, just outside the park entrance at 4,000 feet. (See map on page 90.) They have 10 simple cabins for $40 each. Each has a couple of beds, community showers, (good thing it's not the other way around) and a BBQ. 967-7321 for reservations. Tents are also permitted for free, and there's almost always plenty of space. No reservations. There's a campsite (pit toilet only) in the park called **Kulanaokuaiki** on Hilina Pali Road.

In the park are several campsites that require long hikes. Contact the park directly at 985-6017 to see which ones are open. You can pick up your permits when you get there, and there's usually not a problem in getting them.

Off Saddle Road at a chilly 6,500 feet, cabins are available at **Mauna Kea State Park**. They're $45 per night for up to four people, and have two bedrooms, range, refrigerator, hot showers, toilet and cookware. Some are heated. Call 974-6200 for reservations. They close them for long periods due to drought.

Kalopa Native Forest State Park has decent cabins for $55 and covered campsites for tents. The limited hiking is good, and the park is in beautiful shape.

Many of the beach parks around the island are available for camping with a county permit. They are shown on the map on they next page. Hapuna has A-frame cabins available from the state. There were other sites at press time that were too disgusting to recommend, so we left them off the map.

Waimanu Valley (there's a photo of it on page 175) is utterly remote and stunningly beautiful. No facilities are available. It'll take most of a day to go down into Waipi'o Valley up the trail on the cliff, then down into Waimanu. For this and other **state campsites** call Division of Forestry and Wildlife at (808) 974-4221) or State Parks (974-6200). For **county campsites,** call Parks and Recreation at (808) 961-8311.

Camping Sites—County Sites in Black, State Sites in Red

- Keokea Beach Park
- Kapa'a Beach Park & Mahukona Beach Park
- Waimanu Valley
- Kalopa State Park
- Spencer Beach Park
- Laupahoehoe Beach Park
- Hapuna Beach Park
- Kolekole Beach Park
- Mauna Kea State Park
- Mauna Loa Cabin
- Namakani Paio
- Ho'okena Beach Park
- Kulanaokuaiki
- Halepe and Keauhou Shelters
- Miloli'i Beach Park
- Punalu'u Beach Park
- Whittington Beach Park

If you had to pick the one sport Kona is most famous for, it would probably be its big game fishing. The waters off the Kona coast drop to great depths quickly and are teeming with big game fish. When there's a strike, the adrenaline level of everyone on board shoots through the roof. Most talked about are the marlin *(very hard fighters known for multiple runs),* including blue, stripers and the occasional black. These goliaths can tip the scales at over 1,000 pounds. (Virtually all marlin above 300 pounds are female.) Also in abundance are ono, also called wahoo *(one of the fastest fish in the ocean and indescribably delicious—they strike very hard but tire quicker),* mahimahi *(vigorous fighters—excellent on light tackle),* ahi *(delicious yellowfin tuna)* and spearfish. With calm sunny conditions 300 days per year, quick access to the fishing areas, and strong competition among over 100 fishing companies, Kona has become a magnet for first-timers wishing to try their hand at catching the big one.

A FEW THINGS YOU SHOULD KNOW:

Fish are plentiful year-round but more numerous in the summer, a bit less so in the winter.

The largest blue marlin ever caught in the state was a hull-popping 1,805 lbs.

Most boats leave out of Honokohau Harbor, just north of Kona. A surprising number of the thousand pounders have

been caught just outside the harbor. This is probably because the harbor is flushed every day by freshwater springs, making the water clean and clear. This natural flushing expels the contents of the harbor on a daily basis. Perhaps passing fish like to hang around the harbor entrance to scoop up the results of that day's fish cleaning. Most boats troll nonstop. Licenses aren't required. You will probably have to bring your own food and beverages. Most boats here don't target a particular fish—they just troll for whatever they can get.

Most passengers on Kona fishing boats are novices, so don't feel self-conscious if you have no idea what you are doing. Deck hands will handle all of the arrangements; just sit back and relax.

You will either go on a shared charter (with other folks) or do a private charter. Nearly all charter boats are licensed for six people. Since boats range from 26–60 feet, how big a boat you charter will determine how roomy you feel. The fewer people on your boat, the greater the chance that *you* will be the one reeling in the fish since you share the lines with fewer people.

There are half day (morning or afternoon) charters available, full day, and overnighters. If this is your first time, do a half day to see if boat travel agrees with you. Mornings offer best conditions. Prices start at around $75 per person for a half-day shared charter. You can do a private half-day charter for $250–$400. Full-day private charters go for $400–$650 or more for the big boats. *Usually,* the bigger the boat, the higher the price. Individual boat rates can change often depending on the season, fishing conditions and whims of the

owners. Consequently, we'll forgo listing individual boat rates since this information is so perishable and instead list a few companies that we recommend. Call them directly to get current rates.

If you're easy-queasy, take an anti-seasickness medication. There are people who never get sick regardless of conditions, and those who turn green just watching an old episode of *The Love Boat*. Nothing can ruin an ocean outing quicker than being hunched over the stern feeding the fish. Scopolamine patches prescribed by doctors work best. Dramamine II or Bonine taken the night before and the morning of a trip also seems to work well for many, though some drowsiness may occur. Doctors are starting to cozy up to ginger as a preventative. Try powdered ginger, ginger pills or even *real* ginger ale—can't hurt, right?

Tipping: 10–15% split between the captain and deck hand is customary if you are pleased with their performance. If the captain is a jerk and the deck hand throws up on you, you're not obligated to give 'em diddly.

You should know in advance that in Hawai'i, the fish belongs to the boat. What happens to the fish is entirely up to the captain and they usually keep it. You may catch a 1,000-pound marlin and be told that you can't have as much as a steak from it. If this bothers you, you're out of luck. If the ono or another small fish are striking a lot and there is a glut of them, you might be allowed to keep it—or half of it. You *may* be able to make arrangements in advance to the contrary, but I doubt it.

If you want to catch and release, or tag and release, make sure in advance that your boat will accommodate you. Most will, but some don't. If you do, use

lures—live bait usually results in the fish coughing up its stomach, which kills it.

You might want to go down to the fuel dock at Honokohau Harbor around 11 a.m. or 3:30 p.m. for fish weigh-ins to see what's being caught and by whom. The boats hoist flags on their way back, each one representing a different species of fish caught on that trip.

If you fish from Kawaihae, expect ono and mahimahi rather than bigger stuff.

Whether you catch fish or not, it's great being out on the Kona Coast.

Popular boats can get booked up in advance. Making arrangements before you arrive can maximize your chances of getting a good boat.

Captains and deckhands come and go. Below are some boats that we've had good experiences with or have good reputations as of press time. If you have a contrary experience with any one of them or have an experience with any company that you'd like to share with us, please contact us at the address listed on page 2 so we can stay on top of these boats. The number after each name is the boat length.

For the big stuff try:
Foxy Lady (42')..................325–5552
Sea Genie II (39')..............325–5355
Keneka II (31')...................325–3122
Ihu Nui (35') 325–1513
Marlin Magic (43') 325–7138
Camelot (34')....................325–6421
Hua Pala (35') 325–3277
Sea Strike (31').................329–8135
Reel Pleasure (36')...........882–1413

For light tackle try:
Reel Action (30')...............325–6811
Northern Lights (37') 329–6522
Bottom Fishing (43').........329–4900

To cut through the maze of companies, a reputable charter service company can be invaluable. Unfortunately, these come and go with amazing rapidity. **Charter Services Hawai'i** at 334–1881 or (800) 567–5662 had helpful personnel who gave the facts without the nonsense. As a rule, we are always leery of activity counters—some are helpful and knowledgeable, but some are scoundrels. However, at Honokohau Harbor, you might want to call 329–5735. They are right at the harbor and usually have the skinny on what's going on there.

Kona's famous **International Billfish Tournament** is held in each year in August. Fishermen from all over the world come to compete for top prize. As a result, boats tend to fill up faster during this time.

SHORELINE FISHING

The entire shoreline is available to you. If you want, you can find a secluded spot off any ugly looking lava road on the island. Otherwise, on Hilo side, Hilo Bay, especially near the mouth of the Wailuku River is good. South Point is excellent. In Kailua-Kona, the seawall in front of Hulihe'e Palace is a great place and easy to access. As snorkelers, we've seen schools numbering in the many thousands congregate off this area.

Kona Fishing Tackle (326–2934) and **Yama's** (329–1712), both in Kona, and **Ebisuzaki Fishing** (935–8081) in Hilo are your best sources for supplies.

And remember: Never say, "I'm going fishing." Say, "I am going to the woods." Hawaiian legend holds that the fish will hear and avoid you if you warn them.

The Big Island is rapidly becoming known as *the* island to visit if you want to golf till you drop. This actually presented a problem for us in evaluating the individual courses. It would have been easy to froth at the mouth over most of them because *relative* to courses elsewhere, most are outstanding. But that would have missed the point. So with elevated expectations in mind, we have reviewed the courses *relative to each other*. This is important because if we get less than excited about a particular course, it doesn't mean it's a dump. It just means that you can do better elsewhere on the island.

Prices at the top courses are higher than many are used to. If you stay at a resort near the course, you'll probably be eligible for much cheaper rates.

A FEW TIPS...

Wind is often a factor at Kohala courses, and is usually stronger in the afternoon. Sunshine is *almost* guaranteed in Kohala. Conditions are usually best in the mornings at all courses around the island.

Greens tend to break to the ocean, even when they look uphill.

Kona's driving range near Old Kona Airport is called Swing Zone (329–6909).

Some courses offer big discounts after noon or 3 p.m. Check with individual courses for these or other discounts.

We list kama'aina fees here. These are fees that Hawai'i residents pay. Though less, bear in mind that there are often restrictions on playing times.

MAUNA KEA GOLF COURSE (882–5400)

According to local lore, in the early 1960s, Laurence Rockefeller flew Robert Trent Jones, Sr. to an isolated, barren, mostly unknown place on the Big Island called Kohala. He took him out to an a'a lava field, pointed to the rock and asked, "Can you build me a golf course out of that?" Jones supposedly knelt down, picked up two pieces of a'a and ground them together. They crumbled. He then said, "Mr. Rockefeller—you've got yourself a golf course."

Opened in 1964, Mauna Kea is still the course by which all others are compared. Fairly open and forgiving rolling terrain, this course epitomizes what a Big Island course can be. The layout is brilliant, the location is dazzling, and the course is just plain fun. Number 3 is a signature hole which hugs the shoreline—a very difficult hole. Number 9 shoots downhill toward the hotel. Hole 11, a par three, drops precipitously downhill—consider yourself lucky if you par. 17 is 555 beautiful curving yards. If you were on island visiting us, this is the course we'd take you to. The rolling scenery and the time-tested play seem ageless.

Located at the Mauna Kea Resort just south of Kawaihae—the turnoff is near the 68 mile marker on Highway 19. Fees are $175 for standard, $95 for resort guests. Kama'aina rate is $70. Carts are included, but walking is allowed.

HAPUNA GOLF COURSE (880–3000)

This is the other course at the Mauna Kea/Hapuna Prince resort complex. Designed by Arnold Palmer and Ed Seay and opened in 1992, it features narrower fairways, so bring more balls than you would at Mauna Kea. The course is well marked, well organized, and well kept.

Don't expect to be overwhelmed with hazards, however. The narrowness is your challenge. The course is ensconced in an older lava field filled with scrub, rather than the starker, yet more attractive newer lava fields, such as the Mauna Lani's South Course.

Hapuna is a very pleasant and well-run course, though not overly remarkable. (Services, however, are excellent.) Standard fees are $185, Resort guests pay $105, and the kama'aina rate is $65. Carts are included, but walking is allowed.

MAUNA LANI RESORT (885–6655)

Called the Francis H. I'i Brown South Course and the North Course, these two courses are the result of the 1991 splitting of the 1980 course. North and South each got nine and added nine. Of the two, the SOUTH COURSE is by far the most popular. It is closer to the ocean and is nicely incorporated into the stark lava. Fingers of a'a seem to reach out and grab your ball, so the accuracy-challenged will want to bring more than usual. A'a is a notorious ball eater and shoe wrecker. The course is well maintained and some of the holes are highly memorable. Number 13 is quintessential Hawai'i. Driving toward and along the ocean, make sure you drive *your cart* on the left side for incomparable ocean views. Look back toward hole 7 and the secluded Honoka'ope Beach. A stunning hole by anyone's definition. At 15 you can count yourself among the elite if you can make par. It shoots over a respectable ocean cove onto greens guarded by cleverly placed traps. Par 3...we'll see.

Whereas the South Course is more open and expansive, the less used NORTH COURSE has more trees and a more "traditional" use of lava boundaries. There are several lava tubes sprinkled about, and

Course	Par	Yards	Rating	Fees
Mauna Kea	72	6,365	70.1	$175*
Hapuna	72	6,029	66.8	$185*
Mauna Lani South	72	5,940	68.3	$200*
Mauna Lani North	72	6,086	69.4	$200*
Waikoloa Kings'	72	6,010	68.6	$185*
Waikoloa Beach	70	5,958	68.6	$185*
Hualalai Golf Club	72	6,032	68.9	$155
Waikoloa Village	72	6,142	69.7	$70*
Waimea Country Club	72	6,210	68.3	$60*
Makalei	72	6,161	69.0	$110*
Kona Country Club Ocean	72	6,155	69.1	$110*
Kona Country Club Mauka	72	5,828	68.7	$85*
Discovery Harbor	72	6,326	69.4	$30*
Sea Mountain at Punalu'u	72	6,106	69.8	$42*
Volcano Golf & Country Club	72	6,180	68.6	$62*
Hilo Municipal Golf Course	71	6,006	68.8	$20
Naniloa Country Club (X2)	70	5,615	65.8	$40
Hamakua Country Club (X2)	72	4,920	63.8	$10

* Indicates power cart included in price
Yards, ratings and slope are from the men's regular tees.

the kiawe trees often define the fairway. (Remember to be careful of their penetrating thorns when looking for an errant ball.) Make sure you hit solid on number 4—the scrub-filled lava gorge is laden with muffed drives. Number 17 is a short 119 yards from the tournament tees, but the narrow channel and well-placed traps call for lots of concentration.

Mauna Lani courses are the best maintained courses on the island. If you can only play one, make it the South. Otherwise, you'll find that playing both will offer very different and enjoyable games. Our biggest gripe is that both courses are poorly marked, and the free map is not very accurate. Standard fees for South & North courses at $200. Resort guests pay $105. Kama'aina rate is $95. Discounted during certain times. Between the 73 & 74 mile markers on Highway in Kohala, see map on page 53.

WAIKOLOA RESORT

You have your choice of the WAIKOLOA KINGS' or the WAIKOLOA BEACH.

WAIKOLOA KINGS' (885-4647) is probably our second favorite Kohala course. This links-style course is the tougher of the two. Features include deep bunkers, clever use of lava terrain, and confiscatory lava boundaries. You stand little chance of retrieving your ball in this a'a from hell. They made good use of lava balls (you'll know them when you see them). Golf balls seem magnetically attracted to them.

Hole 5 is deceiving. There are two enormous lava balls nestled in a sand trap larger than many Kohala beaches. The cup is 327 yards away, and if there is a wind at your back and you are in a hard-driving mood, you might make it over the lava—or you might want to

chicken out and use two to get over them...anything to avoid being *behind* them. From most of the course on a clear day, you can see five volcanoes—Kohala, Mauna Kea, Hualalai, Mauna Loa, and Haleakala on Maui. Palms and plumeria are scattered about among the trees. Though challenging, this is a course to be savored.

WAIKOLOA BEACH (885-6060) gets far more golfers than Kings'. That's probably because it is in a location that affords more visibility and because it is closer to the ocean. Kings' is not seen from as many hotel rooms. Waikoloa Beach is a par 70, and its resort style layout is a bit more forgiving. It has less personality than the Kings' but is a fine course nonetheless. Check out the petroglyphs on your left on your way to number 9. On number 9, the wind can play havoc since there is a water border on your left almost the entire 558 yards. Number 15 is whopping 591-yard voyage from the champ tees.

Both courses are well groomed and surprisingly well watered, sometimes to the point of being soggy (as evidenced by the number of golden plovers during the winter months). These two courses can get more crowded than other Kohala courses due to the fact that they actively seek local players. Standard fees are $185, resort guests pay $95, kama'aina rate is $65. After 2 p.m. everyone pays $55. (May be windier.) Near 76 mile marker in Kohala. See map on page 53.

HUALALAI GOLF CLUB (325-8480)

Opened in 1996, this course is private, meaning that only those staying at the Four Seasons Resort or at the adjacent residential community can play.

(Kona Village guests *may* be able to play.) This Jack Nicklaus course is more player-friendly than most of his designs. There's a constant 5% grade toward the ocean, so there's lots of ocean views from the lushly manicured fairways. Very fast greens and a bit less wind than most Kohala resorts. Rates are $155.

WAIKOLOA VILLAGE (883–9621)

Up mauka of the Kohala resort area, three words come to mind here—cheaper, windy, and walking. At $70 for standard rates, it's on the cheaper side of Big Island golf. (But I'll tell you right now that you are better off at Waimea Country Club if the weather is cooperating.) This course is popular with locals who appreciate the $40 kama'aina fares (cheaper with specials). As for the wind, you may see a bird on this course lay the same egg three times. Play *early* if you want to avoid the wind. Lastly, you can walk the course if you so choose, unlike most Kohala courses.

There are more trees here than many other courses. Some like to compare it to a very good municipal course, which sounds fair. It is adequately maintained (though poorly marked—you may even get lost on occasion). Overall, you get what you pay for here.

WAIMEA COUNTRY CLUB (885–8777)

One of the most under-rated courses on the island. You may think you are in Scotland rather than Hawai'i. You are a long way from and above the ocean. *Wide* open fairways, plush, well-watered grass, fog and mist often, and a delicious rolling terrain. These, along with a visitor rate of $60, make it one of the better golf bargains you'll find. The caveat is the weather—it rains a lot here, so call

and ask if it looks like it will be *pumping* that day. Or better yet, just play early. A windbreak of eucalyptus trees surrounds the course. Geese, pheasant, and quail all grace the course's water hazards. Number nine is as picture-perfect as you will find. A graceful curving fairway rambles down, around and up to the green.

If you're scared off by the fees the big boys charge elsewhere, this is a nice alternative—weather permitting. The course is located between the 51 and 52 mile markers on Highway 19 in Waimea.

MAKALEI COUNTRY CLUB (325–6625)

This is one of the lesser known Big Island courses. Located 2,100–2,900 feet upslope, it's cooler and less windy up here than at the Kohala courses. There are beautiful views down the coast, and bougainvilleas dot the cart paths. The course is carved nicely into the forest. Wailing peacocks are scattered about, as well as pheasant and turkeys. Number 4 has a low rock wall to act as a speed bump for low shots. Hole 10 wanders 580 yards with impressive views of the coastline below. Smile when you tee off on number 15—you're being watched. They videotape you, and if you get a hole in one, you get a prize. (It's an easy hole to overshoot.) Makalei is a fun course. You won't get pounding Pacific surf, but you will get a moderately challenging course that's well maintained and easy to recommend. Designed by Dick Nugent. (Any relation to Ted?) $110 for standard fees. Seven miles north of Kona on Hwy 190. Carts are included and mandatory.

KONA COUNTRY CLUB (322–2595)

The four sets of nine here were built over a period of 25 years, and their personalities are all different. Courses are

Over the water and onto the green. Mauna Kea's hole #3 is vintage Hawaiian golf.

split into the **OCEAN COURSE,** and the **MAUKA COURSE.**

The **OCEAN** has some fine ocean and upslope views. Number 12 is a signature hole that skirts the ocean, with enough palm trees to remind you of why you came to Hawai'i. At 13, look for the blowhole near the handicap tees. Note the fantastic corkscrew-shaped palm tree near the white tees at 14. The 124-yard number 17 shoots over a lava gorge—one of the few lava hazards. There is a flock of wild parrots at this course, so keep an eye (or ear) out for them.

The **MAUKA** is more modern, making use of, rather than denying, the natural lava in this area. Number 14 drops 62 feet, over a water hazard and onto the green, with smashing views down the coastline. In fact, holes 14–18 all sport nice coastline views.

Someone must have gotten scared by a lawyer once. There are more warning signs at these courses than any we've seen. Since this is the only course in Kailua-Kona, expect more people here. There are plenty of signs to prod you to keep it moving. *(If you are at this hole, you better have done it in 45 minutes.)* The fairways for both courses could use a little TLC. Greens seem fine. All in all, the course is only fair. If you pay the full standard price, you paid way too much. But check for specials—they often have one or two. Standard fees are $110 for the Ocean, $85 for the Mauka. Carts are included and mandatory.

DISCOVERY HARBOR GOLF AND COUNTRY CLUB (929–7353)

We're still trying to discover the harbor at this course 4 miles from the unreachable ocean. It is the southernmost course in the United States, but it's probably not quite far south enough. Run down and dilapidated, this course is a must-miss. It's now used mostly by the adjacent community. On the positive side, at least you won't have someone prodding you from behind if you want to play slow. Standard fees are $30, Kama'aina rate is $20. Carts included and mandatory.

SEAMOUNTAIN—PUNALU'U (928–6222)

The layout and promise were excellent here, but the course has been a victim to the fortunes (or lack thereof) of the developer. As a result, it had been getting pretty mangy in recent years. SeaMountain was sold in 1994 (for less that a *tenth* of the purchase price), and the course has slowly but steadily improved since then. It's hard to predict what you will encounter, but the price is cheap for a scenic seaside golf course in Hawai'i. If it's in good shape, you'll find the location a real winner. Even if it's not, the fees are still worth it if you are in the neighborhood. Located near Punalu'u Beach on the southeast side of the island 56 miles from Hilo and 65 miles from Kona. Standard fees have been lowered to $42, Kama'aina rate is $24. Carts are included and mandatory.

VOLCANO GOLF & COUNTRY CLUB (967–7331)

Who would ever think that you could have a lush course just 1 mile from the main crater of the most active volcano on earth? Bring your warmies as the 4,000-foot altitude brings a chill to the air. The play is straightforward with few hazards. Mother Nature and the groundskeepers keep the grass green and healthy. Unlike other courses, the afternoons here *may* be better in the summer. Mist and fog sometimes make it interesting, but wind is usually low. Remember to club down since the ball travels farther up here. This is a nice course offering a moderate challenge and a peaceful setting. Standard

fees are $62.50, Kama'aina rate is $27. Carts are included and mandatory.

NANILOA GOLF COURSE (935–3000)

Much of the infrastructure is run down and dilapidated, but the course, aided by the fertile Hilo climate, is in fairly nice shape. The RACK rates seem high given that this is a nine-hole course. Overall, forgettable. Standard fees are $30–$40, Kama'aina rate is $7–$8.

HILO MUNICIPAL (959–7711)

Fairly flat layout and no sand traps (too much rain) are the hallmarks of this course. The play is not overly hard and the setting is quite pretty. It gets soggy after a heavy rain so consider this beforehand. This course is usually pretty crowded and about half walk, so weekends should be avoided for the delays. Standard fees are $20.

HAMAKUA COUNTRY CLUB (775–7244)

Built as a community course in the formerly sugar-rich area of Hamakua, this *small* 9-hole course is popular with locals who come to play and talk story in the "clubhouse." Greens fees are $10. (You're on the honor system—just drop your money in the box in the clubhouse and grab a hand-drawn scorecard.) The holes are very close together and amazingly well tended. The community takes obvious pride in caring for it. You won't find a lot of challenges (and you won't find club rentals or power carts), but you will find a gentle course set in a gentle, friendly community.

From the main highway (19) east of Waimea, turn just before (west of) the Texaco station between the 42 and 43 mile markers and take the frontage road 100 yards to the "clubhouse."

If you've been on a helicopter or air-plane flight on another island, especially Kaua'i, you've been treated to wall-to-wall, tongue-wagging sights. The Big Island, however, has lots of fantastic areas spread about with less interesting areas connecting them. The east side is a lush wonderland, and the west side is dominated by lava. That's why limited tours are so different on each side of the island.

Here, more than most islands, your tour is affected by the passion (or lack thereof) of the pilot. A boring pilot will sound something like this: "On your left is such and such valley, and on your right is such and such hill, and in front is the such and such lava flow." *So what!?* What you really want is a knowledgeable pilot with a command of the island who also knows to speak only when it

Air tours give you a perspective on the volcano that you can't get any other way.

improves the silence. We're prejudiced toward companies that let you ask the pilot questions through a microphone, as opposed to those where the pilots tells you "everything you need to know."

In the past, air tour operators could fly at any altitude they wanted, often producing low-flying *Apocalypse Now!* type flights, but those days are gone. Air tour operators are now restricted to 500 feet over unpopulated areas. But that doesn't mean that you won't walk off the aircraft with drool running down your shirt from the mesmerizing experience. It can still happen, you just aren't *assured* of it anymore. When the music, helicopter, pilot, and sights all come together, it'll still blow you away. We've flown with pilots who have an undisguised passion for the island, and those who may as well be driving a flying bus. Unfortunately, most companies don't use the same pilots all the time, so it's sometimes hard to steer you toward the good ones.

In general, we recommend that helicopter tours be taken from Hilo or Waimea. Tours that leave from Kailua-Kona spend too much time over less interesting areas. That's not to say that there aren't nice things to see from a Kona flight. It's just that to *maximize* your helicopter dollar, you're better off leaving from other the locations.

Don't take a 30–35 minute volcano tour if it leaves from Hilo—you only get a few minutes at the park. The rest is travel time over less interesting terrain.

A-Star helicopters are the most popular. They hold six passengers, with four in back and two beside the pilot up front. The middle seats in the back are so-so; the others are good. Think of the A-Star as a pleasant tour bus. **Hughes 500Ds** have two passengers in the somewhat cramped back and two *outstanding* front seats next to the pilot. This copter feels like a sports car, and the side views from the back are excellent. Windows come off if you want. They are less popular because they are less profitable to operators. **Bell Jet Rangers** are less comfortable with three in back and one passenger up front. The back middle seat is a poor seat indeed. **Bell Long Rangers** carry six passengers with two poor slobs facing backwards—bad design. You will lock knees with the people facing you and sights will be on the opposite side of what the pilot says (and a minute after he says it). We like the Hughes and A-Stars best. We dislike Bell Longs and aren't real fond of Bell Jets.

Afternoon tours are sometimes bumpi-

Company	Phone #	Departure	Helicopter Type	2-Way*
Mauna Kea	885–6400	Hilo, Waikoloa, Waimea	A-Star, Hughes	Yes
Blue Hawaiian	961–5600	Waikoloa, Hilo	A-Star	Yes
Hawaii Helicopters	329–4700	Hilo, Kona	A-Star	No
Tropical/K&S Heli	961–6810	Hilo	Bell Jet	Yes
Volcano Heli-Tours	967–7578	Hilo	Hughes	No
Safari Helicopters	969–1259	Hilo	A-Star	Yes
Kenai Helicopters	885–5833	Hilo, Waikoloa	Bell Jets and Longs	
Mauna Loa	334–0234	Kona	Robinson R22	Yes

Companies toward the top are recommended higher than the ones toward the bottom.
* Indicates whether craft contains a microphone for you to talk to the pilot.

Hamakua Coast by helicopter exposes some of the island's magic valleys.

er. I can tell you that as an ultralight pilot, I do most of my flying on the Big Island in the morning when conditions are usually best. You may want to also.

If you want to get around the altitude restrictions, think about *chartering* the aircraft. It's worth considering if you have a group or if you strike up a friendship with other travelers. It might not cost any more than a tour helicopter, you can leave from Hilo, Kona or Waimea, and *you* get to call the shots. (Leave the doors off if you want if it's a Hughes.) Make sure you rent one that has two-way communications. **K&S** charters their four-passenger Bell Jet for $675 per hour. **Mauna Kea** charges $1,050 for their six-passenger A-star.

THE COMPANIES

Mauna Kea is probably our favorite.

They fly out of Waimea and Waikoloa. They use Hughes' and A-Stars, have two-way communication, and a good attitude toward customers. You can get 45 minutes through the Kohala valleys for $145. Their 2-hour tour is comprehensive and includes the volcano for $310. They also have a 1½-hour "adventure" tour (plus a half-hour briefing) with the doors off the Hughes and jumpsuits for the passengers for $265. These are a very cool alternative to standard tours. They're a bit pricey, but they do a great job.

Blue Hawaii uses nice A-Stars out of Waikoloa, near the Kohala resort area, and Hilo. Two-hour volcano and Hamakua valleys tours, which land at Hilo, are $305. They have the expensive Bose Acoustic Noise-Canceling headphones, complimentary videos of your trip, and a roving microphone to speak with the pilot. They have 45-minute volcano tour flights from Hilo as well for $145. A good outfit.

Volcano Heli-Tours used to leave right from the volcano, providing the most volcano-intensive tour around. Because of that we could look past differences we had with their tours. But at press time they were ordered to begin leaving out of Hilo (just like many others). Now, with part of the trip spent traveling above less interesting areas, the problems seem more glaring. Like no microphone to talk to the pilot, just lots of stories from the pilot who tells you "everything you need to know." The Hughes works well for this tour and their knowledge of the park is beyond most others, but they're not quite as compelling as they used to be.

Hawaii Helicopters is a huge statewide company. In the past we weren't too crazy about their flights—big and passionless. But their current product is unique and pretty cool. You depart from Kona and fly to the volcano. After touring Kilauea, you proceed to Hilo and land. Then it's on a van for a 2–4 hour *land* tour of Hilo. Then back in the bird for a tour of Waipi'o and Waimanu valleys before heading back to Kona. In all you're in the air about 1½ hours plus the ground tour. It's a pretty good way to go if you want to get a peek of Hilo and an aerial tour of the island. $300.

Tropical Helicopters (formerly **K&S**) uses Bell Jet Rangers for their trips from Hilo. 45-minute rides are $99, 1-hour for $158.

Kenai Helicopters leaves from Waikoloa and Hilo. Their tours seem overpriced to us given that they use Bell Jet Rangers and the dreaded Bell Long

Rangers. 40–45 minute Kohala flights are $135, and the 145-minute Volcano/Hamakua waterfall flights are $300.

Safari makes adequate videos of your flight from their A-Star, which leaves from Hilo. Their 55-minute volcano tour is $149; the 45-minute is $115. In the past they've had serious problems when it comes to the accuracy of their narration. But they claim to have solved that now.

Mauna Loa Helicopters is a little different. *You* fly the beast. Consequently, it is described in more detail under ADVENTURES on page 210.

AIRPLANES

Because of its size and relative flatness, airplane tours are an acceptable alternative on the Big Island. Some, like Big Island Air, use large tour planes. Others, like Classic Aviation, use two-passenger open-cockpit bi-planes, which add excitement and adventure to your flight, but they don't go as far.

Big Island Air (329–4868) flies large (9-passenger) planes from Kona on round-the-island tours (well...*mostly* around) for $185. They also have sunrise volcano tours for $135. They do a pretty good job, the routes are interesting, and the pilot does his narrating well. Tours are more rushed than copter tours because they can't hover, but you get a good idea of the makeup of the island. Bumpy at times, so consider motion sickness medicine.

Island Hoppers (969–2000) uses small (four-person) airplanes out of Kona and Hilo for aerial sightseeing. Flights are cheaper and shorter from Hilo ($79) than Kona ($149–$189). Worth considering for the price.

RENTING AN AIRPLANE

Pilots can rent **Koa Air's** (326–2288) Cessna 172 for $88 an hour wet or their 150 for $65. Check rides (minus the usual hot lights and bamboo under the fingernails) extra. Owner will ride with you for an extra $30 per hour. **Island Hoppers** also rents 172s for $89. They have a slick 1998 172 for $119. $124 for the check ride.

The Big Island has plenty of hiking to keep you happy. You can wander through a lush rain forest, walk on a volcano crater floor, puff up a frigid, snow-covered mountain, hike along an empty tropical beach, teeter on the edge of steep canyons, or saunter along an old Hawaiian lava trail. The possibilities and diversity are incredible.

Footwear—We do much of our hiking here in hiking sandals (such as Tevas). For real muddy conditions we use boots lined with Gore-Tex™. And for stream hiking, nothing beats tabis. These look like green fuzzy mittens for your feet and stick to wet, mossy rocks better than any other kind of footwear. (Though without much stiffness, the bottom of your feet tend to get a bit sore.) You'll find tabis for about $20 at Kmart and Wal-mart in Kona, Payless, Wal-mart or Longs in Hilo.

If you're looking for the topographic maps of the island (it takes 74 to cover the island!) then **Basically Books** (961–0144) in Hilo or **Middle Earth** (329–2123) in Kona are your best bets.

We hike a lot and have become big fans of hiking sticks. We each use two on long hikes and find that they greatly ease the hikes and give us better balance. They have saved us several times from falling on nasty lava. Good ones have straps on the handles and are telescopic.

First through lush rain forest, then across the eerie crater floor, the Kilauea Iki hike is smashing!

Hiking at Kilauea Volcano

Much of the best hiking on the island is found in and around Hawai'i Volcanoes National Park. We've described lots of strolls of 30 minutes or less in the volcano section. They include **Bird Park** (a nice 30-minute walk through the forest), **Devastation Trail** (see how the volcano wiped out part of a forest with flying, frothed lava and how it is coming back), **Pu'u Loa Petroglyph Trail** (less than 2 miles round trip, it heads to a massive field of ancient rock carvings—this one takes a bit more than 30 minutes), **Thurston Lava Tube** (see what lava sees as it travels underground) and a few others. We've also described a trip to a pristine **Rain Forest Lava Tube** and a trek to the edge of the smoldering **Mauna Ulu Crater** under ADVENTURES.

Elsewhere in the Park
Kilauea Iki

This is a great hike! If you are only able to do one hike while you are on the Big Island, this is one we'd recommend. It goes from ancient rain forest to a newly lava-paved crater, and back through rain forest. At a little over 3 miles, it can take anywhere from two hours if you hoof it without distractions, to four hours if you stop and gawk as much as we do and enjoy lunch on the crater floor. It is a *reasonably* easy hike (well...maybe moderate) with only about 15 minutes of gentle but constant incline toward the end when you ascend about 450 feet. Before hiking, read some background on this crater and its attention-grabbing past under the VOLCANO section.

We like to start this hike at the Kilauea Iki Overlook and go counterclockwise, through the forest first. The trip is gentler this way and is preferable to going into

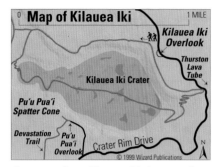

the crater first. (You could also start from the Visitor Center and get there via the Earthquake Trail and Byron Ledge Trail—see page 180.) You will go through a gorgeous and ancient fern and 'ohi'a forest as the trail skirts the edge of Kilauea Iki Crater. Take your time here and enjoy the beauty and grace of the forest and birds. All along are short spur trails offering magnificent views of the crater. Judging size and distance is surprisingly difficult here until you see people walking on the crater floor. The abrupt contrast between the ancient fern forest and the newly created maw of the crater floor couldn't be greater. Though the forest is lush and cool, the 4,000-foot altitude seems to prevent mosquito problems here (though it's always a good idea to bring a repellent, just in case). Before the trail veers inland for a bit, take a look across at Pu'u Pua'i and you will appreciate the scale of the eruptive event. Just keep to the left whenever you encounter a trail intersection. The descent into the crater is somewhat steep, but there are steps carved into the trail in spots and a few railings to help ease the way.

In a heartbeat you go from lush forest to barren lava. The trail bears to your left for a bit, then goes right. Cairns (piles of rock) mark the path across the floor. The lava here is more jagged since it contains remnants of lava spatters rather than the smooth lava farther ahead. Keep an eye out for a small sign pointing to the actual vent, where lava fragments are accumulating. Where steam escapes from cracks, you will notice minerals leaching from the rock. The steam seems unoffensive compared to the nasty stuff that comes out of parts of Halema'uma'u. We like to have lunch near a steam vent about ⅓ way across the crater floor.

The crater floor is quiet and peaceful. You may be hot, cold, wet or dry here, depending on the weather. (Gee, *that's* a useful piece of insight.) Sounds bounce around the crater in an unpredictable way. You may hear the crunching of footsteps when no one is nearby. Plants and trees are already starting to make themselves at home in cracks on the lava floor. It's amazing to stand in this near-dead crater and to see and hear the profusion of life all around you just beyond this hostile field of Pele's destruction.

After you ascend the crater wall, keep to your left along the edge of the crater, and you are back at the overlook. Outstanding!

Napau Crater Trail

Another nice hike is the Napau Crater Trail to **Pu'u Huluhulu.** The trail (occasionally called the Mauna Ulu Trail) is the only place in the park where you can get a glimpse of Pu'u 'O'o, the heart of the recent eruption. (There is an easier view of Pu'u 'O'o outside the park—see page 113.) Mauna Ulu (meaning growing mountain) erupted between 1969 and 1974, adding more than 200 acres of new land to Hawai'i's coastline, and its effects are dramatically seen on this trail. It was Kilauea's second longest flank eruption in recorded history. This trail starts on an old segment of Chain of Craters Road. (Twelve miles of this road were buried by the Mauna Ulu flow and we've shown it on the map on the inside back cover as a stippled line.) This fairly easy trek wanders over the young Mauna Ulu flow, as well as through old forest. You'll notice stone sentries along the way, strangely shaped columns of rock. These are called **lava trees.** When lava from the Mauna Ulu flow coursed its way through here, it occasionally encountered exceptionally wet trees. These resisted the flow and the temperatures long enough for the lava to harden around the tree. When the lava level lowered, these piles remained. You will often see a circle in the middle of lava trees, the outline of the now-dead tree. Sometimes, there are half-circle outlines of the tree. These are on the upstream side of the lava, showing you which way the lava flowed.

At about 30 minutes, you come to Pu'u Huluhulu (shaggy hill), a heavily forested mound. There is a five-minute spur trail leading up to the top. From there you get an awesome view of Mauna Ulu, a third of a mile in front of

Napau Crater Trail Map

you. You may see Puʻu ʻOʻo smoldering off in the distance (quite a bit to the left of Mauna Ulu, partially obscured by the Kane Nui o Hamo Lava Shield—see map). Be sure to look down into the pristine, fern-filled rain forest below you in the crater. It's utterly untouched, looking much like it did a thousand years ago. Looking off in the distance, you can see how the Mauna Ulu flow cut into the heart of the forest, going from green to black in a single footstep.

The view of Mauna Ulu is gorgeous. Looking over at it, you might be tempted to walk over to the top and peer into **Mauna Ulu Crater.** If so, check your insurance and see ADVENTURES.

Most people turn around from here. Past this point the trail goes to the massive Makaopuhi Crater, then to Napau Crater, where there is camping permitted. (You need a permit to go that far.) That's 7 miles one way. Three miles past that is Puʻu ʻOʻo but the trail is currently closed past Napau because the

ground is so unstable at Puʻu ʻOʻo. There is no one there to enforce the rule, but only a fool (or a geologist) would go walking around there. A wrong or unlucky step, and you're toast.

Just before Napau, you will pass the remains of an old pulu factory. Pulu is the soft, down-like fuzz that covers the stems of some ferns. Someone thought it would make a great stuffing for pillows and mattresses, so they built a factory out here. Unfortunately, pulu turns to dust after a few years. Consequently, so did their business.

Earthquake Trail/Byron Ledge

There is a cluster of trails around and below Volcano House. One of our favorite combinations is described below. It sounds more complicated than it is—use the map on page 90. All told, it takes 90–120 minutes and is moderately difficult (if that). You descend, then ascend about 400 feet. This is a good hike to take on a clear day because the

Forests ruled by ferns and ʻohiʻa trees make volcano hiking a time of wonder and magic.

views of the crater can be spectacular.

From the Visitor Center, you can walk around the right side of Volcano House, eventually heading to your left as you pass in front of Volcano House. Parts of the old trail and Crater Rim Road *fell into the crater* after an earthquake in 1983. This part of the road has become part of the Crater Rim Trail. It is eerie to see the road split in half, with guard rails dangling into nothingness. Large, gaping chasms in the old road dispel any notions you may have that ground is inherently stable. Parts of the trail detour from the old road for safety reasons, but it is fascinating to try to safely glimpse as much of the crumbling road as you can, even if through the bushes at times. The best part shows the guard-rail and split road. Watch for this part as it's off the main trail. When the road forks, you'll usually take the right fork whenever you can. See map. The trail will eventually leave the road and descend through 'ohi'a forest. You link up with the Byron Ledge Trail (where you turn right) and continue to the Kilauea crater floor. (The map and trail intersection signs make it much clearer.) On the crater floor, you'll get an idea of the texture of a skimmed-over lava lake. You are only on the crater floor for a few minutes before you head back up. It's not overly steep. On the way back up, you will pass the remains of a recent landslide. Look up from the big rock. You are at eye level and can almost feel the slide coming at you.

At the intersection with **Sandalwood ('Iliahi) Trail,** you have the choice of continuing (which is a little steeper) or taking the Sandalwood Trail. We recommend the latter. It straddles the crater for awhile, featuring great views and several steam vents. Then take the Sulphur Banks Trail back to the Visitor Center.

You might want to add the **Kilauea Iki Trail** to this hike. You can access it early on from the Byron Ledge Trail. See map and description of Kilauea Iki earlier.

Also in the Park...

Consider the **Crater Rim Trail.** It circles the entire Kilauea Caldera and makes for a long day. But segments such as the one between Volcano House and the Jagger Museum are dramatic. The part from the Escape Road to Chain of Craters Road passes through an exquisite fern canopy.

From the end of Chain of Craters road, there may or may not be a trail to an **active lava flow.** See the volcano section for more on that.

There are long, overnight trails (with camping) **Halape, Keauhou,** and **Ka'aha.** Hikes are down the mountain or along the coast and go for many miles. Contact the Park Service at 985–6000 for more information.

KOHALA AREA
Malama Trail to Puako Petroglyphs

Located near the Mauna Lani Resort in Kohala, this 10–15 minute long trail (each way) through a kiawe forest has a few petroglyphs sprinkled along the way. (Kiawe thorns are evil, wicked, and hateful; be careful not to let them penetrate your shoe.) The real payoff is at the end (just past a dirt road intersection) with hundreds and hundreds of lava carvings adjacent to each other in this field in the middle of nowhere. The reasons for the Hawaiians' selection of this site has been lost to the ages. Perhaps the most obvious reason is that the slabs in this area make nice canvases. Regardless, some Hawaiians say that if you close your eyes and listen to the breeze, you can hear the sound of rock scraping against rock.

Kiholo Bay

This is a fabulous place, but access is a little unusual. (See map below.) You can catch a nice glimpse of the bay from the scenic turnout near the 82 mile marker on Highway 19. Through a bizarre (and eyebrow raising) agreement with the state, the wealthy landowners around Kiholo have permission to lock the public access gate whenever they wish. For practical reasons (deliveries, etc.) they *usually* leave it unlocked between 8 a.m. and 4 p.m. on weekdays and lock it the rest of the time. Consequently, one is rarely comfortable bringing a car down here for fear of being locked in. (That's the idea.) Dependable access often means walking this road or the trail from the main highway just south of the 81 mile marker. If you take the latter trail, park near the guard-rail and go straight down 10 feet or so. On the left side heading toward the ocean over a small pile of rocks is a trail. (It had been a road until it was disabled to keep out the less ambitious.) The trail from the highway to Kiholo Bay takes 15–20 minutes. When the trail becomes a gravel road, it will eventually curve to the left. Look for a faint trail from the dirt road to the ocean.

Kiholo Bay is a beautiful and uniquely shaped ocean inlet. It has several points of interest that make it great for exploring. First, the lagoon offers waters that are usually dead calm (but cold and a bit cloudy due to freshwater springs leaking into the bay, kicking up fine silt). Turtles abound here, grazing on limu in the bay. The fishponds inland, called Wainanali'i Pond, are on private property. Turtles swim through the man-made channel to the fishponds at night, perhaps to sleep unmolested. Walking around this part of the bay offers magnificent scenery. You can usually look right into the lagoon water and see the fish.

This whole area was once a gigantic freshwater and brackish fishpond, built by Kamehameha the Great in 1810 after another fishpond (where the airport is now) was destroyed by lava from the 1801 Hualalai flow. Enormous stone walls up to 6 feet tall and 20 feet wide were laboriously erected, creating a deep pool 2 miles in circumference where all manner of deep sea fish were stocked. It was said that half the population worked to complete it and was considered one of the "artificial wonders of Hawai'i" at the time. The lagoon now composing the farthest reaches of Kiholo Bay was once part of that pond, and the water-worn stones were part of the wall. The Mauna Loa lava flow of 1859 traveled *30 miles* to fill in most of the pond and breach the southern wall, creating the lagoon. Fresh water, which initially fed the pond, still intrudes into the bay from springs. Since the water in the back part of the bay is usually as calm as a swimming pool, the snorkeling there, though the visibility is poor, can be surreal. If nobody has been there to disturb the

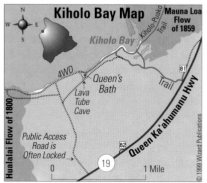

Kiholo Bay Map

Kiholo Bay is a fabulous place to wander around.

water (except for the ubiquitous turtles), the swimmer or snorkeler might encounter what appears to be a pane of glass suspended horizontally in the water about a foot down. That's the lighter fresh water floating on top of the heavier seawater. Left undisturbed, the dividing line between the two can be straight, razor thin, and very visible. If you swim slowly with your hand extended vertically in the middle of the joining of these two layers, the top of your hand will be cold (from the freshwater) and the bottom will be warm (from the seawater).

Walking south along the gravel shoreline, you pass several houses. One is called the **Bali House.** It was built by the guy you see on TV who runs Paul Mitchell hair care products. He paid 200 Balinese workers $1.50 a day for two years to create the intricate carvings and assemble the house. All was then disassembled and shipped to Kiholo Bay, where American and Balinese workers reassembled it. To the shock of many, they used large green logs from the *Borneo rain forest,* which shrank and split in less-humid Hawai'i, and much effort went into responding to the shrinking structure. While being built, the owner was amazingly gracious about letting people tour the house, so many on the island have gotten to see the inside. The Bali House is about midway between the row of houses on the beach, and you *will* know it when you see it.

Continuing south, you'll pass a big yellow house with security cameras, tennis courts, and guards named Bruiser. (It's owned by the guy who invented the pacemaker.) About 100–200 yards south of the tennis courts, only 40 feet from the ocean *and on state land* is a delight known as **Queen's Bath** (Keanalele Waterhole). It's just off the mauka (mountain) side of the trail and easy to miss. There you are, spitting distance from the ocean, in a fabulous crystal clear, spring-fed lava tube bath, open to the sky in two spots. (See photo on page 32.) It is attached to a dry lava tube cave, shown on the map. (By the way, the dry part of the lava tube has numerous petroglyphs carved into it and can be fascinating to visit if you are careful and keep your eyes peeled.) Though filled with fresh water, its level rises and falls each day with the tides. (It goes back farther than it looks—a waterproof flashlight can make exploring it fun.) You can't help but think it doesn't get much better than this. Once you've refreshed yourself in the exquisitely cool water, you can make your way back to your car. By the way, if you have a lot of suntan lotion on, please consider rinsing in the ocean first, perhaps in the bay, to avoid leaving an oil slick in the bath.

The Golden Pools of Ke-awa-Iki

How about a hike that leads to a deserted beach with white sand on one end and black sand on the other? A trail that leads over harsh aʻa, along the beach, past a jewel-like freshwater pool and back to your car in 4 miles. We've taken friends on this hike and they love it. It displays the raw nature of the Kohala coast, has a variety of sights, and rewards you with a cool dip that you'll never forget. (See photo on page 55.)

Slightly north of the 79 mile marker on Queen K (Hwy. 19) there are boulders blocking a road on the fresh (150-year-old) lava leading to the sea. (See close-up map on page 144.) Take the road-turned trail toward the ocean and go around the right side of the fence. (There's a *very* vague trail across the pahoehoe lava to the south of the main trail, but it's too difficult to follow.)

The beach was created when lava from the 1859 Mauna Loa eruption flowed 30 miles, landing at the north end of the beach. The black sand created hasn't had a chance to mix with the previous white beach sand at the southern end, resulting in a nice blend from black to white along the stretch. Just past the south end there are tide-pools to explore if you have reef shoes.

Continuing north (right) you'll come to Pueo Bay. Large amounts of fresh water enter this tiny bay from underground, creating some strange snorkeling conditions. From Pueo Bay you can either take the trail toward the highway (to the right of a very large lava rock) to the pools, or take the other trail to Weliweli Point and link up with another trail. Look for the latter to Weliweli marked with pieces of coral. (The map makes these trails easier to picture.) The pools (there are two of them) can be seen from far away because they are marked by hala trees. (The end of their branches look like palm tree-inspired pompons.) Once at the pools, take a moment to savor the scene. Here in the middle of all this raw harshness is a magnificent oasis—fresh water (no hint of seawater at all) lined with golden-coated lava. (The gold comes from a growth on the rocks; be careful not to damage them by walking on them too much.) Revel and frolic in your unexpected paradise before taking the trail back to your car.

OTHER BEACH HIKES

For other beach hikes, often to secluded spots, check out **Honomalino, Makalawena, Honokaʻope, Green Sand, ʻAnaehoʻomalu** (going south to the freshwater pool), and **Road to the Sea** (the second beach), all described under BEACHES. Also consider the trail between **Spencer Beach Park** and **Hapuna.** It's along the shoreline and is vague only where it crosses the golf course at hole #3.

WAIMEA TO WAIPI'O VALLEY

This hike has some of the tastiest views of any hike on the island and is one of our favorite hikes on the whole island. It leads from Waimea to the top of the back edge of Waipi'o Valley. It's moderately strenuous (if that; it depends on how far you go), has forest and valley views, and is quiet. The trail was cut to facilitate the construction of the Hamakua Ditch system in the early 1900s. The first 40 minutes is through forest. Then you come to a nearly sheer drop-off to Waipi'o Valley. It's amazing how abruptly the back of the valley starts from the plains above. (Surprisingly, the large valleys in this part of the island were often created by unimaginably catastrophic landslides like the one described on page 75, *not* just erosion.) There *may* be a superb waterfall across the valley, if it's been raining. If you are vertiginous, picnic here before returning. Others will want to take the trail along the perimeter of the valley, then through a bamboo grove to a ginger grove (be careful of holes in parts of the ginger matting). Return when you want, 2–4 miles into it, don't try to loop it. The trail is well cut, but be observant. A 2,000-foot tumble into the valley would be ugly. This is a truly great hike when the weather is good, a lackluster hike when the weather is bad. Winter months are *usually* best, but it's *real* hard to predict the weather here and it can change (either way) on a dime. Mornings *greatly* enhance your chance of good weather. The first part of the trail, at the end of White Road in Waimea (right side of map

on page 123) is through a pasture. (Cattle may be present at the beginning.) This is Hawaiian Homelands for the first few minutes, so please be respectful, leave nothing behind, and close the gates. There's debate as to whether the first part is public easement, so be nice.

OFF SADDLE ROAD

This hike, called the **Pu'u 'O'o Trail,** is named after a pu'u (hill) that you won't see 3½ miles north of the trailhead. (Not to be confused with the different, *erupting* Pu'u 'O'o at Kilauea Volcano. *That* exciting hike is described under ADVENTURES, page 212.) This hike is 3½ hours round trip through pahoehoe, a'a and several kipukas (islands of older forest in a sea of younger lava). You'll hear birds and may see animals such as wild sheep or pigs. The trail is vague in spots but generally straight with little elevation change. At about 3 miles, there's a small lava tube cave on your left. This is a good place to eat lunch. Past here you go through a particularly lush kipuka before the trail empties onto a lava field. Tags and cairns (also called ahus, or piles of rocks) have guided you thus far, but the trail gets difficult to follow from here. Although it eventually links up with a dirt road, allowing for a loop hike, it's vague. It's best to retrace your steps from here and come back the way you came unless you're aching to check out the cave. If you are, then link up with the dirt road, and see ADVENTURES on page 216 for a description of this very cool lava tube.

Pu'u 'O'o Trail is occasionally difficult to follow; keep an eye for cairns and tree tags and generally stay in the same direction. The trailhead is on the southern side of the road (right side if you are coming from Kona) on Saddle Road;

park half way between the 22 & 23 mile markers. Elevation is nearly 6,000 feet, so be prepared for potentially chilly weather. This is an OK hike—not a great one—good for breaking up the long Saddle Road drive.

Mauna Loa Summit

Getting to the top of Mauna Loa is tough, no matter which way you slice it. It's 13,677 feet high and there are no roads to the summit. You can do it the hard way, or the *very* hard way—it's your choice. The first is a 3 to 5 day hike from the Kilauea side up the Mauna Loa Trail. The trail starts at the end of the Mauna Loa Scenic Road. This hike has been known to humble even the most conditioned athlete. Though the gradient rarely exceeds 12°, it's 38 miles round-trip through lava and you gain 6,500 feet. Red Hill Cabin is 7½ miles into the hike at 10,035 feet, and Mauna Loa Summit Cabin is near the crater rim at 13,250 feet—another 11½ miles. Some prefer to break this second leg (*ooh*, bad phrase) by overnighting at Water Hole halfway to Mauna Loa Cabin. This trail is in Hawai'i Volcanoes National Park, and you need a permit from them to camp.

The other way up is a *tough* 8-mile round-trip day hike from the **Mauna Loa Weather Observatory** off Saddle Road. (See page 134 for directions.) You start at 11,000 feet, so you won't have a chance to get acclimated—count on altitude sickness from starting so high. (Savvy hikers often car-camp at the weather observatory the night before to acclimate.) This trail is steeper than the Mauna Loa Trail and over rougher terrain, but you can do it in a day if you're into punishment, and the views across the saddle will be superb. Make sure you get an early start.

It's always cold up there, and snow can come at any time of the year without warning. Altitude sickness is common, even among the fittest. For either of these hikes, thorough preparation is the key. Just because you are in the tropics doesn't mean you can take this mountain lightly. The *base* may be in the tropics, but the *summit* is in Alaska. We recommend you pick up a dedicated hiking book that describes these hikes, and how to prepare for them, in detail. *Hawai'i Trails* by Kathy Morey is a good one.

Manuka State Park

A pleasant nature loop walk through native dry and wet forest. Located in the southwest part of the island off Highway 11 just north of the 81 mile marker, it takes 1–2 hours for the stroll, and sights are well marked by forestry personnel. There should be a decent map at the trailhead for you to follow, which includes lots of information. The latter half of the trail has some obnoxious footing on small chunks of 'a'a, so wear sturdy shoes. Otherwise, it's a pretty easy walk. Be sure to check out the lush pit crater. Kids seem to love climbing on some of the gnarled kukui and hau trees along the trail. There are tables and restrooms at the trailhead, a nice place for a picnic. Not the best hiking on the island, but pleasant nonetheless.

Umauma Falls

These exquisite multi-tiered falls are reached by hiking ½ mile in the stream. Tabis (described earlier) work best on wet rocks and are strongly recommended. (Don't go if the water is flowing too hard.) Located 16 miles north of Hilo, take the road inland at the 16 mile marker, turn

Eden? Nope. Umauma Falls.

right and park when the road veers for its first gulch. Enter from the near right (downstream) side of the bridge, then pass under the bridge and ignore the nasty little mutts barking at you from the far side. *Nobody* owns the stream itself. This is unmaintained, so you are on your own. Use your best judgment, and ignore anyone who tells you there aren't any falls up there. We've been lied to by selfish residents who want them all to themselves. By the way, the photo of the falls was taken from the World Botanical Gardens overlook described on page 116. Paying them $5 is certainly easier than hiking it, but being there is glorious.

KALOPA NATIVE FOREST STATE PARK

This is one of the nicer forest hikes on the island, and the park is well maintained for a state park. You go through a beautiful and very lush forest of tall trees and glorious ferns. You'll be skirting along the edge of a large gulch part of the time, then heading down an abandoned JEEP trail back to your car, unless

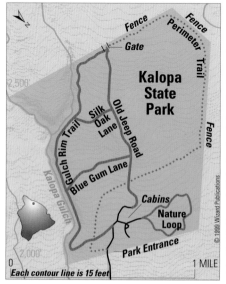

you choose to take the perimeter trail. It is less traveled than the old JEEP road, and the fence is always in sight. This hike is anywhere from 2–4 miles depending on your route, and the elevation gain from the bottom to the top is 400 feet.

This wet forest is heavenly. Take the time to notice the stunning forest around you. If it has thorns (as the brambles do), it's not native. Native plants didn't need to develop harsh defenses since there weren't any large, foraging animals to ward off.

Now a few warnings. It rains about 80 inches per year here, so the weather *may* be a factor. It's often best to go early in the day. The park facilities are maintained by the state, but the trails are not. That duty falls to volunteers who come out every three to six months (or longer) to pretty up the trails, cut fallen trees, etc. That means that if you arrive at the tail end of a maintenance cycle, the trail will be in poorer shape. Our map shows the trails as they are *supposed* to be. Intersections are usually marked, but you may need to keep an eye out for them if the signs have blown down. If you go along the gulch, it'll lead to the fence at the top of the park. (You'll need to cross a small and usually dry gulch about ¼ of the way along.) From the top it leads to the abandoned road (you'll see a gate). Either take the "road" (only a trail now) to the bottom, or continue on the less-used horse perimeter trail. The compacted dirt on the "road" can get pretty slippery on the way down, so be careful. Hiking boots are preferred here.

All in all, this is a great hike for anyone who wants to see the splendor of a Hawai'i forest. If you just aren't up to it, take the ¾-mile nature loop near the parking area. It goes through a native 'ohi'a forest and is worth the stroll. Camping with tents or at the cabins is available here—see CAMPING. Located 40 miles north of Hilo off the main highway. Take the road between the 39 and 40 mile markers and follow the signs. (No signs on the way out, so remember the route.)

HIKES DESCRIBED ELSEWHERE

The hike to **Captain Cook Monument** is listed on page 68; the cold hike to **Lake Wai-au** on top of Mauna Kea is shown on map on page 130. Hiking in **Waipi'o Valley** is described on page 121, plus an ADVENTURE on 210. The awesome hikes through a *pristine* rain forest to the erupting **Pu'u 'O'o Volcano Vent, current lava flows** and a two **lava tube** hikes are all under ADVENTURES, as is the trip into **Pololu Valley** and over to **Honokane Nui.**

Horseback Riding

If you want to let someone else do the walking consider horseback riding. The Big Island has quite a tradition when it comes to horses. There are lots of companies offering wildly different kinds of rides. It just depends on the type of riding and terrain you want to see.

Waipi'o Na'alapa Trail Rides (775–0419) has excellent rides in Waipi'o Valley. (See page 118 for more on this spectacular valley.) Two hours on horseback plus another half hour getting into and out of the valley via 4WD, this is an easy one to recommend. You cross several streams, see breathtaking waterfalls, walk along taro patches, and gen-

erally get a taste of old Hawai'i. $75 per person, 230 pound limit.

Waipi'o Ridge Stables (775–1007) is relatively new and has a very cool product. Instead of going *into* Waipi'o Valley, they skirt the edge, from Highway 240 to Hi'ilawe Falls before circling back. (See map on page 120.) The views from some of the overlooks are extraordinary. $75 for 2½ hours. Eight people max.

Paniolo Riding Adventures (889–5354) has nice quality horses and gear. Their 2½-hour trips are $85 and take you across a wide open working ranch featuring beautiful views. This is not one of those nose-to-tail rides. You go across open country and you can canter if you like. (That means to go faster than a trot for all you city slickers.) The guides aren't patronizing; they genuinely seem to want you to experience the peace of the Hawaiian countryside. Rides have between 2 and 14 people and aren't at all gimmicky. If it's calving season, you might get to see a calf being born. They also have 4-hour picnic rides for $125. Thick dusters and the like are available for free, but it's a good idea to bring a sweatshirt and long pants. Located ²⁄₁₀ mile north of the 13 mile mark on Highway 250 in Kohala. Bring food and water. Easy to recommend.

Kings' Trail Rides (323–2388) brings people down the 2-mile trail to Captain Cook Monument for some outrageous snorkeling, the best on the island. $95. The 1,300-foot descent is constant, and novices might get spooked at riding downhill the whole way. Lunch and snorkel gear (minus fins) are provided. Bring reef shoes for scrambling on the rocks at the water's edge.

Dahana Ranch (885–0057) has 1½-hour tours of their 2,500-acre ranch off the Old Mamalahoa Highway in southern Waimea for $55. You see lush, rolling pastures from open country, not from a trail. You may even get to ride their gentle but *enormous* Brahma bull. Bring warm clothes; it's sometimes misty or rainy in this part of Waimea. (You might want to call them for a weather check.) They also have round-up ride for $100. This is not the kind where you sit there while they do all the work. For at least 2½ hours, your group will do all the hard work from horseback while they bark out orders, and you'll probably have a great time doing it. Eight people are necessary for this. (Call them to see if any others have signed up.) Dahana Ranch has a 300-pound weight limit, and kids over 3 are welcome (except on the round-up ride). Well run by good folks.

Mauna Kea Stables (885–4288) is owned by the Mauna Kea Resort and the Hapuna Beach Prince Hotel. They offer 1-hour tours for $40 and 2-hour tours for $70. They use part of the 225,000-acre Parker Ranch in Waimea and don't use trails. Rider must be at least 8 years old and weigh no more than 210 pounds.

At Kilauea Volcano, **Hauoli Trail Rides** (985–7263) gives 2½-hour ($120), 4½-hour ($182) rides at and around Volcanoes National Park. Very nice setting for riding horses and the owners do a particularly good job. The price is pretty high, but so is the quality. You get what you pay for. They also have a 2-hour ranch ride for $95.

HORSE DRAWN WAGONS

Kohala Carriages (889–5955) takes you on a 2½-hour ride with lunch along a scenic part of North Kohala. At $47.50 it's probably the best of the wagon tour deals. Waipi'o Valley is

toured for an hour by **Waipi'o Valley Wagon Tours** (775–9518) for $40. **Hawaiian Dreams Carriages** (325–2280) takes people down Alii Drive in Kona for $50 for 40 minutes. That's per carriage, not per person. This Kona ride along the busy streets of town, frankly, feels a bit awkward, especially during the day. (Early evening works a bit better.) The Kohala and Waipi'o carriage tours work, but the Kona one seems a little goofy to us.

On the Big Island, kayaking is mostly an ocean affair. Whereas other islands, notably Kaua'i, have rivers to kayak, Hawai'i lacks navigable rivers. But there are several areas on the normally calm Kona coast where kayaking is excellent. Our favorite is across Kealakekua Bay to the Captain Cook Monument. (See page 67 for complete description of the bay.) The one-mile (each way) trip features usually calm waters, lots of spinner dolphins on most trips, and outrageous snorkeling at the monument. This is a *great* trip! Other kayak trips are from Kailua Pier to the north or south, or from Kohala beaches such as 'Anaeho'omalu. Old Kona Airport or Honokohau Harbor to Makalawena is a long, pleasant voyage. (See BEACHES for descriptions and locations of landings.) The area south of Keauhou Bay has numerous cavities (called "sea caves" by the more optimistic companies) that can be fun to paddle by.

Remember that the ocean, even in Kona, can be treacherous and unforgiving, especially during periods of high surf. We don't want to rain on anybody's parade, but if you don't give the ocean the respect it deserves, it can humble you quickly. Only paddle when it's calm, and always be wary near the shore where a rogue wave can beach (or rock) you.

RENTING A KAYAK

Kona Boy Kayaks (322–3600) is the best place to rent. They'll strap the kayak to your roof and off you go. **Aloha Kayak Company** (322–2868), **Kealakekua Bay Kayak** (323–3329) and **Ocean Safaris** (326–4699) also rent kayaks. Expect to pay around $45 per day for a double, $25–$30 for a single. (More in Kohala.) At Kealakekua Bay, put in on the left side of the cement landing near Napo'opo'o Beach Park. Be careful not to damage or walk on the coral when you land at the other side.

There's also a concession to the right of the pier in Kona that rents kayaks by the hour for use in that area. Some Kohala companies rent them by the minute (OK, OK...by the hour). Among them are **Red Sail Sports** (885–2876) and **Ocean Sports Waikoloa**

(885–5555) which rents them at 'Anaeho'omalu Beach. You'll have to cash in your IRA for the Kohala rentals.

If you want a guided trip, try **Hawai'i Pack & Paddle** (328–8911), **Kona Boy,** or **Ocean Safari.** They all have different guided tours. **Hawai'i Pack & Paddle** will give you a complete briefing, paddle with you, provide lunch and snorkel gear (for snorkeling at Honaunau Bay), and show you around Honaunau (Place of Refuge) for $79. They also have two and three day kayak/camping trips to remote areas. **Ocean Safaris** and **Kona Boy** also have tours. Between the latter two, we lean toward **Kona Boy.**

If ocean kayaking is not your thing, **Fluming the Ditch** (formerly Kohala Mountain Kayak Cruise) (889–6922) has a unique way to kayak—in the Kohala ditch. This narrow ditch spends much of its time in mountain tunnels. Along the way you learn about how this engineering feat was accomplished. Five people per kayak. No whitewater here, and don't expect it to be like the logger ride at Disneyland. You won't rush down a steep grade and splash at the bottom. You drift along fairly slow, most of the time, but you may get wet when passing under intersecting streams. Go for the nice views and information, not for a thrill ride. $85 for 1½ hours.

Watch for spinner dolphins during your kayak trip across Kealakekua Bay.

In addition to the standard bus tours listed in BASICS, there's a company that handles things a little differently. **ATV Outfitters** (889–6000) will take you around some private land near the northern tip of the island on ATVs. (You know, those things that look like Tonka Toys on steroids with knobby tires.) For $90 you cruise along for 2 hours, taking in the coastal scenery. They'll provide beverages and long pants (if you left them at home). The ATVs are easy to operate with automatic transmissions. (Riding wimps will do fine on these.) You need to weigh between 90–220 pounds. (The upper number takes into account the fact that most of us lie about our weight. If you're 230, you'll probably be all right.) All in all, it's lots of fun, and the coastal scenery they show you is great.

Aspen has its ski slopes, Washington has its monuments, Orlando has Disney World, and the Big Island has the Kona Coast waters. Quite simply, if you visit the Big Island and don't indulge in Kona waters, you haven't *really* been to the Big Island.

The waters off the Kona Coast are the finest in all the islands. Calmer, clearer, and teeming with fish, residents of other islands turn *blue* with envy. A popular way to see it is on an ocean tour. If you take one of the many tours along the coast, you may see marlin jumping about and turtles. You are *likely* to see dolphins, flying fish off the bow, and whales during whale season. You *will* see smiles from fellow passengers.

You're less likely to get seasick on Kona's calm waters than anywhere else we can think of. Nonetheless, if you take seasickness medication, do it *before* you leave. Some long-lasting medications like Dramamine II or Bonine will help if you take it the night before, as well as the day of a trip. Scopolamine patches need to be prescribed but work well. Some say that greasy foods and citrus are a no-no. Others say take ginger pills, or put a cherry seed in your bellybutton, if you've got the nerve. Boats are usually less crowded on weekends since that's when visitors usually arrive and depart the island. Remember that most single-hull power boats are smoothest in the back.

KEALAKEKUA BAY

The Captain Cook Monument in Kealakekua Bay is a favorite destination. Snorkeling near the monument is perhaps the best you will find anywhere in the state. If you've never snorkeled before, this is the place to start. Experienced snorkelers will be dazzled. A large number of spinner dolphins reside in the bay, and you're likely to see them—perhaps even swim with them, if you're lucky. (They are called spinners because they are the only untrained dolphins that routinely leap clear of the water and spin on their longitudinal axis.) Companies sometimes offer morning or afternoon tours. Take the morning; it's calmer and the water is usually clearer.

Fair Wind II (322–2788) uses a 63-foot power catamaran to bring 100 or so people. They leave from Keauhou Bay, 7½ miles north and stay tied to their mooring for a couple hours of snorkeling, BBQ burgers, and general frolicking. People seem to enjoy the short water-slide into the water and the no-host bar. Restrooms, hose to rinse salt off, shade, ♿ accessible. Nice, easy entry and exit from water, SCUBA and SNUBA also available for extra. Continental breakfast on board. It's not as crowded on board as it looks from a distance. Unfortunately, since they troll along the way, the boat travels too far from the coast to see much of the coastal features. The sail is for decoration—you will be motoring the whole way—but the boat is fairly smooth. This is a good tour, especially for those who are wary about ocean travel. $83 for the 4½-hour morning tour, $48 for the 3½-hour afternoon tour. (An hour less at the bay and snacks instead of a meal.) Avoid seats adjacent to the starboard diving platform; you and your stuff will get splashed. They also have a sunset/night snorkeling cruise described under DINING on page 247.

Sea Quest (329–7238) is totally different. They take six-passengers on their 20 foot rigid-hull inflatables (which is a good design because it absorbs bumps better than a regular rubber raft) to the Captain Cook Monument and beyond to **Honaunau** (Place of Refuge) for snorkeling. It's still bumpier than the Fair Wind II, and there's no shade. (But bumpier means more thrilling.) You won't have all that wandering room that you have on the Fair Wind II, and it's snacks instead of a meal. But these guys go near the coastline and do the best job

of anyone narrating what you are seeing. Along the way they poke the boat into several "sea caves" (more like sea cavities) and show you how they are formed. We like them better than Captain Zodiac below because they snorkel in two spots, aren't nearly as crowded, and take their time on the way back. (They can afford to because they depart from Keauhou Bay, 10 miles closer to the monument than Captain Zodiac.) $67 for the more recommended 4 hour morning trip, $50 for the 3-hour afternoon trip which omits Honaunau.

Fair Wind Raft Adventure (322–2788) is run by the same Fair Wind folks but is similar to Sea Quest. A 28-foot rigid-hull inflatable (which is nicer that Sea Quest's) leaves Kailua Pier and heads to Kealakekua for snorkeling. Unlike most inflatables, there's shade here. They'll stop on the way back for more snorkeling and use the rest of the time exploring the coastline. $64.

Captain Zodiac (329–3199) leaves from Honokohau Harbor 17 miles north of your destination at Kealakekua Bay. One of the four hours is spent at the monument area with snacks provided. $67 per person. This is an adequate tour, but we recommend Sea Quest or the Fair Wind over Captain Zodiac.

Lanakila (326–6000) usually cruises from Kailua Pier to Kealakekua Bay (but sometimes north to Pawai Bay) for snorkeling in their 60-foot trimaran. 10 a.m. to 3 p.m., continental breakfast and small BBQ lunch provided. During slow times they don't book up and won't go unless you bring lots of friends.

OTHER BOAT DESTINATIONS

Body Glove (326–7122) goes to a different location. Their two-deck 50-foot trimaran cruises from Kailua Pier to Pawai Bay, 2 miles north. (See page 151 for complete description of Pawai Bay.) 100 people maximum. Continental breakfast at boarding, deli lunch at site. In addition to snorkeling, they have SCUBA (for an extra fee), both certified and beginner. A good boat, crew, and location make this a good deal, and we recommend it wholeheartedly. Lots of shade, water-slide, restrooms, and a full bar on board. 4½-hour tour ($72), 2½ hours of which is at Pawai Bay. Inner tubes and see-thru boogie boards for the timid. Afternoon cruise to the same place is 3 hours ($48) and snacks instead of a meal. Only ding is that they charge for most beverages. Most boats include this. Of course, the overall price is cheap, so we shouldn't complain.

One of the most unique trips we've seen is **Hawaiian Ocean Adventures** (325–0766). They use a 40-foot speedboat to ply the waters. That alone sets them apart from the other companies. But they also do something no one else we know of has done. They bring kayaks along on the boat, usually speed north from Kona to Makalawena or Kua Bay (two excellent beaches) and then put the kayaks in the water and let you paddle around. They also provide snorkel gear and lunch. Their ad says they use the boats to "gain access to those pristine hidden beaches...that only locals know about." (Guess they haven't read our BEACHES section lately.) It's $70 for the 4½-hour trip. Shorter trips also available.

Kamanu Charters (329–2021) leaves Honokohau Harbor in their 36-foot *sailing* catamaran and heads 2¼ miles south to Pawai Bay. $48, 24 pas-

sengers at most, good snorkeling, and snacks provided. Only a little shade for this 3-hour tour (like Gilligan's Island?). Though an acceptable trip (unless you *have* to sail) you're better off on the Body Glove—better boat, longer trip.

Kailua Bay Charter (324–1749) has quickie tours (under an hour) of Kailua Bay with a glass-bottom boat for $25. No food, just a quick jaunt through the water. Leaves from Kailua Pier.

Kona Paradise Cruises (331–2992) uses a glass bottom boat (called the Coral See) for a "historical" cruise from Kailua Pier to Keauhou Bay (6 miles away) in Kona. They can pack 149 people on the 65-foot boat (but usually don't), and you get snacks and juices onboard along with entertainment and historical narration for $44. Certainly not the cream of the crop, only marginally interesting.

IN KOHALA...

Red Sail Sports (885–2876) uses their 50-foot sailing catamaran to take people out of 'Anaeho'omalu Beach to two of several locations for snorkeling. Motor one way and sail back. Four-hour trip includes continental breakfast and deli lunch for $75. Other tours offered as well included a dinner cruise.

For **Dinner Cruises,** see DINING on page 247. **Submarine** and **semisubmersible,** see page 203.

Parasailing is where you get pulled by a boat while attached to a parachute and a long line. We've done it, and to many people (including us) it *looks* more fun and thrilling than it really is, and doesn't seem worth the money. If you have your heart set on it, **UFO Parasail** (325-5836) will drag you around for $45 for a 7-minute ride, $55 for a 10-minute ride. Tandem rides available.

If you are already into SCUBA, or are interested in trying it out, you've found paradise on the west side of the Big Island. Whereas the east (windward) side of the island offers poorer diving due to river runoff and rough waters, the Kona side is indisputably the best in the state. There are no permanent streams on the *entire* west side (from the northern tip to the southern tip), so runoff is not a problem. Kona waters are mostly shielded from winds and the ocean's prevailing northeast swell, so calmness is the norm. Fish, coral and divers appreciate the warmer water of the Big Island, the southernmost of all Hawaiian Islands. It's 75° at its coldest in February, 82° at its warmest in October. 100+ foot visibility is common.

You have your choice of boat dives or shore dives. Boats mostly leave from Kailua Pier, Honokohau Harbor, and Kawaihae Harbor. Standard dives here are two tanks at two different sites. When we list a price range in the table, it refers to those who have their own gear, and those who need to rent it. The island has no decompression chamber. Everyone knows not to fly after a dive, but don't

forget that the heights of some of our mountains simulate flying as far as your tissues are concerned. Just the saddle *between* Mauna Loa and Mauna Kea is 6,600 feet. And if you decide to drive to Place of Refuge from Kona, you'll reach 1,400 feet—too high if you dove deep.

We tend to like companies that wander toward the boat for the latter part of the dive and allow you to go up when *you* are near the end of your tank, as opposed to everyone going up when the heaviest breather has burned up his/her tank. If you yourself are a heavy breather, Hawaiian Divers may rent their larger tank to you.

So you'll know the perspective that we approach this from, we should tell you what we do and don't like when we go on a dive. On a bad dive, the dive master takes the group on a non-stop excursion that keeps you kicking the whole time. No time to stop and explore the nooks and crannies. Good outfits will give you a briefing, tell you about some of the endemic species here, what to look for, and will point out various things on the dives, keeping it moving but not too fast. Bad outfits kick a lot. Good outfits explain the unique qualities of Hawai'i's environment. Bad dive masters may tell you what *they* saw (but *you* missed). Good companies work around your needs, wishes, and desires. Bad companies keep everyone on a short leash. Good dive masters know their stuff and share it with you. Bad dive masters don't know squat but imply they know it all in order to impress you.

The best boat dive operators are **Dive Makai** and **Aloha Dive** (boat dives only). **Jack's Diving Locker** (boat dives and shop) is also excellent. All are in Kona.

If you've never dived, several companies will introduce you to SCUBA by giving instructions then taking you down on a supervised dive. That's how I started, and I was smitten enough to get certified. **Dive Makai** does the best intros. $119 for one-tank boat dives with *lots* of personalized instruction.

THE TOPS IN KONA

Dive Makai (329–2025) has a boat only, no shop. They give the best briefings on what you will see, and they take a vote on where you want to go (or what kind of environment you want to see). The crew approaches each dive with the excitement of new divers, but with the

judgment of old-timers. The 31-foot Radon is not the fanciest you'll find, but it does the job well, without the jitters affecting smaller boats. They take their time, have a good ascent policy, and are very sensitive to the ocean world. (You won't see them torturing an octopus for your enjoyment like we've seen others do before.) Snacks on board, up to 12 passengers. They also do night dives on request.

Aloha Dive Company (325–5560) is right up there with Dive Makai in terms of attitude and quality of dive; it's a toss-up as to who we prefer. The boat is a fast

DIVE OPERATOR	SERVICES AVAILABLE	PRICE OF 2 TANK BOAT	RENT GEAR SHORE DIVE	CAMERA RENTAL	DIVE COMPUTER	MANTA RAY NIGHT DIVE	DIVE CERTIFICATION	Rx MASKS
ECO-ADVENTURES 329–7116	Dive Shop, Boat & Shore Dives	$97 – $112	$50	$35	$10	$97 – $112 (Includes 1 dusk dive)	$425	Yes
DIVE MAKAI 329–2025	Boat Dives	$95 – $119	No	No	Yes (Required)	None	No	No
KONA COAST 329–8802	Dive Shop & Boat Dives	$80 – $95	$32	$30	None	$65 – $80	$550	Yes
JACK'S DIVING LOCKER 329–7585	Dive Shop, Boat & Shore Dives	$80 – $95	$40	None	$15 Extra	$85 – $100 (Includes 1 dusk dive)	$400 – $600	Yes
HAWAIIAN DIVERS 329–5662	Dive Shop & Boat Dives	$99 – $114	$25	No	*$40* Extra!	$99 – $114	$350	Yes
SANDWICH ISLE 329–9188	Dive Shop & Boat Dives	$75 – $85	$33	$30	$10 Extra	$60 – $70	$450	Yes
RED SAIL SPORTS 885–2876	Boat & Shore Dives	$89 – $109	No	No	None	None	$650	Yes
KOHALA DIVERS 882–7774	Dive Shop & Boat Dives	$85 – $97	$30	None	Included	None	$450 – $600	No
PLANET OCEAN WATERSPORTS 935–7277	Dive Shop, Boat & Shore Dives	None	$30	No	$5 Extra	None	$150	Yes
ALOHA DIVE 325–5560	Boat Dives	$85	No	None	Included	$85	$500	Yes
BIG ISLAND DIVERS 329–6068	Dive Shop & Boat Dives	$80 – $90	$28	No	Included	$55	$450	Yes

30-foot custom built craft that can do 40 knots. (It could use a little more shade area.) This means that they can do dives in areas too remote for other companies. Home-grown local boys Mike and Earl have an enthusiasm about diving that is missing from most companies, and their knowledge of marine life is refreshing. Mike excels at pointing out things you may overlook, while Earl slowly cruises as you do the discovering. Both take their time, and you'll probably do one dive with each guy. Only problem we've experienced is that their calm, laid-back attitude that works so well on the boat sometimes translates into failures to return calls. (Gotta pick up the messages, guys.)

Jack's Diving Locker (329–7585) is a good shop with a 38-foot boat for up to 12 divers and a tiny 23-foot 6-pack when they don't have enough bookings. Good ascent policy, hot shower, and dive masters carry slates. They do a lot of work with novices, but experienced divers will also be pleased. They are also careful with the ocean's critters.

OTHERS IN KONA

Big Island Divers (329–6068) is an improved company since our last edition. Their boat is an unremarkable 28-foot 6-pack. They're better than before, but not great. **Eco-Adventures** (329–7116) is a large outfit with a nice 50-foot catamaran and hot shower. (They also have two other smaller boats.) Standard two-tank dives with deli lunch, 3-tank BBQ dives, manta dives, and a blue water/open water dive where you hang off a tether and wait for pelagics. Nitrox available. They have grown to be very large, and their dives can sometimes feel like you're in a diver processing machine. They also seem to nickel and dime you. Example:

You take a twilight dive; one tank before sunset and a manta night dive. They charge $5 for a flashlight, then tell you can't use it for the first dive, only the second. *Gee, thanks guys!* **Hawaiian Divers** (329–5662) has a nice 42-foot boat (up to 20 passengers, usually less). They also have nitrox. Expect to be vetted; Hawaiian Divers is an advanced, nononsense business, so wipe that smile off your face and straighten those shoulders! Underwater combat extra. **Kona Coast** (329–8802) has two boats—a small one and a big one. Their shop is technically good, but they can be *very* snotty, even for a dive shop. **Sandwich Isle Divers** (329–9188) has an adequate shop, but their 26-foot Radon is *small*. Their attitude is sometimes great, sometimes grating. 6 divers max. **Manta Ray Dives** (334–1154) has a glass-bottom dive boat that also takes snorkelers—manta dive only. (I have to confess to having this overwhelming urge to swim under their boat where the glass is, take out my regulator and pound on the bottom as if I'm trapped.)

IN KOHALA

The diving in Kohala is often richer in coral than Kona. Lush finger coral gardens are plentiful. It's a bit less protected than Kona and sometimes bumpy, especially in winter. Unfortunately, there aren't any operators in Kohala that make us warm and squishy. If we had to choose, we'd probably go with **Kohala Divers** (882–7774). Their 36-foot boat is pretty comfortable. They try to appeal to advanced divers and they're pretty friendly folks. **Red Sail Sports** (885–2876) is a large Kohala Resort area concessionaire with a 39-foot dive boat. Groups are rushed into the water and held on a tight leash. Get out, let's go, next site. We received *no* briefing whatsoever. 18 divers max. Good cookies and cold shower on board. They also do shore dives and have scooters available.

Mauna Kea Divers (883–9298) The good news? They've got a pretty good boat. The bad news—Everything else. Bad shop, bad attitude, bad choice.

IN HILO

Yes, they *do* dive Hilo side. Though the visibility and calmness are *much* better on the Kona side, life is abundant here and often overlooked. You may see more turtles in some spots here than Kona. In the past there was only one shop, and it wasn't much of a choice. Now there's **Planet Ocean Watersports** (935–7277). They have a boat, rent gear for shore dives, and do some very novel dives, including *lava* dives (where accomplished divers can see lava flowing underwater). Call them for any east Hawai'i-related dive questions. **East Hawai'i Divers** (965–7840) gives guided shore dives for $55. Private groups—he promises that you won't see any other divers where he takes you. He dives all over the east side. A good resource.

MANTA RAY NIGHT DIVE

This dive is *so* good, we put it in the ADVENTURES section. If you are a diver or want to be, check out that section and make plans for the dive of a lifetime.

DIVE SITES

Mentioning specific boat dive spots isn't particularly helpful because different companies sometimes use different names for the same spots, and you will usually go where the boat goes. As far as shore dive spots are concerned, here are some beauties you may want to check out on the Kona side. For Hilo side, see Planet Ocean Watersports above.

Crystal Cove—Also used as a boat dive area, it is in Kohala, north of Kawaihae Harbor, off the main highway 100 feet south of the 5 mile marker. It's a 2–3 minute walk on the dirt road (drive all the way with a JEEP), and enter on the right side if the surf's not up. (Entry is not too difficult, but not a breeze either.) Coral garden is thick and lush; depths mostly less than 40. If there's no boat here, you'll have it all to yourself.

Puako—Virtually every dive shop and book tells you to go to the end of the road where the pavement becomes dirt. (You actually turn right *just before* the end.) Go about 25 yards on the dirt, park, and swim out about 50–75 yards. Turn right (north) and you should see several large vertical holes in the reef to drop through to the bottom. Exit the tunnel on the ocean side.

That's fine, but those sources don't know about the far better area. There are several public accesses along here, but the *best* is at telephone pole #120 (kitty corner from the church). (The PUBLIC ACCESS sign is *conveniently* missing, but a check of county records confirms it's public access.) It's narrow, for one car only. (If you don't park on the street, you'll have to work out a way to get the car out if someone parks behind you.) It's 25 feet from car to water and entry is easy. You can see the reef edge from the shore (polarized sunglasses really enhance it), so during the normally calm seas kick almost straight out (slightly to the left) over the fairly shallow reef shelf so you'll end up seaward of the house with the corrugated roof. (Remember where you entered because other entry/exit points are harder on the diver.) Once at the reef wall (150' or so from shore) work your way left (NW) along the wall where countless chasms, arches and small caves coupled with boundless coral, fish and the occasional turtle create a delightful (though shallow 30–40') dive. If you want to go deep (see photo where the boat is hovering), simply leave the coral behind and continue a short ways farther offshore where the sand slopes relentlessly toward the abyss, broken only by vast fields of garden eels. (Approach them slowly, or they'll disappear into their holes.) If you're not too narc'd return to the heavenly reef edge and make your way back. This is one of the few dives where you can go to 135' yet still stay wet for an hour and be within your profile. Snorkelers, too, will enjoy the reef edge.

South Point—If you're a junkyard dog in search of a thrill, South Point has *lots* of fishing relics strewn about the ground. Currents and surf can be unforgiving, so go only when calm. (Winter is sometimes best.) Not-so-easy entry is from rocks to the left (southeast) of the last of the boat hoists. See page 77 for more information on this area. Stay away from point.

Makole'a Beach—One of our personal favorites. The variety, quality and quantity of coral is exceptional. This is a *very* healthy reef, and until now it's never been listed anywhere. We've dived it lots of times and have never seen any evidence that any other diver has been there. (I'm aware that this is about to change.) Unless you want to carry your gear for 15 minutes, you'll need a 4WD vehicle to go over the lava road. This will allow you to drive right up to this black sand beach near Kona. The best diving is about 100 to 200 feet out from the right (north) side of the beach. From there, work your way south parallel to the beach. This is a fairly shallow dive (45 feet) and visibility is not the best in Kona (50–65 feet), but

You could dive Puako every day of your trip and still not see it all.

the quality of the dive site is hard to beat. Follow directions on page 148. Since we're sharing a heretofore unknown dive site (the one that we personally take visiting guests to), please make us proud by being extra sensitive of the pristine reef.

The BEACHES section describes nearly all the beaches around the island. Divers should read the descriptions of Kohala beaches, such as **Kapaʻa Beach Park, Mahukona,** and **Hapuna** (the southern end). In Kona try the Alii Drive **Four Mile Marker** just south of **White Sands Beach** (from the cove head slightly south), **Kahaluʻu Beach Park** (outside the breakwater), **Keʻei,** and **Puʻu-honua o Honaunau** (Place of Refuge).

If you've ever gazed into an aquarium and wondered what it was like to see colorful fish in their natural environment, complete with coral, lava tubes, and strange ocean creatures, you've come to the right Hawaiian Island. Hawaiʻi features a dazzling variety of fish. Over 600 species are found in our waters. Here's our dilemma: If we blather on and on again about how good the water can be on the west side of the island, you're probably going to get sick. But we *have* to! Because this is where Kona really pays off. Usually calm, clear and teeming with fish, the Kona side offers perhaps the best snorkeling in the state.

We'll admit that we're snorkeling junkies and never tire of experiencing the water here. If you snorkel often, you can go right to our list below of recommended areas. But it you're completely or relatively inexperienced, you should read on.

For identifying ocean critters, the best books we've seen are *Shore Fishes of Hawaiʻi* by John Randall and *Hawaiian Reef Fish* by Casey Mahaney. They're what we use. You should see plenty of butterflyfish, wrasse, convict tang, achilles tang, parrotfish, angelfish, damselfish, moorish idol, pufferfish, trumpetfish, moray eel, and humuhumunukunukuapuaʻa, or Picasso triggerfish—a beautiful but very skittish fish. (It's as if they somehow *know* how good they look in aquariums.)

We know people who have a fear of putting on a mask and snorkel. Gives 'em the willies. For them, we recommend boogie boards with clear windows on them to observe the life below.

A FEW TIPS:

- ◆ Feeding the fish is generally not recommended since it introduces unnatural behavior to the reef. That said, some places, notably Kahaluʻu, have experienced feeding for so long that humans are now part of the "natural" order there. Go ahead and feed them at Kahaluʻu, but try to refrain from feeding them elsewhere. It's in your best interest anyway since fish in other locations won't be as receptive to your offerings because they haven't built up the habit. When feeding Kahaluʻu fish, use fish food, rabbit food (cheaper) or a ball of bread rolled tightly in your hand. Contrary to popular belief, frozen peas and potato chips are harmful to fish since they are unable to digest them properly. Dispense the food *sparingly*; too much and they will grab a bite and run. If they have to compete, they will increase in numbers.

- Fish are hungriest and most appreciative in the morning (before their coffee).

- Use *Sea Drops* or another brand of anti-fog goop. Spread it *thinly* on the inside of a dry mask, then do a quick rinse.

- Most damage to coral comes when people grab it or stand on it. Even touching the coral lightly can transfer your oils to the polyps, killing them. If your mask starts to leak or you get water in your snorkel, be careful not to stand on the coral to clear them. Find a spot where you won't damage coral or drift into it. Fish and future snorkelers (not to mention the coral) will thank you.

- Don't use your arms much or you will spook the fish, just gentle fin motion. Any rapid motion can cause the little critters to scatter.

- If you have a mustache and have trouble with a leaking mask, try a little Vaseline. Don't get any on the glass—it can get *really* ugly.

- We prefer using divers' fins (the kind that slip over reef shoes) so that we can walk easily into and out of the water without tearing up our feet. (If you wear socks or nylons under the shoes, it'll keep you from rubbing the tops of your toes raw.)

PRICES

You'll find the least expensive gear in Kailua-Kona. The business can be cut-throat, so look for coupons in the free magazines scattered around the island. If you're going to snorkel more than once, it's nice to rent for a week, leave it in the trunk, and go whenever you have the desire. **Hawai'i Watersports** at (329–0046) has gear for $8 per day, $24 per week. **Miller's Snorkeling** (326–1771) at $7 per day, $15 per week. The snorkel gear at **Jack's Diving Locker** (329–7585) is $7.50 per day, $42 per week. Divers' fins are available. **Snorkel Bob's** 329–0770 (it's near Huggo's restaurant on Alii Drive in Kona) has gear for $2.50–$8.50 per day, $9–$36 per week. Expect to get talked into the expensive stuff here. You can rent

We took this photo at the Captain Cook Monument with a **disposable** underwater camera to give you an idea of the quality you should expect. Remember to get close since the lenses are at a pretty wide angle.

gear from a truck at Kahalu'u Beach Park for use there or at the concessionaire to the right of Kailua Pier.

You won't find inexpensive gear in Kohala. But you can try **Red Sail Sports** at 885–2876, $20 per day for gear. **Ocean Sports Waikoloa** at 885–5555 has a shack at 'Anaeho'omalu Beach. Convenient, but they rent snorkel gear for (hold onto your wallet) a mere $5.25 *per hour* or $15 per day. They rent all kinds of other goodies there at rates that aren't *quite* as confiscatory.

Try to stay in calm areas. If you're in rougher water and a large wave comes and churns up the water with bubbles, put your arms in front of you to protect your head. You won't sense motion, and may get slammed into a rock before you know it.

SNORKEL BOAT TOURS

These can be fun. They'll take you to a good spot, provide gear and show you how to use it, and sometimes provide lunch. OCEAN TOURS on page 192 reviews most of them and includes prices and where they take you. Our favorites are **Fair Wind II, Body Glove** and **SeaQuest.**

The section on BEACHES has complete descriptions of all beaches. Our usual prejudice toward west Hawai'i for water activities applies here. Clarity and calmness just can't compare on the Hilo side, but life can just as abundant there. On the west side, be sure to check out some of these beaches:

Kahalu'u—Easy access and lots of life.
Kealakekua Bay Near Captain Cook Monument—Some of the best snorkeling in the state.

Pu'uhonua o Honaunau—Easy access, excellent area, lots of turtles and coral make it almost as good as the Captain Cook Monument.
Pawai Bay—Very interesting underwater relief.
Hapuna to 69 Beach—Great stretch of reef.
Mahukona—Good underwater junk.
Puako—Very extensive reef.
Kiholo Bay—Strange conditions.
Kapa'a Beach Park—Interesting underwater sights.
Lapakahi State Park—Sometimes exceptional amounts of fish.

On the East Side Check Out:
Punalu'u—Cold black sand conditions but *lots* of turtles.
Kapoho Tide-pools—Calm & unique.

Is this a misprint? Nope. Mauna Kea is 13,796 feet high, and in the winter it gets snow—sometimes a lot of it. **Ski Guides Hawai'i** (889–6747) takes small groups to the top of Mauna Kea. His 4WD is your ski lift, and he acts as guide. For $150 (plus $30 if you need gear) intermediate to advanced skiers get transportation from Waimea, lunch, and lots of fairly short runs down from the summit to where the road loops around. Other runs are available if there's enough snow. Mauna Kea snow (called pineapple powder) is not reliable and neither is the company, so call them when you arrive to see if skiing is available. (It's sometimes tough to get them on the phone.) Granted, the conditions will be better at Aspen. But you can't go straight from the snow to the beach there, now can you? If you want to enjoy the snow yourself (or have trouble finding these guys), you can take a 4WD to the observatory area where everyone but the driver can slide down the mountain on boogie boards or anything you think will do, while the driver takes the vehicle to the bottom to act as a ski lift.

If you're a little hesitant about trying SCUBA, consider SNUBA. That's where you swim below a raft with tanks and a 25-foot hose, regulator in mouth and an instructor by your side. **Snuba Big Island** at 326-7446 (part of a chain) takes you on a shore dive near King Kamehameha Hotel in Kona for $59, City of Refuge in Honaunau for $79, or on one of several snorkel boats for over $100 per person. Groups of 4–6 per trip; expect about 45 minutes of bottom time on the shore dives, a bit less on boat dives. Some of the boat trips listed under **Ocean Tours,** such as **Fair Wind II,** have SNUBA available.

If you feel the need to lose yourself in the fog of a decadent overall body massage and treatment, you're in luck. The **Orchid at Mauna Lani** (885–2000) has a "Spa Without Walls." Couples can enjoy an outdoor sunset massage right at the shoreline. A curtain provides the privacy. They also offer massages with

"electronic brain wave stimulation." You know, where you wear those space-age headsets that are supposed to perform all sorts of miracles. The **Kohala Spa** (885–1234) at the Hilton Waikoloa is a huge (25,000 square feet) full-featured spa with all kinds of options. Enter a twitching ball of nerves, and you'll leave relaxed stupid. **Paradise Spa** (969–3333) at the Hawai'i Naniloa Resort is your best bet in Hilo.

STARGAZING

If you want to go stargazing on Mauna Kea, home to the world's finest and most coveted telescopes, **Paradise Safaris** (322–2366) will pick you up from the west side and take you to the summit for sunset. Then you come down to 9,000 feet for some stargazing through their small scope for $130 per person. They provide hot chocolate and warm coats, and the total time is 7½ hours. It's long but fun. **Star Gaze Hawai'i** (323–9516) will let you peek through their scopes at some Kohala hotels for $10. Kind of hard to get excited about that one.

You won't *Run Silent, Run Deep.* There won't be the sound of sonar pinging away in the background. And it's unlikely that anyone will shoot torpedoes at you. But if you want to see the undersea world and *refuse* to get wet, *dis is da buggah.* **Atlantis Submarine** (329–6626) has a 48-passenger sub which ambles about over a very healthy reef in Kailua Bay. Before your descent to a bit over 100 feet, divers cruise by your windows, feeding the many tropical fish in the neighborhood. This is the opposite of an aquarium—this is *their* world and *you* are the oddity. This $79 40-minute ride is a kick. Kids like it. Adults like it. Even certified divers like us like it. Claustrophobics will probably be too busy staring through the windows to be nervous. Photographers will want to use fast (at least 400 speed) film, and turn off the flash. Mornings are usually best. Wear a bright red shirt, and watch what happens to its color on the way down.

Though not a submarine, **Nautilus II** (326–2003) is called a semi-submersible. Basically, the bottom of the boat is mostly window, affording nice views of fish and reef. (Better than a glass-bottom boat.) For $59 you get a 50-minute tour with a SNUBA (not SCUBA) diver around most of the time picking up critters and feeding the fish. The boat has to hug the northern edge of Kailua Bay, and the sights aren't as good as the submarine. That said, the best views will be on the starboard (right) side going out. $59 is much too steep for this, so hopefully they have a special going on; otherwise spring for the real sub which has much more *ooh-aah* value.

Dudes, the most gnarly surfing on the west side is at **Pine Trees** just north of Kailua-Kona. (See Wawaloli on page 149 for directions.) It takes a 4WD vehicle to get there, but the breaks are outstanding. In Kona, the break off the "little blue church" near **Kahalu'u** is one of the most dependable. **Banyans** on Alii Drive just south of Kona Bali Kai has excellent waves. Other great surf spots are **Ke'ei** and **Old Kona Airport,** described under beaches. You should know that Pine Trees, Banyans and Lyman's (just around the bend) are notorious for the surfers with bad attitudes. Outsiders will be as welcome as reef rash. (By the way, a collection of surfers is known in surfing lingo here as a *quiver.* A little kid surfer who doesn't have a job or a car yet is called a *grommet.*)

In Kona **Honolua Surf Company** (329–1001) and **Pacific Vibrations** (329–4140) rent boards. **Ocean Eco Tours** (937–0495) gives lessons.

If you feel like a lively game of tennis (or you simply like chasing the ball), the Big Island has plenty of courts. The WHERE TO STAY section mentions whether each resort has courts, lighted or not (and the phone numbers for each). The nicest courts on the island are at the **Orchid at Mauna Lani.** This fine tennis complex even has a stadium court. (Crowds are extra.) Rates are $12 per day per person. In Kona the **Hawai'i Tennis Club** (324–7072) near the Kona Surf Hotel is $45 per day. They have lots of services but that's pretty pricey. In Hilo, your best bet is the county **Hoolulu Park** (935–8213). Three indoor and five outdoor courts. Indoor courts (preferred) are $2.

There are 43 *free* municipal courts scattered around the island. Rather than go into mind-numbing detail about all of them, just call the county at 935–8213 and ask for the courts nearest you.

It's common knowledge that humpbacks are common in Hawai'i, mostly between December and March or April. They don't come here to eat (though they do have the occasional pupu). They take advantage of Hawai'i's romantic atmosphere and mate in our waters (so don't stare), returning the following year to give birth. Though more numerous off Maui, the Big Island is still a splendid place to see whales blow and breach. From shore, you may see humpback whales causing a ruckus or just generally frolicking. But out on a boat, you can sometimes get up close and personal. Additionally, there are several other species, including giant sperm whales, pilot whales, false killer whales, beaked whales, pygmy killer whales, and melon-headed whales, that reside here and require boats to see.

Captain Dan McSweeney's Whale Watch (322–0028) is our resident expert. He has spent approximately 1½ zillion hours studying whales off Kona. For $45 you and up to 41 other passengers take their 38-foot boat offshore for 3–4 hours of whale watching and education. Snacks provided, restroom on board. They "guarantee" a sighting or you can come back for free, and *claim* a 90% success rate in finding whales. **Living Ocean Adventures** (325–5556) offers year-round trips of up to 6 people in their 31-foot Bertram (a fishing boat). Like Captain Dan, the owner/operator is always present. Except during humpback season, they troll three lines while they whale watch—if they get a strike, you may get to reel it in. Snacks and juices provided, restroom on board. $54.50 for 3½-hour trip. Several other boat companies listed in OCEAN TOURS under ACTIVITIES provide whale watching during humpback season, but these two companies do it year round and have more experience.

Lastly, during humpback season, we like to swim out beyond the sound of the breakers (say, 100 feet past the breakwater at Kahalu'u Beach) and listen to those soulful giants sing the blues. You certainly won't get to see them underwater, but their concert is often the best in town. (But I sometimes wonder if the fish all around me are thinking, "I *hate* it when the humpbacks come to town. They make such a racket when we're trying to sleep!") You can hear whales from much farther distances if your ears are a few feet underwater. (Hint: hang upside-down.) Some years the whale crowd is pretty raucous, constantly breaching, blowing, and singing. Other years the behemoths may be strangely quiescent.

Windsurfing (also called sailboarding) is done at 'Anaeho'omalu Beach. There you will find rentals on the beach from **Ocean Sports Waikoloa** (886–6666) for $20 per hour, or take an hour-and-a-half lesson for $45.

The Mauna Ulu hike is an 'okole squeezer, not an average stroll.

The activities described below (except for the dolphin encounter) are for the serious adventurer. They can be experiences of a lifetime. We are assuming that if you consider any of them that you are a person of sound judgment, capable of assessing risks. All adventures carry risks of one kind or another. Our descriptions below do not attempt to convey all risks associated with an activity. These activities are not for everyone. Good preparation is essential. In the end, it comes down to your own good judgment.

MAUNA ULU CRATER

This short hike is not for the easily frightened or the faint at heart. Mauna Ulu erupted between 1969 and 1974. When it was all over, it left a smoldering maw 400 feet deep and 600 feet across. (That's a guess—it gets bigger all the time.) This crater is accessible via a 45-minute hike from Chain of Craters Road in Hawai'i Volcanoes National Park. See map on page 179. From there, you just walk up to Mauna Ulu Crater.

We need to stress that this is new land. The part of the hill adjacent to Pu'u Huluhulu *seems* to be the most stable, but that is a relative term. There are several areas where thin, shelly lava breaks beneath your feet. You may only drop an inch or two, but your adrenaline tells you otherwise. There may be even less stable areas around the base. The rim of the crater is nearly straight down and crumbling all the time. If you get too close, it may break off and you may fall in—and then you're *really* out of luck. If all this doesn't dissuade you, you'll get to see a view that is beyond belief. The crater seems raw, like an open wound on Kilauea. It usually steams heavily from several spots. There are empty river banks around it where huge quantities of lava coursed their way down the mountain. There are blobs where lava spattered where it fell, large cracks with heat still escaping. This is as close as you may ever get to experiencing an erupting vent—while it's not erupting. But remember, this hike is what we call an 'okole squeezer. Permits are only required to hike beyond Pu'u Huluhulu to Napau, you *are* allowed to hike to Mauna Ulu without a permit. That's official from the park, but some park personnel sometimes erronously tell visitors otherwise. You don't need permission. Morning is usually best for this hike.

RAIN FOREST LAVA TUBE

In the summer of 1993 park personnel discovered a beautiful, pristine lava tube in the rain forest. Even the ancient Hawaiians apparently never discovered it. Similar to Thurston Lava Tube but with far grander details, it is accessible via a fairly easy one-hour (each way) hike through lush forest. This cave is long and loaded with lava stalactites and other treasures, making it an unparalleled hiking experience. The park wishes to control access, and they have asked us not give directions for fear that some thoughtless jerk might read it and damage some of the delicate features. Consequently they have started *guided* tours of 12 or so people. (Hikes were every Wednesday and some Saturdays at press time.) If you want to be on the list, call them at (808) 985–6017 in advance (it fills up) and make arrangements. Ask for the *Wild Lava Tube* guided hike; it'll knock your socks off.

They will provide helmet lights. (They don't charge for the tour, so bring batteries to help out.) Be prepared to scramble on or around large boulders on the floor that have fallen from the roof over the years. The ceiling is usually 20 feet tall, but severe claustrophobics need not apply. Take your time and expect to spend about an hour to go from one end of the cave to the other.

MANTA RAY NIGHT DIVE

This one may stay with you for the rest of your life. Imagine the following scene: You take a boat to Keauhou Bay, leaving just before sunset. When you arrive, perhaps another dive boat is already there. *Damn,* you think. They'll ruin it. As you slip into the water and approach the action area, numerous lights already there beckon you toward them, like a porch light calling to the moths. Then you see gigantic shadows blotting out the lights. *Mantas!* As you approach, one zooms over your head, missing you by an inch. There you sit, with all the others, mesmerized by the performance before you. One, two, maybe 3 stinger-less manta rays, 6–10 feet across their wings, slowly swirling, looping, and soaring all about you. Like a dance performed by extra-terrestrial beings, these filter-feeding leviathans are more graceful than you could possibly imagine. They seem to understand that they are on stage, and they rarely disappoint. When you think you have gotten used to their size, a goliath 14 feet across may swoop in, its enormous maw scooping up thousands of the tiny, darting shrimp that cloud the water along with the bubbles. You struggle to resist the urge to reach up and touch them—it's best to let them initiate any touching. Above the fray, a sea of needlefish gobble up what they can.

It all started over 20 years ago when the Kona Surf started flooding the area with light, which attracts tiny brine shrimp, a form of plankton. This plankton brings in large manta rays that gobble them by the millions. Consequently, the three or four days before and after the full moon are the days when the mantas are less likely to show—lots of moonlight means the pickins' are easy everywhere. No moon and late rising (waning) moons are best. You will likely have plenty of air left since the dive takes place at about 25 feet and you move very little. Diver etiquette dictates that you leave your snorkel on the boat. The protruding tube can scratch the manta's belly. This is one of those rare dives where a crowd, as long as it's not *too* big, actually make it better. More lights and more wide eyes, though, to be honest, we've noticed that as the number of divers has increased there seems to be more manta no-show nights than before. Snorkelers who try to dive down or the use of scooters can also scare them off. If you started diving because you wanted to feel like you were floating in space, night dives provide that feeling. But for this dive, weigh yourself a bit heavy. You will be plunking yourself among a cluster of boulders, and surge may make you grateful for the extra lead. (Don't assume that if the surf is up boats won't go. Though usually calm, we see boats out there when the surf is high enough to make us grateful we're not there.) Some companies, like **Eco-Adventures,** use ⅓–½ of the 50–60 minute dive for roaming around. Others, like **Kona Coast,** spend nearly all of their time with the mantas. You need to arrange it in advance with them because it's not regularly scheduled. **Manta Ray Dives** (325–1687) leaves from Keauhou Bay for a grueling *four-minute* trip to the site, six nights a week. If you want to snorkel it from shore, tie a green nite stick to your snorkel so boats can see you at night, and don't dive down; stay on the surface. Lastly, if the mantas *don't* show, the site is a boring night dive location. Don't let anybody tell you differently. No mantas, no fun.

At press time the mantas weren't as reliable as they had been in the past and sometimes showed up at another location farther north, so it's a bit iffier. Call Manta Ray Dives listed above as they seem brutally honest as to your chances.

If you've night dived before, *do this one!* If you've never night dived before, consider doing it now! Expect to spend about $60–$80 for this dive—the best money you will ever spend underwater *if they show.*

HONOKANE NUI HIKE

At the north end of the island where Highway 270 ends you'll find Pololu

Valley. (See page 46.) Though the trek into Pololu takes only 15–20 minutes, the more adventurous might want to venture beyond this beautiful valley to the more secluded **Honokane Nui Valley** and its accompanying stream. (Map is on the next page.) From the lookout, it takes most people 90-120 minutes each way to hike into into Honokane Nui. On the far side of Pololu, the trail goes up the 600-foot-high mountain, over the ridge, then drops down into Honokane. The view of Honokane Nui from the ridge top is breathtaking. Be prepared for a wet, sloppy trail going up the ridge from Pololu if it's been raining recently. (It's drier going down into Honokane.) Horseback riders occasionally take this trail and leave a few gifts along the way. Usually, winter is wetter. In Honokane Nui the trail encounters an idyllic bamboo grove. If you're going to go beyond this valley into the next, take the fork to the right just before the bamboo and cross the stream. Otherwise, go through the bamboo, take the left fork at each intersection, and you will eventually encounter the boulder beach. There is

a large deposit of black sand offshore, but it doesn't do *you* a lot of good. Stay out of the ocean here; it'll hurt you. On the far side of the valley is a nice stream and pool—a perfect place to have lunch.

All in all, this is a nice hike when conditions are good. There are some ruins in the valley from days gone by when it was populated. If you are tired, you might be tempted to skirt the water's edge back to Pololu, thereby avoiding the trip up and down the ridge. If it's calm and low tide, you *might* get away with it, or you might get slammed by a rogue wave and washed out to sea, so we don't recommend it unless you're feeling lucky.

Some of the valley trail intersections can get confusing, so be observant. Bring bug juice just in case. Hiking boots are recommended. When you cross Pololu's stream in the first valley, don't do it near the ocean, but rather at a place 100 feet or so back where you can often hop on dry rocks. (Don't cross when it's raging.) Leave for this hike early. Theoretically you could walk all the way to Waipiʻo Valley from here, but

Tucked under a blanket of cloud, uninhabited Honokane Nui Valley is a rich reward for a day hiker.

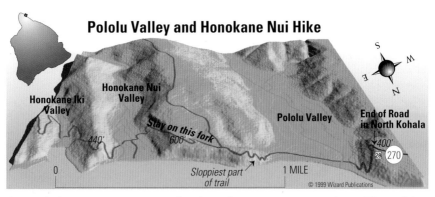

Pololu Valley and Honokane Nui Hike

Honokane Iki Valley

Honokane Nui Valley

Stay on this fork

440'

600'

Pololu Valley

End of Road in North Kohala

400'

28 270

S W E N

0

Sloppiest part of trail

1 MILE

© 1999 Wizard Publications

the trail disappears in spots and only those with mountain goat in their lineage will want to try it. The next valley, Honokane Iki, is accessible via the trail if you have the time. It's small but pretty.

FLY YOUR OWN HELICOPTER

Want to go for a spin in a helicopter and take the controls yourself? **Mauna Loa Helicopters** (334-0234) doesn't offer tours *per se*. They offer *lessons* in their *teeny-tiny* two-seater Robinson R22—one seat for the *real* pilot and one for you. The R22 is a training helicopter, not a touring bird. I've flown in them and the ride is a kick, but not for everyone. You start with half an hour of private flight school where you learn the fundamentals. Then it's off and up where you are given a chance to cruise the skies. The view of the Kona coast somehow seems better when *you're* at the stick. They do the take-offs and landings, and are constantly there to take over if you choke. When you're finished, you'll get a certificate verifying your lesson. Make sure you take the time to practice your arrogant swagger when you get back. (Come on you big-time chopper pilots, you *know* it's true!) Taking people in training copters for lessons/tours is unusual. There's certainly more room for error than with an "ordinary" tour. Nonetheless, my flight on the R22 and

the experience was a hoot. The visibility is better from this little guy than any other helicopter, with no door on the sides (if you wish), and lots of Plexiglas in front. It's expensive, however. A half hour of air time is $150 and an hour is $225.

HI'ILAWE FALLS

How about a hike to a waterfall taller that the tallest building in the world? Hi'ilawe Falls in Waipi'o Valley plunges 1,600 feet with a free fall of around 1,000 feet. Sound intriguing? Well, to get there, you first have to get into Waipi'o Valley on the northeast side of the island. That requires either walking down the 1-mile paved road (with a 900-foot descent), driving a JEEP down, or using a company like Waipi'o Valley Shuttle. (See page 121 for location and more on how to get into Waipi'o Valley. The map of the valley also shows the trail.) At the bottom, take the road to the left until just before it crosses *under* the first stream. To your left you'll see a trail. It's ¾ mile as the crow flies—too bad you got no wings. It took us 45 minutes the first time wearing tabis (described under HIKING) for wet rock walking, but don't count on doing it that quickly if you're not comfortable on wet rocks. A dirt trail exists pretty much the whole way paralleling the main stream, but it crosses the stream in several spots. You're likely to lose it. It's easier to follow coming back, and you'll probably realize all the opportunities you missed to stay on the trail. Just remember that when the trail dumps into the stream due to an obstacle, it either crosses the stream or can be reacquired on the other side of the obstacle. Often, especially during the last ⅓, the trail is on the far (western) side. Watch for it; trail travel is much faster than river rock walking. And remember, this is not a properly maintained trail, but rather a trail of use, so don't expect a fancy trail.

At the falls, the air is filled with the hiss of water dropping delicately into the pool, and the area abounds with broken rock from above. The view is stupendous. If you get beaned by a rock that has fallen 1,600 feet, you can count on doing your best imitation of a fence post.

Different subject, but while you're down in the valley, another waterfall drops almost into the ocean and is located to the right (east) of the end of Waipi'o Beach. Getting to it is described on page 121. Of course, it's unlikely you'd have enough steam left to do the second hike, especially if you have to walk back up Waipi'o Valley Road.

CLOSE ENCOUNTER WITH A DOLPHIN

You may have heard of this one. At the Hilton Waikoloa Village they have a program called Dolphin Quest. They have several Atlantic bottle-nosed dolphins in their lagoon where children and adults can get in the water and interact with them. (Our own local spinner dolphins need deeper water and wouldn't successfully adapt to the program.) You stand on a shallow sandy shore with three or four other folks while the dolphins come up to you. *They* decide if they like *you*. If so, you'll be treated to an experience that you will remember for life. It's hard to express the enthusiasm people have when they

get up close and personal with these ocean-going mammals. But it's undeniable that the encounter is incredibly enriching. You also can't help but notice that the dolphins seem to love their contact with humans as well.

You may be thinking, "Is this program good for the dolphins?" That's a fair question and was a concern of ours. We found out that the company has a similar program in French Polynesia. There, the dolphins have been allowed out into the open ocean (where they could easily swim off at any time). They claim that the dolphins always return "home" to the program. That's a pretty good testimonial. We're not experts, but the dolphins seem pretty happy to us. (We've seen other places where we couldn't make that claim.) The water in their lagoon is replaced with fresh seawater every few hours by massive pumps, keeping it very clean for them and you. The dolphins are very active and playful, reproduce when they are get to the right age (wink, wink), and the trainers seem to show them extraordinary love and affection.

If you're interested call them at 885–1234, ext. 1201. It's not always easy to get in on this. Kids are the most desired customer here. Personnel love to introduce kids, not only to the dolphins, but also to various issues regarding the dolphin's environment (without becoming too heavy-handed). Kids and teens need to make reservations up to 60 days in advance to ensure access. Cost is $85 for 5–12 year olds (around 1½ hours). Teens 13–19 are $85. (shorter program.) Adults must win a lottery for the privilege. Winners pay $115. Lottery-winner no-shows are usually replaced by lucky customers at the Hang Ten Grill or people at the Dolphin Quest office. (If you want it bad enough and are patient, you may be accommodated.) If you want

a private session, called dolphin doubles, two people can do this for $190 per couple during certain times of the year. Other programs are available as well.

If you want to see dolphins *in the wild,* your best chance on the island is in Kealakekua Bay. There are quite a few spinners that live in the bay. While kayaking across to the Captain Cook Monument, you stand a good chance of seeing them. We were once able to slip into the water here where 19 dolphins, including babies, were swimming and splashing all around us. You might also see them on a snorkel trip to the bay.

RAIN FOREST HIKE TO PU'U 'O'O VENT

One of the few laments people voice when visiting Kilauea Volcano is that they can't readily visit Pu'u 'O'o, the origin and lava source of the current eruption. Of course, you can still see lava flowing from up close (Pele permitting) during a visit to the park, but you can't see the *actual vent* where it originates. There are places where a person can get a glimpse of the vent from a distance (see pages 113 and 179), but visiting has been a problem. Unless, of course, you happen to know the way.

Unknown to the vast majority of island residents, the **Ka-hau-a-Le'a Trail** was cut by state workers in 1990 as the quickest and most direct route to Pu'u 'O'o. It just so happens that it passes through the healthiest, most beautiful, and least-hiked rain forest on the entire island. Nowhere will you find a lovelier forest, no matter where you hike.

When we revealed this trail to readers in our first edition, bureaucrats at Hawai'i Volcanoes National Park fumed when they realized that we had pointed out a way to visit Pu'u 'O'o that doesn't go through their park. They even stopped selling this book in the park. Well, *that* certainly isn't going to stop us. Park bureaucrats may not *want* you on this trail because you are beyond their control, but they can't keep you off this *public* trail.

All told it's a 4²/₁₀-mile hike to the edge of the forest from your car. (About 3 miles as the crow flies, but you ain't no crow.) The first half of the hike may as well be through the Garden of Eden. Tree ferns and 'ohi'a trees line the way, bursting with green, many covered with a velvety moss. Even if

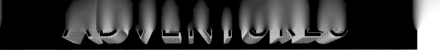

you're not up to the whole hike, a short trek through this forest is highly memorable. There are no big climbs, just lots of tiny hills and dips. This is the rain forest of your dreams. The second half of the forest shows some signs of wild pigs and is not *quite* as perfect. (Only 98% perfect.) When you get to "the big crack" (you'll know), you're a half hour away.

Soon after the crack, the lush forest gives way to small clearings. The trees are looking stressed. Suddenly the forest is dying. Trees are stripped of leaves, grasses are taking over. *Something* is killing the rain forest. Then, through the trees, you see the cause—a sight as awesome as any you've ever encountered. You race to the abrupt edge of the forest and come face to face with Pu'u 'O'o a mile away. The cone, around 500 feet high and built entirely during the current eruption, angrily spews 2,500 *tons* of sulphur dioxide per day, like a snorting exhaust pipe from the center of the Earth. You are on the upslope side, and the lava should be flowing on the opposite side, so you probably won't see that. But if the wind is blowing in the right direction (which it usually is), you will have a view of the beating heart of a volcano. (There's an aerial shot of Pu'u 'O'o on pages 4–5.)

If the wind is blowing toward you (which it usually *doesn't),* you'll notice a sulphur smell. These occasional winds from the south are what's killing the forest edge. Savor this view, revel in it. But don't try to get closer. Don't try to walk up and peer into the lava lake, the risks are unacceptable. If the wind changes, it exposes you to potentially fatal concentrated fumes. If a cloud forms, the fog would disorient you to the point that you wouldn't know your way back to the forest. Plus you might fall from the fragile land into the lava lake—a real bummer. Best to observe it from the forest edge,

soaking up the sight for your memories of tomorrow.

This hike is not for everyone. It is a fairly long day hike, and conditions are usually pretty muddy. (This *is* after all, a *rain* forest.) The trail has been groomed sporadically by state workers, but hunters and other users were keeping it in pretty good shape at press time. We first hiked this trail one week *before* a scheduled grooming by the state and found it well marked and easy to follow with blue tags every few dozen feet along the fairly worn path. A few hunter and pig trails veer off; your path is the most worn path. If you don't see blue tags, retrace your steps until you pick them up. Don't

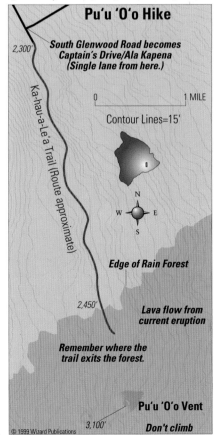

Pu'u 'O'o Hike

2,300' **South Glenwood Road becomes Captain's Drive/Ala Kapena (Single lane from here.)**

Ka-hau-a-Le'a Trail (Route approximate)

0 ————— 1 MILE
Contour Lines=15'

N
W — E
S

Edge of Rain Forest

2,450' **Lava flow from current eruption**

Remember where the trail exits the forest.

Pu'u 'O'o Vent

© 1999 Wizard Publications 3,100' **Don't climb**

continue without seeing the tags. You may be only a few miles from your car, but if you are off the trail, it would be the longest few miles of your life. A compass is comforting, just in case, and the trail is pretty straight all the way out. Of course, we don't guarantee the trail's condition. In fact, we don't guarantee diddly when it comes to hiking. Nature changes quickly. A strong wind storm can return a nice trail back to jungle until workers come back to repair it. We are assuming that you will use your judgment on this. Also, guerrilla gardeners (you know…alternative farmers) sometimes tend their "crops" deep in the forest. They obviously like to stay as far from people as possible. The point is that you shouldn't stray a long distance off the trail for fear of stumbling onto their "farm" (not to mention getting lost in the rain forest).

Start *early* for this hike. You will want to be hiking by 7:30 a.m. to make *sure* you aren't on the trail when it gets dark. (Some who haven't heeded this warning, starting too late, have been caught on the trail at night and needed to be rescued.) We've run into readers on the trail who started at 10 or 11 a.m. and have chastised them for starting too late. Personally, we leave our home in Kona at the *indecent* hour of 4:30 a.m. in order to start hiking by 7 a.m. Time the hike to be back to your car two hours before sunset, just to be safe. It'll *probably* take 2½–4 hours each way, depending on conditions and your hiking skills. You are unlikely to encounter anyone during your hike. Bring plenty of water. Hiking boots (especially waterproof ones) are recommended, and a hiking stick (for probing mud puddles and balance) is *strongly* recommended. Most people will get their feet wet due to occasionally unavoidable puddles. Once at Pu'u 'O'o, make *sure* you carefully note where the

trail ends at the edge of the forest. That's the way back, and you don't want to lose the opening. Lastly, when Pu'u 'O'o finally stops erupting, it won't be *quite* as dramatic. But you can bet it'll still be worth it. The inherent lure of this area will be here for years to come.

To get to the trailhead, take South Glenwood Road between the 19 and 20 mile markers (close to the 20) on Highway 11 (20 miles from Hilo, 95 miles from Kona). It's just south of Hirano Store. The road curves to the right, then left and changes its name to Captain's Drive/Ala Kapena. From the highway it's 3½ miles *to the very end* (including the one-lane part) where you'll find the trail (which may be unmarked), like an extension of the road.

HIKE TO FLOWING LAVA

This one is difficult to describe for the simple reason that we won't know where it is flowing at the time you read this. It may be flowing right at the end of Chain of Craters Road in Hawai'i Volcanoes National Park, making this description unnecessary. But maybe not. The lava flows change location all the time, so we'll tell you how to find out where they are and how to get there.

You can call the park at 985–6000 for an eruption update. Unfortunately they usually don't say *where* it's flowing. You can look at the map posted at the park visitor center. Also, our web site at www.wizardpub.com has updated lava flow info on it. Check it before you leave on your trip to Hawai'i. The flows should be somewhere between the end of Chain of Craters road in the park, and the end of the lava road in Kalapana. If you start from the park, you are probably permitted to hike to the unsupervised flows. They may *imply* that you can't but it is almost always permitted.

What if it's too far from the park? If you look at the map on page 96, you'll see where Hwy 130 ends and a lava road leads out toward a lava-destroyed subdivision. This junky new lava road gets you almost 4 miles closer to the flows and was cut on top of the old public road out to the park boundary. Can you legally drive on it? Well, it was built with private money and state personnel we contacted told us it was on *state* land and they can't stop you from driving on it if you have a 4WD—even though the sign implies it's for residents only. (2WD vehicles *won't* make it.) But another state worker said it was closed because they don't want people visiting the lava flows. *That* doesn't make sense because you *are* allowed to visit those same flows from the park side. The sign itself at the road doesn't even say which residents are permitted, island residents or Kalapana residents. At press time park bureaucrats were quoted in the newspaper saying that they didn't *like* people entering park property from this direction, but the park's own signs in the

area said it was OK to proceed. Perhaps they'd rather not know about it. What does this mean? I don't know. After many phone calls we can't say whether you are technically allowed to use it or not, but we can say that many people use the road all the time. Use your discretion.

At the flows you are presented with several dangers. Lava benches form seaward of the old seacliffs. They can collapse at any time taking viewers with them so *don't* go on the benches. Collapses also can hurl rocks inland. Lava tubes travel under you. Hot water can splash on you. There should be signs where the flows enter the ocean telling you to go no further. Heed them. There may be surface flows, watch for them. Don't *ever* hike here in the dark. There are other dangers as well, such as bad gasses that trade winds *normally* blow to the southwest, and we are counting on your own good judgment to keep you out of trouble. We are not attempting to convey all the dangers present on this hike. You'll have to evaluate some on your

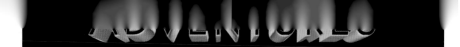

own. The park has a brochure about viewing lava safely that you may want to pick up. This is a thrilling hike of a lifetime but not for the faint-hearted and bad decisions can result in tragedy. Contrary to what you might think, *smaller* lava flows, with less steam at the ocean, are much more dramatic than large ones.

EXPLORE A MILE LONG CAVE

After our first edition several readers asked where they could explore a relatively pristine cave on their own. This one, located off Saddle Road, is one of the best on the island. Formed during the same lava flow of 1881 that threatened Hilo and created the well known, but hardly pristine, Kaumana Cave, 14 miles east, this might well be part of the same tube, though parts are blocked off. There are incredible formations inside, including lava stalactites, channels and shelves that look so perfect and smooth you'd swear they were manmade (though they're not), and numerous surprises.

As a cave (and a relatively young one) this lava tube presents dangers that you need to respect. Though seemingly stable, any cave can have areas where rocks can collapse. Most of the cave is over 10 feet tall but there are opportu-

20 Miles to Hilo →
Saddle Road
21
200
N
Gate
Darker areas are older forest areas
4WD Road (but you'll have to walk it)
Old Pu'u 'O'o Trail
Hill →
Lush fern area →
Cave
© 1999 Wizard Publications
0   1/2 Mile
Contour Lines=15 feet

nities to whack your head. (Personally I wear a hard hat when exploring caves with a head-band flashlight from Walmart attached to the top.) Bring *at least* two strong flashlights (I bring three). The stronger the light, the more enjoyable the experience. You'll miss so much with a weak light and increase your chances of tripping or hitting your head. (I use a SCUBA dive light; Longs Drugs sells them the cheapest.) Getting into the cave from the entrance is a little awkward. And please make sure you don't harm any of the formations or take any souvenirs other than photos from the cave. I'm making some people mad just by telling you where this cave is, so make sure you leave the cave as you found it. (Sorry to sound so preachy, but I can already hear the chorus of critics, who themselves didn't even know about this cave, saying that I shouldn't have revealed this gem.)

To get there, take Saddle Road (200) to the 21 mile marker. On the south side of the road is a short 4WD road that leads to a powerline road (see map). Take this powerline road for 2½ miles. (The power poles are now cut down.) This lava road itself is easy walking but isn't very interesting, and Saddle Road weather may mean misty and wet. Near the cave the road passes through a lush fern area and descends to newer lava. About 200 feet after the decent ends, look to your right for the tube opening. The tunnel passes under the road, and that's the route you want. (The other way, heading uphill, is shorter, less interesting and requires ducking too much.) Because it's a single tube, you can't get lost. After a short distance it opens up to another skylight. Just keep going. Make sure to stop and marvel at the formations along the way; that's what you came for.

After about a mile the cave ends at a rock collapse. Don't try to go farther.

Your table is ready...

By their very nature, restaurant reviews are the most subjective part of any guidebook. Nothing strains the credibility of a guidebook more. No matter what we say, if you eat at enough restaurants here, you will eventually have a dining experience directly in conflict with what this book leads you to believe. All it takes is one person to wreck what is usually a good meal. Many of us have had the experience when a friend referred us to a restaurant using reverent terms indicating that they were about to experience dining ecstasy. And, of course, when you go there, the food is awful and the waiter is a jerk. There are many variables involved in getting a good or bad meal. Is the chef new? Was the place sold last month? Was the waitress just released from prison for mauling a customer? We truly hope that our reviews match your experience. If they don't, please drop us a line, and we will reevaluate the restaurant.

Unlike some travel writers who announce themselves to restaurants (to cop a free meal if the truth be told), we always review anonymously and only expose ourselves after a meal (not literally, of course) if we need additional information. By their reviews, many guidebooks lead you to believe that every meal you eat in Hawai'i will be a feast, the best food in the free world. Frankly, that's not our style. Like anywhere else, there's ample opportunity to have lousy food served with a rotten ambiance by uncaring waiters. In the interest of space, we've left out *some* of the dives. We did, however, leave in a few of these turkeys just to demonstrate that we know we live the real world. Restaurants that stand out from the others in some way are highlighted with this symbol. Restaurants that don't allow smoking are accompanied by the 🚭 symbol.

For each restaurant, we list the price

RESTAURANT INDEX

per person you can expect to pay. It ranges from the least expensive entrées alone, to the most expensive plus a beverage and usually appetizers. You can spend more if you try, but this is a good guideline. *The price excludes alcoholic beverages since this component of a meal can be so variable.* Obviously, everyone's ordering pattern is different, but we thought that it would be easier to compare various restaurants using dollar amounts, than if we used different numbers of dollar signs or drawings of forks or whatever to differentiate prices between various restaurants. All take credit cards unless otherwise noted. When we mention that prices are reasonable, please take it in context. We mean reasonable *for Hawai'i.* (We *know* you pay less back home.) Food in Hawai'i is expensive, even if it's grown here. (You probably pay less for our fruit on the mainland than *we* do here.)

When we give directions to a restaurant, *mauka side* of highway means "toward the mountain" (or away from the ocean). The shopping centers we mention are on the maps to that area.

The difference between local and Hawaiian food can be difficult to classify. Basically, local food combines Hawaiian, American, Japanese, Chinese, Filipino, and several other types and is (not surprisingly) eaten mainly by locals.

Lu'aus, those giant outdoor Hawaiian parties, are described at the end.

Below are descriptions of various island foods. Not all are Hawaiian, but this might be of assistance if you encounter dishes unfamiliar to you.

ISLAND FISH

If you've been fishing today and want to visit your new friend, **MARINA SEAFOODS** (326–2117) at Honokohau Harbor sells fresh fish from the fishing boats and is often cheap. A friend taught us how to paint ahi steaks with mayonnaise which *completely* burns off when BBQ'd but seals in the moisture. You end up tasting only the moist ocean steak.

Ahi–Yellowfin tuna; excellent eaten raw as sashimi.

Ahu–Skipjack tuna, heavier than Ahi.

A'u–A billfish such as marlin or swordfish; steaks are usually broiled or barbecued; meat is firm and white.

Kumu–Goatfish; firm, white meat. Steamed kumu is an island specialty.

Mahimahi–Dolphinfish (not the mammal!), white, delicate, moist, firm.

Mano–Shark; firm, white meat.

Moonfish/Opah–Mild, firm, pink flesh.

Ono/Wahoo–Moderately coarse, white meat that's very moist and delicious.

Snappers–White, firm, yet tender with a mild flavor. 'Opakapaka, Kalekale, and Onaga are the best.

Ehu–Red snapper.

Kalekale–Pink snapper.

Onaga–Red snapper.

'Opakapaka–Pink snapper; especially good to eat.

Ulua and Papio–Jack fish with white, firm, flaky meat.

LU'AU FOODS

Chicken lu'au–Chicken cooked in coconut milk and taro leaves.

Haupia–Coconut custard.

Kalua pig–Pig cooked in an underground oven called an imu, shredded and mixed with Hawaiian sea salt (outstanding!).

Laulau–Pork, beef, or fish wrapped in taro and ti leaves and steamed. (You don't eat the ti leaf wrapping.)

Lomi salmon–Chilled salad consisting of raw, salted salmon, tomatoes, and two kinds of onions.

Pipi kaula–Hawaiian beef jerky.

Poi–Steamed taro root pounded into a paste. It's a starch that will take on the taste of other foods mixed with it. Best eaten with kalua pig or fish. Visitors are encouraged to try it so they can badmouth it with authority.

Poke–Raw fish mixed with seaweed.

OTHER ISLAND FOODS

Apple bananas–A smaller, denser, smoother texture than regular (Williams) bananas.

Barbecue sticks–Teriyaki marinated pork, chicken, or beef pieces barbecued and served on bamboo sticks.

Bento–Japanese box lunch.

Breadfruit–Melon-sized starchy fruit; served baked, deep fried, steamed, or boiled. Definitely an acquired taste.

Crackseed–Chinese-style spicy preserved fruits and seeds.

Guava–About the size of an apricot or plum. The inside is full of seeds, so it is rarely eaten raw. Used primarily for juice, jelly, or jam.

Hawaiian supersweet corn–The finest corn you ever had, even raw. We'll lie, cheat, steal or maim to get it fresh.

Huli huli chicken–Hawaiian BBQ style.

Ka'u oranges–Locally grown. Usually, the uglier the orange the better it tastes.

Kim chee–A Korean relish consisting of pickled cabbage, onions, radishes, garlic, and chilies.

Kona coffee–Grown on the Kona Coast of the Big Island. Smooth, mild flavor; available everywhere.

Kulolo–Steamed taro pudding.

Liliko'i–Passion fruit.

Loco moco–Rice, meat patty, egg, and gravy. Specialty of Café 100 in Hilo.

Lychee–A reddish, woody peel that is discarded for the sweet, white fruit inside. Be careful of the pit. Good small seed (or chicken-tongue) lychees are so good, they should be illegal.

Macadamia nut–A large, round nut.

Malasada–Portuguese doughnut dipped in sugar.

Manapua–Steamed or baked bun filled with meat.

Mango–Bright orange fruit with yellow pink skin. Distinct, tasty flavor.

Manju–Cookie filled with a sweet center.

Musubi–Cold steamed rice, sliced spam rolled in black seaweed.

'Opihi–Limpets found on ocean rocks. Eaten raw mixed with salt. Texture is similar to clams or mussels.

Pao dulce–Portuguese sweet bread.

Papaya–Melon-like, pear-shaped fruit with yellow skin best eaten chilled. Good at breakfast.

Pipi Kaula–Hawaiian style beef jerky. Excellent when dipped in poi. (Even if you don't like poi, this combo works.)

Plate lunch–An island favorite as an inexpensive, filling lunch. Consists of "two-scoop rice", a scoop of macaroni salad, and some type of meat, either beef, chicken, or fish. Also called a Box Lunch. Great for picnics.

Portuguese sausage–Pork sausage, highly seasoned with red pepper.

Pupu–Appetizer, finger foods, or snacks.

Saimin–Noodles cooked in either chicken, pork, or fish broth. Word is peculiar to Hawai'i. Local Japanese say the dish comes from China. Local Chinese say it comes from Japan.

Shave ice–A block of ice is "shaved" into a ball with flavored syrup poured over the top. Best served with ice cream on the bottom. Very delicious.

Smoothie–Usually papaya, mango, frozen passion fruit, and frozen banana but almost any fruit can be used to make this milkshake-like drink. Add milk for creaminess.

Taro chips–Sliced and deep-fried taro; resembles potato chips.

KAILUA-KONA AMERICAN

ALOHA CAFÉ 322–3383

Located in a restored theater building on the highway in Kainaliu (just south of Kailua-Kona), they offer good food at reasonable prices. We like to stop there if we want a big breakfast on our way to the volcano. Most of the seating is on a lanai, and the table all the way to the back has a very nice view all the way down to the coast. The pancakes are exceptionally hearty, and the sautéed tofu makes for a different kind of breakfast. Usually lots of clever specials. Lunches are pretty good, featuring burgers, sandwiches and the like. The place generally has a laid back, funky feel. The service is either great or bad, depending on who you get. Try some baked goods there, or take some with you—they're excellent. **$5–$10** for breakfast, and lunch. Dinner some days for **$10–$20** with a small selection.

BEACH TREE BAR & GRILL 323–3371

Fantastic beachside setting at the Four Seasons at Hualalai 14 miles north of Kona. Mixed menu with grilled fish, pad Thai noodles, burgers and hot dogs, BBQ chicken and tuna salad sandwich. **$12–$18.** Pricey food 'cause you're at a pricey resort.

BILLY BOB'S PARK 'N PORK 323–3371

Elegant dining it ain't, but it's simple, clean and comfortable. The name pretty much says it all, doesn't it? BBQ ribs, chicken, chili, and a few other items. The food used to be excellent, but seems to have slipped since it was sold. Ties optional (if you want one to wipe your mouth). South of the 111 mile marker on Highway 11 a few miles south of Kona in Captain Cook. Dinner is **$8–$12.** No credit cards.

BUBBA GUMP'S SHRIMP CO. 331–8442

Remember the movie *Forrest Gump,* when Bubba describes all the ways you can fix shrimp? Well, the owners of this small chain apparently didn't see it because most of the recipes mentioned in the movie aren't on the menu. But that's OK because this is a really easy place to like. The whole restaurant is based on the movie, and the dishes are named after its characters. Very friendly service, fun and a bit loud. The service can seem a bit unresponsive until you realize that the ping-pong paddle on the table that says, "Stop Forrest Stop" is meant as a signal to the waiter that you want 'em. (Beats the heck out of the old eye-contact method.) The food is mostly fairly good (certainly not great) with lots of shrimp dishes (obviously!), fish, some steak, burgers and salads. The peel-and-eat shrimpers' net catch makes a good appetizer, and they have some very good fresh fish. Their Medal of Honor Margarita is smokin' good, and the portion is hefty. Breakfasts are good here and fairly reasonable. Our only complaint is that they won't take reservations (and long waits are not uncommon). Overall, a fun atmosphere and acceptable food make a good experience. Their location is dreamy. Right on the water on Alii Drive next to Waterfront Row in downtown Kona. **$5–$8** for breakfast, **$7–$15** for lunch, **15–$25** for dinner.

BUNS IN THE SUN 326–2774

Formerly a source for great sandwiches, they seem to have slipped, though the sandwiches are still pretty good and the prices reasonable. Service often indifferent. They bake their own bread (and sell to other restaurants as well), and the bread is their best asset. Avoid the biscuits and gravy; they taste like plastic. In the Lanihau Shopping Center off Palani Road. Breakfast is a reasonable **$3–$6**; lunch is **$6–$8**.

CANAAN DELI 323-2577

Sandwiches, burgers, and pizza in spartan surroundings. The sandwiches, such as the Philly cheesesteak, are more than acceptable, but the pizza can be avoided without worry. Wouldn't mind if they were a bit cleaner. **$4–$7** for breakfast, **$7–$12** for lunch or early dinner. On ocean side of Highway 11 in Kealakekua. No credit cards.

THE COFFEE SHACK 328-9555

 A good place to stop on your way to the volcano—especially if you get an early start (because they do, too). Except when we want a *big* breakfast, this is where we often stop. *Fantastic* view down the slopes of Mt. Hualalai overlooking Kealakekua and Honaunau—try to get a railing table and check out the gigantic avocado tree and the coffee trees below you. (It's nice to sit there drinking coffee from those very trees.) Tables are outdoors but covered, and the place is spotless. Nice selection of coffee drinks, tasty homemade baked goods and breads, a small selection of breakfast items, and a good selection of sandwiches. Try the ham and cheese croissant along with a cinnamon roll for a hearty breakfast. They grow their own coffee and it's tasty. In fact, it's probably best to classify them as a coffee and pastry place that happens to serve a few breakfast items and numerous sandwiches. Lunch can

get busy but breakfast is more relaxing. **$5–$10** for breakfast and lunch. Service is often slow and sometimes surly. Located on ocean side of Highway in Captain Cook just past the 109 mile marker.

COSTCO 334-0770

You'd be surprised to find out how many people eat at this food stand at Costco. Their pizza is surprisingly good (they use pretty good ingredients and the crust is fresh) and it's *very* cheap. $10 for a gigantic pie. They also serve hot dogs, salads and a few other items. You need to be a Costco member to get in. We gave them an ONO because of the value. Can't beat it. North Kona, see map on page 151.

DENNY'S 334-1313

You mean the chain? The cheap Grand Slam breakfast (which is $6 here) and all that? Yeah. Nearly everyone knows what kind of food to expect at a Denny's. This one's no different. The reason we're putting 'em here is that they have an excellent view of Kailua-Kona and the ocean, and they are the first place in town to be open 24 hours. Otherwise, it's the same old Denny's. In CrossRoads Shopping Center at Palani Road and Highway 11.

DRYSDALE'S TWO 322-0070

They serve chicken, burgers, ribs, fish—you get the picture. The food is acceptable (the ribs are usually decent), and the portions are on the large size. With reasonable prices, some outside tables, a casual atmosphere, sports TV, and a full bar, this place is popular with visitors. **$10–$20** per person. No reservations. Open later than most restaurants in case you're hungry when the rest of Kona

closes up. In the Keauhou Shopping Center off Kamehameha III in South Kona.

FLASHBACK'S BAR & GRILL 326–2840

With a great location like this, it should be easy to fashion a good restaurant. But they didn't. It's seems inspired after a Happy Days episode with a '50s and '60s type menu and decor and albums (remember those?) sprinkled all about as music fills the background. Sort of a Hard Rock Café for the quieter set. But the food (which tastes semi-prepackaged) doesn't cut it. I'd hate to get in line behind them at Costco. Sandwiches, burgers, and hot dogs for lunch. Chicken, steak, fish & chips for dinner. Service is equally unremarkable. Lunch is **$5–$13, $10–$22** for dinner. In the heart of Kona on Alii Dr. across from the seawall.

HARBOR HOUSE 326–4166

Ask anyone who frequents Harbor House why they go, and they'll give you a one-word answer— *Schooners!* Located at Honokohau Harbor 2 miles north of Kona overlooking the water and boats, they serve the coldest beer on the island in ultra-thick, 18-ounce frosted schooners for around $3. (Oh, I almost forgot, they serve food, too.) This is a popular place to stop after a fishing or SCUBA excursion. The food consists of average fish and chips, fried calamari, burgers and assorted other fast food. We didn't give 'em an ONO *because of the food,* it's just a great place to have a cold one and watch the tranquil harbor waters while you go over your adventures of the day. **$5–$10.** Head toward the harbor off the highway between the 97 & 98 mile markers and turn right at the buildings. Closes around 7 p.m., the schooners aren't as cold near closing time.

HARD ROCK CAFÉ 329–8866

I guess little Kona has finally made it—we have our own Hard Rock Café. This very successful chain restaurant serves tasty burgers, ribs, pot roast and fish in an ambiance swimming with rock 'n' roll memorabilia. (Good fish sandwich.) Rock music fills the air. The non-smoking tables have the loudest music and no view, while the smoking tables have the best views near the lanai and the volume is softer. If you're looking for a quiet meal and escargot, you *definitely* came to the wrong place. But if you want a fun, tasty and loud meal at a *fairly* reasonable price, *dis is da place.* **$9–$20** for lunch and dinner, open till midnight. No reservations and there's often a wait. On Alii Drive in Coconut Grove Market Place in Kona.

HUGGO'S 329–1493

Gorgeous open air views adjacent to the ocean at Kailua Bay. They are so close to the water because they are grandfathered into the regulations restricting oceanside locations. Pasta, steak, seafood, and some veggie items prepared reasonably well. Try to get a railing table where you look down onto sand, rock, and water. (Preferable over the patio tables.) Decent selection of wines by the glass, and the desserts are outrageous. The adjacent lounge is a good place to enjoy a drink at sunset. We dinged them pretty hard in the last edition for the skimpy pupus. (We said you should take the garlic bread home and starve your parrot.) They sent us a letter saying they were increasing the portions, and they have. Lunch is highly recommended for the good view and food. Try the dinner, if the prices don't scare you off. In all, Huggo's is a good place to eat if you want a great location and reasonably good food. This is the kind of atmosphere many people envision when they contemplate dining out in Hawai'i. And the food is pretty good here, just not great. **$10–$25** for lunch, **$20–$45** for dinner. On Alii Dr., down-town Kona near Royal Kona Resort.

ISLAND LAVA JAVA 327-2161

 The food has improved tremendously since our last edition. (The deadly cinnamon rolls tend to run out, good muffins too.) The coffee is pretty good (though sometimes not very hot). With their views (they're right across the street from the ocean), it's good for a light breakfast and coffee in the morning. Service sometimes poor and some other breakfast items not as good. Birds and flies are occasional hazzard. Alii Dr. in Kona in Alii Sunset Plaza. **$4–$8.**

JAMESON'S BY THE SEA 329-3195

Located next to White Sands Beach on Alii Drive, the setting is wonderful. Their dreamy outdoor railing tables overlook the beach and get you close to the water. (These outdoor "railing" tables are much preferred to the official "outdoor" tables whose view of the ocean is partially blocked by a wall that makes you feel like you're in a hole. Sometimes insects from the beach fly onto the tables; unavoidable, I'm afraid.) The ambiance is first rate. The food is quite variable here—sometimes great, sometimes downright terrible. Some of the dishes seem ill-conceived, others flavorful. (Flavors are not subtle here.) Entertainment is often provided, but sometimes by some pretty bad Hawaiian lounge lizards. *(Give me that crazy, kooky hukilau yeeeah!)* We have some serious objections with Jameson's,

and granting the ONO was a tough call. The portions are too small and the service is responsive but too often snippy. Sometimes we vow not to return but usually change our minds when we want the railing table setting. (And the baked stuffed shrimp.) We like to arrive for dinner about 45 minutes before sunset, though you may not see the sun from the railings. Lunch is **$10–$15,** dinner is **$25–$35.**

KEEI CAFÉ 328-8451

Not really American, sort of a hodge-podge of items from many countries. (I guess that is American.) A little hole in the wall in an out-of-the-way place that serves exceptionally tasty food. You know how you sometimes purposely get into a rut at a restaurant by ordering the same dish because you love it so much? That's how one of us is for the fresh fish (especially ono) on red Thai curry and jasmine rice, the other likes the (spicy) fajitas stuffed with chicken or tofu, salsa, black bean chili sauce and avocado. The decor is nothing, the passing cars from the highway too loud; cheap furnishings, limited hours, tables and menu. But the flavors are unlimited. (Try the eggplant rolls with couscous inside for an appetizer.) Also available are rib eye steak, great pork chops and a few other items. Desserts are not-so-sweet bread pudding, a great mango cake and more. They're only open 5–9 p.m. Tues–Sat for dinner, so make reservations—early if possible. You have to be real aggressive in getting their attention (a flare gun helps), so don't expect attentive service. But the food and reasonable prices will keep you coming back. On Highway 11 just south of Kona in Honaunau near the 106 mile marker. **$10–$20,** dinner only. No credit cards.

KIMO'S FAMILY BUFFET 329-1393

Buffets by the pool at Uncle Billy's Kona Bay Hotel in downtown Kona on Alii Drive. **$6** for breakfast, **$11** for dinner. The quality is not very high, but then neither is the price. It's an OK place to eat all you want for a decent price, making it an acceptable deal for the money.

KONA BEACH RESTAURANT 329-2911

Located in King Kamehameha's Kona Beach Hotel, the restaurant is right next to Kamakahonu Beach and the 'Ahu'ena Heiau, so get a table next to the window which makes a delightful way to start the day. The food is acceptable. For breakfast it's either a buffet for **$10** or off the menu. They have fairly good dinner seafood buffets for $20 Fri and Sat. Otherwise dinner is unremarkable steak, ribs, and chicken. For lunch you eat at **PADDLERS** next door. Average sandwiches and some other entrées there. The kalua pig quesadilla is the best choice there. **$4–$10** for breakfast, **$8–$15** for lunch, **$15–$30** for dinner.

KONA BREWING CO & BREWPUB 329-2739

A cool place to go for some tasty brew and a pizza or salad. 12 taps feature 8 different beers made there as well as 4 guest beers. They range from the mild (Lilikoi Wheat Ale) to the not-so-mild (Fire Rock Pale Ale). Most of the pizzas (except their Hawaiian style) are delicious. *Love* the Ka'u Pesto. Consider the tomato Cajun instead of the regular sauce. In fact they have 5 different sauces and lots of toppings so the possibilities are many. The service could use some improvement, however, but overall this is a great place. On Palani and Kuakini behind Zac's.

KONA INN RESTAURANT 329-4455

Steak and seafood with some stir-fry, pasta and chicken. Nice ambiance—A good place for a sunset dinner. Just a strip of grass separates you from the ocean. For lunch, consider the calamari sandwich—it's by the same people who run the Waikoloa Beach Grill. Dinner uses a dinner menu on one side of the restaurant, and a cheaper "Cafe" (lunch) menu on the other. At dinner, avoid the uncomfortable antique chairs in favor of the highback wicker chairs. **$8–$15** for lunch, **$20–$30** for dinner. The food and service are usually very good. Check out the ceiling fans—all interconnected by an old belt system. Some parents like to bring their keikis here where the munchkins can play on the grass while the grown-ups can dine while keeping an eye on them. Located on the ocean side of Alii Drive in downtown Kona at the Kona Inn Shopping Village. Can't miss it.

KONA RANCH HOUSE 329-7061

A dependable favorite located in an elegantly furnished old Kona Ranch House (oh, I get it!) on the mauka side of Kuakini Highway in Kona, they offer good food, pleasant country ambiance, and no view. It's like eating in a rich uncle's house. Families dine in the Paniolo Room (which can get a bit noisy), reservations are accepted at the quieter Plantation Lanai room. Menus have lots to choose from. Breakfast has everything from biscuits 'n gravy (an old favorite) to eggs Benedict. Egg Beater omelettes if you want. Try the mahimahi and eggs. For lunch there's fish, chicken and crepes. Dinner is steak and seafood or choose the BBQ ribs or pasta. (Try the "krab" cakes.) The best deals are the dinner platters, which

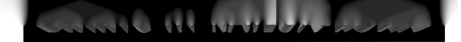

include everything for under $20. Families will like it here. Portions are usually hearty. Service can be a bit slow, but it's usually worth the wait. $7–$12 for breakfast, $8–$15 for lunch. For sale at press time so this review may change.

(TED'S) KONA THEATER CAFÉ 328-2244

Open at 7:30 a.m., this is a good place to stop for breakfast on your way to the volcano. Good, friendly folks. Consider the fresh fish and eggs with Hawaiian sweetbread toast—surprisingly good despite how it sounds. Or the spanikopita with spinach and gorgonzola in phyllo dough. Items have a Greek touch (though the owner's from NY). Lunch includes pita sandwiches, soups, etc. $4–$8 breakfast and lunch. Dinner is $10–$18. On Highway 11 in Captain Cook.

KONA VILLAGE 325-6787

Located at secluded Kona Village between Kona and the Kohala Resort area (see map on page 146), the food here is excellent and pricey. Lunch is a $26 buffet outdoors at Hale Moana. The wind and birds can be a problem, but the food and oceanside view make up for it. Lots of salads, tasty fish, pork or beef, and scrumptious desserts. For dinners indoors you choose from several complete meals for $60 at Hale Moana (Pacific Rim) or $60–$80 at Hale Samoa (which has a dress code—slacks, etc.) These include appetizers, soup, salad, entrée, and dessert, and features seafood or steak in an elegant and romantic atmosphere. Children not allowed at Hale Samoa. Ask them about the time a plane crashed into the Talk Story Bar just before Christmas 1994.

LULU'S 331-2633

With their Caribbean/South Seas type decor, ample portions, tasty food, and giant margaritas, Lulu's works. (Don't confuse them with the disappointing Durty Jakes downstairs.) Numerous sandwiches (love the Maui teriyaki chicken) and burgers, they also have a large pupu selection and some good veggie items. Nice view overlooking the water. (Just pretend you don't see the enormous power lines in the way.) On Alii Drive at Coconut Grove Market Place. (The music from Hard Rock can permeate Lulu's.) $10–$15 for lunch and dinner. The menu lists several other Lulu's locations in the South Seas—such as Tonga—but according to a highly placed source in the Lulu's organization (our waitress), this is the only one.

OODLES OF NOODLES 329-9222

First of all, it ain't really American food. I don't know how to classify them. Exceptionally good food, well chosen combination of flavors and ingredients, bright, cheerful service. Items include Kona-style ahi noodle casserole (which is *impossibly* good), pad Thai, curried coconut pork somen noodles, and more. We haven't had a bad meal here yet. The keiki menu has "ba-sketti," mac & cheese and those under 3 are free. (Bring their driver's license.) Us carnivores as well as vegans will be happy with their selections. In the CrossRoads Shopping Center in Kona at Palani and the highway. $9–$16 for lunch, **add** $2–$4 for dinner.

PAHU I'A 325-8000

Located at the Four Seasons at Hualalai 14 miles north of Kona, this is one of our

favorite restaurants on the island. The lanai tables (which are a bit too close together) are as close to eating on the beach as you'll get, ask for them. The menu is broken into three parts— Hawaiian/Asian, Western, and Hualalai (which are the specials). Items such as the spicy Thai curry with shrimp, scallops, fish and rice are utterly delicious. Their Hualalai warm chocolate cake should probably be outlawed—*nothing* could be that chocolatey. We like to arrive about 45 minutes before sunset to get a good table and to gawk at the superb beachside setting. This is a romantic place. They rarely do anything wrong, but, of course, you pay for that perfection. **$30–$45.** Expensive, yeah. But cheaper than some of the pricier Kohala restaurants. Reservations recommended.

PALM CAFÉ 329–8200

Now you see them, now you don't. Palm Café was a local favorite until they disappeared awhile ago. Now they've rematerialized next to where they used to be. And they're still just as good. A combination of American and Pacific Rim. They're expensive and not ocean front (they're across the street from the ocean) but the food is excellent and nicely presented. Inventive recipes and thoughtful use of ingredients such as fresh fish, lamb and steak make this an easy restaurant to recommend. On Alii Drive in the Coconut Grove Marketplace. Closed Mondays. Dinner is **$25–$40.**

QUINN'S ALMOST-BY-THE-SEA 329–3822

Truth in advertising. You're close to the ocean, but can't really see it. Lunch offers seafood, burgers, and sandwiches. The fish sand-

wich, especially Cajun style, is excellent, as are most seafood items. The clam chowder could use a little improvement. For dinner, it's steak and seafood. Service is quick at lunch time. Consider the quasi-outdoor smoking section, even if you don't smoke, for a nice lunch time nautical green ambiance. Lots of specials here. Most of the food is tastily prepared. We recommend lunch over the pricey dinner. On Palani across from the King Kamehameha Beach Hotel in downtown Kona. **$8–$15** for lunch, **$20–$25** for dinner. Limited parking.

STAN'S 329–4500

Across the street from Kailua Bay on Alii Drive, they have a clean, open air Polynesian theme. Dinner features fish, stir-fry, casserole and steak with occasionally good results. They have a minimum order of $2.50 at breakfast and $7 for dinner. So try to resist the urge to spend one of your valuable vacation days on the Big Island hanging out at Stan's nursing a cup of coffee. **$4–$8** for breakfast, **$10–$15** for dinner. This is a *qualified* ONO. Stan's works for breakfast because of the price and view. Avoid lunch and dinner.

STARBUCKS 329–1166

Don't need to spend a lot of page space for this. Like the Starbucks you have back home. Their baked goods are *excellent;* they get them from Mamane Bakery in Honoka'a. Surprisingly, the Kona coffee we've tried there is not that good. (Too bitter, too hot, too stong, and too expensive.) Hope that changes. Kona Coast Shopping Center on Palani Road.

TROPICS CAFÉ 329–3111, EXT 4

Excellent seaside location for breakfast at the Royal

Kona Resort in downtown Kona. The tables on the terrace looking down the coast are especially coveted. Breakfast buffets are the best value here and are worth the **$11.50** price tag. Buffet omelettes and waffles are made to order, and there are plenty of other selections. You get good food and smashing views. For dinner, Fri—Sun they have a prime rib and seafood buffet dinner for **$21.50**. Otherwise dinner is steak and seafood off the menu. **$20–$30**. The libation-inclined will appreciate the usually excellent (and strong) drinks. Reservations recommended for dinner.

WENDY'S 322-8081

We're a little embarrassed about this. Normally we wouldn't be reviewing a fast food restaurant—love 'em or hate 'em, they're pretty predictable, right? You know, Wendy's...burgers, frosties, a salad bar. Yeah, *that* Wendy's. It's not even a particularly *good* Wendy's food-wise. But this one distinguishes itself by having a million-dollar view—along with $2-dollar hamburgers. Great place to watch the sunset from this location overlooking the ocean from up the mountain, and you may see fish or whales breaching. They even have a telescope for viewing. If you want fast food but still want to experience a touch of the exotic, give 'em a try. **$4–$8**. Located at Keauhou Shopping Center (south Kona) off Kamehameha III.

KAILUA-KONA CHINESE

GOLDEN CHOPSTIX 329-4527

Simple, clean atmosphere and tasty food. The house delight is yummy. Also try the Golden Rangoon for an appetizer. Their plate lunches are an excellent deal at around $5. Lately, if you ask them to spice it up...they will. **$5–$10** for lunch, **$10–$20** for dinner. A tad pricey for dinner, but pretty reliable. On Kaiwi Street just makai (ocean) of Highway 19.

OCEAN SEAFOOD 329-3055

Very clean, quite authentic. Usually well-prepared dishes, fresh ingredients and lots of attention to quality, but sometimes they drop the ball. Most of their clientele are Asian, which should tell you something about the food. Buffets sometimes offered; these are recommended. **$7–$15** per person. Located in the King Kamehameha Mall in Kona. See map on page 59. This is different than their other location on Alii Dr.

KAILUA-KONA FRENCH

LA BOURGOGNE 329-6711

This *tiny* restaurant on Highway 11 between Keauhou and Kona serves tasty and well-conceived dishes, including lamb, duck, venison, and even veal sweet-breads. Only dings: a bit cramped and enclosed with no view. Closed on Sunday. Dinner is **$20–$40**.

KAILUA-KONA GREEK

CASSANDRA'S GREEK TAVERNA 334-1066

As close as you'll get to authentic Greek food on the Big Island (with an island twist). Lunch makes use of pitas, omelettes, gyros, plus burgers and fries. For dinner it's gyros, lamb, seafood, casseroles, and pastas. Pretty good food. Off Alii Drive beside Kona Marketplace. **$6–$12** for lunch, **$15–$25** for dinner.

KAILUA-KONA INDONESIAN

SIBU CAFÉ 329–1112

This Indonesian restaurant is a real find. The food is delicious and distinct. Try the Balinese chicken marinated in tarragon and covered with a peanut sauce. Or the ginger beef. Consider the garlic shrimp with pasta. Hard to go wrong here. Outdoor café style, located in Banyan Court Mall on Alii Drive. $9–$15 for lunch, **add $2** for dinner. Cash only. ⊗

KAILUA-KONA ITALIAN

BASILS RESTAURANTE 326–7836

On Alii Drive across from Hulihe'e Palace. Large selection of pizza, pasta, with a bit of seafood. Pizza is *way* too cheesy. As for pasta, does 11 unremarkable cheese raviolis for $11 sound a bit excessive? The burgers are the best deal. In general, no real compelling reason to eat here. $7–$20 for lunch or dinner. ⊗

BIANELLI'S GOURMET PIZZA & PASTA 326–4800

Some of the best pizza on the Big Island. The atmosphere is pleasant with bicycle, sports, and movie posters everywhere, and the food is excellent. Their selection of pizza ingredients is outstanding (how about some buffalo milk mozzarella on your pizza?) and the quality is usually superb. Try the Chicago style—*ono*. They have all-you-can-eat pasta specials (pick your pasta and sauce) for around $8. Consider the pink sauce. It's *imperative* that you try the Pesto Bread with pine nuts for an appetizer. (Makes me hungry just thinking about it.) Lasagna, manicotti, sandwiches—The $8 calzones are big enough for two though they're a bit too cheesy.

They have a good wine and beer list, as well as a full bar. Service unfortunately can be quite slow, but otherwise you'll be happy with the food and the prices. We try to "rereview" them every few weeks—just to be thorough. Delivery from Keauhou to Kona available. $4–$15 per person. Located in The Pines Plaza on Nani Kailua Road. (See lower part of map on page 59.) One caveat: The food at lunch time is noticeably inferior to dinner-time quality. ⊗

MICHAELANGELO'S 329–4436

Should've stuck to painting. *Very* avoidable Italian food (but with a nice, elevated oceanside setting). Selections include an "all you can eat" spaghetti. The waiter suddenly goes blind when it comes time for the second helping, so wave that arm high. Place could use some spiffing up. Lunch is $8–$18, dinner is $15–$25. In Waterfront Row on Alii Drive.

ROCKY'S PIZZA 322–3223

If you catch 'em on a *real* good day, the pizza is *almost* average. They also serve BBQ sandwiches that taste fairly good the first bite, but seem to get worse as you continue eating, until you wonder if you'll finish it. Some other sandwiches and pasta also available. Overall, prices are too high given the usually surly service and underachieving food. In the Keauhou Shopping Center off Kamehameha III. $5–$20 for lunch and dinner.

KAILUA-KONA JAPANESE

HAPPI YU & YU SUSHI 326–5653

Combination steak house and sushi bar, they consider the teppan yaki their attraction. The quality is high and they take obvious pride, but it seems a bit overpriced to us, given the setting. $10–$15 for lunch, $20–$40 for dinner. On Alii Drive in Waterfront Row but without a real oceanside setting.

SUSHI SHOP 987-8490

(ono) Located next to Zac's in the North Kona Shopping Center, this is the best place in Kona to get good sushi at a reasonable price. Try the sesame roll. Simple hole-in-the-wall (literally) walk-up window, simple outdoor tables. $3–$7. A real find.

TESHIMA'S RESTAURANT 322-9140

(ono) Clean, friendly place with simple but tasty Japanese, American and local items such as bento, teriyaki beef, sushi, and fried fish. There's something for everyone at this family-run restaurant. Only gripe is that they have a habit of bringing all the food at once, typical of restaurants in Japan. Off Highway 11 in Honalo, just south of Kona. Lunch is $6–$10, dinner is $10–$15.

KAILUA-KONA KOREAN BBQ

JENNIFER'S KOREAN BBQ 326-1155

(ono) Excellent place to go for delicious Korean BBQ. (Best in Kona.) It's located on the left side of Luhia Street off Kaiwi Street in the Old Industrial Area of North Kona. See Kona Map. The surroundings are worn but unbelievably clean. Their English is pretty spotty so don't expect much help with the menu. We've liked nearly *every* item we've tried. If you go with the "Lunch and Dinner Plates" the price is a *very* reasonable $7–$10. If you choose the "Yakiniku Plates" (where they cook the meal on your table) the price goes up to $20. But the quality is excellent no matter what you choose. Consider the "side

orders" such as spicy pork for appetizers. Top it all off with some green tea ice cream. This place is a real find. Take out available. Much busier at lunch than dinner. Park around back near the gigantic satellite dishes.

KAILUA-KONA LOCAL

OCEAN VIEW 329-9998

(ono) This place has been here since 1935 (and they haven't changed the linoleum yet). Same family owners, same hearty food. Located across from the seawall in downtown Kailua-Kona, they feature a simple, luncheonette atmosphere, a huge menu, and old-fashioned, filling food. Country fried steak, pork chops, loco moco, kalua pig and cabbage, Chinese dishes, and for appetizer, try the pipi kaula (like beef jerky) dipped in poi—sounds weird but tastes great. This epitomizes a local restaurant. Breakfast ranges from cinnamon toast to hot cakes and Spam. Some may object to the aging surroundings or the sometimes less-than-perky service, but this restaurant is loved by local residents and repeat visitors alike who appreciate getting a full stomach of mostly tasty food for a reasonable price. Not for the cholesterol counters. $4–$7 for breakfast, $4–$12 for lunch, $6–$16 for dinner. They serve smokin' good *frozen* mai tais. Excellent shave ice in the adjacent business. Closed Mondays. No credit cards.

SAM CHOY'S 326-1545

We took flack for not giving Sam Choy's an ONO in our last edition, and we probably will again. People who live here always rave about the place. (But not a single reader has ever stuck up for them in letters and e-mail to us.) The much-beloved Sam is famous throughout the state and has many restaurants. But our experiences usually leave us flat. The restaurant is set up quasi-cafeteria style with very close tables and a loud environment. Service is always rushed and often poor. The food, especially breakfast and lunch, is too oily. Breakfast offers the standard fare (eggs, pancakes) and several local items, such as many types of loco moco (these are huge and described on page 220) and stir fry, beef stew, or poke omelettes. Lunch is teriyaki marinated NY steak (yummy), burgers, loco moco, stir fry, and poke, plus many specials. Dinner works the best but gets expensive (and there's a $12 shared plate fee). Lamb chops, steak, duck and pork all served with various local twists. Sam does a particularly good job with fish. In all, expect crowded, noisy conditions with fatty food for breakfast and lunch (but it's the best place in west Hawaii to try loco moco) and somewhat better conditions at night. Located in Koloko Industrial Area on Kauhola Street just north of Kona on the road before Costco (see map on page 151). $4–$10 for breakfast, $5–$12 for lunch, $20-$30 for dinner (but you can BYOB). If they served dinner only we'd possibly give them an ono, but breakfast and lunch bring them down.

VERNA'S DRIVE INN 334-0449

Actually, if you drive in you can only get coffee or milkshakes. That's because there's a different business in the same building handling those drinks. Verna's doesn't use the drive-in part. Anyway, this is local fast food from this small island chain. Items like saimin (which is pretty good with noodles, teri beef, scrambled eggs and Spam in a broth)

burgers, sandwiches, and plate lunches with chili, teri chicken, stew, etc. It's a good place to try local fast food...just don't expect it fast. Even when you're the only one, service is slow. Shakes are very good but expensive. In Kona on Kuakini and Hanama. $3–$7 for breakfast, lunch and dinner, but $4 for a shake.

KAILUA-KONA MEDITERRANEAN

EDWARD'S AT KANALOA 322-1434

Great food, well presented, and a good atmosphere—that's what you want, right? First the location. With a swimming pool from Kanaloa at Kona Condominiums on one side and the Pacific surf on the other, Edward's sports an unusual but effective location, especially for dinner. At night the pool is quiet, the surf is ever-present, and the sunsets are superb. Pleasant music in the background rounds it out. As for the food, it's expertly prepared. Appetizers include couscous and chicken liver mousseline. Entrées such as lamb, stuffed chicken breast, and squid are delicious. Top it off with flourless chocolate cake or creme brulee. Though the service could use a little fine tuning, the food and nighttime ambiance more than justify the price. Good wine selection. Breakfast is $7–$10, Lunch is $9–$14, Dinner is $20–$35. Located in south Kona, call for directions (too complicated to print). Reservations required for dinner. (Ask for a back "deck" table when you get there.)

KAILUA-KONA MEXICAN

PANCHO AND LEFTY'S 326-2171

We wrote this review several different times, trying to capture our experiences of this dining establishment. We finally decided to abide by the old axiom: If you can't say something nice, don't say anything at all. With this in mind, Pancho and Lefty's is located on Alii Drive. 'Nuff said.

TRES HOMBRES 329-2173
On Walua Road just off Alii Drive in Kona, the atmosphere is good, but the food needs work. Standard assortment of Mexican items, plus some seafood. Service is fine, but the food is underwhelming. **$6–$10** for lunch, **$12–$23** for dinner.

KAILUA-KONA THAI

KONA TAENG-ON THAI FOOD 329-1994
Sorry, but the food's not good enough to warrant the prices. Good menu but uninspiringly prepared. Service is a little cranky. **$10–$25.** Upstairs on Alii Drive across from Kona Marketplace.

ROYAL THAI CAFE 322-8424
(ono) A smooth running machine that puts out extremely good Thai food. Spotlessly clean, crisp and responsive service, and the variety of food is admirable. The red and yellow curries are delicious. Other items include Pahd Thai, lots of vegetarian items, and even Thai dumplings. Try the Thai tea. This is a very easy restaurant to like. In the Keauhou Shopping Center at Alii Dr. and Kamehameha III Hwy. **$6–$10** for lunch, **$10–$20** for dinner.

THAI RIN 329-2929
Used to be tasty Thai food on Alii Drive but it has disappointed us lately. Maybe you'll have better luck. Consider the chicken satay for an appetizer. The Pahd Thai noodles are good. There are

several vegetarian items, and the curry is tops. They'll turn the heat up as much as you want. Lunch is **$8–$15,** dinner is **$10–$20.**

KAILUA-KONA TREATS

FRENCH BAKERY 326-2688
(ono) This is the place to go in Kona for wicked baked goods. Croissants, muffins, danish, and some sandwiches. They also make some pies, and their bread is ono. Open early and they close at 3 p.m. during the week and are closed on Sundays. We often take our visitors here on their last day—a treat before the long plane trip. Also a good place for sandwiches on your way to a picnic. **$4–$8.** Cash only. ☺

KAILUA CANDY COMPANY 329-2522
(ono) Handmade chocolates are the specialty here. Expensive but delicious. Try the a'a lava (dark chocolate with coconut and mac nuts) or the turtles. They also make utterly indecent cheesecake with some world-class flavor combinations sold by the slice. On Kaiwi near Kuakini, old industrial area of north Kona. See Kona map.

MAC PIE STORE 322-4017
(ono) Exceptional pies made with locally grown macadamia nuts and Maui sugar. Similar to a pecan pie but with several flavors. (They're generous with the samples, too.) In Keauhou Shopping Center on Kamehameha III near the south end of Alii Drive.

MRS. BARRY'S KONA COOKIES 329-6055
(ono) *Unfortunately,* they have good homemade cookies and a good variety as well. Try the

chocolate chip/mac nut cookies. Hard to find. See map on page 151. They're on Maiau Road on the way to Costco.

SCANDINAVIAN SHAVE ICE

ONO Good shave ice, but not quite as good as it used to be. For around two bucks you get your choice of 50 flavors of delicious and very *finely* shaved shave ice. Big servings, as well. They use nifty holders and even punched out holes in the tables to hold 'em. Located off Alii Drive in Downtown Kona near Likana Lane. Cash only. For some odd reason they won't let you put ice cream on the bottom anymore, only frozen yogurt. Come on, guys, give us a choice! Though good, the shave ice over at nearby **OCEAN VIEW** is better these days but we didn't put them under TREATS because it's a full-fledged restaurant.

KOHALA

There are a lot of ONO symbols in the Kohala dining section. That's no accident. If you're staying in Kohala, you'll find that the food choices are outstanding. That makes it difficult for us as reviewers. Normally, if we think a place is a dump, we say it's a dump. If the food or service is lousy, we say it's lousy. Unfortunately for us, most Kohala restaurants have great food and service and excellent atmosphere. This makes it hard to review without sounding like a bootlicking commercial for Kohala restaurants. The resorts go to great lengths (and expense) to feed you and keep you eating at the resort. The downside for you is that you can pay dearly for those ONOs. Most of the restaurants here are pricey, and you'll find that eating in Kohala will cost you more than on any other part of the island. It wasn't our intention to gush over so many restau-rants in Kohala, but we can't deny the fundamental quality of their offerings.

The restaurants at the **Four Seasons** and **Kona Village** are in the Kona dining section since they are often frequented by people staying in Kona.

If you want to cook your own meals, you'll soon learn that there are no large **grocery stores** in this area. You will find one, however, a few miles up the road in Waikoloa Village.

When we mention that a restaurant is lunch only, or breakfast and dinner only, you should take this with a grain of salt. Resorts are constantly rearranging these options. Also, you'll find the resorts mentioned are shown on the maps on pages 53 and 140.

For simplicity, we are excluding restaurants in the northernmost part of Kohala (Hawi and Kapa'au). They are described under DINING ELSEWHERE.

KOHALA AMERICAN

THE BAY TERRACE 885-6622

ONO At the Mauna Lani Bay Hotel, the beautiful indoor/outdoor setting and outstanding food make this a winner. The breakfast buffets (**$22**) have an excellent cross section of breakfast items and fresh fruit. Or go à la carte for **$10–$16**. The banana-stuffed French toast with pecans makes my mouth water just writing about it. (You probably didn't need to know that.) Their Sunday brunches are about **$35**. Desserts there include evil selections, such as hot souffles with ice cream, Hanakoa lime pies, and deadly cheesecakes.

BIG ISLAND STEAK HOUSE 885-8805

Steak, ribs, pasta and some seafood. They open at 5 p.m., but don't show up on time because *they* rarely do. Our irritation stems from standing outside *way* too many times, 10 minutes after they are supposed to open, watching them through the glass and waiting for the door to open. Once inside, service is equally uncaring. But, to be honest, the food is good. The ribs are particularly excellent. **$18–$30.** In Kings' Shop in Waikoloa Resort area near 76 mile marker.

BROWN'S BEACH HOUSE 885–2000

ONO Very good outdoor setting near the beach at the Orchid at Mauna Lani. (Sometimes gets a little breezy.) For lunch consider the fish taco or the salmon wrap. Sandwiches and burgers also available. At dinner the seafood is their best bet. They also have duck, lamb and chicken. **$14–$20** for lunch, **$30–$50** for dinner.

THE CANOE HOUSE 885–6622

ONO The indoor/outdoor setting near the ocean at this Mauna Lani Bay Hotel restaurant, coupled with expertly prepared and presented food, make this a memorable choice for steak and seafood. This is a great restaurant by anyone's definition and one we are happy to re-review any time we can. The sunsets from an outdoor railing table are smashing most of the year. Items change often, so we'll refrain from singling any out. It's hard to go wrong here, unless you forget your credit card. Expect **$35–$55,** dinner only. Reservations recommended (make them for an early dinner if you want a sunset).

COAST GRILLE 880–1111

ONO Located at the Hapuna Beach Prince Hotel, the setting overlooking Hapuna Beach is wonderful. We like the outdoor tables near the railings the best. Seafood is the specialty here, and they do it well. With fish caught daily, herbs from their garden, and attentive presentation, your meal here should be superb. The wine list is probably the most extensive on the island. Their oyster bar has several varieties of oysters. The snapper and crab wrapped in ti leaves (laulau), the baked opah, or the seared ahi sashimi with a starter of baked stuffed oysters with cornbread and andouille sausage are guaranteed winners. Put this one on your list of possible sunset dinner restaurants. **$20–$50.** Reservations recommended.

THE GRILL 885–2000

ONO Excellent quality steak, seafood, and chicken. The pesto crusted rack of lamb is delicious. The only problem is that the tables in the non-smoking section are very close together. Consider the smoking section if you want some wiggle room. In the Orchid at Mauna Lani. **$32–$50.** Reservations recommended.

KAMUELA PROVISION COMPANY 885–1234

ONO Steak and seafood at this Hilton Waikoloa Restaurant. The views, especially from the outdoor tables, are fantastic. Inside you'll find an upscale yet casual decor, including two large aquariums full of tropical fish. Start everything off with the pupu platter, which has mac nut shrimp, charred ahi, grilled shrimp sate, and crispy hoisin duck. Dinner selections seem to change often enough that we won't recommend a particular dish. The desserts are very tasty. You may like the elevated outdoor oceanside tables for sunsets, lively indoor tables, or a cocktail at the other outdoor tables near the top of the pool waterfall. Food and service quality are high. Wine list is acceptable. **$25–$50** for dinner. Lunch is over-priced at **$12–$27**. Reservations required for dinner. Resort wear with collared shirts required, but shorts are OK.

KAWAIHAE HARBOR GRILL 882–1368

Fresh fish and some veggie entrées. With a *lovely* view of harbor storage tanks and a drainage ditch and a nondescript atmosphere, the food *better* be pretty good. It's not, and the portions are a joke for what you pay. Shrimp and chips for lunch is $13.50, and for that you get *three* shrimp (four when they're in a generous mood) and some potato wedges. Other entrées are similar. My last fish sandwich there was insanely overcooked ono. (It's hard to ruin ono.) You can do better. Located on the highway on Kawaihae. **$9–$16** for lunch, **$10–$25** for dinner.

KINGS' SHOPS FOOD COURT

If you're going into shock over the price of food in Kohala, the Food Court at the Kings' Shops (take road at the 76 mile marker—see map on page 53) has the usual cast of characters like burger and pizza stands. Chili by Max has adequate chili, cornbread, and hot dogs. The pizza stand has decent thick crust pizza and a few other items. Try a Blizzard at DQ. There's also a Subway. Though more expensive than food courts on the mainland, it's *way* cheaper than your other choices in Kohala. You may want to take your stuff to the outdoor tables overlooking the golf course pond. **$5–$10**.

OCEAN TERRACE 880–1111

Breakfast only at this Hapuna restaurant, which offers nice ocean views.

Buffets **($22)** offer a nice variety of items. À la carte menu includes three-egg omelettes for **$13**, Belgian waffles for **$10**, and steak and eggs for **$16**. Kind of pricey, huh? But the quality is good. (It better be.)

ORCHID CAFÉ 885–1234

Located at the Hilton Waikoloa Village, this poolside restaurant has a limited breakfast menu. Lunch features sandwiches, pasta, pizza, and some Asian dishes. Their best attribute is the soda shoppe, which serves delicious Tropical Dreams ice cream, sundaes, cookies, banana splits—you get the picture. A great place to pick up a treat; the regular meals are adequate. **$10–$15** for breakfast, **$12–$25** for lunch.

ORCHID COURT 885–2000

(ono) Breakfast buffets are $21. They also have various "complete breakfasts" for **$15–$19**, but these seem overpriced. À la carte also available. For dinner they feature a good selection of soups and salads, pastas, steak and seafood and a few pizzas and sandwiches. Dinner is **$15–$30**. Nice setting and good food. In the Orchid at Mauna Lani.

PALM TERRACE 885–1234

(ono) Palm Terrace sports a dashing atmosphere with tables near the indoor garden or outdoor near the pond and waterfall. (We prefer the latter.) This is a buffet place and they do it well. With different themes throughout the week, dinner buffets include Polynesian, Chinese, Paniolo BBQ, Prime Rib, etc. They are usually very busy and serve a huge number of meals, but it's unlikely you'll have to wait too long. The food is usually well prepared and the price—$23 at press time—is more than reasonable. À la carte items also available for those who don't want to do the buffet. As for breakfast, the buffet is $17.50 or $11 for cold continental items. We think the dinner is the better bargain here. Located at the Hilton Waikoloa Village. No reservations.

PAVILION 882-7222

Located at the Mauna Kea Beach Hotel, breakfasts are pricey but outstanding with a huge selection. À la carte includes smoked salmon benedict with sauce Maltese and French asparagus, corned beef hash with poached eggs, or their delicious French toast. Japanese items also available. Full breakfast buffets with tons of selections are $21, Continental buffets (cold items only) are $16. The breakfast view of Mauna Kea Beach is smashing. For dinner consider the island fish, herb crusted rack of lamb, or filet mignon with lobster tail. Children's menu includes hot dogs, the ever-exotic peanut butter, etc. Expect to pay $30–$50 for dinner. Reservations recommended.

THE TERRACE 882-7222

Located at the Mauna Kea Beach Resort, they have an outdoor setting. (Railing tables to the right have better views.) Lunch is not too impressive considering the cost and selection. $10–$15. They also have a **clambake** on Saturdays at the outdoor **HAU TREE** for $65, which includes lobster, crab legs, prime rib—even clams!

WAIKOLOA BEACH GRILL 885-6131

Surprisingly well prepared food for a golf course restaurant. Despite its name, you can't

see the beach (or even the ocean) from here. (But I did see a grill.) Lunch features a limited selection of sandwiches. Try the calamari sandwich—*ono!* Dinners are beef and seafood, with some pasta and chicken. Portions are acceptable, and they have a respectable wine list. Their signature dessert is a very tasty homemade mud pie. Located in the Waikoloa Resort area at the Waikoloa Beach Golf Course. $8–$15 for lunch, $12–$27 for dinner.

KOHALA CHINESE

GRAND PALACE 885-6668

Located in the Kings' Shops off the 76 mile marker, they serve the best Chinese food on the island in a soothing, fairly quiet atmosphere. (I used to work in China and this is where I come when I want the good stuff.) Service is fast—almost too fast at lunch. The lunch combination plates are a good value for Kohala. Large portions at a reasonable price. (Other items are smaller portions for the same money.) Dinner features a huge selection of delicious menu items, traditional and not-so-traditional. For lunch, this is a good place to eat in Kohala without going broke, at least compared to other Kohala restaurants. For dinner, go for broke. Lunch is $9–$15, dinner is $15–$30. 🚭

KOHALA EURO-ASIAN

ROY'S WAIKOLOA BAR & GRILL 885-4321

Some people are born to do certain things. Roy Yamaguchi was born to run restaurants. This growing chain never fails to please. (In the last edition we had a pretty ugly typo when, in praising them, we said they "rarely fail to disappoint." Oops!) The food is delicious, well-conceived and nicely presented. Dishes range from dim sum appetizers, baby back ribs, imu baked pizzas, scrumptious pastas, fish and beef. Specials abound and change nightly. The atmosphere is casual and somewhat noisy. The service is nearly always perfect. Prices are reasonable for what you get. Entrées aren't huge, so consider the delectable appetizers. Reservations strongly recommended for dinner. (Ask for a table near the glass wall overlooking the golf course pond.) Their dark chocolate souffle is legendary. Lunch is **$10–$15,** dinner is **$20–$35.**

KOHALA ITALIAN

CAFÉ PESTO 882–1071

Excellent selection of fine Italian food. Pizzas, pastas and some calzones. Pizza is light—feather-like crust, light sauce, light toppings. It's also delicious and they feature several unique combinations. 9" pizza OK for 1 person. 12" for hearty, man–sized appetites. Try the kalua pig-and-pineapple combination. Pastas can be excellent but are sometimes disappointing. Our only complaint is that they seem to possess a sort of institutional arrogance. They serve quality food with their own unique touch...and they know it. They can be fussy on substitutions. With those caveats, it's a great restaurant and we recommend it wholeheartedly. **$12–$25.** ⊗

DONATONI'S 885–1234

You can arrive at Donatoni's by boat if you wish. As soon as you walk into the fabulously elegant setting, you know you are in for a treat. Tables are assembled in several romantic rooms, one of which has a fireplace. There are outdoor tables, as well. The menu features items such as linguini with fresh seafood in a saffron broth, potato dumplings, lobster, lamb, fresh fish, and several types of pasta. The quality and service are excellent, even for a Kohala restaurant. The wine list is more than adequate. Recommending Donatoni's is a no-brainer. Do it if you feel like pampering yourself with excellent Italian food. Located at the Hilton Waikoloa Village. **$25–$40,** reservations required. Resort wear with slacks required.

KOHALA JAPANESE

HAKONE 880–1111

They have à la carte items here such as lobster, tempura, and steak. Most, however, prefer the buffet. It's $45 and includes a fine assortment of Japanese dishes, including grilled crab legs, chilled tofu, butterflyfish, steamed clams, and buckwheat noodles. There is a sushi bar (not included with the buffet). We gave it an ONO because of the high quality, but you'll be forgiven if the price scares you off. **$35–$60.** Reservations recommended. At the Hapuna Prince Hotel.

IMARI 885–1234

Elegant black-and-copper decor with wood floors and shoji doors all around, you have your choice of three types of Japanese food. Teppan-yaki style (where food is prepared in front of you by a talented, knife-wielding chef), a sushi bar (tables near there will be quieter) or shabu-shabu (where items off the menu are served tableside). The ambiance is thick with

Japanese culture and music, and the quality of the food is very good. If Japanese food is not your thing, they have steak, fish, and lobster. Located at the Hilton Waikoloa Village, reservations required. Dinner is $30–$55. Resort wear with long pants required.

KOHALA MEXICAN

TRES HOMBRES BEACH GRILL 882-1031

Here's a unique ambiance for you—South Seas Mexican. The pleasing decor features lots of personalized surfing and movie posters. The food *can be* good, and the portions range from average (combos) to huge (the black bean burrito). There's lots of attention to detail, and the service is very good. Keikis (kids) will appreciate the separate menu and respectful treatment. Some "healthy" entrées. Top it all off with some deep-fried ice cream. (I know how it sounds, but try it.) We've given 'em ONOs in the past, but they're too inconsistent now. $8–$18 for lunch, $12–$22 for dinner. Nowhere near a beach, despite name.

HILO AMERICAN

FAST FOOD

Hilo's fast food joints are mostly clustered around Puainako Town Center.

FIASCO'S 935-7666

(ONO) American (such as garlic steak melt sandwiches), Mexican (such as sizzling fajitas) and some Italian items, the menu has something for almost everyone and most items are tasty. Some portions, such as the croissant sandwich, are a tad small. The booth seats are strangely low and awkward. $7–$15 for lunch and dinner.

On Highway 11 in Waiakea Center just south of Kamehameha.

HARRINGTON'S 961-4966

(ONO) Overlooking the Ice Pond at Reeds Bay, the setting at night is soothing and romantic. Well-prepared steak and seafood with good service and entertainment some nights make this an easy recommendation. Reservations recommended. $20–$30 for dinner.

KEN'S HOUSE OF PANCAKES 935-8711

A Hilo staple, they offer large portions, adequate food, and a very large selection at reasonable prices. The whole menu is available 24 hours a day—unusual for a Big Island restaurant. Service is sometimes unresponsive because the place can get crowded, and quality has slipped enough recently to strip their ONO. Breakfast and lunch $5–$10, dinner $5–$15. Located on Hwy. 11 near 19.

KK TEI 961-3791

The price is not too· bad for the steak and seafood served with a Japanese flair. Entertainment comes in the form of bad karaoke from across the hall. You can eat your dinner over there if you have the urge to sing "Tiny Bubbles" in front of a crowd. Reservations recommended. $15–$25 (more for steak/lobster combos). On Kamehameha just west of Highway 11.

QUEEN'S COURT 935-9361

(ONO) Located in the Hilo Hawaiian Hotel, their buffets are the pride of Hilo. Seafood Buffet Fri and Sat, Hawaiian Buffet on Sun, and crab legs and prime rib Mon–Thur. I wake up at night thinking about the marinated mahi-mahi. If you're a dessert lover (like us), you'll appreciate the dessert selection. Most buffets include either beer or wine (though they make an exceptional Long Island Iced Tea). This is one of the better meals in Hilo. Prices are **$22–$25.** Reservations are strongly recommended in advance as this is a popular event.

SANDLEWOOD DINING ROOM 969-3333

Located at the Hawai'i Naniloa Hotel, the indoor setting is elegant. Food is hit or miss. For dinner try the scallops with lychee and broccoli stir fried in garlic and soy sauce served over linguine—*Ono!* Lunch offers hot and cold sandwiches, fresh fish, Japanese entrées, and salads. Breakfast is very reasonable at **$4–$8,** lunch is **$6–$8,** dinner is **$20–$35.**

SEASIDE 935-8825

(ono) Most of the freshwater fish is raised right there. In fact, if it didn't overlook the large, serene pond, the atmosphere would be...well, they wouldn't have any. But the pond saves them. Complete dinners come with golden perch, catfish or aholehole (I'm not making that up) and include apple pie for dessert. Ocean-going fish (which they don't raise) are too over-priced to consider. This restaurant has been here for over 75 years and has changed little. Outdoor tables include a show called *count how many skeeters the geckos can eat.* Most of the fish are served whole (head and all), and they often run out of specific fish, but you can call and pre-order. **$12–$25** for dinner. On Kalanianaole Avenue, east Hilo past Banyan Drive.

UNCLE BILLY'S RESTAURANT 935-0861

Ambiance is likeable, whimsical, Polynesian cliché. Entertainment night-ly—they reserve the right to drag you on stage to perform for your fellow diners. Food is fairly good but a bit overpriced. As for service, you'll either be treated like a member of the family...or like an irritating rash. **$4–$10** for breakfast, **$12–$20** for dinner.

HILO CHINESE

NEW CHINA RESTAURANT 961-5677

(ono) Loved by locals who appreciate the simple but good quality and inexpensive Cantonese food in a clean atmosphere. Try the deep-fried pot stickers or the sizzling platter. BYOB. On Kilauea near Ponahawai. **$5–$12** for lunch or dinner. Take out available.

HILO ITALIAN

CAFÉ PESTO 969-6640

(ono) Same as the Café Pesto mentioned in Kawaihae on page 237 but less attitude.

PESCATORE 969-9090

(ono) This place was opened on a bet to see if Hilo could support an authentic Italian cuisine restaurant—and *you* are the winner. It's one of our favorites in Hilo with smartly conceived entrées, such as chicken sautéed with garlic, basil, tomatoes, and artichoke hearts in a sherry cream over pasta. The specials are usually delicious and often come with a dessert (such as the double chocolate truffle cake, which will change your life). Try to resist filling up on the delicious rolls. The atmosphere is subdued Italian. Lunch includes a good choice of pastas and sauces, as well as lasagna or steamed veggies with pasta. This is a no-brainer for a recommendation, though sometimes the service is a tad unresponsive. On the corner of Haili and Keawe. $8–$13 for lunch, $20–$35 for dinner.

HILO JAPANESE

NIHON RESTAURANT 969–1133
The building overlooks Hilo Bay, but they don't make good use of the view. This is a good place to go to be ignored. Prices are too high given the setting and lackluster service. You can do better. Sushi bar plus steak and seafood. $8–$13 for lunch, $15–$25 for dinner. On Banyan Drive.

HILO LOCAL

CAFÉ 100 935–8683
(ono) Possibly Hilo's most popular eating establishment. This is the most successful local restaurant on the island. For over 50 years they've served cheap, tasty, artery-clogging food and are legendary for their loco mocos. (These consist of fried eggs over rice and SPAM or similar meat all smothered with brown gravy.) They have nearly a dozen varieties of loco moco along with burgers, chili, stew, sandwiches, and specials for as little as $1.50. We gave them an ONO because this is quintessential local food. But if you're watching your cholesterol or fat intake, it'll rock your Richter scale like no other place. Grab your food at the window and eat at one of the outdoor tables. Less than $5 for breakfast, $3–$7 for lunch and dinner. On Kilauea near Mohouli.

KA'UPENA 933–1106
(ono) Home of da foot long laulaus. This is the best place on the island to try these delicious island treats. For instance, the super coma laulau (our favorite) is pork, fish, chicken, taro, Hawaiian sweet potato and breadfruit wrapped in ti leaves and steamed. (You don't eat the ti wrapper.) Exceptionally delicious for under $5, or get it with a plate lunch for under $7. The folks are friendly, food is good and cheap; this is local food the way it's meant to be. Located next to the Wikiwiki store on Kamehameha near where Highway 11 starts in Hilo. Poi also available, but it's "BYOR" (bring your own rice).

LOW INTERNATIONAL FOOD 969–6652
This used to be a great place—half bakery, half local restaurant. But quality has gone way down. Famous for their bread selection, baked daily, with flavors such as mango, taro, pumpkin, and the multi-flavored rainbow—a mix of taro, guava, and sweet—the breads just aren't as flavorful as before. The local foods are now forgettable. On the corner of Kilauea and Ponahawai.

HILO TREATS

BIG ISLAND CANDIES 935–8890
Tasty but amazingly overpriced chocolates, cakes, nuts, and candies. On Hinano Street off Kekuanaoa, east Hilo.

HILO HOMEMADE ICE CREAM 969–9559
(ono) Not as sweet or rich as other gourmet ice creams. Lots of exotic flavors from this quaint mom-and-pop shop. On Kalanianaole.

TROPICAL DREAMS 935–9109
(ono) Just as delicious as the Tropical Dreams in Hawi. Located in the Kress Building on Kamehameha Street.

DINING IN PAHOA

GODMOTHER 965-0055

This Italian place is a little strange. You can either have a 12" 4-topping pizza...or have pasta, which they seem to prefer that you order. (The pizza is a good deal at **$12.50**.) The quality of the other items is not quite up to the prices (especially for dinner), but the food is distinctive. The service is squirrely. You'll either like it, or it'll get on your nerves. **$4–$7** for breakfast, **$7–$10** for lunch, **$10–$20** for dinner.

LUQUIN'S MEXICAN RESTAURANT 965-9990

Looks like a dive on the outside. (Come to think of it, it looks like a dive on the inside, too.) Standard Mexican food plus a few specials like tofu enchiladas and tacos (ono), potato tacos and taquitos (also ono), fish and shrimp. Sometimes the food is on the bland side, depends who's cooking. The service is friendly and the portions are large. You're likely, especially at dinner, to spend your evening dining with Pahoa's upper crust—complete with stinky dreadlocks and clothing that hasn't been washed since tie-dye was king. A pitcher of margaritas is $11, and desserts are reasonable but unpredictable. They have the smallest breakfast menu we've seen—three items, each $5. Lunch and dinner are **$4–$15**. You never know what to expect here. This is a good place to go if you are feeling adventurous and want to see some local color, but not if you're feeling persnickety.

DINING IN HAWI

BAMBOO RESTAURANT 889-5555

Located in an old, quaint dry goods building in Hawi, they have an eclectic menu with uniquely prepared foods. Try the pot stickers lined with peanut butter or the Da Kine stew—delicious. You might want to try the lilikoi margaritas. Though the portions are a bit on the small side, the quality is usually excellent and the folks are nice. They have a gallery inside the building offering all kinds of nice, locally carved wood and other products. Definitely worth a peek. Lunch is **$5–$15,** dinner is **$8–$25** per person.

KOHALA VILLAGE RESTAURANT 889-0105

Usually good food at this Hawi restaurant. Mostly burgers and sandwiches plus a few entrées for lunch (good sandwiches). Dinner is pasta, steak, ribs and chicken. A number of good veggie items. Check for specials, good selection of desserts. The prices are fairly good. Hours of operation seem a bit inconsistent. Window seats are best. **$4–$7** for breakfast, **$6–$8** for lunch, **$10–$20** for dinner. On 250 near 270 in Hawi.

MATTHEW'S PLACE 889-5500

This is a teeny-weeny hole in the wall in Hawi. They have a large, homemade style menu featuring local fare, pizza (which is *not* recommended) and the like. Mostly adequate food and reasonably clean. Remember, Hawi is not exactly overflowing with dining choices, so beggars can't be choosy. Located near the Bamboo Restaurant in Hawi, **$5–$10.**

OHANA CAFE AND PIZZA 889-5888

It's probably a waste of time to put this in here since they're only open for dinner (and visitors are rarely up here at night). Their 5" pizzas are a bit overpriced, but other pizzas are very reason-

ably priced. Quality is marginal, but you aren't paying for the best here. Located on Hawi, open for dinner most of the time. Say hey to the cats as they brush against your legs under the table. **$5–$10.**

DINING IN HONOKA'A

CAFÉ IL MONDO 775–7711

Pizza, calzone, lasagna, salads and hot sandwiches. Lots of different espressos. The place has a nice feel and the folks are friendly. When you first sit down, you form the opinion that it will probably be good food. Alas, it's not. Quality is average at best. *I know, I know.* Options are limited in Honokaa. **HERB'S** is bad, **MICHAEL'S** is marginal. This may be your best choice for a sit down meal if **MAMANE** across the street isn't sufficient and **TEX** doesn't work for you. **$3–$10** for lunch, **$6–$10** for dinner.

MAMANE STREET BAKERY & CAFÉ 775–9478

Located in the northeastern part of the island in Honoka'a on the way to Waipi'o Valley. They have a limited selection but produce extremely delicious baked goods. The pastries are worth a detour into Honoka'a if you are out on the main highway. They also have a superlight cheesebread that hits the spot. They take obvious pride in their work and provide baked goods for lots of restaurants and hotels, just don't expect bubbly service. **$2–$6** per person.

TEX DRIVE-IN AND RESTAURANT 775–0598

Every good restaurant does at least one thing well, and Tex is a perfect example. Though most of the food is fairly good fast food, such as burgers, teriyaki chicken, etc., Tex

positively *excels* at making the best malasadas (a Portuguese doughnut dipped in sugar) on the island, served fresh and warm throughout the day. The plain ones are delicious, but now that they have them filled with Bavarian cream or tropical fruits, we never hesitate to stop by when we're in the neighborhood. Located on Highway 19 near Honoka'a and the 43 mile marker. Sometimes the wait (even if nobody is ahead of you) can be long. **$3–$8** for breakfast, lunch, and dinner.

DINING AT KILAUEA VOLCANO

KILAUEA LODGE AND RESTAURANT 967–7366

This cozy restaurant in the sometimes chilly village of Volcano serves delicious food in a warm atmosphere. The owner/chef was a make-up artist on Magnum P.I. when he bought this place. He went to Europe to learn how to cook and has excelled nicely. Items such as fresh fish, steak, tempura, and chicken are all expertly prepared and presented. Expensive, but very good food. We like to get a table near the "International Fireplace." Dinner is **$20–$35.** Smoking on "smoking nights" (when lots of people want to smoke).

LAVA ROCK INTERNET CAFÉ 967–8526

Admirable selection of burgers, sandwiches, chili, salads, chicken, stir fry and more. Many items are veggie and most cost $5 or $6 with generous portions. (Good milkshakes.) Breakfast items include some clever omelettes and French toast with 'ohelo berry. Service is friendly. They have a couple of computers with Net access for $5 per hour, hence the name.

Overall, a very pleasant place. $4–$7 for breakfast and lunch. Old Volcano Road.

STEAM VENT CAFÉ 985-8744

Sandwiches, salads, muffins and the like. Had been a good place to stop when you're on the run in Volcano, though it has disappointed us a lot lately. $6–$11. On Old Volcano Road.

SURT'S 967-8511

Serving European and Asian food, they call it "fusion cuisine." This means sauteed chili squid with basil on one side of the menu and lobster ravioli on the other. Most items are well prepared and intelligently conceived with excellent flavor combinations. (Could use a bit more shrimp with the shrimp scampi though.) Perhaps because they're small and need the turnover, they rush the food to you a bit too quickly. Overall a very good restaurant. Reservations strongly recommended for dinner. $10–$15 for lunch, $15–$30 for dinner. On Old Volcano Road behind Volcano Store.

VOLCANO GOLF AND COUNTRY CLUB 967-8228

At the sometimes misty Volcano Golf Course, the food is surprisingly tasty (though the portions need to be bigger). Burgers, chicken, beef—the stir-fry chicken and teriyaki beef are both good. Breakfast menu is small. The macadamia nut pie (similar to pecan pie) is great. This is an acceptable choice though you have better options in Volcano. $5–$8 for breakfast, $7–$13 for lunch. Dinner on occasion.

VOLCANO HOUSE 967-7321

You won't be overwhelmed with dining selections inside Hawai'i Volcanoes National Park. Their concessionaire, however, does a pretty good job. Breakfast and lunch are buffets, dinners from the menu. Breakfast and lunch are our favorites here, but not because of the food. The staff takes obvious pride, but the lunch food is merely adequate. (Breakfast buffet is pretty good.) But it isn't the food you will remember years from now, it's the view. Perched on the edge of Kilauea Caldera, a window table here offers a drop-dead gorgeous view of the crater that you will savor more than any food you've ever had. (Though we've occasionally seen people, sitting at the window by themselves, with their back to the window—*go figure!)* Don't overlook the room to your left if all the window tables seem taken. Eggs, potatoes, pancakes, sweetbread French toast, cereals and the like for breakfast; fried chicken, rice, fish for lunch. Lunch can be a zoo with buses dropping people off by the dozens at noon. At dinner, hotel guests and area residents create a quieter time. Of course, the view disappears with the sun, but dinner quality is good (though expensive). Pasta, fish, filet mignon, scampi—most are quite well-prepared and at a more leisurely pace. $10 for breakfast, $13 for lunch, $16–$30 for dinner. (Reservations required for dinner.) We gave it an ONO symbol because of the tasty *view,* not the food. (They stopped selling our book at the small shop next door because of that last comment.) In the same building is **UNCLE GEORGE'S**—a snack (and real) bar that sports a similar view. If it's lunch-time, you should probably cough up the extra few dollars and get the buffet described above. If it's not between 11 a.m. and 2 p.m., however, this is a good place to grab a bite and enjoy the view. Their selection dwindles as the sunlight does. $5–$10.

DINING IN NA'ALEHU

SANTANGELO'S PIZZA & BAKERY/ NAALEHU FRUIT STAND 929-9009

This is an excellent place to stop on your way to or from the volcano from the west side of the island. A bakery/pizza parlor/general store, everything is good here except the pizza—it's a bit soggy and a little bland. But they have tasty sandwiches and delicious and reasonably priced baked goods (we've tried them all just for you—aren't we dedicated?) Try a Ka'u orange—generally, the uglier the orange, the better it tastes. They also have health food ingredients, exotic and local spices, and an overall good feel. $4–$8 per person. Generally open during daylight hours. If the macadamia nut shortbread is fresh, get two.

DINING IN WAIMEA

BREE GARDEN 885-8849

They don't serve brie at the Bree Garden (named after the owner/chef). The food is usually very tasty and well presented. Pastas, sandwiches, some BBQ, and lots of specials at lunch. Lamb, pasta, steak, chicken and veal for dinner. Unfortunately, having good recipes is not enough. If the staff doesn't care whether you're happy or not, you probably won't have a good meal. Service is slow and underwhelming. They sometimes seem annoyed that you are there and make their displeasure known by their unresponsiveness. With their bright and pleasant surroundings and good food, this could be a good place to eat. But until they get a personality trans-plant, we'll have to hold off on our endorsement. **$8–$12** for lunch, **$15–$30** for dinner. Located in Waimea behind the Texaco gas station.

EDELWEISS 885-6800

When's the last time you got your fill of fine German food? Burgers and sandwiches at lunch are complimented by bratwurst, wiener schnitzel and venison, all served with skill by Chef Hager, formerly of the Mauna Kea Resort. Lamb, German sausage, pasta al fresco—the menu is eclectic. *Lots* of specials. Expect to stay full for hours from the decidedly rich entrées. Rich and heavy works in cooler Waimea, but don't try going to the beach afterward or you may split wide open. Open Tuesday–Saturday for lunch and dinner. **$8–$12** for lunch, **$15–$30** for dinner. On Highway 19 between Lindsay and Opelu.

HAWAIIAN STYLE CAFÉ 885-4295

Never was there a place so aptly named. This is proba-bly the best deal on the island when it comes to *quantity* and heartiness. Let me give you an example. Two eggs, your choice of meat, plus hash browns or rice. Then add either toast or two fluffy pan-cakes (the size of hub caps). All for $5. Now that may be obtainable back on the mainland, but it's utterly *unheard* of in Hawai'i. Two of the enormous pancakes alone are $2. (They'd be $10 at a Kohala resort!) They're open from 6 a.m to 1 p.m. on weekdays, closed Saturdays and open 7:30 a.m. to noon on Sundays. Closed last Sunday and Monday of each month. The early lunch features thick burgers obscured by a towering mound of fries, as well as some other items. The atmosphere is laid back with a few tables (which probably aren't cleared or cleaned as often as they should be) and a large sit-down counter. This is how Mom used to cook before she found out it was bad for you. Sometimes we miss it. **$3–$8.** On Highway 19 between Lindsay and Opelu across from Edelweiss. See map of Waimea on page 123.

KOA HOUSE GRILL 885-2088

With a name like Koa House, you expect lots of Hawaiian koa wood everywhere. And you're not disappointed. Lunch works best here, as dinner is a bit overpriced. For lunch, their best item is the kalua pig sandwich with delicious Hawaiian lilikoi BBQ sauce. Burgers and a fish sandwich are also available. Bananas Irwin makes a good, but highly overpriced dessert. (All the desserts are too pricey.) Dinner is a steak and seafood affair with some pasta. **$7–$10** for lunch, **$16–$30** for dinner. In Waimea on north side of Highway 19 east of Waimea Center.

LEILANI BAKERY 885-2772

Average baked goods served without a smile. For a place that serves food, they have an annoying habit of closing for lunch. In Waimea Center in Waimea.

MERRIMAN'S 885-6822

Everyone knows Merri-man's, and everyone raves about it. And for good reason. Peter Merriman is an excellent chef, and the service is usually just right. (But not always.) Lunch includes Hawaiian jerked chicken (don't worry, it tastes better than it sounds), Pita Merriman sandwich (clever, huh?), and fish sandwich. Dinner features lamb, châteaubriand on black beans with kiawe-smoked tomato sauce, and fresh fish prepared several ways.

For dessert, consider the congo bars (keep your knife). If you're in Waimea and want some tasty food, give them a try. Go there for lunch if you're on a budget. A bit crowded at times. Located on Hwy 19 in Waimea. Reservations recommended. **$8–$16** for lunch, **$15–$35** for dinner.

MORELLI'S PIZZA 885-6100

When you walk in and notice that the regulars are eating sandwiches, not the pizza—take the hint. The pizza is lifeless. Crust is light, crunchy, and tasteless, and the sauce was inspired by it. Stick with the baked sandwiches, which are almost adequate. Lunch and dinner are **$5–$10.** In the tired Parker Ranch Center in Waimea.

SUGAR N' SPICE 885-0548

Located on the Highway across from Kamamalu Street. They have outrageous chocolates flown in from several vendors around the country. Locally made ice cream as well. It's expensive here, but one of the best sugar buzzes you'll find anywhere. (Try the chocolate covered blueberries—*oww!)* Selection varies; sometimes great, sometimes sparse.

NIGHTLIFE

Not in the same league as what you'll find in Honolulu or any other big city, but on the Big Island we don't exactly spend *all* our evenings watching old reruns of Gilligan's Island. (Well...maybe Fridays.) There *is* life after sunset here.

The liveliest is **KONA.** Every Friday the Entertainment section of the local news-paper, *West Hawai'i Today,* lists every-thing that's happening for the week ahead. Very handy. Much of the action takes place on Alii Drive. It's easy to walk downtown and check out what's shakin'. Directions to these places are in their reviews. For cocktails, the **BILLFISH BAR** at the King Kamehameha Hotel is are famed for their cheap drinks. Try a frozen mai tai at **OCEAN VIEW**, usually very tasty. **HUGGO'S** can be very romantic and they often have live music. The **WINDJAMMER LOUNGE** at the Royal Kona Resort (329–1111) is an excellent place to have a cocktail overlooking the water. They often feature music and dancing. **KONA BREWING CO. & BREWPUB** (329–2739) on Kuakini and Palani behind Zac's is a good place for a cold, locally made beer. 12 different brews. **C.W. BOAR'S RESTAURANT & SPORTS BAR** (329–2445) on Pawai Place in the Old Industrial Area off Kaiwi St. has live music most nights or karaoke.

The **ALOHA THEATRE** in Kainaliu often has fun local plays. Call 322–9924 for more information.

BIG ISLAND COMEDY CLUB (329–4368) is a roving comedy act. Call to see where they are performing.

IN KOHALA, nightlife is a resort affair (so to speak). Many of the mega-resorts have lounges. An example is the **HONU BAR** at the Mauna Lani Bay Hotel (885–6622). Very upscale with billiards, chess, and a dress code, so lose the tank top. The **SECOND FLOOR LOUNGE** is a lounge/disco at the Hilton (885–1234) and is open from 9 p.m.–1 a.m. Good places to have a drink include **KAMUELA PROVISION COMPANY** at the Hilton, **BROWN'S BEACH HOUSE**, **OCEAN BAR** and **POLO BAR/PANIOLO LOUNGE** at the Orchid, and the **BEACH TREE** at the Four Seasons (325–8000). They also have a fun Surf & Sand BBQ on Saturdays.

IN HILO, your best bet is at the **WAI'OLI LOUNGE** (935–9361) in the Hilo Hawaiian Hotel. They often have good local bands performing contemporary Hawaiian music. (But the drinks have been small, weak, and overpriced the past few times we were in.) **HARRINGTON'S** (see review) is a very romantic spot on the water. **UNCLE BILLY'S** (see review) has a hula show at 6 p.m. and 7:30 p.m.

LU'AUS

We've all seen them in movies. People sit at a table with a mai tai in one hand and a plate of Kalua pig in another. There's always a show where a fire dancer twirls a torch lit at both ends and hula dancers bend and sway to the beat of the music. To be honest, that's not far from the truth. Lu'aus can be a blast and, if your time allows for one, they are highly recommended. The pig is baked in the ground all day creating absolutely delicious results. Shows are usually exciting and fast paced. Although lu'aus on O'ahu can make you feel like cattle being led to slaughter, the lu'aus on the Big Island are smaller, more intimate affairs of usually 100–200 people. Most lu'aus are all you can eat and drink (including alcohol) for a set fee (except where noted below). If the punch they are serving doesn't satisfy you, they usually have an open bar to fill your needs.

Different resorts hold their lu'aus on different nights. These change with the whims of the managers, so verify the days we list before making plans. Many lu'aus advertise that they are rated number one. By whom? At any rate, this is what we thought of them.

IN KONA, your best bet is undoubtedly the **ROYAL KONA RESORT** (329–3111) M, F, Sa—$53. Excellent food with a good variety (turkey for the cholesterol counters, but we gluttons will want to "pig out" on the main course). The location is smashing, right next to the water. The other Kona lu'au at **KING KAMEHAMEHA'S KONA BEACH HOTEL** (329–2911) is a little disappointing. The food and show are merely adequate, and you have to stand around for a while outside the grounds observing some arts and crafts before you are let in. They hawk a number of items during the entertainment. With some changes, this could be a great lu'au given its excellent location. Tu, W, Th, Su—$54.

Outside Kona, 10 miles to the north, the **KONA VILLAGE LU'AU** (325–5555) on Fridays is the most expensive lu'au on the island. It's $74 *plus* drinks, and the cash bar is expensive. (But the drinks are good.) If you arrive early, you'll have to cool your heels outside the gate near Highway 19—Kona Village jealously guards its privacy. The grounds are very pleasant and the lu'au pit is charming. We wouldn't mind if there was a little less self-promotion (for that much money, it should be commercial-free), but no one can deny that this is a *great* lu'au. The food is good, the show is good, and the location is good. We just wish that the price was good.

IN KOHALA, the **MAUNA KEA** lu'au (882–7222, ext. 5801) is on Tuesdays for $68. The grounds are superb—right near the water, and you can wander over to the manta ray area after it's over and watch those leviathans do their dance. The food and show are also excellent, making this an easy-to-recommend event. Though not a lu'au, they also have a **clambake** on Saturdays at the outdoor **HAU TREE** for $68 which includes lobster, crab legs, prime rib, and clams. The **OUTRIGGER WAIKOLOA RESORT** (886–6789) has good food at a more reasonable price. The show is merely fine, but the food is exceptional,

delicious, and varied. Located adjacent to the fishponds at 'Anaeho'omalu. Su & W—$60. The libationary inclined should note that they stop serving drinks a bit early. The **LEGENDS OF THE PACIFIC** Polynesian show at the Hilton Waikoloa Village (885–1234, ext.54) on Fridays is not a lu'au per se. No pig buried in the ground here. The show is pretty good and the food is tasty, but they need more Hawaiian dishes and more selections. Only one drink is included. In general, you can do better for $60.

DINNER CRUISES

Dinner cruises off the Kona Coast are a nice alternative. **CAPTAIN BEANS' CRUISES** (329–2955) is owned and operated by tour giant Roberts Hawai'i. Known locally as the classic booze cruise, you and up to 291 other passengers (on the bottom deck) leave Kailua Pier on a 150-foot boat and head south. $52 includes pickup in Kona, add $8–$11 for Kohala pickup. They do a surprisingly good job, with lots of interactive entertainment. (Try not to fall off the tables when you dance on them.) The food is basic but pretty tasty (though they could use a dessert). One tip: Keep your plate full; tables sometimes run out. If you want a cocktail, you'll want to bypass the anemic punch they serve and take advantage of the open bar instead. The boat is smooth, and with the constant entertainment it's easy to forget you are on a cruise, so walk to the railings after dinner and enjoy the coastline—watch for flying fish. All in all, it's a hoot. Most on board seem to have a good time. No one under 21 allowed.

RED SAIL SPORTS (885–2876) leaves 'Anaeho'omalu Beach in the North Kohala Resort area for a 2-hour sunset cruise. Appetizers and open bar included for $49.

Room with a view…

Your selection of where to stay can be one of the more important decisions you'll make in planning your visit. To some, it's just a place to sleep and rather meaningless. To others, it's the difference between a good vacation and a bad one.

There are four main types of lodgings on the island: hotels, condominium resorts, bed and breakfasts, and single-family homes. The overwhelming majority of visitors stay in one of the first two types. Hotels offer more service but lack kitchens. Condos usually have full kitchens and more living area but usually lack daily maid service. Many condos have minimum stays—usually three nights. This varies between different rental companies. If your group or family is large, you should strongly consider renting a house for privacy, roominess, and plain ol' value. There is a list of **Rental Agents** on page 263, each happy to send you a list of homes they represent. For **B&Bs,** see the end of this section.

If you have internet access, we have included our own aerial photos of nearly every hotel and condo on the island, so you'll know if oceanfront *really* means oceanfront. On some of the photos we have labeled the different buildings so you can pick out the one you want. Point your browser to **www.wizardpub.com.**

When describing condos, three-bedroom/two-bath units are described as 3/2, two-bedroom/one-bath units are described as 2/1, etc. Differentiation between half baths and full baths is not made. The price spreads for rooms of a given size are due to different views, different locations within the resort, and occasional seasonal fluctuations. So when you see that a 2/2 unit rents for $110–$140, you should figure that $140 units have a better view or are closer to the water. The terms Ocean Front, Ocean View, and Garden View are used rather capriciously in Hawai'i, so we have avoided them. Unless otherwise noted, all condos come with telephones, complete kitchens, coffee makers, lanais (verandas), cable TV, ceiling fans, and have cribs available upon request. None have A/C, and maid service is usually every few days or less unless otherwise noted.

As for hotels, unless otherwise noted, all *do* have A/C, telephones, small refrigerators, lanais, cable TV, and cribs available. None have room service unless we mention it.

All prices given are RACK rates, meaning without any discounts. Tour packages and travel agents can sometimes get better rates. Most places offer discounts for stays of a week or more, and some will negotiate price with you. Some won't budge at all; others told us *no one* pays RACK rate. Also, be aware that these prices are subject to taxes of about 11%.

The gold bar indicates that the property is exceptionally well priced for what you get.

Solid Gold Value

The gem means that this accommodation offers something *particularly* special, not *necessarily* related to the price.

A Real Gem

Throughout the book we talk about the positives associated with the various areas. In deciding where to stay, here are three negatives for each major location worth considering:

Kohala: Food will cost you more. You are far from the town of Kailua-Kona and its available resources. You are far from the volcano.

Kailua-Kona: Vog will be more of a nuisance in Kona. Traffic, while not *nearly* as bad as the mainland, can be troublesome at commute time. There's more noise along Alii Drive.

Hilo: Activities are less numerous. The ocean is less pleasant. Rain will probably be a companion.

KOHALA

Kohala is famous for its **mega-resorts.** These destination resorts have tons to see and do on the premises, pricey restaurants offering superb atmosphere and cuisine, and almost unending sunny weather. The developers have created oases in the lava desert where lava once stretched uninterrupted for miles.

You will notice that accommodation prices are high in Kohala. These snazzy resorts don't come cheap. We leave it up to you to decide if it's in your budget. A lot of them have REAL GEM icons next to them. We like to think of ourselves as stingy with these, but facts are facts— these *are* gems. But like the genuine article, these gems come at a price.

Picking the best mega-resort in Kohala is not a straightforward process. All 8 have radically different personalities, so *your* personality is key to which one you'll like best. Most of these resorts do a great job at creating an atmosphere. They question is, is it *your* atmosphere? In our view, the Mauna Lani Bay Hotel has the best exotic tropical feel. The Orchid at Mauna Lani has the richest, most luxurious feel. The Hilton Waikoloa Village has the most jaw-dropping elaborate, yet family-oriented feel. The Mauna Kea has the best beach location. And 10 miles south of the main Kohala resort area, Kona Village has the most "authentic" old Hawai'i feel. The Four Seasons has some of both Mauna Lanis assets. Rich and luxurious yet also a great tropical feel. Most of these resorts are world class, and we don't say that lightly. Choosing one just depends on what you want.

Kohala Hotels

FOUR SEASONS RESORT
(800) 332–3442 or (808) 325–8000

243 rooms, 8 tennis courts (4 lighted), 6 conference rooms, 4 pools, keiki (kid) pool, lava snorkel pool, 4 spas, coffee makers in rooms, free valet parking, free child care, *private* golf course, health spa, 3 restaurants. The Big Island's newest luxury resort, it shines, even among its superb competitors. 243 rooms among 37 one and two-story bungalows in several semi-circles with 6–8 rooms per building, plus a few golf course buildings. They used a lot of local materials, giving the resort a very Hawaiian feel. Every unit (even golf course units) has a nice ocean view. (Building 25 is closest to the water.) Second-floor rooms have better ocean views, but first-floor rooms have a pleasant garden on the other side of the bathroom glass with a second private *outdoor lava shower* ensconced in the garden where water gurgles over a short lava ledge. What a great place to have your morning shower! This makes the first floor a better value than the higher-priced second-floor rooms. Overall, rooms are of average size, nicely furnished with cool slate floors and sea grass mats.

A Real Gem

One feature we've never seen anywhere else is a large lava anchialine pond with 2½ million gallons of fresh and salt water. Connected to the ocean, its level rises and falls each day with the tide. Inside are 40 species of fish, including several spotted eagle rays. You won't find a safer place to snorkel in the state. It's great to be there when they feed them.

If you bring your keikis, you'll find licensed child care service for young'uns 5–12 is free. The resort is the only one with a *truly* private golf course. Only guests and residents of the development are allowed to play, so tee times are spaced farther apart. (See review under Golfing on page 169. In short, it's a very nice player-friendly Jack Nicklaus course for about $145.) The same goes for the full spa, which offers enough luxuriating decadence to melt your toenails. The resort fronts a beach, but the swimming is poor due to a lava shelf. They do have a manmade quasi tide-pool at the shore for wading in. However, just a short stroll south is Kuki'o Beach with somewhat better swimming.

Services here are extraordinary, even for a Kohala resort. (An example: chilled towels at the pool and Evian spritz service. How's that for pampering?) The swimming pools are scattered around the resort. Some, such as the main lip-less infinity pool, are cleverly constructed so that, while swimming, it seems to be part of the ocean. Their restaurants, such as Pahu I'a, are excellent. No surprise there. Rooms are $450–$650. Suites are $775–$5,700! ♿ 🚭

HAPUNA BEACH PRINCE HOTEL
(800) 882–6060 or (808) 880–1111
350 rooms, 4 conference rooms, pool and spa, 2 golf courses, health club, restaurants, free valet parking. Owned by the same company that owns the nearby Mauna Kea, the Hapuna was built next to one of the best beaches on the island. Their kitty-corner location denies the resort the true beachfront designation the Mauna Kea has, but you can access Hapuna Beach with ease. You are ushered into the resort by an impressive array of royal palm trees, and the grounds are impeccably groomed. They spent a lot of money here, and it shows. The staff at the Hapuna is impressive, extremely professional, and friendly. They even stock the rooms with video games for the keikis. But we must need an eye exam. We've been in some ocean view rooms and couldn't see the ocean anywhere. We were assured that "the ocean is out there." Gee, that's comforting. The swimming pool is the lipless variety (called an Infinity Pool), with the water coming right up to the top—nice effect. Things are pretty spread out, so expect to do a lot of walking. The resort itself is hard to describe. It has all the amenities and is pleasant, but it has a starkness to it that we can't quite put our finger on, yet can't deny. This place just doesn't work for us. It doesn't radiate the dreamy warmth that some of the other resorts do, and their reliance on Japanese visitors (which are scarce these days due to their gloomy economy) gives it an empty feel. Rooms are $345–$520. Suites are $925–$6,500. ♿ 🚭

HILTON WAIKOLOA VILLAGE
(800) 221–2424 or (808) 885–1234
1,241 rooms, 3 pools, 3 hot tubs, valet parking, health club, spa, beauty salon, 8 tennis courts, racquetball court, two golf courses, 24-hour room service, 6 restaurants, tons of shops, tram and a boat service.

A Real Gem

Where do we start? How about *wow!* This is the one you've probably heard about. This resort, built in the late '80s and spread over 62 acres, is the most elaborate of them all. (By the way, despite its name, it is not located in or next to the town of Waikoloa Village.)

Over a thousand rooms in three separate towers are joined by a tram and boat network right out of Disneyland. A swimming pool has a pounding waterfall and an Indiana Jones-type swinging bridge overhead. There is a dolphin pool where lucky guests can get in the water with dolphins. (TIP: No-shows are often replaced by lucky customers at the nearby Hang Ten restaurant.) The whole experience is described in ADVENTURES on page 211. Artwork is spread all over the resort. Parrots are also scattered about. There are multiple concierge desks around to assist in booking activities, making reservations, or pointing the way to a particular part of the resort. The one thing the Hilton doesn't have is a Mauna Kea type beach. (They have a manmade inland lagoon beach instead.) But 'Anaeho'omalu Beach is a half-mile walk or drive south. There's a large lagoon where guests float around in kayaks, paddle boats, and rafts. In terms of amenities, the Hilton Waikoloa is an excellent place for families. Kids will *never* get bored here. There's a shallow swimming pool with a sand beach at one end, a video game room, a water slide, sand volleyball court, and enough activities to wear out any teen or crumb cruncher. Consider a ground floor cabana room in the Lagoon Tower in front of the dolphin pool where kids can frolic on the grass.

Large groups will find the group facilities superb. From their 24 conference rooms to the ballroom the size of Waikiki to their business services area, which rents everything from computers to cellular phones—if you're here for business, they can accommodate you. The restaurants here are excellent. Fine Italian, Japanese, American—even a decent ice cream soda shoppe. There are 8 lounges, a theme nightclub...We could go on and on, but we're running out of room.

The resort might seem overwhelming at first. It cost over a third of a *billion* dollars to construct, and a staggering 1,400 employees are needed to run it all. You won't see all of them running around, however. That's because they go from here to there via an extensive underground tunnel network. Tunnels have dashed lines separating the lanes—even shoulders—and when you're down there, you're likely to run into your chef in uniform cruising along on a three-wheeled bike.

The entire resort is oriented inward, resulting in a destination that is self-contained. Some people who visit the Hilton Waikoloa snort that it's not real. Frankly, they miss the point. It's not *supposed* to represent reality. It's fantasy, escape, a leap into never-never land. You wouldn't sniff that Disneyland is phony, would you? The designers of the Hilton Waikoloa Village did a great job of achieving their objective—making an out-of-this-world playground/fantasyland for adults and kids. If that's what you are looking for, you will find it here in abundance. If you want to experience a calm piece of authentic old Hawai'i, you've come to the wrong place.

Regular room prices rose a lot over the last couple of years, so look for packages. Rates are $400–$530. The 55 suites range from $875–$4,920. &. ⊗

KONA VILLAGE
(800) 367–5290 or (808) 325–5555

125 units, 2 pools and spas, 3 lighted tennis courts, restaurants, child care service (ask), health club, refrigerators, lu'au, airport pickup and drop-off service, *meals included*. This is a

A Real Gem

rather unique place on the Big Island. Located between Kona and the main Kohala resort area, this resort was built in 1965 as a place to get away from it all. (And back then it *was* away from it all.) No phones, TVs, or radios—they even have their own electrical generators and wells. Nestled next to a fine salt-and-pepper beach, most rooms are charming thatched, free-standing bungalows (some are duplexes). Some are right on the beach, especially the Royal Alii Hales on the left side. A few rooms are adjacent to pockets of black sand. The layout is similar to what Gilligan's Island would have looked like with more people and more money. Rooms scattered about with trees, hammocks, and a large exotic fishpond filling in the scene. The rooms along the tranquil ponds *define* serenity. We like them as much as the oceanfront rooms. All 82 acres are surrounded by a fresh sea of stark black lava. Service and staff are top notch—you want it, they'll get it. You'll get a FAX of the news delivered to your door daily. You can sign for anything, so leave your wallet in the room safe. An astounding percentage of their guests are repeats. Their Friday lu'au (which is included) is one of the best, and the food at the restaurant is great. This is the sort of place you want to come to if you are burned out, want peace and relaxation, and don't plan to get out a lot. Many guests don't even rent a car. They just lounge around the well-tended grounds the whole time or get picked up for activities. Lots of resort activities are included. Check out the manta ray that hangs out near the coconut tree light at night. This is a good place for honeymooners, and they have nice wedding services. They've won plenty of travel awards—justly so. They are synonymous with perpetuating the "old Hawai'i feel." This resort used to be super secluded. But the quiet was broken when the Four Seasons, a golf course, and a residential community moved in next door. Expect a little less peace (and isolation) than in years past. They still have the no-nonsense guards at the entrance and on the beach to keep outsiders out. The price is high here, but it *includes meals* (or at least a high food credit). They had a major renovation not long ago that added jacuzzi bathtubs in some rooms and more room amenities. But don't expect flashy rooms. Simple, small, spartan, and clean with a funky hut design and tiny bathrooms. By the way, the golf course next door *probably* won't be available to you. (They seem to have a somewhat tense relationship with the Four Seasons.) Ask them about the time a plane crashed into the Talk Story Bar just before Christmas 1994. Rates *for two* are $450–$795. Price rises a lot for more people since meals are included. ♿ 🚭

MAUNA KEA BEACH HOTEL
(800) 882–6060 or (808) 882–7222

310 rooms, pool, 11 tennis courts, free valet parking, 24-hour room service,

A Real Gem

lu'au on premises, conference room, health club, 2 golf courses, restaurants, child care service. This was the first resort to grace the Kohala lava desert area, and a large part of their business is repeat customers. Built by Laurence Rockefeller in 1965, it set the standard for all that came afterward. The Mauna Kea has traditionally been one of the most popular resorts on the island, but their reliance on Japanese visitors (whose economy was in the tank at press time) shows in the form of closed restaurants and an emptier feel. You may be able to get good package deals. Though the rooms are quite small and far from elaborate, the resort is restful and pleasing. Many people like the slow pace here. They have the best beachside location on the island, with the marvelous Kaunaʻoa Beach (usually called Mauna Kea) right at its doorstep. This beach alone qualified it for A REAL GEM, as far as we're concerned. On the right (northern) side of the beach a bright light brings in large manta rays at night. You can see them from a lookout just above the water. The luʻau has a *great* setting. While other resorts now outshine the Mauna Kea, it still stands the test of time. Rooms are $345–$525, suites are $570–$1,125. ⅃ ⊘

MAUNA LANI BAY HOTEL AND BUNGALOWS (800) 327–8585 or (808) 885–6622

350 rooms, 18 tennis courts (8 lighted), VCRs, 24-hour room service, 6 shops, 3 conference rooms, ballroom, several restaurants, 2 golf courses, free valet parking, pool and spa, steam room, health club, child care service. This is one of those resorts that is hard for us to review without sounding like a drooling commercial. If you read our other reviews, especially in other parts of the island, you'll see that we're not shy about finding fault with resorts. But this one's different. In short, this is one of our favorite resorts in Kohala. As soon as you walk in, you are greeted by the magnificent atrium around which the building is centered. Palm trees and flowing pools stocked with fish and turtles create an instantly calming atmosphere. It's open air yet shielded from the sun. Right away some-

A Real Gem

thing is different. Instead of standing at the counter to check in, you have a seat at one of the desks and sip fruit juice while all the particulars are handled by the staff. Then it's off to your room, which is on the small side but immaculate and smartly designed. Oceanfront rooms have dazzling views. Ocean-view rooms on the fishpond side (especially the D wing) have gorgeous views of the lush fishponds that preceded the resort. These ancient fishponds are fantastic to wander through and are part of the most interesting grounds of any resort on the island. (Consider wandering back to sparkling Secret Pond for a quick dip. It's shown on our map on page 53.) The Mauna Lani deserves high marks for the way they incorporated the resort into the richly historical area.

The hotel raises endangered green sea turtles, and every July 4th they release them into the wild. (It's a heck of an event.) The entire resort fronts two man-made sand beaches, one quite protected, the other less so. The beaches aren't as good as Mauna Kea's beach, but the rest of the resort more than makes up for it. As with many resorts they have flags to describe ocean conditions. And as with the others, their lawyers must have confiscated the green flags because we've never seen them, even when it's flat. Along the beach are numerous covered cabana chairs. Watching the sunset from these (with an optional beverage from the nearby Ocean Grill and Bar) is unforgettable. There are also plenty of hammocks sprinkled about. Keikis (kids) will find their own jacuzzi—shallower and cooler than the grown-up variety. Their restaurants surpassed our expectations.

The staff here is exceptionally accommodating, and services are plentiful. Snorkel gear is free and lots of activities are available. The golf courses, along with the Mauna Kea Golf Course, provide the best golfing on the island.

If you just won the lottery (or don't need to), their five **bungalows** represent the pinnacle of accommodations. Not like "common" presidential suites on top floors, these stand-alone units come with private 24-hour butler service, your own swimming pool and spa, and 2,600 square feet of tongue-wagging indoor opulence. When movie stars come they often rent one or two of the two-bedroom, three-bath bungalows for a month or so. Price? $4,200–$4,750 per night, depending on if it's oceanfront. Oh, what the heck! Might as well spring for the oceanfront, huh?

The rest of us mortals will take the standard rooms. $350–$620, suites are $970. (Discount packages available to make it more palatable.) 🔥 🚭

THE ORCHID AT MAUNA LANI
(800) 325-3589 or (808) 885-2000

541 rooms, 10 tennis courts (7 lighted), VCRs, 24-hour room service, lots of shops, 18 conference rooms, ballroom, several restaurants, 2 golf courses, valet parking, pool and spa, health club, beauty salon, child care service. Well, here we go again. We try not to blather on about a resort—It hurts our credibility. But when it's right, it's right. The Orchid (formerly the Ritz-Carlton) has an intoxicating richness that permeates everything. The lush grounds have a very sculpted and precise feel. Nothing is out of place. The inside is just as flawless. The lobby, halls and rooms are all richly furnished with lots of wood and fine carpet—even the elevators seem affluent. The overall effect is European elegance

A Real Gem

with a tropical touch. The cleaning staff here deserves medals. I *dare* you to try to find something that isn't spotless. The entire staff seems obsessed with pleasing you. Restaurants are what you'd expect, on the higher end with delicious results. The manmade beach is usually calm and protected. Lots of activities are available. The tennis complex is the best on the island, and the two Mauna Lani golf courses are humbling and world renowned. You can get a massage next to the ocean at the "spa without walls" where the sound of the surf helps you relax. (As if you'll need any help.)

The Orchid is exceptional in every way. It has become popular with business travelers, but if you're looking to be pampered, consider it. It's not the most Hawaiian resort on the island, but it might be the ritziest. Rooms are $385–$650. (RACK rates may seem high, but if you ask for a "Suresaver Rate," they'll knock $80–$100 per night off most rooms.) One-bedroom suites (which are *very* nice) are $700–$1,400. Larger suites available. 🔥 🚭

OUTRIGGER WAIKOLOA BEACH RESORT
(800) 688-7444 or (808) 886-6789

545 rooms, 6 tennis courts, room safes, room service, on-site child care, 7 conference rooms, valet parking, pool and spa, health club, golf course, lu'au, and 2 restaurants. Formerly the Royal Waikoloan and located next to 'Anaeho'omalu Fishponds and Beach (see BEACHES) on 15 acres of well-maintained grounds. The new Outrigger ownership has done wonders turning a formerly tired resort into a nice place to stay. Though the rooms are smallish (little over 300 sq. ft.), they're comfortable and have a few interesting ammenities like Web TV. The pool has a keiki pool offshoot that's lined with sand at one

end forming a tiny kids beach. The other end features a small waterslide. They have a pretty good lu'au on the premises. The "oceanfront" rooms are pretty far from the ocean, so the garden view rooms are their best bargain. Rooms are $210–$290, suites are $425–$1,000. ♿ 🚭

Kohala Condos

Your choice of condos in Kohala is limited to upscale ones. You won't find a cheap dive among them.

THE ISLANDS AT MAUNA LANI
(800) 642–6284 or (808) 885–5022
46 units, A/C, pool, spa, daily maid service. If we could give two GEM icons we would! The two-story

townhouse-type units are posh with high end furnishings (like Sub-Zero refrigerators), bathrooms large enough to taxi

A Real Gem

a small plane, bathtubs with bay windows, private garages, etc. This very quiet and secluded, gated property is located on the Mauna Lani North Course. (Not oceanfront—hey, you can't have it all.) When you make your reservations, they will ask you what kind of groceries you want and deliver them to your room. Two-bedroom units are 2,300 square feet. The grounds are manicured and the pool area, with its dashing waterfall, is inviting. If you are looking for upscale privacy and your budget won't allow the $4,200 bungalows at the Mauna Lani (in other words, if you aren't filthy with it), this is a very nice alternative. Room rates, *which include a full-size car and stocking of the kitchen with food,* are $395–$450 for a 2/3, $525–$650 for a 3/3. 3 night mini-

mum. Just between us, they could get a lot more.

MAUNA LANI POINT
(800) 642–6284 or (808) 885–5022
116 units, A/C, pool, spa, daily maid service. This is a tough one. The interiors are nice with expensive furnishings, huge master bathrooms, pleasing layouts, good location, and relaxing views across the golf course. That said, it's probably a bit overpriced. The units are not "perfect" enough for this price. Some of the amenities we normally associate with Mauna Lani properties aren't here. Don't get us wrong. These are fine units and you'll probably like it here. It's just that you can do better for the money. 1/2 units are $290–$370, 2/3 units are $375–$475, 3/3 units are $650.

MAUNA LANI TERRACE
(800) 822–4252 or (808) 883–8500
80 units, A/C, pool, spa, keiki pool.

Most units overlook the ancient fishponds, creating an amazingly tranquil setting. Some units have ocean views,

A Real Gem

as well. Buildings J, K, and L often have nice sunset views. Units have higher end furnishings. 2 and 3-bedroom units are the better units. The complex is right next to the Mauna Lani Bay Hotel with all of its services. The grounds are nicely groomed. 1/2 units are $320, 2/3 units are $430, 3/3 units are $610. ♿ 🚭

VISTA WAIKOLOA
(800) 822–4252 or (808) 883–8500
123 units, A/C, pool and spa. Considering the calibre and the fact that it's in Kohala, this is a pretty good deal.

Units are large and nicely furnished, the layout is pleasing, grounds are well groomed, the bathrooms

Solid Gold Value

have nice deep tubs. Views aren't overwhelming—distant ocean. But if you want a condo in Kohala, this is as close as you'll come to inexpensive yet pleasant. 2/2 units are $245–$300. ♿ 🚭

SHORES AT WAIKOLOA
(800) 822–4252 or (808) 883–8500
120 units, A/C, pool, spa. Though the grounds are better here, the units are smaller and aren't as nice as Vista Waikoloa. The furnishings aren't as expensive either. (Shower curtains instead of clear glass shower doors, etc. You get the picture.) You're better off there. 1/1 units are $205, 2/2 units are $240–$275. 🚭

KAILUA-KONA

The resorts in Kailua-Kona and the surrounding area aren't of the same calibre as the glitzy mega-resorts of Kohala, but neither are the prices. You'll find that you can stay and eat in Kona a lot cheaper than Kohala. Condos are far more numerous here than hotels. Some condos are a downright bargain, while others can only be recommended to in-laws.

Most accommodations in Kailua-Kona are along Alii Drive. This road fronts the shoreline offering splendid ocean locations and sunsets. The penalty for staying on Alii Drive is auto noise. Cars and motorcycles scoot by, sometimes creating unpleasant reminders in *some* condos that you are still in the real world. (Other condos keep their rooms far enough from the road to keep them blissfully quiet.)

The important thing to remember about renting condos, especially in Kona, is the fragmented nature of the market. Each unit usually has a different owner, they all use different rental agencies to manage them, and it changes all the time. (Spreadsheets, blinding headaches, and blurred vision are all necessary to figure it out.) Therefore, when *we* review them, we may look at 10 units and get 10 winners. *You* may rent one and get a dump because the owner is using furniture from a landfill and carpet from the finish line at the Ironman Triathlon. You never truly know what you're going to get.

The high season in Kona is December through March, and most condos charge more at that time.

If you're looking for a good deal and have a little time before your trip, the classifieds in the *West Hawai'i Today* newspaper (329–9311) on the west side, or *Hawai'i Tribune-Herald* (935–6621) on the east side often have incredible deals from individual owners of condos and houses. (We have links to them from our web site.) From the mainland, you can buy an individual paper or get a short-term subscription. It'll cost you a few dollars, but you may save hundreds or even thousands of dollars on your accommodations. Just remember that you won't have the security of working with an established rental agent or company.

Kailua-Kona Hotels

(ASTON) KEAUHOU BEACH RESORT
(800) 922–7866 or (808) 322–3441

A Real Gem

318 rooms, 6 tennis courts (2 lighted) room service, conference room, pool, keiki (children's) pool. This was a tired, worn

resort until new owners bought it in the late '90s and fixed it up quite thoroughly. Originally built in 1970, the hotel borders Kahalu'u Beach on one side and a tide-pool on another. Many of the rooms have nice views. The oceanfront rooms are *worth every penny.* They're the only rooms on the Big Island that are *directly* over the water. Just look down and you may see turtles and eels swimming in the shallow tide-pool. Other rooms are fairly nice for the money. For the location it's a good deal. Rooms are $155–$270. ♿ 🚭

KING KAMEHAMEHA'S KONA BEACH HOTEL
(800) 367–6060 or (808) 329–2911

457 rooms, 4 tennis courts (2 lighted), a dozen shops, pool and spa, lu'au. Built in the mid '70s, the King Kam (as it's known locally) is a Kona fixture. Located next to the Kailua Pier, the hotel is fronted by the tiny but calm Kamakahonu Beach. The 'Ahu'ena Heiau shown on page 57 is also on the grounds. This area was the home of King Kamehameha during his latter years, and his legacy has been adopted by the hotel. Paintings of him and other royal family members are strewn about the resort. The lobby is laid out like a mall, emphasizing the multitude of shops available. Some are worth stopping for. The rooms are average here, and the service could use some improvement. Overall, the King Kam is starting to show its age but is still a fairly fine hotel. You'll probably be pleased with it as a selection. The King Kam is the center of the universe every October when the Ironman Triathlon takes place. Most of the athletes stay here, as do many from the television crew, and rooms are hard to get then. Rooms are $120–$195, suites are $350–$550. ♿ 🚭

KONA SEASIDE HOTEL
(800) 367–7000 or (808) 329–2455

234 rooms, 2 pools. This hotel, located

Solid Gold Value

across the street from Kailua Bay in the heart of Kailua-Kona, is one of the better deals on the west side. The buildings, built over time several decades ago, are immaculate. Tidiness is a welcome obsession here. The simple grounds are constantly groomed, the rooms are more than acceptable. You won't find water-slides, glass elevators, or an atrium the size of Kaua'i, but you *will* find a pleasant hotel staffed by friendly folks with a central location at a cheap rate. If that's what you are looking for—stop looking. Standard rooms in the oldest building are $98. Rooms increase to $115, with kitchenettes for $125. They will almost always offer 20% off the RACK rates, so ask for this promotion. ♿ 🚭

KONA SURF RESORT
(800) 367–8011 or (808) 322–3411

At press time this resort—the first swanky resort built in the area—was worn, dreary and had just been closed by its owners until buyers could be found to rescue and renovate the property. If you have fond memories of this resort in its prime, don't visit it. It will only depress you.

KONA TIKI (808) 329–1425

15 rooms, pool. This small hotel, built in

Solid Gold Value

1953, is an old-style Kona hotel. All rooms have incredible oceanfront views right next to the water. How close? The swimming pool

is permanently salty from waves washing over the rock wall. At night guests are invited to blow the conch shell and light the tiki torch. Continental breakfast is free. The guests usually end up forming a loose family of sorts. You won't find the usual array of amenities. Missing are phones, air conditioning, TV—they don't even take credit cards. (They *do* have a BBQ with a dynamite view for you to use.) This is the kind of place that visitors looking for a smashing oceanfront location, simple room, and *very* reasonable prices will come back to over and over. Rooms are $57–$62. Kitchenettes are $68. Three-day minimum at times.

ROYAL KONA RESORT
(800) 222-5642 or (808) 329–3111

452 rooms, 4 tennis courts (3 lighted), coffee makers in rooms, pool and keiki pool, 5 conference rooms, hair salon, lu'au, room service. This is a good choice for any

A Real Gem

one who wants a nice oceanfront location in downtown Kona and doesn't want to spend a fortune. You can walk anywhere from here. Owned by tour giant Pleasant Hawaiian Holidays, rates are reasonable—even more so if you book a package through Pleasant. (See BASICS.) Built in 1968 but well kept, this former Hilton has pleasant grounds, the rooms are clean, and the restaurant is a good deal with dynamite views from the terrace tables. Of the three buildings, the Beach Building is the quietest in terms of human activity. The Boom Boom deck is a good place to sit and listen to the sound of the surf. They don't have a beach, but there is a saltwater lagoon to swim in. Their lu'au is excellent. All in all, you seem to get a bit more than you

pay for here. Rooms are $140–$210, suites are $250. ♿ ⚲

UNCLE BILLY'S KONA BAY HOTEL
(800) 367-5102 OR (808) 329-1393

147 rooms, pool and keiki pool. If you're just looking for a place to stay with no frills but a convenient downtown location, it's worth considering. They are fairly basic, and the rooms could be a touch cleaner, but they have some good room and car packages. Avoid their sister property, the Kona Inn, across the street. By the way, where *is* Kona Bay? (The hotel is across from *Kailua* Bay.) Rooms are $84–$94; add $28 and you get a car.

Kailua-Kona Condos

ALII VILLAS
(800) 367-5168 or (808) 329-6488

129 units, small pool. Units are fairly small but with prices starting at $80–$95

Solid Gold Value

for 1/1 units, the value can be excellent. Shop around with different rental agents. If you get a garden view for $80 or an ocean front for $100, it's a Solid Gold Value. If you pay $100 for a garden view room, ignore the gold icon.

BANYAN TREE
(800) 367-5168 or (808) 329-6488

20 units, pool. All units are ocean front with the sound of the surf below you. Rooms are adequately furnished and maintained. If you want the master bedroom facing the ocean closed off from the living room by shoji doors, don't get an end unit where the bedrooms are toward the back. Near a surf spot, there may be surfers hanging out in front of the place. 2/2 units are $145.

Casa de Emdeko
(800) 367-5168 or (808) 329-6488
106 units, 2 pools (1 saltwater), central A/C. The design

Solid Gold Value

and decor is a weird, out-of-place Spanish permutation, but the rooms are a good deal from several rental agents. Get as close to the ocean as you can. The rock-enclosed saltwater pool is fed by well water and is pretty cold but very picturesque with a great location. There's a small, elevated, sandy sunning area and a clubhouse with BBQs. Though slightly worn (building maintenance could use a boost), the price is right for what you get. 1/1 units are $90–$100, 2/2 units are $140-$150.

Country Club Villas
(800) 799-5662 or (808) 322-6696
90 units, 3 pools, tennis court. Units are large and comfortably furnished. Many units are right on the golf course with distant ocean views from the large lanais. 2/2 units are $150.

Kanaloa at Kona
(800) 688-7444 or (808) 322-9625
166 units, 2 lighted tennis courts, 3 pools, room safes. Upscale units with amenities, such as showers with two heads and large jacuzzi bathtubs in the 2 and 3 bedroom units, outdoor wet bars, Jenn-Air ranges with indoor grills, etc. 2/2 units are quite large, 3/2 units simply add an open loft. The restaurant by the pool, Edwards at Kanaloa, is excellent (See DINING.) Our only complaint is that they seem to nickel and dime you on the small stuff, like charging for the safe, $1 to *receive* a FAX and air conditioning that is an extra $30 *per day*. For these prices they should include these. Nice location on the shore. Overall, you

should be pleased here. 1/2 units are $225–$255, 2/2 units are $260–$290, 3/2 units are $310. 2 night minimum. ♿ 🚭

Keauhou Kona Surf & Racquet Club
(800) 799-5662 or (808) 322-6696
193 units, 3 tennis courts, pool. There are older townhouses and newer condos. Huge variation in rooms here, even among the condos. Many oceanfront units, like buildings 4 & 5, have outstanding rooms with incredible locations. On the other hand, some of the buildings have tacky rooms with poor maintenance. The townhouse units are older and more weathered. The swimming pool is larger than most condo pools, and the tennis courts here are lighted. There are several interesting archeological sites on the grounds. 2/2 units are $125–$220, 3/2 units are $150-$250.

Keauhou Palena
(800) 367-5168 or (808) 329-6488
56 units, pool. Right on the golf course, but fairly cheap quality units and furnishings. You can do better elsewhere for the money. 1½/2 units are $95. ♿

Keauhou Punahele
(800) 367-5168 or (808) 329-6488
92 units, pool and spa. Toward the end

Solid Gold Value

of Alii Drive, this place is very quiet and peaceful (boisterous kids are not as welcome here as at other places). Most (but not all) units are expensively furnished with large lanais. Grounds are well kept. Very clean, very quiet, very tidy, very good deal. Not ocean front. 2/2 units are $104–$125, 3/3 units are $165 (good value on the 3/3).

KEAUHOU RESORT
(808) 322-9122
48 units, 2 pools (one shallower for kids). Grounds are nice, rates are acceptable. Bedrooms aren't entirely shut off in some cases; two-story townhouse layouts are preferable. Overall, adequate. 1/1 units are $97–$107, 2/2 units are $123–$145. Knock off about $25 during the summer, which creates a pretty good value. 5 night minimum or pay extra for cleaning. ♿

KONA BALI KAI
(800) 535-0085 or (808) 329-9381
(800) 367-5168 or (808) 329-6488
155 rooms, pool, small spa. With some units on both sides of Alii Drive, the oceanfront units can be a very good deal, depending on who you rent from. The complex is run by Marc Resorts (the top phone numbers), but units rented from SunQuest (second set of numbers) can offer dramatically cheaper rates (see rates below). Bear in mind that with the latter you won't get daily maid service. Units are smallish, but the resort seems well run and the views are excellent. Almost gave it a SOLID GOLD VALUE. Units across the street are not worth the discount—go for oceanfront. 1/1 units from SunQuest are $110, 2/2 units are $145. Marc rates are $169–$229 for 1/1, 2/2 units are $239–$279. ♿ ⊘

KONA BY THE SEA
(800) 922-7866 or (808) 327-2300
86 units, A/C, room safe, pool and spa, daily maid service. Unlike most condos, the rooms are mostly the same. Nicely furnished, quiet, with pleasant grounds. The oceanfront saltwater pool mentioned on page 60 is next to the grounds. This is a nice resort but the RACK rates are a bit steep, so try to get a package deal or a discount. 1/1 units

are $235–$290, 2/2 units are $290–$345. ♿ ⊘

KONA COAST RESORT
(800) 799-5662 or (808) 322-6696
323 units, tennis court, central A/C, 2 pools, 3 jacuzzis, pool-side restaurant.

Solid Gold Value

This complex was built in multiple phases. The units in the first phase (where the rental pool comes from) can best be described in one word—large. Large kitchens, large bathrooms, large bedrooms, large living rooms, large lanais. It was for this reason and the many facilities that we gave it a SOLID GOLD VALUE, especially the 1/1s. Grounds are very nice. Most of the other units are smaller timeshares and are not relevant to this review. 1/1 units are $150, 2/2 units $220, 3/2 units $250.

KONA ISLANDER INN
(800) 622-5348 or (808) 329-3333
145 units, A/C, pool and spa. Designed more like a hotel than a condo (but rooms are individually owned), these basic rooms lack a kitchen. Just a microwave, coffee maker, and small refrigerator. Cheap, but not a dump. There used to be a front dest but it's closed. The number listed above is for the on-site rental agent. 1/1 rooms are $35–$79.

KONA ISLE
(800) 799-5662 or (808) 322-6696
60 units, pool, A/C. Very small, but you could do a lot worse for the money. Units are clean, and the complex is ocean front. There's a small sandy area with hammocks and BBQs sprinkled about. Be sure to check out the genuine oceanfront saltwater pool next door mentioned on

page 60. If you paid under $90 for a 1/1 unit (or under a $100 for an oceanfront unit), you did OK.

KONA MAGIC SANDS
(800) 622-5348 or (808) 329-3333
35 rooms, pool. The place is kind of a dump, but it's cheap and right on the ocean. (Some units are much better than others.) You can see and hear the ocean right from your bed. Units are *very* small. The bed area seems to be formed from a converted lanai in some rooms. But you can't beat the oceanside price of $65–$95.

KONA MAKAI
(800) 367-5168 or (808) 329-6488
102 units, 2 tennis counts, A/C, pool and spa. Units are smallish but the price is good. The grounds are pleasant. 1/1 units are $90–$95. 2/2 units $120–$130. &

KONA NALU
(800) 367-5168 or (808) 329-6488
15 units, central A/C, tiny pool. This is the oceanfront location you've been dreaming of. Their three-story building sits right on the shoreline. Each unit has flawless ocean views from the master

A Real Gem

bedroom, as well as the huge lanai. Open the drapes and the sliding glass doors, and soak up the view as you hear the pounding of the ocean. The units are large and fairly well furnished. 2/2 units are $167–$190. What a deal!

KONA REEF
(800) 367–5004 or (808) 329–2959
(800) 367–5168 or (808) 329–6488
130 units, A/C, pool and spa, BBQs. Buildings A and D are fairly quiet, but

units next to Alii Drive are noisy. The rooms are not bad, but the grounds could use some punching up. You're probably best off going with SunQuest (the second numbers) as opposed to the direct number listed first above. (The direct number will cost you much more and you may get less aloha.) 1/1 units with Sunquest are $99–$125. Castle rates are $139–$210 for 1/1. 2/2 units are $233–$265.

KONA SEASPRAY
(808) 322–2403
4 units, pool, spa. With their glorious location almost across the street from Kahalu'u Beach Park, this is a great place to stay if you

A Real Gem

have any interest in swimming or snorkeling. (Easily accessible, convenient, and with good underwater scenery, Kahalu'u is the most user-friendly snorkel spot on the island.) Units are large and nice inside, views of the bay and Ku'emanu heiau are excellent, and the poolside BBQ makes a great spot to congregate after a day of exploring. 1/1 units are $95–$105, 2/1 unit is $115–$145. Easy to recommend. They also have 4 units next door at Kahalu'u Reef that we weren't able to review at press time.

ROYAL KAHILI
(800) 799–5662 or (808) 322–6696
32 units, pool. Small but tidy units in this four-story building across the street from the ocean (but not much of a sea view). Don't worry, there's an elevator. Pretty decent value for the money. 2/2 units are $140.

(Aston) Royal Sea Cliff Resort
(800) 922-7866 or (808) 329-8021

150 units, tennis court, A/C, room safe, 2 pools (1 saltwater), spa. All the units decorated the same and fairly large. The recreation area has an outdoor kitchen and BBQs, and there's daily maid service. Like Kona By The Sea, they have lots of packages available so you shouldn't end up paying RACK rates. 1/1 units $200–$255, 2/2 units $230–$295. Large oceanfront villas are $560–$630, which is overpriced. If you get one, ask for 2,500 sq. ft. model—same price. ♿

Sea Village
(800) 367-5168 or (808) 329-6488

Solid Gold Value

132 units, tennis court, pool and spa. Quiet location, nicely kept grounds and rooms. There's a large grassy BBQ area next to the pool that makes a fine place to cook that fish you caught today. 1/1 units are $95–$120, 2/2 units are $135–$150, 2/3 units are $155.

White Sands Village
(800) 367-5168 or (808) 329-6488

108 units, 2 tennis courts, A/C, pool, spa, BBQs. This fairly old building is right across the street from White Sands Beach Park, which is usually swimmable. They get a few extra points for that (but don't expect much of an ocean view from most rooms). Smallish 2/2 units are mostly adequate. (The washer and dryer is directly across from the toilet—that's different.) 1/1 units are $95, 2/2 units are $115–$130. 🐳

Rental Agents

Most rental agents have 3 or 5 day minimum stays. You also will not get daily maid service unless you pay extra. We've

been particularly impressed with the candor of SunQuest Vacations. They seem to tell it like it is. The internet can be a good source for specials and promotions.

SunQuest Vacations
(800) 367-5168 or (808) 329-6488

West Hawaii Property Services
(800) 799-5662 or (808) 322-6696

Hawaii Resort Management/Kona Hawaii Vacation Rentals
(800) 622-5348 or (808) 329-3333

Hilo Accommodations

Your choices in Hilo are much more limited than on the western side of the island. The number of overnight visitors here is a fraction of what the Kona side gets. The hotels are older here, so don't expect the swankiness of the Kohala resorts. But you shouldn't expect Kohala prices either. Hotels can be had quite cheap in Hilo, so even if you are staying on the western side, you should strongly consider staying at least a night here when you are exploring this side or visiting the volcano. That'll keep Hilo from becoming a blur during an around-the-island driving frenzy.

Most of the hotels are located along Banyan Drive. Many have outstanding views of Hilo Bay.

Country Club Hawai'i Condo Hotel
(808) 935-7171

150 rooms. So what are they—a hotel or a condo? They are a hotel with rooms owned by individuals, so expect variations among the rooms. If you don't expect squat for service here, you won't be disappointed. Many rooms are dumpy and not worth the price. Consider the other offerings in Hilo. Rooms are $65–$95.

DOLPHIN BAY HOTEL
(808) 935-1466

18 rooms, TV (no cable). One of the better bargains in Hilo. Rooms are clean and have complete kitchens. Unusual Japanese tubs are in most units (except standard). The lack of telephones may make arranging your day awkward, but the room quality and kitchen at this price make it easy to recommend. Located in northern Hilo. (See Hilo map.) Rooms are $66–$76, one and two bedrooms units are $86 & $98. Only quibble is that there was a bad crowd habitually hanging out in the neighborhood as we went to press.

HAWAI'I NANILOA HOTEL
(800) 367-5360 or (808) 969-3333

325 rooms, 2 pools, jacuzzi, conference room, free airport pickup, health spa. Oceanfront units have nice views, with the Waipi'o Wing the closest to the ocean. Their spa has a sauna, steam room, weight room, massage room, etc. This was a grand hotel at one time, but now they are a bit worn, feeling the effects of low cash flow and a ticking clock on leased land. Their RACK rates are a bit high, but check for specials. They often have an advance purchase deal that is a heck of a bargain. Rooms are $100–$160, suites are $190–$240. ♿

HILO HAWAIIAN HOTEL
(800) 367-5004 or (808) 935-9361

285 rooms, conference room, pool. This is the nicest hotel in Hilo. Built in 1975, their location on Banyan Drive overlooking Coconut Island affords them nice views. Their buffets are the best in Hilo, drawing lots of people from other hotels, as well as residents, and usually sells out in advance. Their lounge has nightly entertainment

A Real Gem

often featuring excellent local musicians (save us a seat when Bruddah Waltah is playing), but the drinks are small and anemic. They are owned by the Nissan Car Company. Visitors driving other rental cars will be towed. (Just teasing!) Rooms are very comfortable and nicely decorated; the buildings are well maintained. Check for specials. Rooms are $107–$141. Family suites (a good deal) are $177. Other suites are $273–$350. ♿

HILO SEASIDE
(800) 367-7000 OR (808) 935-0821

135 rooms, pool. Clean, simple rooms from this Banyan Drive hotel across from the ice pond. Rooms are $88–$110, with kitchenettes for $120. You can almost always get a 20% discount. Ask for it. Add $30 for a car.

UNCLE BILLY'S HILO BAY HOTEL
(800) 367-5102 or (808) 935-0861

144 rooms, pool. Owned by the same family as the Kona Bay Hotel, rooms are decent sized and clean, but their last price increase put the RACK rates a bit too high. The lobby is funky—sort of a '50s Hawai'i as the mainland saw it. Building maintenance could use a little boost. Superior type rooms are the best value. If you go oceanfront, get a wraparound. Units are $84–$112, kitchenettes are $94–$122. Car packages are available for about $28 more. Seniors get an automatic room upgrade. ♿

VOLCANO VILLAGE

The town of Volcano Village has a limited number of places to stay, but the choices you *do* have are superb. All three qualified for A REAL GEM. If you are spending a week on the Big Island, at least

A Real Gem

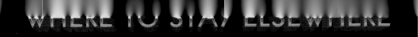

one night should be spent here. This is the most convenient place to stay when you explore the volcano. You can take your time and do the volcano justice. Remember, it gets chilly here at 4,000 feet, so bring something warm and waterproof. There are lots of B&Bs in Volcano Village, so check out the service mentioned on the next page or our web site.

CHALET KILAUEA
(800) 937–7786 OR (808) 967–7786

If pressed, we could review this place with one word—wow! Built in 1942 but thoroughly remodeled, this inn is remarkable for its elegance, attention to detail, and style. Everything is perfect. There are 5 rooms. The Continental Lace Suite is their very romantic bridal suite with double jacuzzi bathtub in the bathroom. The TreeHouse Suite is two story; a wooden spiral staircase leads to the bedroom with its dreamy view. The bathroom has a jacuzzi bathtub, TV, and a fireplace in it! On Wright Road. They also have other properties, such as a simple B&B for $55–$65 (good for families on a budget), houses and cottages off grounds, the Lokahi Lodge, and more. We like the suites at the inn best, but Lokahi is a fairly good deal at $125. The extra touches are far to numerous to mention (including outrageous marble bathrooms and afternoon tea in the common area). Wear the warm, fuzzy bathrobes to the outdoor spa. Rooms are cleaner than most operating rooms, and the grounds are lush and tidy. All rooms have TVs and VCRs. Gourmet candlelit breakfasts included (tall people duck). Arrange in advance for an enchanting stay. Suites at the Inn are $135–$395 (no minimum). Call them for their complete price list of all properties.

KILAUEA LODGE (808) 967–7366

12 rooms, centrally heated, fireplaces in

some. Opened in 1938 as a YMCA youth camp, this quaint lodge was converted in 1986 by Albert and Lorna Jeyte. (He was a make-up artist on Magnum P.I.) The whole thing is very well done. There are different types of rooms such as the Honeymoon Deluxe (very romantic), Hale Maluna building (snug rooms with fireplaces and incredible skylights in the bathrooms) and a cottage. The grounds are lush and well tended. The staff is top notch. Breakfast is included in the price. No phones or TVs. $110–$145. ♿ ⊗

VOLCANO HOUSE (808) 967–7321

42 units. This hotel/lodge is located on the rim of Kilauea Caldera inside Hawai'i Volcanoes National Park. They are a protected park concessionaire and our expectations were low, but we're pleased to say that this hotel, like the park itself, is surprisingly well run. The rooms are small but clean and warmly decorated with koa furniture. They have phones, but no TVs or radios. At night most people either head down to the lava flows (Pele permitting), relax at the bar, watch the movie about the volcano shown at 7:30 p.m., or just curl up by the fire in the lobby fireplace, said to have been burning continuously since 1874 (though they "move" the fire when they need to clean the fireplace). Some of the rooms (especially 30–33) have excellent crater views. No minimum stay. The lobby gets unbelievably busy at lunch but quiets down at night. The cheapest rooms are in the 'Ohi'a building (its downstairs rooms, 46–50, have better layouts) where there's a cozy little lobby with its own fireplace. You may have to light that one. Check out the incredible wood used in the couch and chairs—a great place to sprawl out and read, similar to the way Mark Twain may have when he stayed here. Crater view rooms are $165, no

crater view is $95 or $135. They also operate 10 cabins at Namakani Paio Campgrounds mentioned in CAMPING.

WAIMEA

Things get chilly up here at 2,500 feet, as well. You have your choice: There's the 31-room **Kamuela Inn** (885–4243). This charming and quaint inn is smaller than the Waimea Country Lodge. It's clean and the setting is well groomed. Rooms in the older section are are $59–$72, kitchenettes are $89–$99, newer section is $79–$85, with suites for $185. The better bet is the **Waimea Country Lodge** (885–4100). 21 clean, spacious rooms with phones and high, knotty pine ceilings. Rooms are $86–$92, Kitchenettes are $100. If you don't get a kitchenette, get a Superior.

SOUTHEAST PART OF THE ISLAND

These two places are on the south side of the island, and a long way from other towns. In Na'alehu you'll find the **Shira-kawa Motel** (929–7462), 12 rooms, full kitchens in some, hot plates in others. On the positive side, it's run by nice people. On the negative side, it's a dump and overpriced for what you get. $30 for a single, $35 for doubles, $42 for kitchenettes. and $50 for the 1 bedroom.

Located near Punalu'u Beach is **Colony One at SeaMountain** (800) 488–8301 or (808) 928–8301. 75 units, pool and spa, golf course. This condo complex is in the heart of SeaMountain, a troubled development project away from everything. Units are individually owned, and the variation is tremendous. You may find a rotary phone and a '70s color scheme in one unit and somewhat newer furnishings in another. Overall, the units are mostly fairly adequately *(enough qualifiers there, Andy?)* maintained and cleaned, and the grounds are pleasant.

But you can do better for the money. Only for those bent on staying away from it all. Not beachside. Studios are $95–$108, 1/1 units are $120–$135.

WAIPI'O VALLEY

Lush and secluded, Waipi'o Valley is described in detail on page 118. If you want to stay there, you have two choices. **Waipi'o Treehouse** (775–7160) is utterly unique. Perched high up in a marvelous monkeypod tree near Papala Falls toward the back of Waipi'o Valley, when you climb the steps you find a small and very basic tree room with screened-in windows and a kitchen with utensils. You provide the food, and the place is all yours. The luxury is supplied by Waipi'o Valley, not the owners. Consider only for the novelty. $250 for one night, price goes down a bit with longer stays.

Tom Araki's Waipi'o Motel (935–7466) is a *very* simple 5-unit building. Shared bathroom and two shared kitchens. No electricity. B.Y.O. food for the gas appliances. Spartan rooms have beds and a table. Not much else. But given the price and location, you get what you pay for. Tom was in his 90s when he passed away at press time, so we don't know if this price will stay. $15 per night.

Topside is the nearby **Hotel Honoka'a Club** (800) 808–0678 or (808) 775–0678. 19 rooms (#10 and #16 are the best), this place is tiny, ancient, and clean. $45–$65, they also have hostel beds for $15 per person.

BED AND BREAKFASTS

Rather than describe the countless B&Bs scattered about the island, you're better off calling **Hawai'i's Best B&B** (800) 262–9912. We have lots of links to B&Bs on our web site, but it's not practical to personally review them the way we do other accommodations.

Index

Index

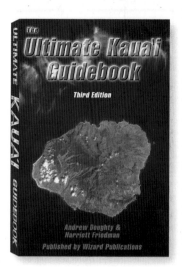
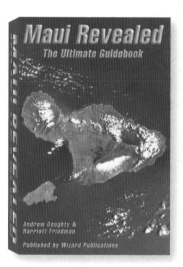